CONTEMPORARY ISSUES IN ISLAMIC LAW

CONTEMPORARY ISSUES IN ISLAMIC LAW

Abdul Haseeb Ansari

SERIALS PUBLICATIONS
NEW DELHI (INDIA)

Edition: 2011

ISBN: 978-81-8387-257-7

Published by
SERIALS PUBLICATIONS
4830/24, Prahlad Street, Ansari Road
Darya Ganj, New Delhi-110002 (India)
Phone : 23245225. Fax : 91-11-23272135
E-mail: serials@sify.com

Contents

Preface

In its restrictive sense, the *Shari'ah* comprises rules governing relations between man and Allah (s.w.t.), commonly known as rules of *ibadat,* and rules governing human relations and human behaviours, commonly known as rules governing *muamalat*. They are basically revealed rules enshrined in the Qur'an and Prophetic traditions (*Sunnah*). *Corpus juris* developed by various schools of thought (*madhahib*) is known as the *fiqh*. It is for this reason that they suffer from difference of opinions (*ikhtilafat*). They are, in fact, detailed rules. It is, therefore, not advisable to use the *Shari'ah* and the *Fiqh* interchangeably. However, it is notable that in rules pertaining to *ibadat*, there are minimum *ikhtilafat* among the *Aimmah* (plural of *Imam*). Rules of *Shari'ah* have to be understood in light of the purpose they have to achieve (*maqasid* of *Shari'ah*). Interpreted rules have been put as various legal maxims (*kawaid al-kulliyyah alfiqhiyyah*). In fact, legal maxims are abridged forms of certain set of related rules. In fact, Islamic law is the modern and more acceptable terminology, which is commonly used for the *Shari'ah*. In Islam, law is not a frozen code. It can further be developed and it is being developed by jurists (*Ulama*) by means of legal reasoning (*ijtihad*), interpretation (*taweel*), Juristic preference (deeming provisions, *istihsan*), public interest (*maslalah mursalah*), legal verdict (*fatwa*), collective opinion (*Ijma*), analogy (*qiyas*) and opinion (*ray*). Rules to meet the challenges of contemporary problems are developed by application of one or some of these means. But these man-made rules for their validity have to be in conformity with the basic sources of law, i.e. the Qur'an and *Sunnah*. As the door of *ijtihad* had never been closed there have been and there might be, in future, multiplicity of opinions on one question of law. For some, there is no problem in it. They say that let there be multiplicity of opinions. The best one among them, which in the public interest will ultimately prevail, and the rest will go into oblivion. Some others say that in order to avoid multiplicity of opinion that might cause confusion and uncertainty for certain period of time, collective *ijtihad* (*ijtihad* through *ijma*) should be preferred. This seems to be a preferable opinion. But for this, we will have to narrow down the scope of *ijma,* i.e. *ijma* of a town or *ijma* of a country. This seems to be correct approach as to get *ijmah* of jurists of the whole world is simply utopian.

The book "Contemporary Issues in Islamic Law" comprises a number of research papers dealing with certain contemporary issues and suggesting amicable solutions to them, which can serve the *Ummah* the best. A brief account these are as follows:

> In chapter one, Israr Ahmad Khan in "Ibn al-Arabi's Interpretation of the Qur'an: An Evaluation of Its Legal Validity", states that several *tafsir* works have been written from the jurisprudential angle. One such exegesis of the *Qur'an* is *Ahkam al-Qur'an* by Abu Bakr ibn al-'Arabi. This work has covered almost all the chapters of the Qur'an. But only those verses have been touched that have legal bearing. It is based on highly well defined and widely recognized methodology. It represents the approach of *Maliki* School of Islamic law. It also contains criticism of the remaining three schools of law, *Hanafite*, *shafi'ite*, and *Hanbalite*. He has made a humble attempt to discuss how significant Ibn al-'Arabi's contribution to the legacy of Islamic law is. For that matter, only six important issues have been selected for the deliberation.

Salim A. Fara in chapter two entitled "An Islamic Repose to the 'Human Rights' Discourse: An Analysis of the Problem and Proposal for an Alternative Dialogue", discusses various human rights from the Islamic law perspective and concludes that although there are divergences in human rights in civil law and Islamic Law, yet a compressive and harmonized set of human rights is a possibility.

In chapter three entitled, "Command Theory of Legal Positivism and *Hukum Shar'i*: A Comparison" Abdul Haseeb Ansari and Saad Abu Elgasim write that as opposed to the natural law theory, which presupposed a metaphysical basis of law, which required 'Is' and 'Ought' relationship between the law based on the absolute source and man-made law, positivists, especially Austin and Bentham, propounded their command theories. Law for them is the command of the sovereign. Among them, Austin's theory is charged with absolutism, as he believed that the sovereign is indivisible, illimitable and has no superior to him. Also, law for him is enforced based on penal sanction. For these reasons, Austin has been extensively criticized. Contrary to his theory, Bentham's command theory is flexible. He believes in constitutional limitation on the sovereign. His sovereign is subject to the law made by him. But his theory has also been criticized, as being impracticable in many countries. In the Islamic jurisprudence, the concept of *hukum shar'i* seems to be similar to these command theories. But apart from other points of difference, in Islam, Allah (s.w.t.) is the sovereign and human beings, including *khalipha* of the state (head of the state), are vicegerent. It entails that man-made laws for their validity have to be in conformity with the Qur'an and *Sunnah*. The chapter critically examines the command theories of Austin and Bentham and compares them with the concept of *hukum shar'i*. It finds that the Islamic command theory can be practiced in Islamic states having any form of government.

Norhashimah Mohd Yasin in Chapter four entitled "Islamic Commercial Contract Cases Heard in Civil Courts under Common Law: A Case Study of Malaysia and England", discusses about the judicial solicitude on commercial contracts in the United Kingdom and Malaysia and concludes that issues pertaining to transaction under the *Shari'ah* should be decided by the *Shari'ah* courts. On the contrary, judges deciding over disputed must have in-depth knowledge of Islamic law. She appreciates the positive development in Malaysia.

In Chapter five, entitled "Judicial Precedents: An Expository Study of Civil Judicial System and *Shari'ah* court system" Abdul Haseeb Ansari writes that in common law countries, judge-made laws, are one of the potential sources of law. Initially, the perception in England was that judges do not make law, they simply interpret the law. This traditional view could not endure long. Judges of 20th Century changed this notion and thus immensely helped in manifest ways in development of the common law. This position was maintained in most of the decolonized states. In some countries such as in India, this position was maintained in the Indian Constitution. In a country like Malaysia, British Common Law had value even after their independence. But some of the judges and legal scholars emphasized on having an indigenously developed common law suited to Malaysian conditions. The doctrines of *stare decisis* and judicial precedent significantly contributed in bringing about certainty judge-made laws. The position in the classical *Shari'ah* was different, and these doctrines had no value. But some countries, including Pakistan, maintained these doctrines applicable to the judicial systems of the country. This could be possible there because the judicial system in Pakistan is integrated. In Malaysia, they are being followed only in the civil court system. The chapter suggests that these doctrines should be applied to *Shari'ah* court system also, as they bring about certainty in law, show respect to senior and more experienced judges, and are in the public interest (*maslahah mursalah*).

Hikmatullah Babu Sahib in chapter six entitled "Islamic Law and Modernity: Conflict and Reconciliation" writes that the pressure of modernity is forcing many to reconsider their traditional values and laws. Laws, which were once considered sacred, have been modified as to their interpretation and application in accordance with the demands of modernity. Islamic law, too, is under immense pressure to accommodate the changes in consonance with the modernity. At the core of this debate is the position of women and their *shar'i* privileges. Many have argued for the reconsideration of these issues and have called for re-examination of the original *shar'i* texts. Has Islamic law, being a universal law, ignored this important aspect of justice? Can Islamic provisions be subject to influences dictated by the time and space? Will such changed provisions be still considered sacred? Is Islamic law essentially anti-modernity? These are some of the questions this chapter has looked into. Thus, this chapter represents an effort to find out the areas of conflict and explore their course of conciliation. It also examines the concerns raised by some of the modernist Muslim scholars who have advocated for fresher interpretation of Islamic Law.

Sayyid Muhammad Yunus Gilani in chapter seven entitled "Jurists and Legislators in Islam: Origin and Classification of the *Ulama*", writes that There is no religious hierarchy or priestly class in Islam. However, despite the absence of any church, priests and sacraments[1], with the passage of time there emerged in the Muslim world a class of religious luminaries who possessed legislative, social and political authority. These scholars or religious leaders govern almost all the aspects of the human life for at least in theory the religion and community are inseparable in Islam. They interpret the Qur'an and *Suunah*, and need be, derive laws from these sources. They also make entirely new rules based on analogy to meet the challenges of the contemporary world, provided they do not violate Qur'an and *Sunnah*. They may have expertise in any of the disciplines, but collectively they are known as *Ulama*. The chapter attempts to trace the origin and to discuss the classification of *Ulama*. A review of the existing literature leaves room for and demands for this direct and detailed historical, etymological and critical study of the institution of *Ulama* and its classification in the context of juristic and legislative functions.

In chapter eight entitled "Contemporary Issues in Terrorism and Their Islamic Perspectives: A Comparative Assessment", Abdul Haseeb Ansari states that various issues pertaining to global terrorism have been extensively debated. The most complex area of discussion has been to arrive at a widely acceptable definition because no definition can serve everyone's aspiration. It does not mean we should not make further efforts to arrive at a universally viable definition. It is rightly said that a feasible definition can be reached only when reasons, which compel groups of people to resort to terrorism, are given due consideration, as no one wants to risk his life. It is, therefore, necessary to explore the reasons of terrorism and hit at its roots, rather than giving it a symptomatic treatment in the name of 'war on terrorism' or a 'long war'. The chapter discusses about various reasons that are considered to have created impediment in reaching a universally acceptable definition. It is true that there cannot be all-encompassing definition, but we can have one that covers the maximum of them. It is not within the scope of the chapter to discuss various definitions. The chapter simply considers them collectively from the Islamic perspective. It also makes efforts to suggest a workable definition. It has now been proven that Islam encourages religious tolerance and peace and amity among the people of all faiths rather than encouraging terrorism. The chapter sheds light on the Islamic aspects of terrorism, and goes further to compare the western law and practice pertaining to taking captives, treatment of prisoners of war, and providing them appropriate access to justice with their Islamic conceptions, which will be a unique exposition. For this purpose, original sources of the *Shari'ah,* based on relevant Qur'anic verses (*ayat*) and *Sunnah* (Prophetic traditions) have been resorted to.

Hafiz Ali Ismail in chapter nine entitled "The Contract of Ja'alah and the Modern Banking Business: A Juristic Analysis", writes that in the context of Islamic law of contract, Ja'alah may be classified as a unilateral contract that entered into in the absolute discretion of a person. The scope of its practice, at the present time, particularly in the banking system is limited. Like other types of contracts Ja'alah has an essential requirement of formation that is the subject-matter. The contract's main features as discussed by jurists of various schools include valid performances which are not only capable of being subject-matter of the contract, but also are much relevant to the modern banking business. This discussion by the jurists had taken place long before the emergence of the modern banking. In this paper, an attempt has been made in such a way to identify all types of performances which are relevant to our modern banking business.

Nayel Musa Shaker Al-Omran in chapter ten entitled "Judicial Control in the Islamic System", writes that in Islam, judiciary has relatively more power than civil law courts because in the Islamic judicial system, doctrine of precedent in not applicable. In civil law systems it is stressed that judiciary should be separate from executive and should be independent. But it is a fact that in many countries, although constitutions prescribe that the judiciary will be independent, it has to face pressure from the executive. Islam ensures rule of law, separation of power and independence of judiciary. The chapter discusses various aspects of these cardinal aspects of the Islamic judicial system.

Norhashimah Mohd. Yasin in chapter eleven entitled "Regulation of Islamic Banks and Allegations of Lax Control of Money-Laundering", discusses whether Muslim countries are lax in their supervision of Islamic banks with regards to their international obligations under, for example the Financial Action Task Force (FATF) Recommendations, to combat money-laundering. It looks at the regulatory and supervisory framework of anti-money laundering in the two countries at the forefront of Islamic banking – Malaysia and Bahrain. The relevant money laundering legislation of both counties, as well as the guidelines issued by the respective central banks are examined. There is also a brief look at the issues of Islamic charities with accounts at Islamic banks as well as money transfer emphasizing that *hawala* is not part of Islamic banking). Any relevant resolutions by Fatwa Committees and whether or not there is any contradiction with money laundering legislation are also examined. She concludes with establishing whether Malaysia and Bahrain meet international requirements for combating money laundering, particularly with regard to Islamic banks.

In chapter twelve entitled "Woman in the *Shari 'ah* Courts: A Study of Malaysia and Indonesia", Ramizah Wan Muhammad writes the status of woman as a *Shari'ah* court judge according to the classical Muslim jurists has to be discussed. She begins with the historical background of the status of woman before and after the advent of Islam. In the Holy Qur'an there is a chapter on women which shows that the women have a special place in *Shari'ah.* However, in the case of a woman judge, there are differing juristic views, but their views are open to interpretation. The chapter makes such attempt to justify the notion that a woman can be appointed as a judge of the *Shari'ah* court. She also looks into the contemporary situation in Malaysia and Indonesia, where Islam is the religion of the majority of the population, and it is recognized as the religion of these states. The function of the government that looks after the interests of the community in the absence of the original legal rulings in the Divine revelations is also discussed. The chapter discusses the importance of *Shari'ah* court as an institution to dispense justice regardless of who the judge is. Most of the time, the culture and norms of a certain community are the impediments to the success of each country and not simply of one's belief.

In chapter thirteen entitled "Contract Documentation under Islamic Law: redefining its Role" Suhaib Walid Sharaiyra, elucidates that documentation is one of the least discussed methods of contract authentication under Islamic law, presumably due to the lesser degree of importance it was given as an instrument of evidence and perhaps even contract formation and conclusion. This is unfortunately evident in the scarcity of literature, especially modern literature, which addresses contract documentation, even though its importance is manifested in the revelation of Allah (s.w.t.) where documentation was made a requirement in the longest verse of the Qur'an. This lack of academic focus on matters of documentation, the writer believes, has played a vital role in the misuse of contractual documents for the benefit of traders and companies and to the exploitation of the public. Hence, the purpose of writing this chapter is to illustrate various features of contract documentation including the requirement, purpose and method of documentation, under Islamic law, in an attempt to redefine the role which written contractual documents play and the more pressing need for such a process nowadays, as compared to the early stages of its history and its usage in the early stages of Islam. Such discussion is hoped to assist in spreading awareness of the force which contractual documents have and the need for such an issue to be given due consideration.

Abdul Razak Abdullahi Hashi in chapter fourteen entitled "Administrative Ethics of Corporate and Public Administration from the Qur'anic Perspective" states that according to the Islamic perspective of management and administration, administrative and managerial ethics of public administration is imperative for social and economic prosperity of the community. The Qur'an which is the verbal speech of Allah, states that achievement of social growth towards knowledge-based culture and economic prosperity is impossible without having efficient and ethical professionals of managers and public administrators. The Qur'an has employed the terms to denote those who hold public offices and at the same time offered various professional and managerial ethics which the *ajir* and *ulul amri* should have. The Qur'anic expressions of managerial and administrative ethics include *amanah* or integrity and trustworthiness, *al-quwah* or strength and competence, and *alim,* i.e., skilful in the professional knowledge, qualification and experience. Furthermore, perfection and quality, continuation of *amal salih* are also among the Qur'anic managerial ethics of public administration. The Qur'anic expositors or the *mufasirun* have unanimously agreed to these Qur'anic managerial characteristics to encompass such values as integrity, transparency, good governance, accountability, commitment, attitude, reasonableness, fairness and devoid of conflict of interest. This chapter aims to explore the Qur'anic managerial ethics and professional characteristics of managers and public administrators, while modern theories of leadership and management will be highlighted and compared to that of the Qur'an. Textual and comparative methods will be applied in this study.

Prof. Dr. Abdul Haseeb Ansari
Ahmad Ibrahim Faculty of Laws
International Islamic University
Malaysia

List of Contributors

1. **Dr. Abdul Haseeb Ansari** is a Professor of Law at Ahmad Ibrahim Kulliyyah of Laws, International Islamic University, Malaysia. *ahaseeb@iiu.edu.my*

2. **Dr. Abdul Razak Abdulahi Hashi** is an Associate Professor at Department of Ususl al-Din and Comparative Religion, Killiyyah of Islamic Revealed Knowledge and Human Sciences, International Islamic University, Malaysia. *Nashaat99us@yahoo.com*

3. **Dr. Hafiz Ali Ismail** worked as an Assistant Professor at Ahmad Ibrahim Kulliyyah of Laws, International Islamic University, Malaysia. Presently, he is associated with one of the Sudanese Universities.

4. **Dr. Hikmatullah Babu Sahib** is an Associate Professor at Department of General Studies, Kulliyyah of Islamic Revealed Knowledge and Human Sciences, International Islamic University, Malaysia. *hikmatullah@iiu.edu.my*

5. **Dr. Israr Ahmad Khan** is a Professor at Department of Qur'an and *Sunnah* Studies, Kulliyyah of Islamic Revealed Knowledge and Human Sciences, International Islamic University, Malaysia. *israr@iiu.edu.my*

6. **Nayel Musa Shaker Al-Omran** has recently obtained his Ph.D from Ahmad Ibrahim Kulliyyah of Laws, International Islamic University, Malaysia. He is a former lecture of Sudan University. *nyelshaker@yahoo.com*

7. **Dr. Norhashimah Mohd. Yasin** is a Professor at Ahmad Ibrahim Kulliyyah of Laws, International Islamic University, Malaysia. *Norhashimah_iiu@yahoo.com.au*

8. **Dr. Ramizah Wan Muhammad** is an Assistant Professor at Ahmad Ibrahim Kulliyyah of Laws, International Islamic University, Malaysia. *ramizah@iiu.edu.my*

9. **Dr. S. A. Farrar** worked as an Associate Professor at Ahmad Ibrahim Kulliyyah of Laws, International Islamic University, Malaysia. Before that, he had worked as a lecturer with the universities of Manchester and County. He is currently working with Faculty of Law, University of Sydney. *salim.farrar@sydney.edu.au*

10. **Saad Abu Elgasim** is a research scholar at Ahmad Ibrahim Kulliyyah of Laws, International Islamic University, Malaysia. *Almosafir101@yahoo.com*

11. **Dr. Sayyed Muhammad Yunus Gilani** is a Professor of Islamic Studies, University of Kashmir, India. Presently working with the International Islamic University, Malaysia. *dryunusgilani@gmail.com*

12. **Dr. Suhaib Walid Sharaiyra** has recently obtained his Ph.D from International Islamic University, Malaysia. *suhaibwalid@hotmail.com*

1

Ibn al-'Arabi's Interpretation of the Qur'an: An Evaluation of Its Legal Viability

Israr Ahmad Khan

Introduction

Prominent Muslim jurists are divided along juridical lines. They generally respect one another. Yet, they view their own respective schools of jurisprudence as the most valid and strongest of all. *Hanafi* scholars consider the views of Abu Hanifah, Abu Yusuf and other founders as superior to those of non-*Hanafi* schools of *fiqh*. Experts of Shafi'i school believe in the preeminence of the decrees of al-Shafi'i over the others. Followers of Ahmad ibn Hanbal are satisfied with their leader's approach. *Maliki* authorities feel exultant with the *fatwas* of Malik ibn Anas and others of *Maliki* school. These intellectuals have also tried to justify their respective *fiqhi* schools. For that matter, they have interpreted the *Qur'an* accordingly. As a result, there has come up many a legal exegesis of the Islamic Scripture. One such exegesis is *Ahkam al-Qur'an* by Ibn al-'Arabi. It represents *Maliki* school of Islamic law. It is deemed as an important source not only for the students and teachers of *Maliki* denomination but also for those interested in Islamic law as a whole. This article attempts to introduce this source of Islamic law, on the one hand and evaluate its legal significance, on the other. It is not possible to accommodate in this short article all the legal views of Ibn al-'Arabi. The scope of this research is limited to some important dimensions of Islamic law discussed in Ibn al-'Arabi's above-mentioned work.

Ibn al-'Arabi: A Short Biographical Sketch

His name is Abu Bakr Muhammad ibn 'Abd Allah. He was born in the year 468 A.H./1076 A.D. at Ishbelia, a town in Muslim Spain. His father 'Abd Allah ibn Muhammad, who belonged to elite class of the city, was himself a well-known expert of Maliki school. He is generally known as Ibn al-'Arabi. One may mistakenly take him to be the great mystic figure. It is to be born in mind that the mystic figure was Ibn 'Arabi and not Ibn al-'Arabi, the difference being "al". The former is popularly known as Muhiyy al-Din Ibn 'Arabi, whereas the latter as Abu Bakr Ibn al-'Arabi. He accomplished his primary and secondary education in his native place. Thereafter he embarked upon educational tour of a number of places like Egypt, Syria, Iraq, and Makkah. He met and learned from almost all the known scholars of those places various prevalent disciplines. His hard work and sincerity yielded fruits. He very soon became well grounded in *usul al-fiqh* (Islamic legal theory), *fiqh* (Islamic law), *hadith* (traditions of Prophet Muhammad), *kalam* (Islamic philosophy), *tafsir* (interpretation of the *Qur'an*), and Arabic literature. When he returned to his town, he stood tallest of all the other scholars there. It was not merely knowledge, which impressed his people very much but also his honesty, integrity, generosity, humility, humbleness, truthfulness, trustworthiness and sincerity towards promises earned people's love and respect for him. Initially, he devoted his time and energy to teaching Islamic law, and preaching the messages of the *Qur'an.* A large number of people used to turn up to listen to him, not only the local but also foreigners. He was appointed as the judge of his city. He soon became famous for his unique manner of writing the judgment and its quick and effective implementation. The wrong doers and anti-social elements of the city got scared of the way he executed justice. After he was relieved of his position, he once again turned to the dissemination of his knowledge. He penned down many works. The most outstanding work is his exegesis of the *Qur'an*, *Ahkam al-Qur'an.* He lived a life of seventy-five (75) years. He died in the year 543 A.H./1148 A.D.[1]

Ahkam al-Qur'an: A Brief Introduction to Its Methodology

Ibn al-'Arabi has touched almost all the chapters (114) of the *Qur'an* in his exegesis but has interpreted only those verses that have any legal bearing. After he takes a verse for interpretation, he divides his discussion into various issues. He, then, deals with them one by one in brief or in detail. At times, he stops with one or two issues and if the need be he continues conceiving as many as thirty-eight (38) issues. For instance, the verse 2:187 spells out the position of the nights in the month of fasting. Ibn al-'Arabi has identified from there nineteen (19) issues for discussion. Indication to the number of issues he makes immediately after the quotation of the verse in view. He puts every issue as a sub heading. It is his tackling of these issues under particular verse that serves as his interpretation of the *Qur'an.* Wherever it is possible, the first issue he brings about is the background of revelation of the verse. The other derived issues are related to semantic dimension of certain words, meaning of every component of the chosen verse, and legal aspects. Under legal aspects, he refers to various views of scholars and treats them critically. The universally acceptable methodology of Qur'anic interpretation comprises around eight principles: (1) The *Qur'an* interprets the *Qur'an.* (2) Traditions of the Prophet (s.a.w.) are the practical explanation of the *Qur'an.* (3) The Companions were the ear and eye-witnesses of revelation of the *Qur'an.* (4) The views of Companions' disciples are significant. (5) Socio-historical background of the revelation of the *Qur'an* plays a crucial role in unfolding the truth. (6) Judeo-Christian sources, at times, fill in the gap of historical narratives. (7) Classical Arabic literature of the time of revelation is highly valuable for understanding the *Qur'an.* (8) Independent logical reasoning opens the hidden vistas of the *Qur'an*. Ibn al-'Arabi has employed all these methods except the 6th one. He has completely avoided consulting Judeo-Christian sources. As for the tradition of the Prophet (s.a.w.), he has been very strict. Unlike other commentators of the *Qur'an*, he has not used weak and concocted traditions. He was a follower of Imam Malik ibn Anas, the founder of *Maliki* school of Islamic law. It is very evident from his treatment of the Qur'anic verses that the only objective of this task is to support, strengthen and further validate *Maliki* opinions on Islamic issues. In addition to the above-mentioned principles, he has brought in the views of other jurists in general and Abu Hanifah and al-Shafi'i in particular. He has debated their views to the point of refutation.

Scope of Ahkam al-Qur'an

The latest edition of *Ahkam al-Qur'an* is available in four volumes. The first volume covers only four chapters (*al-Fatihah, al-Baqarah, Aali Imran, and al-Nisa'*). The verses selected for interpretation are five (5) from *al-Fatihah*, one hundred three (103) from *al-Baqarah*, twenty seven (27) from *Aali 'Imran*, and sixty four (64) from *al-Nisa'*. The second volume includes five chapters (*al-Ma'idah, al-An'am, al-A'raf, al-Anfal, and al-Tawbah*). The verses discussed are forty two (42) from *al-Ma'idah*, thirty (30) from *al-An'am*, twenty eight (28) from *al-A'raf*, thirty one (31) from *al-Anfal*, and fifty six (56) from *al-Tawbah*.

The third volume comprises interpretation of twenty four chapters, dealing with six verses from *Yunus*, thirty two (32) from *Hud*, twenty seven (27) from *Yusuf*, four (4) from *al-Ra'd*, five (5) from *Ibrahim*, ten (10) from *al-Hijr*, twenty two (22) from *al-Nahl*, twenty seven (27) from *al-Isra'*, twenty four (24) from *al-Kahf*, seven (7) from *Maryam*, nine (9) from *TaHa*, two (2) from *al-Anbiya'*, twenty (20) from *al-Hajj*, thirteen (13) from *al-Mu'minun*, twenty nine (29) from *al-Nur*, eleven (11) from *al-Furqan*, nine (9) from *al-Shu'ara'*, nineteen (19) from *al-Naml*, nine (9) from *al-Qasas*, four (4) from *al-'Ankabut*, three (3) from *al-Rum*, five (5) from *Luqman*, three (3) from *al-Sajdah*, and twenty six (26) from *al-Ahzab*.

The fourth volume consists of seventy-three (73) chapters. The number of verses interpreted are three (3) from *Saba*, two (2) from *Fatir*, four (4) from *Yasin*, three (3) from *al-Saffat*, fifteen (15) from *Sad*, four (4) from *al-Zumar*, three (3) from *al-Mu'min*, seven (7) from *Fussilat*, eight (8) from *al-Shura*, seven (7) from *al-Zukhruf*, four (4) from *al-Dukhan*, three (3) from *al-Jathiyah*, three (3) from *al-Ahqaf*, three (3) from *Muhammad*, five (5) from *al-Fath*, seven (7) from *al-Hujurat*, two (2) from *Qaf*, three (3) from *al-Dhariyat*, three (3) from *al-Tur*, one (1) each from *al-Rahman*, and *al-Waqi'ah*, four (4) from *al-Hadid*, seven (7) from *al-Mujadalah*, nine (9) from *al-Hashr*, seven (7) from *al-Mumtahanah*, two (2) from *al-Saff*, two (2) from *al-Jumu'ah*, four (4) from *al-Munafiqun*, five (5) from *al-Taghabun*, six (6) from *al-Talaq*, three (3) from *al-Tahrim*, one (1) from *al-Mulk*, three (3) from *al-Qalam*, four (4) from *al-Ma'arij* , three (3) each from *Nuh* and *al-Jinn*, eight (8) from *al Muzzammil*, four (4) from *al-Muddaththir*, six (6) from *al-Qiyamah*, six (6) from *al-Dahr*, three (3) from *al-Mursalat*, three (3) each from *al-Naba'*, *'Abas*, and *al-Mutaffifin*, two (2) from *al-Inshiqaq*, four (4) from *al-Buruj*, five (5) each from *al-Tariq* and *al-A'la*, two (2) from *al-Ghashiyah*, six (6) from *al-Fajr*, five (5) from *al-Balad*, one (1) from *al-Shams*, three (3) each from *al-Layl, al-Dhuha*, and *al-Inshirah*, four (4) from *al-Tin*, six (6) from *al-'Alaq*, three (3) each from *al-Qadr* and *al-Bayyinah*, two (2) from *al-Zalzalah*, three (3) from *al-'Adiyat*, two (2) from *al-Takathur*, one (1) each from *al-'Asr* and *Quraysh*, three (3) from *al-Ma'un*, two (2) from *al-Kawthar*, one (1) each from *al-Nasr* and *al-Masad*. Five (5) chapters (*al-Najm, al-Fil, al-Ikhlas, al-Falaq, and al-Nas*) have been taken into consideration only from the angle of some unrelated issues, having no legal connection.

The issues discussed in all the four volumes are: independent reasoning, inheritance, prisoners of war, sale, trade, neighbor, protection tax, war, pilgrimage, communication of Prophet Muhammad's tradition, shelter in the sanctuary of *Ka'bah*, child care, authority, Pregnancy period, Menstruation, alcohol, debt, blood-money, basis of foster relation, usury, liberation of slave, pawn, obligatory and voluntary charity, adultery, extent of covering the female's body, sorcery, position of the previous revealed law, witnessing, martyr, prayer and the mosque, fasting, divorce, purification, voluntary confinement in the mosque, waiting period for the divorcee and the widow, rationality, spoil of war, retribution, court judgment, unlawful edible items, dower, dedication, maintenance, marriage, exchange of gift, will, endowment, orphan, swearing, generosity to parents, fleeing from plague, migration (in the first volume); inheritance, captive, faith, sale, protection tax, war, pilgrimage, wine, slaughtering the animal, apostasy, obligatory and voluntary charity, adultery, theft, witnessing, hunting, mosque and prayer, truce, fasting, divorce, knowledge, contract and agreement, spoils of war, retribution of injury, judgment, robbery, treasure of wealth, homosexuality, unlawful meat, consultation, intercalation, time and reason of will, ablution, orphan, swearing, pre-Islamic practices (in the second volume); labor charge, inheritance, seeking permission, sale, greeting, war, pilgrimage, punishment, the incidence of false allegation, authority, pregnancy, menstruation, wine, etiquette of slaughtering the animal, usury, apostasy, slavery, obligatory charity, adultery, theft, poetry, witnessing and confession, martyr, prayer and mosque, legality of hunted meat, fasting, surety, divorce, purification, divorce through comparing the wife with mother, waiting period, contract and agreement, impact of the evil sight, retribution, judgment, lie, guardianship, expiation of oath, punishment of homosexuality, legality of skin of the dead animal, mutilation, pawning, consultation, coercion, dower, dedication, parentage, marriage, gift, ablution and bath, representation, orphan, swearing, merry making activities, exposure of the female body (in the third volume); inheritance, treatment of captive, faith, sale, sale-deed, war, pilgrimage, authority, child care, liberation of slave, obligatory charity, theft, poetry, witnessing and confession, compensatory contribution, fish hunting, prayer and mosque, divorce, purification, speculation, waiting period, divorce through comparing the wife with mother, pregnancy, spoil of war, lucky draw, retribution, legality of obedience to unjust authority, unlawful dress and ornament, consultation, coercion, dower, dedication, maintenance, marriage, ablution, endowment, swearing, pre-Islamic practices (in the fourth volume).

Legal Significance of Ibn al-'Arabi's Interpretation

Discussion on all the issues raised and debated by Ibn al-'Arabi in his work, *Ahkam al-Qur'an* is an encyclopedic task. In the following lines, only few issues will be focused on to see the viability of Ibn al-'Arabi's approach.

Marriage Related Issues

The verses 4:23-24 read: "*Forbidden to you (for marriage) are: your mothers, your daughters, your sisters, your fathers' sisters, your mothers' sisters, your brother's daughters, your sister's daughters, your foster mothers who gave you suck, your foster sisters, your wives' mothers, your step daughters born of your wives with whom you have established conjugal relationship—but there is no problem on you if you have not established conjugal relationship with them to marry the step daughters—the wives of your real sons, and two sisters in wedlock at the same time, except for what has already passed; Allah is oft-forgiving, most merciful. Also the married women, except those who fall under your rightful possession in war. Thus Allah has ordained for you. With the exception of these women all others are lawful for you for marriage.*"

The *Qur'an* has explicitly counted the women with whom the marriage is totally prohibited. As it is clear from the above quotation, seven categories of such women hail from the blood relation, two from the foster relation, two from the marriage relation, two from the in-laws, and the remaining one is unrelated.

The Forbidden Women for Marriage

Ibn al-'Arabi while making legal interpretation of the above two verses of the *Qur'an* (4:23-24) shares the decree of *Maliki* school of law concerning the total number of forbidden women for marriage. According to him, forty (40) categories of women are prohibited. Fourteen have been mentioned in the *Qur'an* as quoted above. All these fourteen, except the woman already married to someone else, are forbidden forever. The total number of women who are forbidden permanently is twenty-five. The remaining twelve permanently forbidden women are: foster daughter, foster sister, foster mother's sister, foster father's sister, foster brother's daughter, foster sister's daughter, the wife and her paternal aunt together, the wife and her maternal aunt together, the woman separated through cursing (*mula'inah*), the woman with whom the knot has been tied during her waiting period, wife of the father, wives of the Prophet (s.a.w.) [They are all like mothers of the believers; this category is now dropped due to its non-availability]. The women who are forbidden temporarily are fifteen in number: the 5th wife, the married woman, women in her waiting period, woman during her menstruation period after the delivery, the pregnant, former wife divorced thrice, non-Muslim woman, non-Muslim slave girl, Muslim slave girl if her master is capable to pay the dower to the free woman, slave girl of the son, the woman in the state of pilgrimage attire, the sick woman, the minor female orphan, the woman with whom the knot has been tied at the time of Friday prayer call, and the woman with whom the knot has been tied at the time of Friday sermon.[2]

Two categories from the permanently forbidden women, the one who got separated from her husband through cursing and the other with whom the knot was tied during her waiting period seem to be controversial. Abu Hanifah does not consider the cursed woman permanently forbidden. To him, the separation through curse is just like divorce. If the woman thus separated repents and withdraws her curse for the cursed husband, she may be allowed to return to her husband.[3] Ibn al-'Arabi rejects this argument and advances a tradition of the Prophet (s.a.w.) on the authority of 'Abd Allah ibn 'Umar: "The account of both of you (the cursed husband and the cursed wife) is now in the hands of Allah. One of you is a liar. You (the husband) have no way to her."[4] Ibn al-'Arabi seems to have misunderstood the statement of the Prophet (s.a.w.). He does not forbid the cursed woman forever. What appears from his saying is that the reason for separation between the wife and husband is the curse. If this factor does not remain in place due to any reason, as Abu Hanifah argues, there is a way for both of them to resume their conjugal link.

The reason for the woman with whom the knot has been tied during her waiting period being forbidden forever, according to Ibn al-'Arabi, is that the person concerned married her before she turned lawful for another marriage; the unlawful act rendered the woman permanently unlawful for the person concerned.[5] It seems strange on the part of Ibn al-'Arabi that he deems the knot during the waiting period as the factor for her being permanently forbidden for the person with whom she has tied the knot. Undoubtedly, the marriage before the completion of the waiting period is unlawful, but to consider it the factor for the woman to turn permanently unlawful may not be reasonable. He himself has used a legal principle on some other occasion that the unlawful act does not cause the lawful to become unlawful.[6] This principle may also be applied to this case. Such marriage, indeed, stands legally null and void. But after the completion of the waiting period the interested couple may be allowed to reenact the marriage. There should not be any problem in it.

Inclusion of Muslim slave girl, the woman in the pilgrimage attire, the sick woman, the minor female orphan, the slave girl of the son, and the two women with whom the knot is tied during the Friday prayer call and the Friday sermon respectively seems strange in the list of the temporarily forbidden women. The Muslim slave girl is forbidden, according to Ibn al-'Arabi, for the one who is capable to pay the dower. He argues that the marriage with Muslim slave girl is conditioned with two conditions, non-availability of the wherewithal to pay the dower and the fear of committing unlawful sexual act.[7] He has derived this argument from the verse: "*And whoever of you has not the means to wed free, believing woman, they may wed believing slave girls*" (4:25). This verse does not seem to be putting the condition for marriage with the female slaves, but it merely refers to a practical situation in which one should prefer to safeguard one's chastity through tying the knot with female slave. Abu Hanifah does not see the propriety of the conditions for marrying slave girls.[8]

The marriage with the woman in pilgrimage attire is not looked at negatively by scholars like Abu Hanifah and others. The basis of this approach is the Prophet's (s.a.w.) marriage with Maymunah bint al-Harith during the hajj rituals. But Ibn al-'Arabi doubts the authenticity of this report of the Prophet (s.a.w.)-Maymunah marriage as recorded by al-Bukhari.[9] He cites another tradition as recorded by Malik ibn Anas: "The person in the pilgrimage attire should not marry, nor some one else should make the arrangement for his marriage in that condition". The main reporter of this report is Nubayh ibn Wahb who is considered by al-Bukhari as weak. But Ibn al-'Arabi insists on his authenticity probably because the tradition has been recorded by Malik ibn Anas, the founder of *Maliki* school of law.[10] Ibn al-'Arabi's stand seems to be valid. Most of the well-known experts on the biographical dictionaries such as al-Nasa'i, Ibn Sa'd, and Ibn Ma'in consider Nubayh ibn Wahb an authentic reporter.[11]

The sick woman should not be married, according to Imam Malik. Abu Hanifah and al-Shafi'i allow the marriage with sick woman. Why should the sickness be the reason for her not being able to wed? The minor female orphan is also a controversial category. Abu Hanifah finds her marriage valid on the condition that her guardian should do it on her behalf. Imam Malik and al-Shafi'i do not consider it lawful.[12] The marriage at the time of Friday prayer call and the Friday sermon is a valid reason for Ibn al-'Arabi to declare it null and void. Is it unlawful to do that? Probably, Ibn al-'Arabi founds his view on the command in *Surah al-Jumu'ah* (62:9): "*O you who believe! When the call is proclaimed for the prayer on Friday, rush to the remembrance of Allah and leave off the business. That is better for you if you did but know!*" Then from the angle of Ibn al-'Arabi even a business transaction during that time should be declared invalid. He perhaps views any transaction at the time of Friday call and sermon unlawful. In a place where one and the same time is fixed for the Friday prayer call and the Friday sermon in all the mosques there, Ibn al-'Arabi's decree seems to be acceptable but in a town where different times of the two religious rites are different, his judgment may not be valid. It was better for Ibn al-'Arabi to talk about the proper and valid timings for the solemnization of marriage than to include the women married at the improper time in the list of prohibited women for marriage.

Invalid Marriage for the Father and the Son

There is no doubt that the women of the son are forbidden forever for the father (4:23). Likewise, the son cannot marry his father's women. It has been categorically prohibited in the Qur'an: "*And marry not women whom your fathers married*" (4:22). Ibn al-'Arabi has raised a subsequent issue concerning other factors prohibiting the father and the son to marry certain women. If the father commits adultery with his son's wife, she becomes forbidden for both the son and the father for marriage. The son can no longer continue his matrimonial relation with his wife who has been sexually exploited by his father. Ibn al-'Arabi vehemently advocates this view. To him, marriage with such women is totally prohibited for both the son and the father.[13] If this unlawful sex relationship is based on the consent of the partners concerned, it is valid to declare the women concerned forbidden for both. But if the father has raped his son's wife, it does not seem to be reasonable to separate her from her husband if he is willing to continue the marriage. Likewise, if the son rapes the wife of his father, she may continue with her husband if he wants to do so.

Ibn al-'Arabi says: "If a woman has been merely touched by the father or the son, she is unlawful for both because the touch is, according to *Maliki* scholars, like sexual act".[14] *Maliki* and *Hanafi* scholars view touching the woman as unlawful as sex with her. Al-Shafi'i differs from them. He does not equate the touch or hug of a woman with the sex. Ibn al-'Arabi rebuts the opinion of al-Shafi'i on the ground that what is prohibited is *nikah* (wedding) which simply signifies intimacy hence the kiss, the embrace and the oral sex all fall under the imports of *nikah* (marriage).[15]

Ibn al-'Arabi considers a woman who has been merely gazed with sexual enjoyment by both the son and the father as forbidden for both. He thinks that the sexual gaze is like intimacy and meeting, which brings carnal pleasure.[16] It is too much. How can it be proved that the gaze was sexually driven, and not mere an innocuous look? Mere gaze does not imply promiscuity. If this view of Ibn al-'Arabi is made the criterion, the marriage will become too hard a provision to practice.

Yet, Ibn al-'Arabi includes the son's slave girl in the list of temporarily forbidden women. She should appear in the list of the permanently forbidden women. Does Ibn al-'Arabi see no problem in the marriage between the son's slave girl and his father after she is freed or bought over by the father?

Significane of the Equality in Marriage

The verse 28:27 reads: "*He said: I intend to wed one of these two daughters of mine to you, on condition that you serve me for eight years.*" This is the statement of Prophet Shu'ayb to his would be son in law, Moses. While interpreting this verse and the succeeding one (28:27-28) Ibn al-'Arabi has raised and discussed thirty issues. The 22nd issue is the equality in marriage (*kifa'ah*). He has referred to the controversy of *Maliki* scholars over whether the equality between the bride and the groom should be in terms of the piety, the wealth and the family background together, or any one of them. He views the piety as the only dimension to be taken into consideration for marriage. He advances this verse to support his approach: "*Verily, the most honorable of you with Allah is the one who is the most pious among you*" (49:13). Another argument he gives is the marriage of Moses. He says that Moses was an expatriate, strange, alone, and poor, yet Shu'ayb proposed to wed him to his daughter only on the basis of his piety.[17] It does not seems fair on the part of

Ibn al-'Arabi to pass this sweeping judgment about the position of Moses. The reason does not agree that Moses' father in law did not enquire about his family background and the place of origin; he must have come to know about his princely upbringing in the palace of Egyptian king and his link to the Children of Israel. Apart from that Moses was, as is evident from the history, physically very strong man. Thus when Shu'ayb proposed to Moses, he knew that he was proposing to a man of high family background, of royal linkage, a healthy man, and of course an honest person. One may hardly disagree with Ibn al-'Arabi that the first thing to be assessed in the bride and the groom is the piety but other dimensions are also important such as family background, health, academic position, wherewithal etc. Ignorance of these additional aspects may, at times, lead to the matrimonial conflict.

The Position and Amount of Dower

Muslim jurists unanimously consider the dower a necessary part of the marriage. Ibn al-'Arabi subscribes to this unanimous idea on the basis of the *Qur'an*: (1) "*So wed them with the permission of their guardians and give them their dower in accordance with what is reasonable*" (4:25); (2) "*Lawful to you in marriage are the chaste women from among the believing community and the chaste women from among the people of the Scriptures before you if you have given them their due dower*" (5:5); and (3) "*And there will be no sin on you to marry them if you have paid their dower to them*" (60:10).[18]

While interpreting the verse 4:20 ("*And if you intend to replace a wife by another one and you have given one of them a great amount of dower, do not take back anything thereof. Would you take it wrongfully and with sin*?"), Ibn al-'Arabi emphasizes that the husbands have been prohibited to take anything back from what they have already given to their ex wives. The reason of this prohibition is that the dower the husband pays to the wife becomes the property of the wife.[19] The practice in the today's Muslim societies is in contrast with this Qur'anic injunction. In most cases, the husbands confiscate, after the divorce, all that they give to their wives. Actually, the above verse commands the believers not to take any thing from their divorced women.

The above verse (4:20) uses a word "*qintar*" (great amount of wealth). Ibn al-'Arabi has devoted several pages to discuss the meaning of this term and its practical application in Muslim society. His discussion is presented here briefly.

As it appears from this verse (4:20), there is a room for the huge amount of dower in marriage. 'Umar ibn al-Khattab, the second Muslim Caliph once wanted to fix the amount of dower and declared that none should specify the dower more than twelve (12) *awqiyah* (the then denomination of gold coin in Arabia). A woman raised objection to it on the ground of the verse (4:20). 'Umar agreed with her and withdrew his decree on the matter. The Prophet (s.a.w.) paid the dower to his wife Umm Habibah 400 or 800 *dinar* (another denomination of gold coin). 'Umar himself is reported to have given 40,000 *dirham* (silver coin) as a dower in his marriage to Umm Kulthum bint Ali. The Prophet (s.a.w.) had solemnized the marriage of a man to a woman without mentioning the amount of dower. When this man neared his death, he left a will to give a particular property to his widow as a substitute for the dower. The widow sold that out. The price she received was around 100,000 *dirham*. 'Urwah ibn al-Zubayr paid 40,000 *dirham* to her wife al-Barqi bint Hani as dower. A rich person namely Mutarrif married a woman on 10,000 *awqiyah* as dower. There are also examples of very little amount of dower paid. The Prophet (s.a.w.) solemnized the marriage of a woman on only an iron ring as dower. In another case the Prophet (s.a.w.) allowed a woman to accept a pair of shoes as dower. 'Abd al-Rahman ibn 'Awf married a woman merely by paying a small amount of gold (equivalent to five *dirham*).

Scholars are not unanimous on the precise amount of the wealth called as "*qintar*". There are around ten different views on this matter. Some consider it as thousands of *dinar* or dirham and some are of the view that this implies huge wealth without specific limit. Ibn al-'Arabi does not give any weight to any of these views. But he agrees that "*qintar*" signifies" the wealth which is too much in weight.[20]

It seems quite surprising that Ibn al-'Arabi makes the above verse (4:20) the basis of his discussion on the dower in marriage. In the verse there is a mention of an exceptional case and not every case where the amount of dower is in the form of huge wealth. In the verses of the Qur'an, in which the dower-payment has been made obligatory for the groom in marriage (e.g. 4:25; 5:5; 60:10), the term used for the dower is "*ujur*" (plural of "*ajr*" meaning reward). The amount of reward depends upon the situation of both the groom as well as the bride. It may be, at times, less and, at some other times, more. That is why the Prophet himself paid a huge dower for his own marriage but very little for the marriage of some poor Companions. Ibn al-'Arabi has quoted a tradition of the Prophet on the authority of 'Uqbah ibn 'Amir that the Prophet (s.a.w.) said: "The best marriage is the one which takes place with ease".[21] Dower payment is an intrinsic part of the institution of marriage. Easy marriage may also mean easy approach in the agreement of dower amount.

Divorce-Related Issues

The verse 2:229 reads: "*The divorce is twice, after that either you retain her on reasonable terms or release her with kindness. And it is not lawful for you to take back anything from what you have given them, except when both the parties fear that they would be unable to keep the limits ordained by Allah. If you, then, fear that they would not be able to keep the limits ordained by Allah, there is no sin on either of them if she gives back (the dower) for her release.*"

In this verse three important rulings have been passed: (1) The divorce should be given only twice after which there is still a room for the resumption of conjugal relation, (2) If the divorced woman is released, the ex husband does not have any right to lay claim over what he had given to his wife, and (3) In case of uncompromising situation between the wife and husband, the wife may buy her freedom (*khul'*) through returning to the husband the bridal-money (*mahr*).

Number of Divorce

Ibn al-'Arabi, in his deliberation over the above verse (2:229), at times, agrees and, at some other times, disagrees with other scholars over the issue and the nature of the number of divorce as ordained by the *Qur'an*. He identifies the above verse as a revelation to protect the women from abuse at the hands of husbands. As he explains, in the pre-Islamic period the people would divorce their wives hundreds of times and withdraw it hundreds of times with a view to meting out psychological torture to the latter; Allah corrected this practice of the people through his command. He criticizes al-Shafi'i for his view that three divorces pronounced together are valid. He stresses that one of the conditions of the valid divorce is its occurrence at intervals. For that he makes the word of the verse "twice" (*marratan*) as a proof. He argues that if two or three divorces are given in one single sitting, it is only once, not twice. To strengthen his approach further he cites the Prophet's (s.a.w.) judgment in the case of 'Abd Allah ibn 'Umar who divorced his wife during her menstruation period. The Prophet (s.a.w.) asked him to retain his wife until the completion of the menses followed by another two menses period as well as that of purity; and he allowed him, then, to divorce her in the state of purity without having any physical contact with her. Ibn al-'Arabi's third argument in his favor is the view of Malik ibn Anas and Abu Hanifah that the legally valid divorce is only twice.[22] The chance for the resumption of conjugal relation, Ibn al-'Arabi maintains, after two divorces always remains in place. He does not agree to the view of al-Shafi'i that the release of the divorced wife after two divorces constitute the third and the last divorce. He rejects the tradition attributed to the Prophet (s.a.w.)— "The release with kindness is the third divorce"—as unreliable. He finds the permission of the third divorce in the other verse: "*And if he divorces her, she is, then, not lawful for him until she marries another husband.......*" (2:230).[23]

Position of the Property Given to the Wife by the Husband

The above verse (2:229) prohibits the husband to take back anything from the wealth the husband has given to the divorced wife before divorce. Some scholars are of the view that the prohibition applies only to the dower (*mahr*) but Ibn al-'Arabi looks at this as applicable to all kinds of wealth the husband ever gave the wife during their happy days.[24] Syed Mawdudi interprets the provision in view in these words: "The husband does not have any right to take back whatever he has given to her wife including the dower, ornaments, clothes etc. In principle the demand to return the gift or the present is in conflict with the Islamic ethics. This mean attitude has been likened in a hadith to the dog's licking away its own vomited out stuff. Obviously, it is very shameful for the husband to demand of his divorced wife to leave behind every thing he gave her. The etiquette Islam has taught is that the man while bidding farewell to his divorced wife should rather give her something."[25]

Provision of Separation on woman's Initiative (Khul')

As has been mentioned earlier, the verse (2:229) prescribes for the married woman a lawful way to buy her freedom from the marriage. Like other jurists, Ibn al-Arabi does believe in the significance of *khul'*. But he disagrees with others like al-Shafi'i who consider the uncompromising situation between wife and husband as the condition for the application of *khul'*. The statement in the above verse (2:229)—"*if you fear that they would not be able to keep the limits ordained by Allah, there is no sin on them if she buys her freedom through payment*"—seems to be making the *khul'* linked to the extremely adverse matrimonial relation. Ibn al-'Arabi is of the view that this verse does not spell out about the condition of *khul'*, but about the general reason leading to the use of the provision of separation. According to him, even without any such reason woman is entitled to ask for separation if she is not willing to continue the marriage.[26]

Al-Shafi'i considers the *khul'* dissolution of marriage (*faskh*), not divorce (*talaq*). Ibn al-'Arabi rebuts this decree and declares *khul'* as divorce. He does not see any chance of resumption of conjugal relation after *khul'*. For this matter he refers to a tradition. When a wife of Thabit ibn Qays complained to the Prophet (s.a.w.) about the cruel treatment at the hands of her husband and wished to have separation, the Prophet (s.a.w.) advised her to return the orchard, which her husband had given her as dower, to her husband and asked Thabit ibn Qays whether he agreed to the separation in exchange of the return of the dower. When both the wife and the husband agreed, the Prophet announced separation between them.[27]

The Provision of Remarriage

The verse 2:230 ("*And if he has divorced her [the third time], she is not, then, lawful for him until she has married another husband. If the other husband divorces her, it is no sin on both of them to reunite*") puts a very hard condition for the remarriage after the husband divorces his wife thrice. This provision in legal terminology is called "*halalah*". Ibn al-'Arabi talks on this occasion about two things: (1) the position of marriage with another husband and divorce without consummation, and (2) the divorced woman's own initiative for another marriage. Sa'id ibn al-Musayyib allows the remarriage merely after the marriage without sex with the other husband followed by the divorce. Ibn al-'Arabi insists that the term *nikah* (marriage) implies both the wedding and the consummation hence the woman's remarriage with the first husband will not be valid without the second husband consummating the marriage before he divorces her. He also derives the idea of woman's own initiative to marry another husband.[28] It means the divorced woman should not be forced to marry another person. The statement—"*until she marries someone else*" (2:230)—gives the right of marriage to the woman, and not to anyone else. Had Ibn al-'Arabi used *hadith* he would have further strengthened his view. On the authority of many sources such as Ali, 'Abd Allah ibn Mas'ud, Abu Hurayrah, and 'Uqbah ibn 'Amir it has been reported that the Prophet (s.a.w.) cursed the man who persuades another man to marry his divorced wife and divorce her so as to remarry her.[29] Syed Mawdudi considers such marriage and remarriage unlawful sexual act.[30]

The Divorced Woman's Rights to the Residence and the Maintenance

The verses 65:4-6 clearly put the matter concerning the waiting period and the residence plus maintenance for the divorced women, whether pregnant or not. This divine command does not appear ambiguous, yet Muslim jurists have unnecessarily fallen victim to the controversy. As for the residence and maintenance for the two categories of divorced women, the pregnant and the non-pregnant divorced only twice, scholars are unanimous that the husbands must provide to them. The controversy surrounds the question whether the non-pregnant divorced woman who has been divorced thrice deserves both the residence and the maintenance. There are mainly three views among them about the divorced woman's right to residence and maintenance. First, she deserves both the residence and the maintenance. *Hanafi* school of law has adopted this stand. Second, she has the right only to the residence but not to the maintenance. This is the decree of Malikites and Shafi'ites. Third, she is to be provided neither the residence nor the maintenance. This is the view mainly of Ahmad ibn Hanbal.[31]

Ibn al-'Arabi tries to maintain the view of Malik ibn Anas. He favors the second view. He insists that the non-pregnant divorced woman who has been divorced thrice cannot lay claim to the maintenance on the ground that she has been accorded the right only to the residence. His basis is the above-mentioned verses (65:4-6). His argument is that the *Qur'an* prescribes only the residence for the non-pregnant divorced women. The logic he follows is this: "When Allah mentioned the residence, He applied it to all kinds of divorcees. But when he stated the maintenance, He conditioned it with the pregnancy. Thus, it is clear that the thrice-divorced woman does not have any right to the maintenance."[32] One might, then, argue that Allah did not also mention the residence for the pregnant. Ibn al-'Arabi brings out, in response to this observation, a simple reasoning. He says: "The once or twice-divorced women have the right to the inheritance; and they cannot go out of the house during their waiting period except with the permission. The residence was not commanded for them. It is because the residence is the logical corollary of the maintenance. Allah says: "*If they are pregnant, spend on them until the delivery*" (65:6)."[33]

One might apply the same line of argument as used by Ibn al-'Arabi to validate the non-pregnant women's right not only to the residence but also to the maintenance. The same verse (65:6) begins with this statement: "*Lodge them where you live, according to your means, and do not harm them so as to straiten them*". Psychologically, when the divorced wife has been allowed to remain in the house of the husband during her waiting period, she stands allowed to share in the other facilities of life including food and clothing. It does not make any sense that the husband is ordered to provide residence for his divorced wife but prohibited from arranging for her maintenance.

Unlawful Sexual Act and Its Punishment

The *Qur'an* is very sensitive to the ethical dimension of human life. It provides a number of moral principles for the mankind so as to maintain the social fabric. One of such principles is "keep away from all kinds of sex relation out of wedlock": (1) "*And those who guard their chastity except from their wives or (the slaves) that their right hand possesses*" (23:5-6); (2) "*And come not near to the unlawful sexual intercourse. Verily, it is an indecent deed and an evil way*" (17:32).

The *Qur'an* treats such sexual offence very seriously and prescribes ways to discipline the offenders: (1) "*And those of your women who commit illegal sexual intercourse, take the evidence of four witnesses from amongst you against them; and if they testify, confine them to houses until the death overtakes them or Allah ordains some other way*" (4:15); (2) "*The male and the female guilty of illegal sexual intercourse, flog each of them a hundred stripes*" (24:2).

Scholars and jurists have unnecessarily covered this simple Qur'anic prescription with complicated debates making the issue of punishment for adultery the bone of contention. Ibn al-'Arabi took part in this disputed discussion adamantly. While trying to communicate the message in one of the above-quoted verses (4:15), he declares that it is a verse too difficult to understand. He claims that the entire Muslim *ummah* is unanimous over its ever time applicability. He rejects the idea of its abrogation on the ground that the abrogation applies only to a situation where two statements on the same issue are essentially different; the other statement on the same issue as this verse is 24:2 which prescribes punishment of flogging to the adulterer; there is no conflict between the two verses (4:15 and 24:2); they are rather complementary to each other.[34]

The first part of the verse (4:15) talks about the procedure of proving the guilt of the women involved in adultery; the second part thereof sheds light on the immediate penalty imposed on the guilty persons; and the last part thereof ("*or Allah ordains for them some other way*") assures the believers to receive some way out of this problem. While enlightening his readers on this last part of the verse, Ibn al-'Arabi enters into the debate of what is acceptable and what is not regarding the penalty for adultery as prescribed in some traditions of the Prophet (s.a.w.). Muslim and others have recorded a tradition on the authority of 'Ubadah ibn Samit that the Prophet (s.a.w.) said: "Take from me. Allah has ordained a way for the women. The unmarried offender will be punished by a hundred lashes and banishment of one year.[35] The married offender will be flogged a hundred lashes and stoned to death." It is very clear from this tradition that the adultery deserves double punishment. For the unmarried it is flogging and the banishment; for the married actor it is flogging and stoning to death. Ibn al-'Arabi takes two stands, one for the married offender and the other for the unmarried offender. As for the double penalty for the unmarried offender, he submits to the above-mentioned tradition. Abu Hanifah considers the double punishment for the unmarried offender in conflict with the *Qur'an* hence he declares the tradition abrogated and retains the command of the *Qur'an* (24:2). Ibn al-'Arabi disagrees with him and seeks to favor the relevance of the tradition. But Ibn al-'Arabi does not want to apply the double punishment to women actors due to the banishment being highly injurious to the chastity of the women. For the punishment to the married offenders, he does not favor the double punishment because he did not find the Prophet (s.a.w.) flogging the actor before stoning to death.[36] What a double standard! Amin Ahsan Islahi rejects the report of 'Ubadah ibn Samit as concoction made by the heterodox people.[37] It seems quite strange that the Prophet himself declared the way ordained by Allah and he was the first to disobey it. The theory of abrogation is not a valid basis to explain this discrepancy between the word and the practice. If the Prophet (s.a.w.) did not carry out the double punishment for the married actor, he must not have said about the double penalty. The Prophet (s.a.w.) did prescribe the double punishment to some unmarried offenders. It may not necessarily be in the light of the way ordained by Allah but it might have been a measure of extra punishment keeping the nature of the offence in view. When Allah promised to guide to a way for the sexual problem (4:15), it is logical to conclude that the way must have been revealed in the *Qur'an* itself and that revelation is 24:2. With the revelation of the punishment for the adultery in 24:2, it became clear that the only penalty for the sexual offence is flogging, and nothing else. Ibn al-'Arabi classifies, like other jurists, the sex offenders into the married and the unmarried. It is an evident discrepancy in the jurisprudence. If Allah did not specify the category of the offenders, scholars do not have any right to insert their speculations in the Islamic law.

Punishment of the Armed Robbery

The *Qur'an* seeks to establish an environment in the human setting where none is wronged; and where everyone's life, property, and honor are safe. For that matter the *Qur'an* prescribes harsh punishments for the usurpers of others' life, property, and honor. The offence of unjust killing carries death penalty (2:178). The theft is deterred by cutting off the hand of the thief (5:38). When a woman's honor is outraged, the guilty upon conviction is to be publicly humiliated by flogging (24:2). The *Qur'an* also deals very seriously with the issue of armed robbery. The punishment for the armed robbery may be derived from the verse 5:33 ("*The punishment of those who wage war against Allah and His Messenger, and strive with might and main for mischief through the land is execution, or crucifixion, or the cutting off the hands and the feet from the opposite sides, or exile them from the land*").

Ibn al-'Arabi finds the provision of this verse (5:33) applicable to the armed robbery. According to Malik ibn Anas, Ibn al-'Arabi's legal mentor, the Qur'anic term "*muharib*" as occurred in the above-quoted verse implies a person who waylay, terrorize people in general, and creates chaos in the land whether he kills someone or not. For such person the *Qur'an* orders either of the four punishments, execution, or crucifixion, or amputation, or deportation. Malik ibn Anas sees in these four options the freedom of the judge to decide in accordance with the situation. Ibn al-Arabi has quoted an example from the Prophet's (s.a.w.) tradition referring to the punishment of robbery. Some people approached the Prophet (s.a.w.) seeking his help for their problem. The Prophet (s.a.w.) sent them to a place where the camels of the government were taken care of. These people reached there and enjoyed living there for a reasonable period of the time. One day they killed the in-charge of the camels and took away the camels. Upon this the Prophet (s.a.w.) sent his people to pursue them and nab them. When they were caught and brought to the Prophet (s.a.w.), they were all sentenced to death. Ibn al-'Arabi has also quoted two cases, which he decided during his tenure as the judge. First, some armed robbers waylaid some people, took away a woman from them, and gang raped her. When this case was brought to Ibn al-'Arabi, the judge, he decided it in the light of the above-mentioned verse (5:33). The jurists contested this judgment of Ibn al-'Arabi and said the offenders were not "*muharibin*" (waylayers). Ibn al-'Arabi, then, argued that the robbery of a woman's chastity is more serious offence than that of the wealth; the people will not mind if all of their wealth is taken away in order to save the honor of their wives and daughters. Second, a case of theft was brought to him. The thief had entered a house along with his accomplices; he threatened the head of the family with a knife, putting it on his chest, and his partners took away the wealth. He passed the judgment equating the thieves with the "*muharibin*" (armed robbers).[38]

In the today's so called sophisticated and highly enlightened world the armed robbery on the highways and bank robbery cases in the cities and towns are quite common phenomena. Armed robbery in fact amounts to creating chaos in human society and to terrorization of the people. The only suitable penalty, the reason appeals, for such offenders is what Ibn al-'Arabi suggests in the light of the *Qur'an*.

Property Distribution and the Settling of the Deceased's Debt

The *Qur'an* is in most cases very brief while directing man in his multi-dimensional life. In one or two occasions only the *Qur'an* puts forward the matter concerned in detail. One such issue, which it has dealt with all the necessary detail, is the property distribution. It shows the gravity of the matter. While giving the detail of who should get how much from the deceased's property the *Qur'an* explicates that the distribution of the property should be carried out only after the execution of the will as well as the debt of the deceased: "*After the payment of all the legacies and debts*" (4:11 & 12).

Ibn al-'Arabi considers this provision of settling the debts first as a very serious provision in the law of property distribution. To him, the payment of debts has been given priority to the distribution of property because it is far better than any other good deed. He quotes a tradition recorded by great *hadith* scholars like al-Bukhari on the authority of Jabir ibn 'Abd Allah. After the death of his father, Jabir requested the Prophet (s.a.w.) to pay the debts of his father with his own hands. The Prophet (s.a.w.) accepted the request and went to Jabir's orchard where all the money creditors had gathered to get their dues back. The Prophet (s.a.w.) made the payment to all those who had lent anything to the deceased.

Ibn al-'Arabi mentions three incidents recorded by al-Bukhari and others. First, the Prophet (s.a.w.) led the funeral prayer of someone who did not have any debts. Second, he led the funeral prayer of someone who had debt and left wherewithal to settle it. Third, he declined to lead the funeral prayer of the one who had debt and did not leave anything to pay it off.[39]

These incidents speak volumes of the seriousness of the unpaid debts. In Muslim societies today there is little attention to the payment of the debts owed by the deceased. The inheritors distribute the property without taking into consideration the Qur'anic instruction on settling the debts from the deceased's property before its distribution among the lawful claimants. The inheritors are afraid that the debt settlement may reduce the size and value of the property hence they will lose materially. Why do they forget the permanent loss on their part if they do not pay off their father's debts out of his own property, which he left behind.

Alcoholism: Bane for Human Life

The *Qur'an* seeks to ensure the welfare of the society as well as the individuals. It bans all those things that may harm the individual and social life of man. Qur'anic prohibition on certain food items and drinks is one such measure. The *Qur'an* has prohibited man to drink wine due to it being very destructive to the human body, mind and the social relations. There are three verses talking about the position of wine: (1) "*They ask you concerning alcoholic drink and gambling. Say: In them is a great sin and some benefits for men, but the sin of them is greater than their benefit*" (2:219); (2) "*O you who believe! Approach not the prayer when you are in a drunken state*" (4:43); and (3) "*O you who believe! Intoxicants and gambling................are abomination of Satan's handiwork. So avoid that in order that you may be successful*" (5:90).

Ibn al-'Arabi mentions the controversy surrounding the meaning of the Qur'anic term for the wine, "*al-khamr*". There are mainly two views regarding the application of this term. First, according to Abu Hanifah and others from Kufah, the term *al-khamr* applies to only the wine prepared of grape; and the drink made of other fruits and sources is "*nabidh*" (non-alcoholic beverage). Second, according to the jurists of Makkah and Madinah, all the drinks that bring pleasure and cause intoxication fall under *al-khamr* (wine). Ibn al-'Arabi criticizes Abu Hanifah's approach in this matter. He argues that all the intoxicants are wine hence all of them are unlawful. In order to further strengthen his stand he advances two arguments. First, the day the wine was forbidden the people broke their wine pots, which were full of the beverage made of the date fruits. Second, 'Umar declared that the alcoholic drinks that were banned were basically made of five sources, grape, dates, honey, wheat, and barley.[40]

Conclusion

Ibn al-'Arabi's work *Ahkam al-Qur'an* is of great legal value. It has touched on almost all the relevant legal issues related to religious life, social order, economic undertaking, political matter, cultural phenomenon, educational system, and moral problem. In the above discussion some legal issues concerning marriage, divorce, property distribution, armed robbery, alcoholism etc. were discussed in detail. Ibn al-'Arabi's arguments seem to be very strong but, at times, weak. He has used, at times, sarcastic remarks against great jurists like Abu Hanifah and al-Shafi'i. It is not appropriate for his position as a scholar. Respect for others is a known etiquette in the academic and intellectual life. Most of the time Ibn al-'Arabi is very brief in his arguments. It is because, as it appears from his frequent references and suggestions, he has discussed the same issues in some other works. Had he repeated the same information in his *tafsir* work his interpretation of the *Qur'an* would have been more useful. In the Arab world there is a very popular trend to edit and annotate the old works. Ibn al-'Arabi's work of *tafsir* is in great need of editing and annotation so as to let it become comprehensive.

Notes

1. Al-Zirikli, Khair al-Din, *Al-A'lam* (Dar al-'Ilm li al-Malayin, Beirut, 1999), vol. 6, p. 30; Al-Dhahbi, Muhammad Husayn, *Al-Tafsir wa al-Mufassirun* (no date and place of publication), vol. 2, pp. 448-449; Muhammad 'Abd al-Qadir 'Ata' (editor), *Ahkam al-Qur'an* of Ibn al-'Arabi (Dar al-Kutub al-'Ilmiyyah, Beirut, 1996), p. Arabic letter "Ha", under the title "Ahkam al-Qur'an and its Author".

2. Ibn al-'Arabi, Abu Bakr, *Ahkam al-Qur'an* (Dar al-Kutub al-'Ilmiyyah, Beirut, 1996), vol. 1, pp. 494-495.
3. *Ibid.* p. 495.
4. *Ibid.*
5. *Ibid.*
6. *Ibid.* p. 496.
7. *Ibid.* p. 502.
8. *Ibid.* p. 501.
9. Al-Bukhari, Muhammad ibn Isma'il, *Sahih* (Dar Ihya' al-Turath al-'Arabi, Beirut, 1400 A. H.), vol. 3, kitab al-Nikah, p. 366, hadith no. 5114.
10. Ibn al-'Arabi, *Ahkam al-Qur'an*, vol. 1, p. 496.
11. Ibn Hajar, *Tahdhib al-Tahdhib* (Dar al-Ma'rifah, Beirut, 1996), vol. 5, pp. 592-593.
12. Ibn al-'Arabi, *Ahkam al-Qur'an*, vol. 1, p. 496.
13. *Ibid.* p. 476.
14. *Ibid.* p. 477.
15. *Ibid.*
16. *Ibid.*
17. *Ibid.* vol. 3, p. 507.
18. *Ibid.* vol. 1, p. 508.
19. *Ibid.* p. 469.
20. *Ibid.* pp. 469-472.
21. *Ibid.* p. 470.
22. *Ibid.* pp. 257-260.
23. *Ibid.* pp. 260-261.
24. *Ibid.* p. 263.
25. Mawdudi, Syed Abul A'la, *Tafhim al-Qur'an* (Markazi Maktabah Islami, Delhi, 1983), vol. 1, p. 175.
26. Ibn al-'Arabi, *Ahkam al-Qur'an*, vol. 1, pp. 263-264.
27. *Ibid.* p. 264-267.
28. *Ibid.* pp. 267-268.
29. Mawdudi, *Tafhim al-Qur'an*, vol. 1, pp. 176-177.
30. *Ibid.*
31. *Ibid.* vol. 5, pp. 573-575.
32. Ibn al-'Arabi, *Ahkam al-Qur'an*, vol. 4, p. 287.
33. *Ibid.*

34. *Ibid.* vol. 1, p. 457.
35. Muslim, *Sahih* [with the commentary of al-Nawawi], (Dar al-Ma'rifah, Beirut, 1997), vol. 6, kitab al-Hudud, pp. 189-191, hadith nos. 4390-4393.
36. Ibn al-'Arabi, *Ahkam al-Qur'an*, vol. 1, pp. 461-464.
37. Islahi, Amin Ahsan, *Tadabbur-e-Qur'an* (Taj Company, Delhi, 1997), vol. 5, pp. 365-366.
38. Ibn al-'Arabi, *Ahkam al-Qur'an*, vol. 2, pp. 92-100.
39. *Ibid.* vol. 1, pp. 442-444.
40. *Ibid.* pp. 208-209.

2

An Islamic Response to the "Human Rights" Discourse: Analysis of the Problem and Proposal for an Alternative Dialogue[1]

S. A. Farrar

Introduction

The "Human Rights"[2] discourse is founded upon the notion of the inherent equality and dignity of every human being. As fellow members of the human family, it purports to offer Muslims a powerful rhetoric in the articulation of their grievances, a mechanism for securing their needs and wants from a state or states, and a protective shield in their battles against inequalities, injustice, oppression and exclusion. In the wake of the troubles triggered by the 9/11 attacks and the continual suffering caused by military invasions and occupations of Muslim lands, "Human Rights" emerges as a contemporary language of resistance.

Yet there is unease in Muslim communities, both lay and academic, that an embrace of "Human Rights" doctrine in totality would undermine attempts to live an Islamic life and for states to operate according to Islamic principles. Muslims are aware that "Human Rights" has been used as a sword against them just as much, if not more, than as a shield in their defence. Thousands of marchers protesting in Ankara and Istanbul in support of secularism and *against* an "Islamist" presidential candidate invoke their "Human Rights."[3] They, and others opposed to the establishment of an Islamic State in Muslim lands, utilize the doctrines of "Human Rights" to denounce the *Shari'ah*, especially its apparent denial of freedom of belief, its alleged oppression of women and the perceived severity of its system of punishment (the *Hudud*).

"Human Rights" also figures frequently in the political rhetoric of the "War on Terror," in support of the military wars being fought against and between Muslims in Iraq and Afghanistan, and in criticisms of the so-called "axis of evil" Similarly, it appears as a cultural and ideological ally in the cultural war being fought by the United States and the UK in the Middle East, Asia and elsewhere. It provides both the philosophical template upon which liberal reform programmes are exported to the Muslim world as well as some of the intellectual tools for re-interpretations of Muslim texts which Americans and Europeans regard as compatible with their perspectives and values.[4] It appears to operate as an attempt to de-legitimize existing Muslim governments (especially which purport to govern in accordance with the *Shari'ah*), to challenge long-held traditions, practices and beliefs and to posit a plausible replacement consistent (in their view) with a broad interpretation of Islam and with approaches of the "modern world".[5]

In short, the concern is that the "Human Rights" discourse reads as a contemporary manual for a neo-colonialist and imperialist agenda. Such a concern may be more apparent than real, but it flags up the importance of examining and exploring the compatibility of "Human Rights" with an Islamic framework and with the rules of the *Shari'ah* - the *Fiqh*[6]- in order to see where Muslims can position themselves in the ongoing debate.[7]

This essay is divided into three main sections. The first section begins by setting out and comparing the conceptual categories and fundamental premises of "Human Rights" with Islam and its *Shari'ah*. The second section contextualizes the discussion through an analysis of the Convention on the Elimination of all Forms of Discrimination against Women (CEDAW) and the problem of "dress codes".[8] In the third section, the author summarises the essential problems and suggests meaningful ways forward for the respective camps in the ongoing debate.

The "Human Rights" Discourse

"Human Rights" is a universal discourse; a neutral, non-partisan critique that claims to uphold the inherent dignity of the individual human being. It holds that every human being has an equal and "inherent" right to freedom and dignity, and that the list of rights it protects and promotes are distributed equally and universally irrespective of gender, race, religion and ethnicity. It is said that by virtue of being "human" one receives these "rights".[9] Although there are different views on the origins of "Human Rights"[10], the modern foundation stone for "Human Rights" doctrine is the Universal Declaration on Human Rights (UDHR). This has been the principal philosophical source and inspiration for other conventions and multi-lateral treaties, such as the International Covenant on Civil and Political Rights (ICCPR), the International Covenant on Economic, Social and Cultural Rights (ICESCR), and the Convention on the Elimination of all forms of Discrimination against Women (CEDAW), which comprise International Human Rights Law.

The efforts of the "Human Rights" lobby since the end of World War II to secure universal acceptance of the idea of "Human Rights", at least politically, appears to have been a success. In addition to the UN, regional organizations such as the Council of Europe, the Organization of African Unity and the League of Arab States, have all adopted the ideals of "Human Rights" and drafted their own treaties in order to improve "Human Rights" standards in their particular regions.[11] This has included the Organization of the Islamic Conference (OIC) which in 1990 adopted the Cairo Declaration on Human Rights in Islam.

Political acceptance in no small degree has been facilitated by globalization and the power of the world wide media in our information age. No government, irrespective of its political persuasion, wishes to be described and pilloried as a violator of "Human Rights," so much so that governments prefer to dispute whether such violations have occurred rather than the notion of "Human Rights" itself.[12] Although conceptual conflicts remain between "Human Rights" and different traditions,[13] most of the disputes have arisen over their interpretation and substantive content. In other words, and to quote Mashood Baderin, the debate has been about *universalism* in "Human Rights" rather than its *universality*.[14]

By virtue of the fact that they are deemed inherent, many advocates of "Human Rights"–especially in the West–argue that there is a base standard and necessary content from which member state governments can never depart. Although it is obvious that cultures around the world have different world views and concerns, they maintain that governments cannot excuse persistent inequalities, oppression and marginalization in their societies on the basis of "cultural difference". The provisions of "Human Rights" treaties such as the UDHR, ICCPR and CEDAW are intended to improve the living conditions and quality of life for every individual in society, and apply irrespective of their race, ethnicity, culture or religion. Defences of cultural relativism, they argue, would lead to dilution of fundamental and necessary protections and absolve governments of their responsibility to promote a "larger freedom."[15]

Opponents of this view maintain that even if one is committed to the ideals of "Human Rights", they cannot be implemented in isolation of cultural and religious contexts. Gender roles, common understandings, ritual practices and community networking often operate as gatekeepers, blocking unwanted external influences and admitting others only to the extent that they can be adapted and claimed as "their own".[16] Failures to recognize this reality not only fuels fears of neo-colonialism,[17] but can also perpetuate the very practices which the ideals of "Human Rights" are meant to address.[18] Proponents of cultural relativism, therefore, argue that cultural and religious traditions themselves must be allowed to mediate between "Human Rights'" texts and government responsibilities in order to implement "Human Rights'" imperatives effectively. This does not mean that cultural and religious traditions remain static; indeed the presence of the "Human Rights" instrument, they argue, provides a reference and educational resource that promotes a new cultural hermeneutic; a new internal dynamic of "rights" promoting sustainable change and reform.[19] But it does imply that desirable reform will be less likely if "Human Rights" advocates ride rough shod over local tradition.

Although these differences in interpretation of "Human Rights'" have existed since the adoption by the General Assembly of the UDHR and explain the general wording of many of its articles, they are united in one important aspect. They are committed to the idea of "Human Rights" and to a philosophical, political and legal framework in which substantive claims of "Human Rights" can be secured.

To what extent, if at all, is a religious tradition, such as Islam, with its own sources, methods of interpretation, substantive doctrines, formulated rules and principles, consistent with this discourse?

The Islamic Discourse of Rights (Huquq)

If one studies books of *Fiqh*, it soon becomes apparent that Muslim scholars write primarily in terms of "obligations" rather than "rights". For example, they will write:

يجب على كل مكلف اداء جميع ما اوجبه الله عليه،
... و يجب و ترك جميع المحرّمات

(This means: It is obligatory for every accountable person to perform all that which Allah obligated him to perform...and to avoid committing all prohibitions)[20]

A person is called "pious" (*taqiy*) if he/she performs all obligations (*wajibat* or *furud*[21]) and avoids all prohibitions, rather than when they have fulfilled all rights incumbent upon them. Nevertheless, it would be false and incorrect to conclude that "rights' talk", even as conceived within the western discourses, does not exist. First (although there is no necessary connection), for many obligations there are correlative rights.[22] For example, it would not be wrong in terms of judgment to rephrase the above quotation and to state that Allah has a "right" that we obey Him and a right that we refrain from disobeying Him.[23] Similarly, although the texts state that solvent Muslims are "obliged" (*yajibu ^alayhim*) to pay *Zakat* to the 8 categories of persons stipulated in the Qur'an, it would also be correct to say, as a correlative, those 8 categories of persons are "entitled", that is–they have the "right" to receive *Zakat*.

Second, Islamic Law[24], the *Shari'ah*, refers explicitly to rights in scholarly elaboration of *Huquq Allah* (the Rights of Allah) and *Huquq an-Nas* (the Rights of People).Yet these rights are understood in religious rather than secular terms; they are but a reflection of one's obedience to God and to His Prophet.[25] The former are universal, eternal and immutable; the latter dependent upon context and generated through societal relationships. These relationships, however, remain structured by the rules of the Shari'ah and ultimately return to the immutable revealed religious sources. The Prophet, (صلى الله عليه وسلم) was asked by a man who was the best amongst the Muslims and he replied:

مَنْ سَلِمَ الْمُسْلِمُونَ مِنْ لِسَانِهِ وَيَدِهِ.

"The one who saves his fellow Muslims from his hand and his tongue".[26]

The Islamic scholars construed from this *Hadith* that there are rights[27] between people (*Huquq An-Nas*), such as not to be beaten or verbally abused,[28] in addition to the rights which Allah has over us (*Huquq Allah*), such as not to associate partners with Him, prayer and fasting. Some of the Rights of People derive from the mere fact of our Muslim faith –as the wording of the *Hadith* implies. This is because the existence of certain rights are not free after the performance of certain obligations, the most important of which, from a Muslim's perspective, is not to associate any partners with God and to believe in Prophet Muhammad as His final Prophet and Messenger. This entails that the person who performs that primary obligation has a preferential status over the one who neglects it.

The latter does not mean, however, that persons who do not profess Islam are without any rights. Their rights originate in the principles of "*Ahd*"(covenant) or "'*Aqd* " (agreement) with which Muslims are duty bound to comply.[29] If the promise is freely given, it generates an obligation (*fard*) on the part of the Muslim to fulfill the terms of his agreement and provides a corresponding right and legitimate expectation for the non-Muslim that those terms will be implemented as stated. The precedent of the Holy Prophet (صلى الله عليه وسلم) in the Treaty (*Sulh*) of *Hudaybiyah*[30] indicates that such agreements may be entered into by the leaders of Muslim states even if the terms may at first seem unfavourable. This would enable Muslim states and a collection of Muslim states to make agreements that confer specified benefits and protections on non-Muslims and to forego some of their own rights for a clear benefit (in the Treaty of *Hudaybiyah* it facilitated the spread of Islam in non-Muslim states). Even after the time of the Prophet, (صلى الله عليه وسلم) the Caliphates and Sultanates that ruled up until the end of the reign of Sultan Abdul Hamid II operated on this basis.[31]

It should be clear from this that Islam has its own discourse that is compatible with discourses of "human dignity". [32]

Allah says in *al-Qur'an*:

و لقد كرمنا بني ادم

(And Allah ennobled the Children of Adam)

The nobility of Adam, the original human being, was such that even the Angels (who are free from sin), were ordered to prostrate to him in deference to his status and superiority.

The dignity to be accorded the human being was preserved in the principles which underlay the Islamic rules conveyed by all of the Messengers of Allah: from Adam and Musa, through to 'Isa and *Sayyidina* Muhammad (صلى الله عليه وسلم). The Islamic scholars (such as al-Ghazzali, and some others) termed them: the five essentials or *Maqasid ash-Shari'ah*; namely: the preservation of life, lineage, property, intellect and religion. All of the rules which they brought, in their different ways, sought to protect these five essentials. This did not mean that life and property, for example, could never be taken or that matters of religion not be regulated. For instance, to have a rule which allows the ruler to take the life of another if the latter has killed without a right is an acknowledgement of the importance attached to life and the need to deter others from taking it. It is not an affront to the dignity of life itself. The rules prohibiting and punishing fornication and adultery uphold the importance of family ties, community bonds and the clear devolving of property to one's descendants. They also indicate how different we are from animals and serve to demarcate the human being from the animal. The rules on apostasy and the prohibition on leaving Islam remind the human being at all times of his primary responsibility to God and of the purpose of his creation. To turn one's back on the ultimate truth having been shown the straight path is not only treasonous (as he has betrayed His Creator and Lord) but also a denial of the origin of all of the rules that proclaim the dignity of the human being.

The Problem

The essential dilemma is that both *Shari'ah* and "Human Rights" are universal discourses. As "Human Rights" claims to be universal, it cannot bow to divergences that originate in another normative framework. Moreover, as these rights are deemed inherent, they are non-negotiable. It may allow alternative conceptions to a degree and different interpretations of its substantive content, but it will deem illegitimate values, principles and laws that go against its fundamental premises. It is not up to a particular religion or belief system to pick and choose those aspects with which it agrees and to ignore the rest. Indeed, the "Human Rights" agencies of the UN understand the doctrine in this way. This is why in 1993 the Vienna Declaration pronounced: "all human rights are universal, indivisible and interdependent and interrelated." The pluralism it supports, therefore, is limited and selective.

The *Shari'ah* also has universal application. It offers a complete code and way of life (*Deen*) for the human being and enjoins the believers not to judge by other than that Code, whether through the format of "Human Rights" or otherwise[33]. Through its five ontological modalities: the *haram* (prohibited), *makruh* (disliked), *mubah* (permitted), *wajib* (*fard*) (obligatory) and *mandub* (*sunnah*) (optional and rewardable), working in conjunction with the twin concepts of *fard-ul 'ain* (personal obligation) and *fard-ul kifayah* (communal obligation), the *Shari'ah* is able to regulate and guide both private and public life. Moreover, its combination of temporal punishment (through *Hudud*, *Qisas*, *Ta'zir* and *Kaffarah*) with dire consequences for body and soul in the Hereafter should any person commit prohibited acts or fail to perform obligations (irrespective of whether that punishment is carried out[34]), along with its refusal to bow out of political life[35], provides an holistic and integrated approach to human governance, taking into account both physical and spiritual concerns. Its completeness appears to leave little room to accommodate "Human Rights."[36]

Of course, if the substance of a "Human Rights" doctrine coincides with the interests protected and promoted by the *Shari'ah*, one might argue that in applying that "Human Rights" doctrine one is implementing the *Shari'ah*; indeed, one might argue that the former is a contemporary procedural mechanism for carrying out the latter in nation states which rarely support or defend Islamic interests. The differences, it might be said, are more in terminology and sources than with substance. But even those who argue for the incorporation of "Human Rights" within a so-called Islamic paradigm accept fundamental differences remain.[37] The problem is real and not hypothetical as Muslims are mindful of the Prophet's saying:

من احدث في امرنا هذا ما ليس منه فهو رد

("We reject that which is introduced into this religion of ours when it is not from it.").[38]

Their loyalty and obedience are to the laws and values which "belong" to Islam; that is, those based in *Ayats* of the *Qur'an*, the sayings of the Prophet, the *Ijma'* of its top scholars (the *Mujtahidun*) and *their* juridical reasoning (*Ijtihad*). It is not up to us take some part of the religion and to ignore the rest, as the *Qur'an* addressed the Jews before them,

أفتؤمنون ببعض الكتاب و تكفرون ببعض

(Do you believe in a part of the Book and reject a part?)[39]

Moreover, logic dictates that two universal discourses cannot co-exist because co-existence implies a degree of compliance and submission. If one principle of "Human Rights" law is not in accordance with Islamic doctrine, by necessity that "Human Rights" law must then be amended to conform with Islamic doctrine if the *Shari'ah* is to maintain its universalism. Similarly, if the *Shari'ah* is contrary to "Human Rights" doctrine, followers of the latter would argue that the *Shari'ah* must also be reformed.[40] If, in the process of juridical reasoning (*Ijtihad*), the relationship between text (*Nass*) and intellect (*'Aql*) were reversed, so that the latter was given precedence over the former, there would be no barrier to using conventions and treaties on "Human Rights" as a subsidiary source of interpretation to the *Qur'an* and *Sunnah*. But such a process would be very controversial and encounter considerable resistance as the history of the Mu'tazilah bears witness.[41]

It will be apparent from the case study below that while "Human Rights" offers an opportunity to articulate grievances and to change posited laws of nation states in line with the *Shari'ah*,[42] there remains an impasse not simply at the theoretical and conceptual level, but also in the day to day disputes and encounters between "Human Rights" advocates and Muslims who wish to continue with their traditional way of life.

A Case Study: Gender Equality and the Problem of Dress Codes

Non-discrimination and the principle of equality is said to be "the starting point for all other liberties."[43] The Universal Declaration on Human Rights (UDHR)[44] and the International Covenant on Civil and Political Rights (ICCPR), do not differentiate between men and women and emphasize that the rights mentioned therein are general in character.[45] Article 3 of the ICCPR obligates States to ensure that both men and women enjoy equally all of the civil and political rights stated in the Covenant. The Convention on the Elimination of all Forms of Discrimination Against Women (CEDAW) explicitly advocates equality for women and advances a programme of reform that aims to change traditional roles between men and women and to prohibit all forms of discrimination.[46] In order to ensure reforms are actually implemented by States Parties, CEDAW also places an obligation to submit reports to the Secretary General of the UN once every four years and for those reports to be considered by the Committee set up under CEDAW[47] consisting of experts selected by States Parties.[48] It is no under-statement to say that the pursuit of gender equality is now one of the major pillars of International "Human Rights" Law.

The *Shari'ah* also addresses equality between men and women. During the Last Sermon, the Holy Prophet (صلى الله عليه وسلم) reminded his male companions of the reciprocal nature of rights in Islam. He stated:

إن لكم على نسائكم حقا ولنسائكم عليكم حقا

(It is true that you have certain rights in regard to your women, but they also have rights over you[49])

Thus for a Muslim state to acknowledge in its legislation the rights accorded to men by the *Shari'ah* and to ignore the rights accorded to women by the same source would be a type of discrimination prohibited in Islam.

But this does not entail absolute equality and the granting of the same rights and obligations. Rather, the law is one of "equivalence" because of inherent differences between men and women,[50] the additional responsibilities conferred on men[51] and the differentiation of roles prescribed in the *Qur'an*.[52] The emphasis which Islam places on roles, however, and that these are in part determined by our gender and inherent differences, does not sit easily with the framework of universal rights envisaged by the ICCPR and the Convention on the Elimination of all Forms of Discrimination against Women (CEDAW). Role differentiation is seen as a contributing factor to the oppression and marginalization historically endured by women, especially in traditional societies. This is made clear by the Human Rights Committee in its General Comment on Article 3 of the ICCPR. It states:

> *"Inequality in the enjoyment of rights by women throughout the world is deeply embedded in tradition, history and culture, including religious attitudes... States parties should ensure that traditional, historical, religious or cultural attitudes are not used to justify violations of women's right to ...equal enjoyment of all Covenant rights."*[53]

It should be noted that the Human Rights Committee uses the expression "religious attitudes" and does not distinguish between this and "religious law." Yet there is a vast difference between the opinions and biases of a people *inspired* by religion (a "religious attitude"), and the formal rules of "law" or *shar'* which apply to all, irrespective of cultural practices and gender biases or preferences. The pre-eminent Islamic scholars, the *Mujtahidun*, deduced these rules from the sources sincerely and as an act of worship. They were not done in order to perpetuate historical oppression of one gender or community over another. Rather, they believed that in formulating a rule they were discovering and clarifying what Allah had revealed to His Prophet in order to guide the people.[54]

Dress codes and the idea that men and women should have to dress modestly and appropriately are matters that fall within the *Shari'ah* and have been the subject of much adverse comment by "Human Rights'" activists.[55] The general position in the *Shari'ah* is that men are obliged to cover what lies between their navel and their knees, and women must cover all of their bodies apart from what is "apparent," namely their faces and their hands. There are differences in the schools as to whether men can wear shorts and whether women are allowed to reveal their feet, but all the schools agree that the remaining parts of the male and female body must be covered when in the presence of other than the spouse and relatives of the opposite sex whom one is prohibited from marrying.[56]

Rather than viewing the codes as an impartial and gender-neutral prophylactic, a protection against the sexual objectification prevalent in contemporary societies[57], activists tend to construct the dress codes as part of an historical and traditional pattern of discrimination against women, a form of restraint against a woman's self-expression and an indication of her subordinate role. The "religious law" is converted into the prohibited "religious attitude" because the woman is required to cover more of her body than a man. Indeed, they regard it as one of the most visible aspects of a woman's oppression and second-class status. Linguistically[58] and physically, the veil is seen as demarcating and isolating the woman from the mainstream of society.[59]

Textual support for their opposition to Islamic Dress Codes seems to derive from General Comment 28, paragraph 13, in which the HRC directs:

> *"13. States parties should provide information on any specific regulation of clothing to be worn by women in public. The Committee stresses that such regulations may involve a violation of rights guaranteed by the covenant, such as article 26, on non-discrimination; article 7, if corporal punishment is imposed in order to enforce such a regulation; article 9, when failure to comply with the regulation is punished by arrest; article 12, if liberty of movement is subject to such constraint; article 17, which guarantees all persons the right to privacy without arbitrary or unlawful interference; articles 18 and 19, when women are subjected to clothing requirements that are not in keeping with their religion or their self-expression; and, lastly, article 27, when the clothing requirements conflict with the culture to which the woman can lay a claim."*

Yet of itself, and in isolation of the wider cultural conflicts and mechanisms for enforcement, paragraph 13 is not necessarily against the Islamic dress codes. The Committee does not state that dress codes are violations of the Covenant per se. Rather, they "may involve" a violation of the rights in the Covenant depending on the extent of the dress code and any differentiation between men and women. No one is saying, for example, that a State is not allowed to punish a woman who walks the streets naked. An objection would exist, however, if a man walked naked in the streets and was exonerated while a woman was punished by the courts for doing the same.

Moreover, there is nothing in the *Shari'ah* that would necessitate corporal punishment (article 7), imprisonment (article 12) or even a power of arrest (article 26). Failure to follow Islamic dress codes, in relation to both men and women, is not an offence which carries a fixed penalty (*Hadd*). Rather, any corrective measures taken by the authorities would be discretionary in nature (*Ta'zir*) and could entail merely a reprimand. Further, if provision for this reprimand were posited in the legislated law of a Muslim State, it could be enforced by way of summons rather than through a power of arrest. If there were community concerns as to the integrity of the *Shurta*, or the local police, and their ability to administer the rules fairly, there is no reason why a *Hakim* or local magistrate could not be so empowered.

Even if one returned to the motivating concern of "Human Rights'" activists in this area, namely the "invisibility" of women in the Muslim State and their objection to the *Burqah* and *Niqab* (in particular) as a symbol of their social exclusion, there is nothing in the authoritative Islamic texts which mandates either the *Burqah* or the *Niqab*. First, there is not a single *ayah* from the *Qur'an* or a *Hadith* which requires either form of headwear to be worn by women generally.[60] Rather, the *Qur'an* directs women to draw their veils over their chests and not to display their beauty "other than that which is apparent."[61] This suggests that the face and the hands need not be covered. This remains the case even if the woman is very beautiful. It is narrated in the *Saheeh* of Ibn Hibban[62] that at the time of the Prophet a beautiful woman used to come to the *Masjid* in order to pray. Some of the men would arrive late and stand in the last row for the congregational prayer so that when they bowed during their prayer, they would peek under their arms and look at the beautiful woman behind them. In spite of the obvious distraction to their prayer, the Prophet did not order the woman to cover her face. Rather, the following *ayah* of the *Qur'an* was revealed:

و لقد علمنا المستقدمين منكم و لقد علمنا المستئخرين

(*Allah* knows who among you stands in the first row and who among you stands in the last.) [63]

Second, the same judgment is supported in the *Hadith* of the Prophet. It is narrated in the *Saheeh* of Al-Bukhariyy that during the *Hajj* season, a beautiful woman came to the Prophet in order to ask him something. Behind the Prophet was his cousin al-Fadl (the son of al-'Abbas), who was also of fine appearance. The woman and al-Fadl began to look at each other with desire, prompting the Prophet to physically turn al-Fadl's face to one side. In spite of her beauty, the Prophet did not reprimand the woman and tell her to go and cover her face. In explaining his actions to al-Fadl's uncle, the Prophet said:

رأيت غلاما حدثا و جارية حدثة فخشيت أن يدخل بينهما الشيطان

(I saw a young man and a young woman and I was worried that the devil would seduce them.)[64]

The scholars reasoned that had it been an obligation for her to cover her face, then the Prophet would have ordered accordingly. If a man were consumed with desire, the obligation was upon him to look away, not for her to cover up. As the *Qur'an* said:

قل للمؤمنين يغضوا من أبصارهم

(Say to the male believers: Let them lower their gazes)[65]

Third, it should be noted that both Ibn Jarir at-Tabariyy[66] and Qadi 'Iyad al-Malikiyy,[67] among others[68], report a juridical consensus (*Ijma'*) that a woman is not obliged to cover her face. This means that some of the opinions of the later scholars (*al-Muta'akhhireen*)[69] mandating the *Niqab* should not be given any weight.[70] This does not mean, however, that wearing *Niqab* or the *Burqah* is not a good practice. Indeed, the Hanafi jurist Ibn 'Abidin in his *al-Hashiyat* also reported a consensus that it is *recommended* by the Islamic texts. But one cannot deem obligatory what is merely recommended.

In summary, there is room for manoeuvre between the Islamic rules on dress codes and the texts on "Human Rights" and that the adoption of the latter would not necessarily entail abolition of the former. In fact, it could be argued that paragraph 13 of General Comment 28 may be used to *support* Islamic dress codes. The paragraph mentions that a state party should provide information on clothing regulations "when women are subjected to clothing requirements that are not in keeping with their religion or self-expression... and when the clothing requirements conflict with the culture to which the woman can lay a claim." This would seem to suggest that Muslim women in countries where CEDAW is directly incorporated into their law would be able to challenge laws and regulations which prevent them from taking office, entering an educational establishment, or holding any government job unless they remove their *Hijab* or *Niqab*. In theory, those provisions could be used in legal and political challenges by Muslims against such regulations passed by governments of Turkey,[71] France, Germany and the UK,[72] who are State Parties to CEDAW, and whose existing reservations would not prevent reference to such laws.[73] They could also be the subject of critical comment by the Committee which reviews the reports submitted by States Parties every four years, and be used to ratchet up the pressure on those States to reform.

But CEDAW reflects an alternative value system located in individual freedom rather than duty, responsibility and the need to fulfill a role (see above).[74] It resists all attempts by States, or local cultures using the state legal apparatus, to limit a woman's self-expression. Should a woman wish to wear the *Hijab*, *Niqab* or *Burqah*, the state should not, by force of law, prevent her from doing so nor impose regulations that would have the effect of excluding her from civil and political institutions. But by the same token, if the state wanted to *impose* such forms of dress so that women were denied the option to follow or not to follow the dress codes that would also be contrary to the Convention. In principle, this would seem to include all forms of the veil.

This leaves Muslims in a dilemma in that it appears one cannot be had without the other. Although Muslim states might enter reservations to protect their laws, it would seem doctrinally inconsistent for Muslims to utilise and to support the use of the very same articles to enable following of the dress codes in other states. Such an approach smacks of "double speak" of which

Muslim states accuse western nations in their approach to "Human Rights".[75]

Further, principles of International Law in the interpretation and validation of reservations to "Human Rights'" treaties as currently applied, would prevent such a challenge in practice in any event. According to the International Court of Justice in the *Reservations to the Genocide Convention* case,[76] and prevailing juristic opinion, interpretation of the "objects and purposes" of a Convention is left to the particular state itself to determine and to choose whether the State holding that reservation is a party to the Convention or not.[77] If, for example, Saudi Arabia wanted to challenge the legality of the prohibition of *Hijab* in Turkish universities under International Law, Turkey could point to Saudi Arabia's reservation to CEDAW and argue that it is incompatible with the latter's objects and purposes. This would enable Turkey to hold that Saudi Arabia is not a party to the Convention.[78] While that would not stop members of the CEDAW Committee charged with reviewing reports submitted to them from making critical comment[79], it is doubtful whether that procedure would be effective as representatives of States more closely orientated on Islamic tradition are under-represented on the Committee.[80] It would also depend upon the willingness of the offending State to take remedial measures. When reports detailing Turkey's compliance with CEDAW were brought before the Committee, it is notable that only one member of the Committee made an adverse comment on dress codes enforced in public Turkish universities and the Turkish representative was able to dismiss the criticism. First, he said that it was matter for the universities to decide rather than the government. Second, even if it was a matter for the government, the wearing of the headscarf (*Hijab*) was a religious symbol and contrary to Turkey's secular democracy. And third, their position was not in opposition to the opinions of the European Court of Human Rights which had upheld similar regulations.[81]

The problem which the above case study illustrates is that even if the texts of treaties are open to interpretations compatible with *Shari'ah* and could even help to allow Muslims to follow its norms, current structures within the UN militate against those interpretations being given any currency.[82] When one considers the multiplicity of issues which come before these committees (such as the CRC[83] and the Committee of CEDAW), it is unlikely that all of the issues which Muslims would like discussed will be given equal emphasis. Even if dedicated time were allotted to consider more deeply matters related to religious compliance, there are no Islamic scholars on these Committees who could fulfill that function effectively. Furthermore, the appointment of such scholars[84] could lead to another set of problems which would need to be resolved through a detailed framework of rules specifying the weight to be given to their opinions and how conflicts between them and the rest of the Committee could be resolved. Any perceived imbalance in the procedure in favour of one side or the other could also lead to accusations of bias and undermine the very reason for their inclusion. It is highly likely the new composition and decision making structure of the Committee would become so complex and protracted, that the work of the Committee would grind to a halt.

This leads us to the uncomfortable conclusion that while greater recognition of Islamic values and precepts is possible within the perspectives of International "Human Rights",[85] the structural reforms required within specialized committees to make this a reality would make it very difficult to realize in practice. The recent reforms to the structure of the UN and the introduction of the new Human Rights Council, to be appointed by an absolute majority of the General Assembly, with a specific mandate to review the records of all member States (and not just those belonging to a so-called "axis of evil") and to promote genuine interactive dialogue, may well soften the impact on Muslims of a renewed emphasis on the implementation of "Human Rights". Yet it is uncertain how the new structure would filter down to the more specialized committees charged with enforcing specific treaties and conventions.

The Way Forward

A number of authors such as Monshipouri, An-Na'im and Baderin[86] have suggested part of the problem lies with the interpretative mechanisms of the *Shari'ah* and that any rapprochement between the two discourses requires fresh interpretations or, at the least, new formulations of *Ijma'* (consensus) in order to accommodate most of the concerns of International "Human Rights". I have suggested elsewhere that these proposals would not carry the traditional Islamic establishment with them and likely to encounter considerable resistance, especially in Sunni heartlands.[87] Moreover, the idea that Muslim peoples need to "reform themselves" when there is no guarantee of their Islamic rights being secured in non-Muslim States is more reminiscent of a colonial agenda than an international system of law based upon mutuality and reciprocity.

The above discussion indicates that an Islamic response to the "Human Rights" debate needs to be mobilized outside the current framework for enforcing International "Human Rights" Law and outside of the UN in order to protect the integrity of the *Shari'ah* and its Doctrine.[88] This does not mean that all dialogue between Muslim and non-Muslim States should end or that we cannot reach workable agreements on substantive and practical matters[89] which relate to "Human Rights" concerns. But these agreements need to be reciprocal in nature, as was the Treaty of H̲udaybiyah, and to carry concrete benefits for both sides. They also must be enforceable through existing domestic and regional mechanisms.

Before this can happen, the structural imbalances in power between non-Muslim and Muslim States have to be addressed. All agreements involve negotiation and the results of negotiation are invariably affected by the economic, political and military muscle wielded by the respective parties to that negotiation. The current stalemate obtaining between Palestinians and Israelis and the political support given by the United States and the European Community to Israeli positions in the negotiation process illustrate the importance of power brokers.

The most obvious source of power-broking is the Organization of the Islamic Conference and for negotiations to take place through its auspices. Established in 1973 and with a current membership of 57 Muslim States, a third of current UN membership, the OIC offers considerable potential to fulfill this task. Following the collapse of the Caliphate in 1924, with its combined resources it is the only body at the international level and which claims "strict adherence to Islam and to Islamic principles"[90] for its operating values, that is able to compete regionally and with individual superpowers. Since 1975, the OIC has gradually enhanced its international status and occasionally been invited to the negotiating table by the UN.[91]

Because it claims to represent the interests of Muslim states as diverse as Turkey, Saudi Arabia, Indonesia and Iran, it naturally avoids extremist positions and openly calls for consensual decision-making between Muslim states and for dialogue between Muslim and non-Muslim states. The OIC-EU forum launched in 2002 and recent calls to revive these talks,[92] along with the recent decision of the US President to appoint a special envoy to the OIC[93] provide clear indications that both sides are beginning to realize the important role which the OIC can play in improving relations between Muslim and non-Muslim states and in enhancing the relationships between non-Muslim states and their Muslim citizens. It also serves as a reminder to the OIC itself that if it is to assume its global and regional role, it cannot continue to be divided by nationalist interests and must seize the *ummatic* nettle. [94] The recent meeting of the Third Extraordinary Session of the Islamic Summit held in Mekkah between 7-8 December 2005 and its call for the Islamic Conference of Foreign Ministers to actively promote good governance and the values of "Human Rights" in its Member States on the lines set out by the 1990 Cairo Declaration on Human Rights in Islam and the need for a binding covenant as to the same,[95] indicate how seriously the OIC regards this task and this it is not empty rhetoric.

The OIC Member States themselves have also begun to take positive steps in their domestic laws. Malaysia, one of the OIC Member States, has started to address local and international concerns through a synthesis of "Human Rights" with the values of *Shari'ah* in its criminal justice system. The Royal Malaysian Police, which have written the words *Allah* and *Muhammad* above their crest, have embarked on a process of internal reform, and are attempting to incorporate some of the recommendations outlined in the Royal Commission's Report on the Royal Malaysian Police in 2005 and the Report of the Commission to Enquire into the Standard Operating Procedural Rules and Regulations in Relation to the Conduct of Body Search in Respect of an Arrest and Detention by the Police (2006).[96] Both of these reports emphasized the need for transparency, accountability, "human rights' policing" and a renewed focus on the values of *Shari'ah*. While many of the details are still to be worked out and implemented,[97] the old complacency and inactivity is being replaced with a new determination to reform outdated structures and better orientate operational values.

Although many criticisms can be made of the OIC, including its inability to draft a constitution for the proposed International Islamic Court of Justice, and the failure to establish the important International Islamic Law Commission,[98] it remains the best avenue for negotiating, drafting and enforcing agreements between Muslim and non-Muslim States in matters relating to "Human Rights". If it is to seriously assume this role, however, the EU, other regional bodies (such as ASEAN) and individual States such as the USA, China and Russia, must draw up special treaties with the OIC in which these States will agree to legislate and enforce particular matters which the OIC indicate must be addressed in their respective jurisdictions. The EU already has a well established and sophisticated enforcement mechanism with its Member States, but there would need to be special arrangements with other regions and other States where the legal mechanisms for enforcement are less transparent and doubts may persist as to their efficacy.

As for the Muslim side, each of the 57 Member States of the OIC need to confer specific authority on the OIC to negotiate and draft treaties on their behalf and to comply with the terms of any agreement entered into.[99] Monitoring of agreements would need to be carried out by a new enforcement organ of the OIC which would also have the power to sanction Member States and, ultimately, order their expulsion from the OIC for fundamental and repeated failures to comply with the terms of its agreement. In light of a number of economic initiatives among OIC member states and the new moves for international *Halal* markets, exclusion from the OIC and subsequent isolation could have serious economic and political repercussions for the State concerned. Failure to establish such an enforcement organ, however, would lead to skepticism amongst non-Muslim States and reluctance on their part to enter into binding agreements with the OIC. It is essential, therefore, for the OIC to reform its infrastructure and to focus on matters of enforcement – both in terms of its relations with non-Muslim States and with its own Members.

Conclusion

The majority of the above discussion has focused on the difficulties of reconciling concepts of International "Human Rights" with the precepts and principles of the *Shari'ah* – the Islamic Law. It has been argued that while both discourses have a number of meeting points, sharp divergences still exist both in theory and in practice. But it has also been suggested that these obstacles are not insurmountable at the international and regional level in that both Muslims and non-Muslims recognize[100] that agreements made between States are binding upon the parties. The effectiveness of such agreements from the perspective of both sides will depend upon the quality of the negotiation process,[101] the implementation of a detailed enforcement regime and the extent of mutuality and reciprocity.

Mutuality and reciprocity is important not merely in terms of substance but also symbolically. It sends out a message that common standards are being applied in each other's jurisdictions and announces the end of political and legal hypocrisy. If non-Muslim States wish to continue restricting Muslim rights to practice their religion–including the wearing of *H̲ija̲b* and *Niqa̲b*, the application of Muslim family law and inheritance, burial rights, *Waqf* (Islamic trusts) and circumcision[102], and to implement disproportionate and discriminatory anti-terror and immigration laws, they cannot expect Muslim States not to differentially regulate the lives of non-Muslims in Muslim States, let alone attempt to prevent Muslims applying their own legal tradition in their own lands in relation to their own Muslim citizens. The historical criticism of Orientalists[103] that the Islamic State discriminated against non-Muslims through the imposition of *Jizyah* (the Capitation Tax), the discriminatory dress codes, the non-availability of the death penalty and of equal compensation in the event of a Muslim killing a non-Muslim is off the point, quite apart from being only a partial truth and an argument pulled out of context.[104] The point is that both sides have and continue to discriminate to protect and promote, as they see it, the values of their particular societies. In the context of most European countries, and France in particular, it is their secular tradition and the notion of formal equality before the law.[105] In the context of most Muslim countries, it is their religious tradition and the values of the *Shari'ah.*[106] It is only through mutual exchange, understanding, genuine debate, effective negotiation and agreement that our societies can avoid further fall-out from 9/11.

Even if the reforms I mention are implemented, conflicts will continue to arise internally in Muslim States, and many of them because of the religious-secular divide that we see regionally and internationally. Just as at the international level, interpretative mechanisms and legislative measures sensitive to locality, local beliefs and common religious practices will be required to resolve them[107] along with a detailed framework of enforcement, including a monitoring system, to ensure they are realized in practice.

Notes

1. This article is based on a paper prepared for the Law and Society Conference, Humboldt University, Berlin, 25-27 July 2007.
2. The term "human rights" is placed in speech marks to indicate that the concept is not self-evident or uncontested and remains a matter of controversy in the Islamic world.
3. Newspaper reports note that 600 NGOs sponsored and supported the recent marches in Ankara and Istanbul in support of a secular state and in opposition to the "Islamist" presidential candidacy of Abdullah Gul. Retrieved from *Al-Jazeera*, 29 April 2007, see: *http://aljazeera.com/me.asp?service_ID=13300.*
4. According to David Kaplan, the United States has regarded the implementation of Human Rights as a key policy directive in their fight against Islamist extremism and has set aside substantial funding to support organizations fighting their ideological war. For example, USAid funds 30 organizations in Indonesia alone which promote liberal thinking and "Human Rights" in Islam. See further, D. Kaplan, "In an Unseen Front in the War on Terrorism, America is Spending Millions…To Change the Very Face of Islam," (USNews.com, 25/4/2005).
5. This parallels and almost matches the "rule of law" propaganda articulated by Orientalists in the 1950s when newly independent Muslim countries were searching for constitutional models to orientate their fledgling states; see further, S.A. Farrar, "Islamic Jurisprudence and the role of the accused: a re-examination", *Legal Studies* (2003), Vol. 23, No. 4, 587-604, at 592-3. As for the role of western academics in supporting European and American geo-political objectives, see

generally Edward Said (cf *Orientalism*: London, Penguin, (1995)) and *Covering Islam*: London, Vintage, (1997), in particular.

6. Linguistically, "fiqh" means knowledge and encompasses more than that pertaining to "rules" (*ahkam*); hence why Abu Hanifah termed his treatise in relation to the Islamic Creed, "*Al-Fiqh-ul Akbar*" (the Greatest Knowledge). In the Shari'ah literature, however, it has the technical meaning of the religious judgments (*Ahkam*) derived from the Islamic sources (*Nusus-is Shari'ah*). This means that for any Muslim response to have the epithet "Islam*ic*", it should be based on those sources and within the overall framework of Islam rather than upon extraneous considerations and sources.

7. This indicates that "Human Rights", both in terms of concept and conception is not uncontroversial in the non-Muslim "western" world either. Critical Legal Scholars and postmodern philosophers, in particular, have been very critical. See further, Costas Douzinas, *The End of Human Rights–Critical Legal Thought at the End of the Century*: Oxford, Hart Publishing, (2000), chapter 1; Jacques Derrida, *Spectres for Marx*: London, Routledge, (1994), p. 94.

8. I do not suggest that this is the only problematic area. But in light of the ongoing controversy in Iran and recent legislative amendments in the Indonesian state of Aceh, the issue seems an appropriate one in which to explore the conceptual, legal, cultural and political difficulties which this paper seeks to address.

9. See: J.Rehman, *International Human Rights Law; A Practical Approach*: Dorset, Pearson, (2003), p. 6; Mashood A. Baderin, *International Human Rights and Islamic Law*: (2003), Oxford, OUP, p. 16.

10. See Henkin, A.H. (ed), *Human Dignity: The Internationalization of Human Rights* (1979), p. ix; Stephen P. Marks, "From the 'Single Confused Page' to the 'Decalogue for Six Billion Persons': The Roots of the Universal Declaration of Human Rights in the French Revolution" *Human Rights Quarterly*, (1998),Vol. 20, pp 459-514; Maurice Cranston, *What are Human Rights?*: London, Bodley Head, (1973); Michael Perry, *The Idea of Human Rights:* New York, OUP, (1998), chap 1.

11. See: the European Convention for the Protection of Human Rights and Fundamental Freedoms (1950), the African Charter on Human and People's Rights (1981), and the Arab Charter on Human Rights (1994).

12. See Baderin, *op.cit.*, p. 23.

13. I argue this includes Islam; see below. For conceptual difficulties with Judaic law; see Robert Cover, "Obligation: A Jewish Jurisprudence of the Social Order," *Journal of Law and Religion* (1987) Vol. 5, 65.
14. Op.cit., p. 23. Again, I do not mean by this that the concept of "Human Rights" is acceptable in Islam.
15. See the speech of Kofi Annan, "In larger freedom: towards development, security and human rights for all," *Report of the Secretary-General*, United Nations, General Assembly, A/59/2005, para 17.
16. See Homi B. Bhabha, *The Location of Culture*: New York, Routledge, (1994).
17. See R. Higgins, "The Continuing Universality of the Universal Declaration" in P. Baehr, C. Flinterman, M. Senders (eds), *Innovation and Inspiration: Fifty Years of the Universal Declaration of Human Rights*, Amsterdam, Royal Netherlands Academy of Arts and Sciences, (1999).
18. Although the governments of Turkey are more often cited as violators than protectors of "Human Rights", their failed attempts to secularize and "modernize" the Turkish people using the full state apparatus is a good comparative example of the enduring nature of traditional religious practices and their ability to navigate around hostile externalities. See further, Ihsan Yilmaz, *Muslim Laws, Politics and Society in Modern Nation States: Dynamic Legal Pluralisms in England, Turkey and Pakistan*: Aldershot, Ashgate, (2005).
19. See, Abdullah Ahmed An-Na'im, "Human Rights in the Muslim World," *Harvard Human Rights Journal* (1990), Vol. 3, 13. For a critical account of An-Na'im's theory, see S.A. Farrar, "Revelation, Philosophy and International Human Rights: Reconciling the Irreconcilable?" (2005), *IIUM Law Journal*, Vol. 13, No. 2, 259-291.
20. Sheikh 'Abdullah al-Harariyy, *Mukhtasar 'Abdullah al-Harariyy al-Kafilu bi-Ilmi –d-Deen ad-Daruriyy* Dar al-Mashari', Beirut, (2004), p. 18.
21. Within the School of Ash-Shafi'iyy, the term "wajib" and "fard" have the same meaning, and are used inter-changeably except in matters pertaining to the Pilgrimage (Hajj). In the school of Abu Hanifah, however, the term "fard" conveys a higher degree of obligation and refers to those matters founded upon explicit verses of the *Qur'an* (*qat'iyyah*) or upon *hadiths* with mutawatir chains of narration. The "wajibat" still refer to obligations, but the degree of sin for the one who fails to perform them is less.

22. On the relationship between "rights" and "duties" in western jurisprudence, the normal starting point for discussion is the famous work of Hohfeld, *Fundamental Legal Conceptions As Applied in Judicial Reasoning* (1919).
23. Religiously, however, it would not follow that as human beings have 'rights' that *Allah* has 'obligations'. This would be a renunciation of the principles of *At-Tawhid* because it would wrongly imply that *Allah* has a partner to obligate Him with matters.
24. I do not imply by this term other than the *Shari'ah*. Distinctions between "Islamic Law" and the *Shari'ah* are frequently made in Orientalist literature distinguishing between the administrative regulations and rules issued by Muslim sovereign rulers (*Qanun*) and the rules derived from the revealed sources (the *Qur'an* and *Sunnah*).
25. The customary rules set up by communities independently of the *Shari'ah*, alternatively called *'adat* or 'urf, may generate expectations of compliance, but no "rights" as such unless dictated by the *Shari'ah* itself. Custom is only regarded as a secondary source and even then the custom generally referred to is the practice of the Arabs at the time of the Prophet (صلى الله عليه وسلم). See further, Sheikh Muhammad Zahid al-Kawthari, *al-Maqalat al-Kawthari*: Cairo: al-Maktabah al-Azhariyah li al-Turath, (1994).
26. This is a *mashhur* hadith (ie it has at least 3 different narrations which convey the words of the Prophet in exactly the same way). The particular narration above is found in the collection of Sahih *Muslim*, Kitab-ul Iman, Bab Bayan Tafadili-l Islami wa Ayyu Umurihi Afdal, Hadith no. 57.
27. I do not intend, in this brief paper, to elaborate on the content of those rights between Muslims nor how we necessarily categorise them as flowing from the "*maslahah*" or from the *Maqasid* of the *Shari'ah* directly. This has been mentioned by other writers, but needs closer examination and detailed explication which is beyond the remit of this paper. It needs to be stated, however, that modern writers who refer to these concepts tend to look to change the Islamic law to conform with Human Rights norms – rather than vice versa. The argument advanced in this paper is that Islamic law needs to stand on its own rather than as a reflection.
28. The explanation of An-Nawawi, (see: *Sharh Saheeh Muslim*) clarifies that the hadith means a "perfect" Muslim (*Kamil*). The meaning of the *hadith* narrated through Jabir المسلم من سلم المسلمون من لسانه ويده, therefore, is implicit. It does not mean that a Muslim who violates the

rights of his fellow Muslim is no longer a Muslim; rather, he is a sinner.

29. The principles related to *sulh* (settlement) are also relevant, as the precise terminology of the Treaty of Hudaybiyah indicates. These enable a Muslim to forego some of his rights for a perceived benefit.

30. See: I.A. Jamahali, *Diplomatic Relationship in Islam: Its History and Relevance to the Contemporary Muslim Society:* Kuala Lumpur, ISTAC, International Islamic University Malaysia, (2005); Abu Khalil, Shawqi, *Sulh al-Hudaybiyah: Al Fath al-Mubin*: Damascus, Dar al-Fikr, (1983).

31. For an example, see: the Draft Treaty of Amity and Commerce 1536, drawn up between Sultan Suleyman 1st and King Francis 1st of France. This is referred to by J.C. Hurewitz , *The Middle East and North Africa in World Politics: A Documentary Record*, i. *European Expansion*, 1535-1914, Princeton, 2nd Edition, (1975).

32. See: Javaid Rehman, *International Human Rights Law*: Harlow, Pearson, (2003), p. 6. Steiner and Alston, *International Human Rights in Context:* Oxford, OUP, (2000),; Mashood Baderin , *International Human Rights and Islamic Law*: Oxford, OUP, (2004). This does not mean that the rules are based on "human dignity" as that would imply they are centred on the human being when, in reality, they are centred on the human being's worship of God. Rather, these rules are *consistent with* a discourse based on "human dignity".

33. See *Surah al-Ma'idah*, ayah 44. This does not mean that those who judge by other than the Law of *Allah* are not Muslims; rather, they are big sinners (see Sheikh 'Abdullah al-Harariyy, *Bughyat at-Talib*, Vol. 1, Beirut, Dar al-Mashari'a', (2004), pp 76-78).

34. Avoidance of punishment in the Hereafter is dependant upon a person fulfilling the *arkan* (essential elements) of *at-Tawbah* (repentance). These are: regret, cessation of the prohibited act and the firm determination never to commit it again. Although temporal punishment may ensue following a confession (*iqrar*) which is often associated with remorse and repentance, there is no necessary connection between punishment in this life and punishment in the Hereafter. See further: S.A. Farrar, "Islamic Jurisprudence and the role of the accused: a re-examination," *Legal Studies*, (2003), Vol. 23, No. 4, p. 601.

35. This explains the detailed treatises on political governance within the Islamic State by al-Mawardi, At-Taraboulsi, and others. It also offers an interesting parallel with Christianity and Canon Law which gradually disassociated itself from the workings of the state ("render

unto Caesar what is Caesar's"), preferring spiritual guidance from a distance (see in particular the works by Thomas Aquinas).

36. *Surah al-Ma'idah*, ayah 3 is the last verse of the *Qur'an* to be revealed and it means: "Today, I have completed your religion for you." It should be noted, however, that this verse does not mean that the *Shari'ah* ended on that day; rather, the eternal framework in which the *Shari'ah* would be developed was completed when this last ayah was revealed. It implies, ultimately, that everything must return to the Holy Qur'an rather than to the philosophical speculations of "Human Rights'" theorists. See further, S.A. Farrar, (2005), op.cit.
37. See further, Mashood Baderin ,op.cit; Mahmood Monshipouri: "Islam, Democracy and Human Rights: the Continuing Debate in the West", *Middle East Policy*, (1994), Vol. 3, No. 2,: 22-39; *Islamism, Secularism and Human Rights*: Boulder and London, Rienner, (1998); Abdullah Ahmed An-Na'im, *Towards an Islamic Reformation: Civil Liberties, Human Rights, and International Law*: Syracuse University Press, (1990).
38. This hadith is narrated in the Saheehs of al-Bukhariyy and Muslim; see an-Nawawi, *Al-Arb'auwna Al-Nawawiyyah fi al-Ahadith an-Nabawiyyah*, 3rd Edition: Beirut, Dar al-Masharia', (2002), p. 12 (Hadith no. 5). See also note 29 above.
39. *Surah al-Baqarah*, ayah 85.
40. This is advocated explicitly by an-Na'im and Monshipouri, op.cit. Baderin does not go as far, but his formal rejection of *Ijma'* (juridical consensus) as an irrevocable source of the Shari'ah in order to incorporate "Human Rights" amounts to a very similar position in practice; see further, S.A. Farrar, "Revelation, Philosophy and International Human Rights: Reconciling the Irreconcilable?", (2005), *IIUM Law Journal*, Vol. 13, No. 2, pp 283-284. The work of M.H. Kamali offers a similar perspective; see further: *Freedom of Expression in Islam*: Kuala Lumpur, Ilmiah Publishers, (1998); *The Dignity of Man: The Islamic Perspective* : Cambridge, The Islamic Texts Society, (2002); *Principles of Islamic Jurisprudence*, Cambridge, UK, The Islamic Texts Society, (2003).
41. S.A. Farrar, *ibid.*, pp. 268-269. This does not mean that Mu'tazilah thinking will not influence sections of Muslim Society. It does presume however that in the long-run it will not be able to dislodge traditional schools and 'madhhabs' which continue to thrive despite many attempts to "renew" the religion in the past.
42. It should be mentioned that this would be possible only in those countries where International Law is given both horizontal and

vertical effect; namely where citizens can invoke provisions of International Law directly through the domestic law without necessitating the governing state to raise the case on behalf of its citizen in the international courts.

43. See Bayefsky, A.F., "The Principle of Equality or Non-Discrimination in International Law," *Human Rights Law Journal* (1990), Vol. 11, p. 1.
44. See: Article 1 ("All human beings are born free and equal in dignity and rights"); Article 2 ("Everyone is entitled to all the rights and freedoms set forth...without any distinction of any kind, such as...sex"); Article 7 ("All are equal before the law and are entitled without any discrimination to equal protection of the law"); Article 16 ("1. Men and women of full age, without any limitation due to...religion, have the right to marry...They are entitled to equal rights as to marriage, during marriage and at its dissolution").
45. See: Article 2 ("1. Each State Party to the present Covenant undertakes to respect and to ensure to all individuals within its territory... the rights recognized in the present Covenant, without distinction of any kind, such as...sex"); Article 23 ("4. States Parties to the present Covenant shall take appropriate steps to ensure equality of rights and responsibilities of spouses as to marriage, during marriage and at its dissolution."); Article 26 ("All persons are equal before the law and are entitled without any discrimination to the equal protection of the law. ...the law shall prohibit any discrimination and guarantee to all persons equal and effective protection against discrimination").
46. For a full general discussion of the policies and problems surrounding CEDAW, see Steiner and Alston, op.cit., pp 158-236. See also, J. Rehman, op.cit., pp. 350-375.
47. See Article 18.
48. Although selected and nominated by the States themselves, it should be noted that they are not government representatives and operate in their personal capacities; see J. Rehman, op. cit., p. 364.
49. This *Hadith* is found in most collections of *Hadith*. This wording is taken from At-Tirmidhi, *Hadith* no. 1083.
50. *Surah al-Baqarah*, ayah 228.
51. Men are obliged to financially support their wives and pre-pubescent children; it is not incumbent upon the wife to support the husband or his children. According to the denominational schools of Ash-Shafi'iyy and Malik, when the husband is no longer in a position to

maintain the wife, he no longer has "authority" over her and the marriage contract is breached; see Abu Hayyan al-Andalusiyy, *Al-Bahr al-Muhit*, Vol. 3, pp. 336-337.

52. See: *Surah An-Nisa'*, ayah 34.
53. General Comment 28, para 5.
54. See S.A. Farrar, *op. cit.*, (2005), p. 270.
55. See, for example, the comments in Malaysia by the pressure group, "Sisters in Islam", which claims to address these issues from Muslim perspectives (http://www.sistersinislam.org.my/lte/11112005.htm).
56. This does not mean that there are no clothing restrictions in relation to one's own family or when in the presence of persons of the same sex. Indeed, it is prohibited for a daughter to reveal her genitalia to her father and vice versa; likewise for a mother and son, father and son, mother and daughter, etc unless there is a necessity. The clothing restrictions are according to the specific context and relationship.
57. It could be argued that the restrictions on clothing even between family members as stated above, militate against sexual abuse in the home.
58. It is interesting to note the number of western texts claiming to document oppression of women by Muslims which have the title, "Behind the Veil". Among others, see: "Behind the Veil in Arabia; Women in Oman"; "Behind the Veil; A Nurse's Arabian Nightmare"; "The Bomber Behind the Veil."
59. The frequent and visceral criticism of the Taliban's enforcement of the *Burqah* (full face veil) and secularist criticism of Turkish Presidential candidate Abdullah Gul, whose wife wears a *Hijab*, and recent media criticism of Iran's enforcement of Hijab, are good examples. For a full discussion of the legal, sociological and cultural context of the Hijab in France, see Mohammad Mazher Idriss, "Laïcité and the banning of the 'hijab' in France," *Legal Studies,* (2005), Vol. 25, No. 2, 260-295. For comment on recent developments worldwide, see: "Muslims and the veil: the meaning of freedom", *The Economist,* May 10th 2007.
60. This is not the case with the wives of the Prophet. As Abu Dawud in his *Sunan* has explained (see Kitab al-Libas, Bab fi qawlihi ^azza wa jalla, و قل للمؤمنات يغضضن من أبصارهن) they were obligated to cover up completely in front of other men (even if blind). He also states specifically that this judgment pertained only to the wives of the Prophet, and did not apply to all women.
61. *Surah al-Nur*, ayah 31.

62. See Vol. 1, p. 309, al-Ihsan bi-tadrib.
63. *Surah al-Hijr*, ayah 24.
64. See Ibn Hajr al-'Asqalaniyy, *Fath al-Bari*, Vol. 4, pp. 77-78.
65. *Surah al-Nur*, ayah 40.
66. See *Jami'u al-Bayan fi Tafsir al-Qur'an*, Vol. 9, p. 54.
67. He reports a consensus that a woman is not obliged to cover her face, but men are obliged to lower their gazes; see *al-Ikmal*. Zakariyya al-Ansariyy, from the Shafi^yy school, also refers to the consensus reported by Qadi 'Iyad; see *Sharh Rawdah at-Talibin*, Vol. 3, p. 110. In relation to other comments made by Zakariyyah al-Ansariyy in the same passage, see the note below.
68. The Imam of the Haramayn, al-Juwayni, also reported the consensus that a woman is not obliged to cover her face and hands, and it is for men to lower their gazes; see Ibn Hajar al-Haytamiyy, *al-Fatawa al-Kubra*, Vol. 1, p. 199.
69. Those scholars who said that women must cover their face, such as Zakariyya al-Ansariyy (*op. cit*), ar-Ramli and an-Nawawi, did not say that the woman's face is "'awrah"; rather they said that it must be covered to prevent seduction between men and women and to protect the general *maslahah*. However, this view does not give due weight to the consensus and is not reported to be the opinion of any *Mujtahid* – within the school (*Ashab al-Wujuh*) or without restriction (*Mutlaq*). This opinion also contradicts the *saheeh* hadiths mentioned above.
70. It needs remembering that the Prophet informed, "My Ummah would not agree upon an error" (the hadith is narrated by at-Tirmidhiyy and others). The term "My Ummah" in the *Hadith* refers to the complete Mujtahids (like ash-Shafi'iyy, Malik, Ahmad, Abu Hanifah, etc.) and not to scholars of a lower rank, including even scholars of *Usul al-Fiqh*. See further, al-Hattab ar-Rai'iniyy al-Malikiyy [d. 954 A.H.], *Qurrat al-'Aini bi-Sharh al-Waraqat Imam al-Haramayn*: Beirut, Dar al-Mashari^, (2001), p. 71. This suggests the statement of Professor Baderin that "the Shafi'iyy and Hanbali schools of Islamic jurisprudence generally hold that women must veil up their whole person in public, away from the view of strangers" (*International Human Rights and Islamic Law, op cit.*, p. 64), relying upon some modern generalist works, is not accurate. See above note.
71. One suspected motivation behind the "Islamist" Turkish ruling party's enthusiasm for joining the European Union is that it would help to erode the "fundamentalist secularism" of much of Turkey's ruling elite and enable Muslim women, among others, to express their religious identity in all spheres of life.

72. A recent circular from the Department of Education in the UK now prohibits teachers from wearing the Niqab on the grounds that it obstructs the effective carrying out of their teaching and pastoral responsibilities.
73. I do not mean by this that any legal challenges using these instruments would be successful, but rather they could be referred to in support of domestic legal and political arguments thereby increasing pressure on the forces of the state to effect legal change.
74. This returns to the point on the so-called universality of "Human Rights"; supra.
75. Malaysia ratified CEDAW in 1995 and initially made a number of reservations on the basis that those provisions were contrary to Islamic Law. Following the Beijing Conference in 1997, however, six of those reservations were withdrawn even though some of them remain incompatible with the *Shari'ah*; see Nor Aziah Mohd Awal, "CEDAW and Islamic Law: Its Application in Malaysia", (2007), *4th ASLI Conference* May 2007, Jakarta, Conference Papers, p. 941. Even the International Islamic University in Malaysia has not been spared the critical scrutiny of its dress codes inside its own campus, following Malaysia's adoption of CEDAW; see *The Star*, 10 November, 2005; *New Straits Times*, 10 November, 2005; "Sisters in Islam", http://www.sistersinislam.org.my/lte/11112005.htm.
76. ICJ Reports, 1951, p. 15; 18 ILR, p. 364.
77. This has led some critics to question the sincerity of some Muslim States who have signed and ratified CEDAW; see S. Sardar Ali, *Gender and Human Rights in Islam and International Law: Equal Before Allah, Unequal Before Man?*: Boston, Kluwer Law International, (2000).
78. This is separate from the difficulty of finding an appropriate avenue for determining legal address as Saudi Arabia does not accept the ICJ as a suitable judicial body to determine disputes. By virtue of the principle of reciprocity, France would be allowed to rely upon Saudi Arabia's reservation which would preclude any recourse to the International Court. It should also be noted that Saudi Arabia is not listed by many as a State Party to the CEDAW even though it formally ratified the Convention in 2000 (it has yet to submit any report).
79. In the case of those countries which have signed up to the Optional Protocol, that would include the rights of individual women or groups of women to make their own petitions to the CEDAW Committee where their national courts have not granted any remedy.

80. There are no representatives of the more "conservative" Muslim countries from the Gulf or Saudi Arabia on the Committee. Turkey, Algeria, Bangladesh, Tunisia and Egypt (as well as Malaysia and Indonesia) have all been represented but rarely more than 3 at any one time in a Committee of 23 persons. See further, the CEDAW website: *http://www.un.org/womenwatch/daw/cedaw/members.htm.*
81. See further, the report of the Committee Meeting at the United Nations Information Service: *http://www.unis.unvienna.org/unis/pressrels/2005/wom1480.html.*
82. An overview of the Committee's attitude in the recent past towards Islamic practices, can be obtained by reading their responses to the reports of member States. For example, see the 2003 CEDAW Committee Report on France and its discussions surrounding "traditional customary practices, including polygamy" (paras 37 and 48).
83. The reason why the *Hijab* was brought up as an issue affecting the rights of children was because it was thought the French Government's policy in 2004 to ban all religious symbols in government schools might adversely affect the right of Muslim children in France to have free education. The French Government was asked to explain its position before the Committee in 2005 and noted that most of the problematic cases (550) had been resolved through dialogue at the local level; see further, the UN Committee Report and Recommendations: *http://www.unhchr.ch/html/menu2/6/crc/doc/co/France-CO2.pdf* (in particular, paras 25-26). It was not addressed before CEDAW because France's periodic report had yet to be submitted.
84. A problem would arise immediately as to who would qualify to be a "scholar" and who would be the legitimate authority to nominate and then appoint them.
85. A similar conclusion is made by Mashood Baderin, *op.cit.*, pp 234-235. He maintains that differences between the two discourses could be reconciled through adoption of the 'margin of appreciation' doctrine. For my response to this approach, see S.A. Farrar, op.cit, (2005), pp. 281-289.
86. See also M.H. Kamali, *op.cit.*
87. See: S.A. Farrar, *op. cit.*, (2005). The real problem lies not with the definition of consensus, but with the failure of modernists and new movements to comply with the recorded instances of consensus and the separation of the intelligentsia from the Mujtahids. It is interesting to note the OIC's recently promulgated 10 year Programme of Action

rejects "flouting the tenets and pillars of the religion and the well-established schools of jurisprudence" (Article 4.2).

88. I do not mean by this that the UN is necessarily a defunct body nor that it cannot play a useful role, especially where world security is at stake. But many of its current functions could be more efficiently handled regionally and bi-laterally.
89. See the Treaty of Hudaybiyah and the treaties entered into by Muslim Sultanates referred to above.
90. See A. Ahsan , *The Organization of the Islamic Conference (An Introduction to an Islamic Political Institution)*: Herndon, Va. U.S.A., International Institute of Islamic Thought,. (1988), p. 19.
91. See M. Baderin, *op. cit.*, p. 227.
92. See the Report on the Witton Park Conference, "Challenging Stereotypes in Europe and the Islamic World: Working Together for Constructive Policies and Partnerships", 2-3 May 2006, (retrieved on 30 June 2007 from: http:www.oic-oci.org/English/article/wps06-27.pdf). The Conference was held in association with the General Secretariat of the OIC. See also, the Report of the OSCE–ODIHR Roundtable Discussion, "The Representation of Muslims in Public Discourse", Warsaw 9 May 2006 (retrieved on 30 June 2006 from: http:www.oic-oci.org).
93. This was announced on June 27, 2007 during his visit to the Islamic Center in Washington (see http:www.oic-oci.org).
94. Apart from unified positions on the Arab-Israeli conflict, the early years of the OIC were marked by failures to come to any consensus on many of the regional conflicts occurring in the Muslim World; see A. Ahsan, *op. cit.*, pp. 120-123.
95. This was openly advocated by Professor Baderin, *op.cit.*
96. This is also known as the Report on the "Nude Squats" controversy.
97. Although certain compromises were made, many of the reforms suggested by the two Commissions were incorporated in the Criminal Procedure (Amendment) Act 2006. As of 1st July 2007, however, its provisions are not yet in force. For further details on the reform process, see S.A. Farrar, *The Criminal Process in Malaysia: Cases and Materials,* Vol.: Kuala Lumpur, Pearson and Prentice Hall, (2007).
98. According to the Eleventh Conference of Foreign Ministers in Islamabad, the International Islamic Law Commission was meant to have its head-office in Baghdad. The Iran-Iraq war, two Gulf Wars and continuing instability in Iraq, however, have prevented this from

coming into operation. If the member states of the OIC can agree on alternative location and a proper constitution for the International Islamic Law Commission, it could provide a pivotal role in the *Shari'ah* / "Human Rights" discourse. Among its agreed objectives are: (1) conduct research in fields that would enhance the *Shari'ah*; (2) examine laws and draft laws referred to it by member states or sub-committees in light of the *Shari'ah* and pronounce whether or not these are in accordance with the *Shari'ah*; and (3) devise ways and means to secure representation in order to put forward the Islamic point of view before the International Court of Justice and other institutions of the UN which entails Islamic interests. See further, A. al-Ahsan, *op. cit.*, p. 36.

99. There is nothing specifically in the Charter of the OIC which provides for this power. Although it could be implied from the Objectives of the Charter which include taking "necessary measures to support international peace and security" and helping "to strengthen the struggle of all Muslim peoples with a view to safeguarding their dignity independence and national rights", it could also conflict with its Principles outlined in Article II. These emphasize, among other matters, that the OIC must "respect the sovereignty, independence and territorial integrity of each member state." It would be necessary, therefore, that the Charter of the OIC be amended in order to confer this power on the OIC unambiguously.

100. This is recognized in International Law under the principle of *Pacta Sunt Servanda*.

101. This includes equality of bargaining power, mutual understanding and necessary expertise on both sides. The realization of the Islamic International Law Commission as a fully functioning subsidiary organ of the OIC will be an important step towards developing a better understanding of non-Muslim perspectives as well as providing the necessary *Shari'ah* imput on matters relating to International Law and "Human Rights".

102. Until recent medical research validated by the World Health Organization indicated that male circumcision protected against transmission of HIV, there was a sizable lobby calling for the banning of male circumcision and not just the universal prohibition of female circumcision. See further: *http://www.who.int/hiv/topics/malecircumcision/en/index.html*. See also: S. Rennie, A. Muula and D. Westreich, "Male Circumcision and HIV Prevention: Ethical, Medical and Public Health Trade-Offs in Low-Income Countries," *Journal of Medical Ethics* (2007), Vol. 33, 357-361; David and Michael Benatar:

"Between Prophylaxis and Child Abuse: The Ethics of Neonatal Male Circumcision," *The American Journal of Bioethics* (2003), Vol. 3, No. 2, 35-48.; Dena S. Davis, "Cultural Biases in Responses to Male and Female Genital Surgeries", *American Journal of Bioethics* (2007), Vol. 3, No2, 15; M. Fox and M. Thompson, "Short Changed? The Law and Ethics of Male Circumcision," *International Journal of Children's Rights*, (2005) Vol. 13, 161-181; M. Fox and M. Thompson, "A Covenant with the Status Quo? Male Circumcision and the new BMA Guidance to Doctors", *Journal of Medical Ethics* (2005), Vol. 31, 463-469.

103. For representative samples of the Orientalist canon, see the work of Bernard Lewis, *Islam – from the Prophet Muhammed to the capture of Constantinople:* London and Basingstoke, Macmillan Press, (1974); *Islam in History: Ideas, People and Events in the Middle East:* 2nd Edition, Chicago, Open Court, (1993). See also: N. Coulson, *A History of Islamic Law:* Edinburgh, Edinburgh University Press, (1964), and *Conflicts and Tensions in Islamic Jurisprudence:* Chicago, University of Chicago Press, (1969). See further, J. Schacht, *An Introduction to Islamic Law:* Oxford, Clarendon Press, (1964).

104. A close reading of Ash-Shafi'iyy's *Kitab al-Umm*, would indicate that the need for differential clothing between Muslim and non-Muslim was left to the *Ijtihad* (individual legal reasoning and discretion) of the Ruler and was not a necessary part of the Islamic State's legal framework. As for the *Jizyah*, according to Ash-Shafi'iyy also, the amount could be as little as one dinar and to be paid after the elapse of one lunar year. Ultimately, however, al-Mawardi writes that the amount would be fixed to accord with peoples' means (see *Ahkam as-Sultaniyyah*, (The Laws of Islamic Governance), p. 210, Ta-Ha, London.). The Jizyah system, therefore, made little practical difference to the taxation system which Muslims and non-Muslims are currently subjected to in the modern world. Also it needs to be remembered that Muslims would pay *Zakah* which was not payable by non-Muslims. In relation to *Qisas* and *Diyyah*, it is the ruling of the school of Abu Hanifah that there is no distinction between a Muslim and a non-Muslim.

105. British and French legislation, for example, although formally applying to all British and all French, indirectly discriminate against Muslims and their way of life. In the case of the former, they criminalize polygamous marriages and practitioners of female circumcision (no distinction is drawn between cultural practices of female genital mutilation and the sunnah, as practiced in Malaysia and

Indonesia); they invalidate Muslim marriages and divorces, and refuse to recognize Islamic rules of *Waqf* and Inheritance. In the case of the latter, the doctrine of *La¿cité* (which roughly translates as "secularism") bans the display of all religious symbols in government schools and institutions (though its implementation depends upon the particular judgment of the Head of the relevant institution), a ban which disproportionately affects and discriminates against Muslim women who wish to wear the *Hijab*. A Catholic is not obliged under Papal laws to display a cross whereas a Muslim woman is obliged under Islamic Law to wear a *Hijab*. The rule's impact, therefore, is differential and indirectly discriminatory.

106. Hence the differential rules on blasphemy, apostasy and freedom of expression. The *Jizyah* capitation tax did not just help fill the Muslim treasuries, it was also symbolic of their religious separation; see *Al-Qur'an, surah at-Tawbah*, ayah 29.

107. This necessitates further research into legal pluralism and development of doctrines that are beginning to emerge in Muslim States struggling to reconcile Islamic tradition with cultural modernism. See further, the Malaysian case: *Meor Atiqulrahman bin Ishak (an Infant, by his guardian ad litem, Syed Ahmad Johari bin Syed Mohd) & Ors v Fatimah bte Sihi & Ors* [2006] 4 MLJ 605. See also the commentaries on this case by Abdul Aziz Bari: "Turban and the Constitutional Right to Religious Freedom: The Ruling of the Federal Court in *Meor Atiqulrahman,*" *The Law Review*, (2006),pp 554-569; "Islam in the Federal Constitution: A Commentary on the Decision of *Meor Atiqulrahman*" [2000] 2 MLJ cxxix-cxlii; "Enforcement of Shari'ah in Malaysia: Divine Provisions in a Constitutional Democracy" in Hussin Mutalib (ed), *Islam and Democracy: The Southeast Asian Experience* (2004), Singapore: Centre for Contemporary Islamic Studies (CCIS) and Konrad Adenauer Foundation (CAF), pp. 33-52.

3

Command Theory of Legal Positivism And *Hukum Shar'i*: A Comparision

Abdul Haseeb Ansari & Saad Abu Elgasim

Introduction

The crux of the natural law school is that all the theorists do not dissociate moral rules from legal rules; rather, they generally relied on 'Is' and "Ought' relationship. According to them, 'Is' comprises rules based on either divine wisdom or human reason, and 'Ought' encompass as man-made law. For their validity, man-made laws, existing or to be made in future, have to be in conformity with divine commands or reasons. Since both are based on absolute wisdom, they are just and good rules, i e, they are moral laws. They have three characteristics: universality, immutability and eternity. Once any man made law proves to be in conformity with the original law, it becomes part of that law, and then falls within the ambit of natural law. For this reason, natural law thinkers subscribe to the idea: morality is the basis of the law.

Although legal positivists have not totally negated the importance of moral reasons as part of the content of law - for example, Austin's 'law properly so called' includes law made by God; he says that disobedience to evil laws is legitimate if it would promote change for good. HLA Hart expounds that ...legal positivism...is in no sense a necessary truth that laws reproduce or satisfy certain demands of morality, though in fact they have often done. HLA Hart, who is a modern positivist and who has confronted with Devlin on the findings of Wolfenden Report, at page 206 of his book *The Concept of Law* writes: "...the certification of something legally valid is not conclusive of peoples obedience, ...however powerful the authority is, its its demands must in the end be submitted to a *moral security*..." Positivists do not subscribe to the idea of 'Is' and 'Ought' relationship; for them, morality is not the basis of law. Law for them is made and not discovered; it thus does not have the basis of absolute wisdom. Positivists rest the premise of their theory on 'command': for Austin, it is commanded by a sovereign; for Bentham, it is commanded by a legislative authority; and for Salmond, it can be command of the judiciary (for him, "the central idea of juridical theory is not *lex* but *jus*, not *gestez* but *recht*"; "laws legal character becomes potent only when they are recognized and applied by the court in the administration of justice").

Legal rules and moral rules are different from each other. Law is made and not discovered. A law may or may not have a moral basis. Its validity depends on its enactment by a legitimate authority; it can be a sovereign authority or a subordinate authority having power to make law. Stephen Guest puts it in the following words: "...We are able (right or wrong) to see at least this difference between moral and legal rules: that with legal rules more significance is attached to their status as law by facts about their creation and not their content. That is not to say that there are no moral rules, which owe their status to such facts, since promises create moral obligations is in way that is independent of their status; rather, it is that more significance is attached in the case of law. We are less inclined to question, as we might a promise, the content of legal rules when we ask ourselves the question, should we carry it out, or avail ourselves of the facility it offers, or obey it. It is a strange idea, for example, to ask whether we should do what is morally right; but not so strange to ask whether we should do what is legally required of us or it is legally permitted that we do. This distinction arises from our attaching so much significance to the status of legal rules." This is the reason why a positive law differs from being a moral law. It also adds force to positive law. Positive law has always been one of the potent sources of law; rather, the most potent source of law.

In his essay entitled "Positivism and Separation of Law and Morals", published in (1958) 71 *Harvard Law Review* 593-601, Professor HLA Hart's outlined the following five cardinal points to reflect various dimensions of legal positivism: (1) Laws are commands of human being. (2) There is no necessary connection between law and morals. (3) The analysis of legal concepts is (a) worth pursuing, (b) distinct from (though not hostile to) sociological and historical enquiries and critical evaluation. (4) A legal system is a 'closed logical system' in which correct decisions may be deduced from predetermined legal rules by logical means alone. (5) Moral judgments cannot be established, as statements of fact can, by rational argument, evidence or proof.

In Islamic jurisprudence, major part of law is derived from the injunctions from Allah (swt) contained in Qur'an and *Sunnah*. They are *hukum shar'i* (commands of Islamic law). In Islam, sovereignty is with Allah. They, thus, have the basis of divine wisdom. There can be man-made law also-as a government, being the representative of Allah (swt)–can make law from time to time for the sake of imparting justice. However, man made laws for their validity have to be in conformity with the divine injunctions.

It is evident from the two jurisprudence, Islamic and Western, that the basic approach of the command theory in them is different from each other. The paper discusses the command theories in both of them, and then compares them. It also discusses the scope of application of command theories in the contemporary states.

Command Theory

For the proponents of the command theory, law is the command of the sovereign. The command theory is based on imperialism and absolutism. Among early proponents of this theory are Hobbes and J. Bodin, but the theory took its proper shape in Austin's positivism. Generally, for Austin, a sovereign has to be a human being having power to make law and to enforce it on the basis of coercion; he also believed in law made by God, but he did not lay much emphasis on it. However, for Jermy Bentham sovereignty depends on the form of government, it can be one person or assemblage of persons.

Early Development of Command Theory

The basic idea of command theory is based on absolutism propounded by J. Bodin and Thomas Hobbes. Since Hobbes had thought of a sovereign having absolute power with him and to be above the law and the Church, so that he could be able to protecting the country from insurgency and to keep the people united. He believed in the idea that 'it is the fear of the king that rules; not the king'. It is for this reason that he defined law as 'dictates of right reason conversant about those things which are either to be done or omitted for the constant preservation of life'. Sovereign (one person or an assemblage of persons), who has been given power by the people, on the basis of a social contract entered into by the people, to rule, to make law (so that people could be brought out of their conditions which had become, according to him, nasty, brutish, solitary and short) and to take violators of laws to the task; and people have to show the allegiance to the sovereign. Sovereign rules the country wielded with law in one hand and the sword in the other hand. He writes that if the king becomes week and unable to protect its subjects, he can be deposed. But looking at the whole theory propounded by him, it does not seem to be possible. In his *Leviathan* Hobbes writes "Civill lawes is to every subject, those rules, which the common-wealth has commanded him, by word, writing or other sufficient Sign of the Will, to make use of, for the distinction of Right, and Wrong. That is to say, of what is contrary, and what is not contrary to the Rule...The Legislator in all common-wealths, is only the sovereign, be he one man, as in a Monarch, or one assembly of men, as in a Democracy or Aristocracy. For the Legislator, is he that maketh the Law. And the common-wealth only, prescribes, and commandeth the observation of those rules, which we call Law: therefore the common-wealth is the Legislator. But the common-wealth is no person, nor has capacity doe anything, but by the Representative, (that is, the Sovereign) and therefore the Sovereign is the sole legislator. The Sovereign of common-wealth, be it an assembly or one man, is nor subject to civill lawes. For having power to make and repeal lwaes, he may when he pleaseth, free himself from that subject, by repealing those Lawes that trouble him, and making of new; and consequently he becomes free like before. For he is free, that can be free when he will: nor is it possible for any person to be bound to himself; because he that he can bind; can release; and therefore he that is bound to himself only, is not bound...".

JG Riddall in Jurisprudence writes, "And before Hobbes, Bodin in *Six Books of Republic* had written, '...it is the distinguishing mark of the sovereign that he cannot in any way be subject to the commands of another, for it is he who makes law for the subject, abrogates law already made, and amends obsolete law. No one who is subject either to the law or to some other person can do this. That is why it is laid down in the civil law that the prince is above the law, for the word law in Latin implies the command of him who is invested with sovereign power...If the prince is not bound by the laws of his predecessors, still less can he be bound by his own laws. One may be subject to laws made by, but it is impossible to bind oneself in any matters which is the subject of one's own free exercise of will...It follows of necessity that the king cannot be subject to his own laws.'..."

Bentham's Positivism/Utilitarianism

Jermy Bentham was a positivist. For him, law is generally made; it does not have a metaphysical basis. For him, law is the command of the sovereign, who can be 'any person or assemblage of persons to whose will a whole political community are (no matter on what account) supposed to be in a disposition to pay obedience, and that in reference to the will of any other person'. His main concern was to protect the legal system from the effects of the French Revolution, which had its widespread effect; people had started talking about natural rights of men. He referred this to as 'nonsense on the stilts'. By this he meant that the nonsense of the deductive reasoning that fallaciously lay behind the doctrines of natural rights had been raised on a pedestal–a place where according to him they did not belong. His *expository jurisprudence*, which means an examination of the law as it is posited (commanded). He supports the idea of critical examination of the law on the basis of its utility eg, 'the greatest happiness of the greatest number'. This also gives us insight in finding what law ought to be. This is known as *'expositorial jurisprudence'*. Both of them are related to each other in the sense that without investigating into the past law, we cannot make any guess about the future law. Although law is made by the sovereign, it has to be tested on the basis of two sovereign masters, *pain* and *pleasure*. Thus, if a law brings pain, it will be a bad law; on the contrary, if it brings pleasure, it will be a good law. And the ultimate goal to be achieved by law is the greatest happiness of the greatest number. His emphasis is on the happiness of the greatest number; it means if there are two groups of people in a society and if from the group, which is in minority and poor, things are taken and given to the other group, which is already rich, Bentham will have no problem. But this will be great injustice to the poor group. This is also against the equitable distribution of the resources of the country, which is considered to be a tool in modern countries of redistribution and bridging the gap between the rich and the poor. His pain and pleasure theory is also criticized for the following reasons: (1) Pain and pleasure are subjective elements; (2) They are relative terms; (3) They are not the sole factor for determining the validity of law; (4) They are just one of various factors for validating a law; and (5) If everyone pursues his own pleasure, it might be detrimental to others, who need, rather who need protective discriminatory support from the sovereign/ government.

Bentham writes "...to define all law in terms of facts–the political facts of power, human prescription, punishments and rewards–only then could be devised a scientific theory of legislation based on the principle of utility." Bentham gives four kinds of commands: command (example: lie down); prohibition (example: do not lie down); non-command (example: you may refrain from lying down); and non-prohibition (example: you may lie down). John Austin, who was a disciple of Bentham, supported command theory with greater emphasis on penalties for disobedience of the law made by the sovereign. However, he believed in positive and negative sanctions. For laying more emphasis on negative sanction, like that of Austin's, his theory, in effect, is known as the coercive order of law eg, one who violates the law commanded by the sovereign, will have to face appropriate punishment inflicted on him by the subordinates of the sovereign.

Law for him is 'an assemblage of signs declarative of a volition conceived or adopted by the sovereign in the state, concerning the conduct to be observed in a certain cause by a certain person or class of persons, who in the case in question are or are supposed to be subject to his power'. Thus, for him, source of law is the will of the sovereign, which can be: he himself conceives law and issues commands; he can adopt law of the previous sovereign; and he can adopt law in advance to be issued in future by his subordinate authorities, including judges.

Austinian Theory

John Austin was a disciple of Bentham as well as a friend and follower of John Stuart Mill. He was the stanch supporter of the command theory of law supported with coercion, suitable punishments. Austin propounded his theory of law in *Province of Jurisprudence Determined,* published in 1832, the year of Bentham's death. Austin has identified law, positive (to do something) or negative (abstain from doing something), with the sovereign. There cannot be law without a command to that effect issued by the sovereign. Mainly, a command has three elements: a wish, a sanction, and the expression of the wish. If there in no sovereign there cannot be any law. Likewise, existence of law testifies existence of a sovereign. He writes, "Every positive law or every law simply and strictly so-called, is set by a sovereign individual or a sovereign body of individuals to a person or persons in a state of subjection to its author." According to Austin, laws are in the form of commands, active (by positive endeavor of the sovereign) and tacit (implied, for example, continuation of commands of the previous sovereign, and law made by judges under tacit authority), general (to the subjects in general) and specific (to a group of person for a specific act). Law, according to him, can be classified as properly so-called and improperly so-called. The first category of law can be issued by the sovereign himself or by a person having authority to make law given by the sovereign, or by God. Law improperly so-called is given by a person who does not have authority to make law. They are: command of others (positive morality), law by analogy (positive morality), and law by metaphor (laws of nature). Law given by other than the sovereign is positive morality because they are made by someone who does not have the authority to make law. They are generally exemplified by dress codes, metaphor, rules made by parents and rules of clubs and societies. Law properly so-called is backed by sanctions. Penalty is inflicted on the violator of a law. It is thus an integral part of the law. In short, Austin's command theory has three significant aspects: sovereign, command, and sanction.

Sovereign by Austin is a person, a physically determinate person, who is habitually obeyed by the bulk of the members of the society. In addition to this, he is indivisible, illimitable and continuous.

Austin is known for criticisms of his 'law as coercive order' and 'law is the command of the sovereign, and no sovereign means on law'. However, he has few supporters. Among them, Professor Morison is prominent. He is of the opinion that the central ideas of Austin's command theory have been misinterpreted or misunderstood. Austin's command theory, especially law as a coercive order, has been subjected to an extensive criticism. Some general criticisms are: (1) There are some laws that are not based on commands. The best examples are the law of testamentary succession and the law of contract. For that matter, customary law is also not based on command and yet it is practiced (2) A sovereign may unconsciously allow a law to be practiced. There may not exist even a tacit command for it. (3) A sovereign may not necessarily be source of all laws. Law exists even when there in no sovereign. (4) Austin has not been concerned with early societies. (5) A law to be a command has to pass through certain procedural requirements. These requirements are necessary to be observed. It is truer in modern states, including monarchies and dictatorships. Salmond and Hart have been prominent among Austin's critiques. It will be appropriate to examine their criticisms.

Criticism by Salmond

Sir John Salmond has been critical to Austin's command theory. He has rightly written that some are imperative principles; and some others, are not in the form of commands issued by the sovereign. He has, thus, unduly stressed on the command aspects of law-making. According to him, Austin's imperative theory did not take cognizance of justice, which is the paramount purpose of law, he unduly stressed on imperative aspect of law-making by saying law is the command of sovereign, and he has also ignored the ethical purpose of law, which is an essential element of law for ensuring justice. Salmond believes that judicial precedent and custom are also sources of law and they respectively produce case law and customary law. They are applied by the courts although they are not enacted by any sovereign or legislative body. Salmond's criticisms are not beyond comprehension. In fact, laws also have the basis of customs; or in certain situations, they reflect the ethical aspects of law. Likewise, all laws are not commands; nature of some legal rules can be mere enabling. Salmond's criticisms are truer in modern states, where there are several sources of law: legislation, customs, judge-made law, and revealed law. To some extent, his criticism gets support from Maine, as he says sovereign cannot necessarily be the source of law. Law exists even in the absence of a sovereign. Main is of the opinion that interdependence of law and sovereign is not always true. But he exaggerates this idea when he writes in *Early History of Institution* that 'some sovereign never made law. The rules which regulated the life of his subjects were derived from their immemorial usages, and these rules were administered by domestic tribunals in families or village communities'. For this reason, Maine was replied by Salmond saying that 'Austin did not anticipate an early society where source of law was customs and religion; his theory is for states. The rules to which Maine refers to are not properly law. They are the defective and deformed predecessors of the more perfected type that constitute the positive law of the more civilized states...'. The author is of the opinion that Austin's imperative theory fails in almost all modern states, including states that have dictators or kings. For example, in the Middle-East, kingship follows the revealed law. Rather, the revealed law is the test of law. Any law that violates the revealed law is considered to be invalid. Certain laws which are based on religious norms but have been abrogated, amended or modified based on *ijtehad,* looses its previous identity. Likewise, based on human endeavours, which are permitted in Islamic jurisprudence, entirely new rules can be made. Moreover, as in an Islamic state, sovereignty is with Allah (swt), king or *khalipha* or any other sovereign acts in a representative capacity, his command is actually the command of Allah (swt). In fact, his law gets power and validity from Allah's laws that he has revealed for the mankind.

Criticism by HLA Hart

Among Austin's critics, HLA Hart is eminent. In his *The Concept of Law*, Hart has extensively criticized Austin's command of law. Some of his criticisms are worth quoting here: (1) Law is not simply based on coercion. It is inapplicable to a large section of a modern legal system. To support his criticism, he quotes laws pertaining will, contract, marriage, and jurisdiction of courts. (2) Austin has monolithic model of law. According to him, in a developed legal framework, there are two sets of rules, primary rules and secondary rules: primary rules lay down standards of human behaviours, and secondary rules are procedural and remedial in nature. Secondary rules are there to identify, amend primary rules and apply in resolving disputes (These is named by him as the secondary rules of adjudication). Primary rules acquire the unity of a system through their union with secondary rules. (3) The sovereign, according to Austin, is not bound by his own command. Hart is a stanch supporter of rule of law. Legislator(s) exercises his law-making power given to him by law. The idea of command will explain a coercive order addressed to another in special circumstances, but why a statute applies generally and also applies to its framers. (4) The continuance of pre-existing laws cannot be explained on the basis of command. (5) Austin's habit of obedience fails to explain succession to sovereignty because it fails to take account of differences between 'habit' and 'rule'. Habits only require common behaviour, which is not enough for a rule. A rule has an internal aspect, ie people use it as standard by which to judge and condemned deviations; habits do not function in this way. Hart maintains that the significance of rule has been neglected. Succession to sovereign occurs by virtue of acceptance of a rule entitling the successor to succeed, not because of a habit of obedience. Thus, Austin's command-duty-sanction thesis fails to explain why, if a gunman threatens X with 'Your money or your life', X may be obliged to handover his purse, but has no obligation to do so. The reason is one has an obligation only by virtue of a rule. For Hart rules of obligation are different from other rules in that they are supported by great social pressure because they are necessary to maintain the society. (6) Hart did not reject customs altogether. According to him, in the preliminary stage of development of law, where only primary rules exist, they are not formally promulgated by any sovereign. This is a pre-legal condition. In a developed society, existence of only primary rules is simply a luxury. These rules may have basis of social practice or religious belief. (7) Austin's characteristic features of a sovereign is do not exist in modern societies. Now, there is rule of law and sovereign acts under limitations prescribed in the constitution of the country. Dicey is also of the opinion that absolute sovereign is a rarity now. He expounds that the actual exercise of the sovereign power is under two limitations, external limitation (For example, Sultan of an Islamic state can make law which does not violate Qur'anic injunctions) and internal limitation (This emanates from the nature of the power of the sovereign itself). Austin also confused with *de facto* and *de jure* sovereign authorities.

Austin's successors either have abandoned his command theory or have accepted it in a limited sense. For example, Holland concentrated on enforcement of law by a sovereign political authority. Salmond takes law as consisting of the rules recognized and acted on by courts of justice. Hart, as stated above came out with 'primary rules and rules of recognition. It can thus be concluded that although in modern states laws are generally made by the law-making authority, customs, religious injunctions, and judge-made law are also valid sources of law. Also, a sovereign authority works under the laws of the state. It is different thing that among all sources of law, legislation is the most potent source and might override other sources of law.

Bentham and Austin Compared

The comparison between the two positivists and proponents of the command theory of law can be delineated under the following points:

1. General–Bentham rejected the 'Is and 'Ought' relationship, which is the basis of the natural law thinking. According to him, they are separate and may be termed as 'expository' and 'censorial' aspects of jurisprudence. Austin also supported this idea but laid more emphasis on the expository aspect of law. We can say that Austin's approach was narrow and less pragmatic. He seems to be more supportive to the authority of the sovereign, thus does not suit to modern states. Contrary to this,

Bentham's approach is relevant and can have place in contemporary jurisdictions. RWM Dias supports this view by writing 'A comparison of Bentham and Austin lead to the conclusion that the former provided a deeper and more adaptable theory'. Also, Betham avoided the absurdity of law properly so-called and law improperly so-called.

2. Sovereign–Both of them have laid emphasis on sovereignty, as the sovereign must command habitual obedience from his subjects. However, Bentham's view is refined than that of Austin. He does not subscribe to the negative aspect of the sovereignty that people habitually obey the sovereign, but *the sovereign is not in the habit to obey anyone.* Austin's sovereign is neither limitable, nor divisible; he is an absolute one. On the contrary, Bentham's concept of sovereignty is flexible. He alludes to the idea that sovereignty is limitable as well as limitable, as he subscribes to a federal form of government, where legislative and other powers are divided between a federal government and state governments. Thus, Bentham's concept of sovereignty is pragmatic and closure to modern states, which are governed by a constitution(s); and if a state has federal form of government, the power to issue commands is divided between the federal government and states governments. In such a situation, it can be argued that the courts of the country should have the power to review legislation, and to determine whether they are in conformity with the constitution. Bentham points out another kind of limitation where law is made by the sovereign but is not internalized by the subjects of the sovereign.

Salmond has also criticized the sovereignty concept given by Austin. He challenges the Austin's idea that a sovereign has all powers of issuing commands having no superior authority; and stands separate from the state. According to him, Austin erroneously thought that if a sovereign is restricted or confined to a limited sphere, he is not a sovereign. Salmond is of the opinion that sovereignty need not mean unlimited supremacy as supposed by Austin. He seems to have agreed to the idea of divisibility of the sovereignty, but a sovereign (Parliament or State assembly, as the case may be) in that situation should have power to issue commands freely (make law) without having a superior authority. Dicey, Duguit and some other jurists have also given different concepts of sovereignty.

It is notable here that in an Islamic state, sovereignty is will Allah (swt). *Khalipha* or the king is just a representative of Allah (swt). Thus, God is superior to him, and he does not have absolute power to issue commands. His power has an inherent limitation that all his decrees will have to be in conformity with Qur'an and *Sunnah* (Prophetic traditions). It is notable here that Austin has recognized divine law; it does not have inherent superiority over commands issued by Sovereign.

3. Obedience–According to Hart, Austin's notion of obedience of the people to the sovereign is deficient. Hart has pointed out three situations: a sovereign dies and a new sovereign, may be his son, takes over and issues command; the new sovereign issues one command and dies; on the death of a sovereign anther sovereign is elected. In all the three situations, according to Hart, the requirement of habitual obedience lacks. In the first situation, when the new sovereign stays in the office for sometimes and issues commands and people obey his commands, we can say that there is habitual obedience of his commands. This situation will not be there if he dies in short time after issuing only few commands. All these situations, therefore, are governed by a set of rules of succession. These rules exist without habitual obedience of the people. In modern states, Austin's theory fails, as habitual obedience is not a requirement for a law to exist. A law is valid if it has been made by a sovereign authority and conforms to his (or its) legislative power enshrined in the constitution. Bentham's notion of habitual obedience is only positive, as his sovereign is not above the law. We have noted above that Bentham believes in divisibility and limitability of the sovereign power. It is so under a constitutionally limited government. It can, therefore, be inferred that Hart's notion that there are certain rules that govern succession of sovereignty is closer to Bentham's idea of divisibility and limitability of the sovereignty.

4. Command–Both Austin and Bentham base theory imperative theory on commands issued by the sovereign. As noted above,

Bentahm's commands can be classified into to two: one, command (positive) and prohibition (negative); second, non-command and non-prohibition. The first two are backed by negative sanction. They seem to be more satisfactory than Austin's command theory, which does not have these details. However both theories suffer form some inherent deficiencies. Bowel Genn in his *Jurisprudence* writes, "For Austin it is difficult to see many laws as being the 'expression of a wish'. Can a body like parliament really be said to wish; what if the majority of the parliament of members do not know the contents of the law? What if a big majority opposed it? What if majority was gained by issuing a 'whip'? In short, can a sovereign body really be said to 'wish'?

5. Sanction–Austin has laid total emphasis on negative sanction (penal sanction). An individual subject is under duty to carry out the legal command if non-compliance is inflicted with penal sanction. He does not visualize situations where people have no duty. In reality, there are laws, for example enabling laws (Law on solemnizing marriage, law to enter into a contract, law to make a will. For Hart, they are power conferring rules) from which no legal duties arise. Bentham subscribe to the idea of positive and negative sanction. For him, commands may or may not be supported with sanction, but they are not necessary for existence of a law. However, for both of them, legal obligations require backing of penal sanction. Truly speaking in modern states all kinds of sanctions work for enforcement of laws. Even a reward can be a sanction. Likewise, there can be laws without any sanction.

To sum up, although the root of command theory existed in fifteenth and sixteenth century, it was thoroughly discussed and expounded in its biggest possible form by Austin. His command theory seems to be more influenced by Hobbes than his predecessor Bentham. However, as we have noted above, his theory was extensively criticized, as it is not suited to modern states. Bentham is also not free from criticism; he had broader vision and his theory is therefore pragmatic and more suited to many modern states, except Islamic states where sovereignty vests in Allah (swt). Modern positivists have not totally rejected the command theory. Also, they do not totally reject natural law. Most of them believe in natural law, but for them, natural law is that which is natural to man; it is made by man for man; and it does not have any metaphysical basis. Perhaps this theory has been propounded to protect the basic (fundamental or inherent) rights of the man.

Shari'ah Concept of *Hukm* (Command)

Hukm shar'i is a concept that refers to a theological as well as a regulatory relation that exists between two parties. One is the lawgiver (*al-hakim*) and the other is the law subject (*al-mahkum alayh*). Like any other relation, its main three elements are the two parties to it in addition to its subject matter. Because of the theological and regulatory nature of *hukm shar'i*, its three elements in addition to its definition and classification have been the interest of both Muslim theologians as well as jurists. Just as they have been, they shall be the interest of this section as any reasonable and fair exposition of the concept concerned requires.

The definition of *hukm* has been disputed by two main groups, viz. theologians (*usuliyyin*) and jurists (*fuqaha*). On the one hand, Muslim theologians have defined *Hukm* as: the communication of the lawgiver (*khitab al-shar'i*) concerning the conduct of the legally competent persons (*afal al-mukallafin*) by way of demand (*al-iqtida*), option (*al-takhyir*) or declaration (*al-wad*). On the other hand, Muslim jurists have defined it as: the effect of the communication of the lawgiver concerning the conduct of the legally competent persons by way of demand, option or declaration. As an illustration, the verse: "Establish prayer" (Qur'an, 2: 42) according to Ussuliyin is the *hukm shar'i*, that is to say, the text itself. Whereas according to *Fuqaha* the requirement of the text is the *hukm shar'i*, that is to say, what is understood from it, viz. the obligation of prayer.

Usuliyyin, being concerned with the macro issues of *Shari'ah* as a way of life and a legal system seen within a methodological framework, have considered the communication of the lawgiver containing the rule which regulates the conduct of the *Mukallaf* to be *hukm shar'i*. Whereas *fuqaha*, being concerned with the micro issues of *Shari'ah* seen within a practical framework, have considered the rule prescribed through the communication of the lawgiver to be *hukm shar'i.* After all, it is intelligible to arrive at these two different perceptions of *hukm* for the latter's being approached by two different disciplines, and this is what might have caused Ibn Al-humam and Al-taftazani, as quoted by Haji Mohammed in his Ph.D thesis entitled "Rights and Duties in *Shari'ah* and Common Law", to consider *Hukm* to be a homonym *(mushtarak)* which applies to the communication, its effect and, on top of that, the effect of the communication.

Classification of *Hukm*

Hukm shar'i has been classified into two main categories, namely, defining rule (al-*hukm al-taklifi)* and declaratory rule *(al-hukm al-wad'i).* These categories can be deduced from the definition of *Hukm* which is expressive of them and the subdivisions of one of them. At the end of our way back from the categories derived from the definition we can split up the definition into two definitions corresponding to the two categories *hukm shar'i.* The two categories of *hukm shar'i* derived from its definition, their subdivisions and the definition given to each one of them are necessary to be dealt with.

Defining Rule *(al-hukm al-taklifi)*

Al-hukm al-taklifi may be defined as: the communication of the lawgiver concerning the conduct of the legally competent persons by way of demand or option. Primarily, *al-hukm al-taklifi* demands of the *Mukallaf* either to perform a certain act or to forbear from performing it, or provides him with the choice between performance and forbearance. If the demand to perform a certain act occupies a decisive mode of expression, it is called obligation *(al-wujub).* But if it occupies an indecisive one, it is called recommendation *(al-nadb).* Conversely, if the demand to forbear from committing a certain act is conveyed by a decisive mode of expression, it is called prohibition *(al-hurmah).* But if it is conveyed by an indecisive one, it is called reprehension *(al-karahah).* Finally, if the communication of the lawgiver places the *Mukallaf* exactly in the middle between the two poles of performance and forbearance, and places in his hands the freedom to decide against anyone of them he may lean, it is called permission *(al-ibahah).* Ultimately, *al-hukm al-taklifi* occurs in the five varieties of obligation, recommendation, prohibition, reprehension and permission.

The evidence's degree of definitiveness in terms of its meaning (*dalalah*) has caused to divide *hukm Taklifi* into five types as we have just seen. The evidence's degree of definitiveness in terms of its authenticity (*thubut*) in addition to its meaning, however, has caused the Hanafis to divide *Hukm* into seven categories: If the demand to perform a certain act is definitive in terms of its both authenticity and meaning, it is called absolute obligation *(al-fard)*. But if it is not definitive in terms of its authenticity, it is called obligation *(al-wujub)*. Recommendation *(al-nadb)* is what it is called if it is not definitive in terms of its meaning. Correspondingly, if the demand to refrain from doing a certain act is definitive in terms of both its authenticity and meaning, it is called prohibition *(al-hurmah)*. But if it is not definitive in terms of its authenticity, it is called reprehension by way of religious prohibition *(al-karahah al-tahrimiyyah)*. Reprehension by way of religious scruple *(al-karahah al-tanzihiyyah)* is what it is called if it is not definitive in terms of its meaning. Lastly, if the communication gives the *Mukallaf* the option between commission and omission, it is called permission *(al-ibahah)*.

The distinction made by the Hanafis is not only terminological, but it has its practical jurisprudential consequences. For example, the recitation of some part of the Qur'an in prayer, according to the Hanafis, is absolutely obligatory. However, the recitation of *Surat Al-fatihah* is obligatory only, for it has been established by an unauthentic tradition. Based on that, failing to recite any part of the Qur'an in prayer renders it void because such an obligation has been established by an authentic evidence being the Qur'anic verse which reads: "So recite what is available from the Qur'an" (Qur'an, 73: 20). On the other hand, failing to recite *Surah Al-fatihah* does not render the prayer void because this obligation has been established by an unauthentic tradition which reads: "Whoever does to recite *Surat al-fatihah* in prayer will not be credited with having observed the prayer".

The distinction has also its theological consequences. But with respect to these, the Hanafis and the *Jumhur* are alike. According to both, who denies *fard*, for instance, is considered an infidel (*kafir*), but who denies *wajib* is considered impious (*fasiq*).

The Hanafi distinction has been described as strange for its acceptance would entail an unacceptable result. What is considered an obligation on our part, according to the Hanafis, is considered at the same time an absolute obligation on the part of the companion who narrated the tradition. That is because he was sure about its authenticity for he hearted it from the prophet (saw) himself. Moreover, it would render it obligatory on the part of some of the companions and absolutely obligatory on the part of the others. In addition, such a distinction is not supported by any evidence from the Qur'an or the *Sunnah*, except for pilgrimage, in which a distinction has been drawn between the requirement of a command and the requirement of another. According to this exception, the acts that the *mukallaf* is required to perform in pilgrimage (haj) are divided into those whose abandonment would render pilgrimage void and those whose abandonment would not. While the former are termed constituents *(arkan)* the latter are termed obligations (*wajibat*).

The above-mentioned two criticisms of the Hanafi distinction are not sound. As for the first criticism, it is quite intelligible to hold that what is absolutely obligatory on the part of the companion of the prophet (saw) might be obligatory on our part. That is because the companion was sure about its authenticity and had to act according to it. Whereas we are not, and therefore we are not as obliged by it as the companion was, for each one has to act according to what he believes to the best of his knowledge. Likewise, it might have been absolutely obligatory on the part of some of the companions and obligatory only on the part of the others. In addition, this is not a unique phenomenon, if not an ordinary one. The week prophetic tradition is not binding on us according to Muslim scholars. However, it might have been said by the prophet (saw) and because of that the companion who narrated it was no doubt obliged by it contrary to us.

As for the second criticism, such a distinction could not have been made by the *Shari'ah* itself, for its commands are supposed to have been communicated on the basis of the presumption that they are all authentic. But if any doubt arises over their authenticity, that would be a worldly historical matter with which scholars have to deal exercising *ijtihad.*

Disregarding whether the Hanafi distinction is sound or not, the five-fold classification of *Hukm Taklifi* as proposed by the majority opinion (*Jumhur*) will be discussed briefly in the next paragraphs.

Obligation (Al-ijab)

Al-ijab is the communication of the lawgiver which demands of the *mukallaf* decisively to perform a certain act. The effect resulting from it is called al-*wujub*. The act characterized by *al-wujub* is called *al-wajib* (the obligatory). Paying obedience to the command by the *Mukalla*f leads him to be rewarded by the lawgiver, whereas disobeying it renders him liable to be punished by the same authority. One of the patterns of conduct to which Muslims have been commanded to conform is what had been conveyed by the following *Quranic* verse: "O you who believe, fulfill the obligation" (Qur'an, 5:1).

Being a subdivision of *hukm taklifi*, which itself is a division of *hukm shar'i*, has not saved *al-wajib* from being further subdivided into various subdivisions one of which is its subdivision in to personal obligation (*wajib 'ayni)* and collective obligation (*wajib kifayi). Wajib 'ayni* is what had been addressed to the *Mukallaf* personally whereby his duty to perform the prescribed act can not be discharged by someone else on his behalf. Good illustrations of this are the obligation to perform prayer and the obligation to fulfill contracts. *Wajib kifayi*, however, is what had been addressed to the Muslim community in general whereby if some of its members discharge the duty the rest of the community would be absolved. Performance of *jihad* and *ijtihad* can be referred to as illustrations.

Al-wajib is also divided into what is dependent on a time limit (*wajib muwaqqat)* and that one which is free from any time limit (*wajib mutlaq)*. The obligation to fast in the month of *Ramadan* is *wajib muwaqqat* for it must be observed within a specific time limit. Whereas the obligation to expiate is *wajib mutlaq*, for it can be observed at any time provided before one dies.

Recommendation (Al-nadb)

Al-nadb is the communication of the lawgiver which demands of the *mukallaf* indecisively to do a certain Act. The effect that results from it is also called *Al-nadb*. The act characterised by *al-nadb* is called *al-*

mandub (the recommended). While performing the recommended act earns the *mukalaf* spiritual reward, contrary to *wajib*, does not entail any liability for punishment for not performing. This is accentuated by this verse: "O you who believe, when you contract a debt for a fixed time, write it down" (Qur'an, 2: 282).

Prohibition (Al-tahrim)

Al-tahrim is the communication of the lawgiver which demands decisively of the *mukallaf* to refrain from committing a specific act. The effect ensuing from it is called *al-hurmah*. The act characterised by *al-hurmah* is called *al-haram* (the prohibited). Contrary to *al-wujub,* entitlement to reward results from the omission of the act; however, liability for punishment results from its commission. Commanding the *mukallafin*, Allah (swt) has said: "O you who believe, devour not usury doubled and redoubled" (Qur'an, 3: 129).

Reprehension (Al-karahah)

Al-karahah is the communication of the lawgiver which demands indecisively of the *mukallaf* to abstain from doing a certain act. The effect that ensues from it is also called *al-karahah.* The act characterised by *al-karahah* is called *al-makruh* (the reprehensible). Omission of reprehensible acts causes the mukallaf to be rewarded, while their commission results in no punishment imposed upon him. Of the acts which have not been strictly prohibited is what had been conveyed by the following Quranic verse: "O you who believe, when the call is proclaimed to Friday prayer on Friday, hasten to the remembrance of Allah and leave off trading" (Qur'an, 62: 9).

Permission (al-Ibahah)

Al-Ibahah is the communication of the lawgiver which demands of the mukallaf neither to perform a certain act nor to forbear from performing it. Like it, its effect is called *al-ibahah.* The act characterised by al-ibahah is called *al-mubah* (the permissible). With respect to *al-mubah*, The question of reward or punishment does not arise in terms of its commission or omission. Giving the *mukallafin* the option, Allah the almighty has said: "And if the prayer is finished, you may disperse through the land and seek the bounty of Allah" (Qur'an, 62: 10).

Declaratory Rule (Al-hukm Al-wad'i)

Al-hukm al-wad'i may be defined as the communication of the lawgiver which declares a thing to be a cause, a condition or an impediment to another thing.

According to this definition, *al-hukm al-wad'i* establishes a relation between two things. The first thing, on the one hand, may be a cause, a condition or an impediment. On the other hand, the other thing, which is the effect of the cause, the object of the condition or what had been impeded by the impediment, is always *hukm taklifi*. The death of a person is not a happy occasion, but nevertheless it is a good illustration of the three kinds of *hukm wad'i*. While the relation of kinship between the deceased and the heir is the cause of inheritance, the death of the relative during the life of the heir is a condition for it. However, the homicide of the *slain* relative is the impediment to the murderer's entitlement to a share from his victim's estate.

The establishment of a relation between two things being the essence of *hukm wad'i* has caused some scholars to add to the three kinds mentioned above validity *(sihhah)* and invalidity *(butlan). The same reason* has caused Al-ghazali to add specific performance *(ada)* and non-specific performance *(qada)*. It has also caused the Hanafis to add wisdom *(hikmah)*, effective cause *('illah)*, sign *('alamah)* and constituent *(rukn)*. To the first three kinds agreed upon, however, the treatment will be confined.

Cause (Al-sabab)

Al-Sabab maybe defined as: that one whose existence entails the existence of *hukm*, and whose non-existence entails the non-existence of *hukm*.

The existence or non-existence of the effect entailed by the existence or non-existence of the cause must be conceived of as *Shari'ah* causality and not a logical one. The decline of sun, for example, is the cause of the obligation of offering noon prayer not because of the inherent capability of the sun's decline to cause such an effect, but because Allah (swt) has said: "establish regular prayers at the sun's decline" (Qur'an, 17: 78). Similarly, theft is the cause of hand amputation not because such an effect can be characteristically imputed to such a cause, but because the Lawgiver has enacted theft as the cause of the prescribed punishment provided in the following verse: "The man and woman who are guilty of theft cut off their hands as a recompense for what they have earned" (Qur'an 5: 38). Therefore, *al-sabab* has been described as that by existence of which a thing exists and not by its authority.

Al-*Sabab* is of two kinds: the first one is that which is not an act of the *mukallaf* and does not lie within his power; such as the coming of *Ramadan* as the cause of fasting; and the second one is that which is an act of the *mukallaf* and lies within his power; such as murder as the cause of retaliation.

Although the act constituting a cause may be optional, the effects entailed by it are not necessarily so. For example, although entering in to a marriage contract is permissible, payment of *mahr* is obligatory regardless of the assent or dissent of the husband.

Condition (Al-shart)

Al-Shart may be defined as: that whose non-existence entails the non-existence of *hukm,* and whose existence does not necessarily entail the existence of *hukm. Al-Shart* has been classified into three kinds, namely, philological, rational and *Shari'ah.* Philological *shart* is what had been stipulated by language such as the stipulation of the wife's stepping out of the husband's house as a condition for divorce. Rational *shart* is what had been required by reason (e.g. the requirement of body as a *shart* for life). Lastly, *Shari'ah shart* is what had been stipulated by *Shari'ah.* This can be exemplified by the stipulation of purity as a condition for the validity of prayer as provided in the following Quranic verse: "O you who believe, when you rise up for prayer, wash your faces and your hands up to the elbow, and wipe your heads and feet up to the ankles" (Qur'an, 5: 6).

Of the three kinds of *shart* mentioned above, the last one, which concerns us here, has been further classified in to *shart* which is a compliment of *sabab*, and *shart* which is a compliment of *hukm. Shart,* which is a compliment of *sabab,* is that one which qualifies the *sabab* to cause its effect. For example, custody as a *shart* for theft is the cause of hand amputation, and unlawfulness as a *shart* for murder is the cause of retaliation. On the other hand, *shart* as compliment of *hukm* is the one whose fulfillment enables *hukm* to get established. As an illustration, the death of the relative during the life of the heir is a *shart* for inheritance, and the vender's power to deliver the goods to the purchaser is a *shart* for the utilization of the goods by the purchaser.

Impediment (Al-man'i)

Al-Man'i may be defined as: that whose existence entails the non-existence of *hukm*, and whose non-existence does not necessarily entail the existence of *hukm*.

The elimination of *hukm,* which is the *Shari'ah* effect of *man'i*, may take place either directly or indirectly. It takes place directly if the *man'i* was involved. It is what *usuliyyin* call *man'i al-hukm*, for it impedes *hukm* from getting established. For instance, if a father kills his sun intentionally, retaliation would not be taken on him, for fatherhood is an impediment to retaliation. On the other hand, the elimination of *hukm* takes place indirectly if the *man'i* involved is what jurists call *man'i al-sabab*, for it disqualifies *sabab* (reason) to cause its legal effect. For example, the ownership of the minimum amount of property, which is the cause of *zakah*, would not give rise to its legal effect if the owner is indebted. Therefore, debt is considered to be a *man'i*.

The Lawgiver *(Al-Hakim)*

The duality envisaged in modern constitutions, which brings with it the perception that the state is the lawgiver and a subject to it, does not exist in *Shari'ah*. In *Shari'ah,* both the state and the individual are subjects of the *hukm* (law) issued from the Hakim (Lawgiver) who is Allah (swt), and whatever legislative powers exercised by the state are considered conferred upon the state by the Hakim, and do not emanate from it. This concept of law is based upon and substantiated by various Qur'anic verses two of which are the following ones: "The command rests with none but Allah" (Qur'an, 6: 57); and "And whoever judges not by that which Allah has revealed, they are disbelievers" (Qur'an, 5: 44).

However, in some of the works of *usul al-fiqqh* (Basic priciples of *fiqh* or Islamic Jurisprudence) one may come across the statement that the Mu'tazilites hold that *hakim* is the human reason. The mu'tazilites' assertion seems to be capable of being accomodated within the *Shari'ah* concept of *hukm* if we bear in mind that the term *hakim* is used in two senses. In the first sense, *hakim* means the lawgiver from whom *hukms* are issues. In the second sense, *hakim* means the revealer or discoverer by which *hukm* is known.

In regard to the agreement of Muslim scholars, the two senses in which the term *hakimb* is used are not alike. As for the first sense, the *Qur'anic* verses illustrated by the above-quoted ones have left no chance for Muslim scholars to disagree. But as for the second sense, Muslim scholars are divided into three categories, namely, the Ash'arites, the Mu'tazilites and the Maturidites. On one end of the spectrum, the ash'rites have held that *shari'ah* is the revealer of the divine law as it is based on divine injunctions. On the other end, the Mu'tazilites have held that human reason is the revealer. In between, the maturidites have introduced a compromising formula of the two extreme views.

One must not think that human reason has been proposed by the Mu'tazilites as the *shari'ah's* rival in regard to the determination of Allah's will whereby *Shari'ah* can be overridden by human reason. What the Mu'tazilites wanted to say is that since it has been unanimously held that whatever Allah commands is good and whatever Allah forbids is evil, human reason can, independently of *shari'ah,* know the will of Allah with respect to human acts on the basis of its ability to discern the nature of acts being either good or evil.

The Asharites have maintained that human acts can not be characterised by goodness or evil whether because of their essence or some external attributes to them, for the goodness and evil of human acts change with the change of individuals and circumstances. For example, truth is good, but it is evil if it would lead to the murder of an innocent person by a tyrant. Conversely, lie is evil, but it is good if it would save the life of that innocent person. Therefore, *Shari'ah* is the only means through which the value of human acts can be ascertained; because their goodness depends on their being commanded and their evil depends on their being forbidden.

Despite their disagreement in terms of the nature of goodness and evil of human acts being inherent in them, external attributes to them or relative qualities change with the change of individuals and circumstances, the Mu'tazilites have agreed on the reason's capability to discern them without any help from the *shari'ah.* For example, man is not in need for the revelation to know, though it may confirm, that the beneficial lie is good and the harmful truth is evil. However, they concede that the goodness or evil of some acts can not be distinguished through a means other than the *Shari'ah* such as the goodness of fasting on the last day of *Ramadan* and the evil of fasting on the first day of *Shawwal.*

In principle, the Maturidites have agreed with the Mu'tazilites on the acts aptitude to b characterized by goodness or evil and the reason's capability to discern the good or evil character of acts. Nevertheless that does not necessarily mean that the commands of reason must coincide with those of the *Shari'ah.* That is because reason is prone to error especially when it comes to the determination of the value of highly ambiguous acts.

The aforementioned theological dispute has its serious corollaries pertaining to man's accountability in the hereafter. For the Ash'arites and the maturidites, accountability is conditional upon the reaching of call, that is, the revealing of scriptures and the sending of prophets. Therefore, those who lived during the interval in the series of prophets do not account for what they had done. In contrast, the Mu'tazilites have not regarded the reaching of call as a condition for accountability for the possession of intellect ought to have urged those who lived during the interval in the series of prophets to do what is good such as the belief in Allah, and to refrain from doing what is evil such as infidelity.

The Subject Matter of *Hukm* (*Al-mahkum Fih*)

The subject matter of *hukm (al-mahkum fih)* is the act of the *mukallaf* (the subject) to which the communication of the lawgiver relates. In other words, it is the act of the *mukallaf* which might be characterized by one of the subdivisions of either *al-hukm al-taklifi* or *al-hukm al-wadi.* Three conditions have been stipulated for the validity of *al-mahkum fih.* They are as follows:

1. The knowledge of the act. For the *mukallaf* to be expected to pay obedience to the communication of the lawgiver addressed to him, the act constituting the subject matter of that communication must be known to him specifically. Therefore, the general commands mentioned in the Qur'an had not been binding upon the *mukallafin* until they were detailed by the *Sunnah* of the prophet

(saw). As an illustration, the verse: "Establish prayers" (Qur'an, 2: 43) had not been binding until the prophet (saw) said: "Pray as you have seen me praying". However, the knowledge of the act required by this condition is the possible knowledge and not the actual knowledge. In other words, the act commanded is binding upon the *mukallaf* as long as he is capable of knowing it even if he does not know it actually. The capability of knowing the act implies the *mukallaf's* adulthood, sanity and having the access to the source of knowledge either personally or through asking the specialists.

2. The knowledge of the source of the command. If the need for the first condition is logical, the need for this condition is moral. The knowledge of the authority from whom the command issues establishes the legitimacy of the act which gives rise to its abidingness upon the *mukallaf* that urges him to act accordingly. Like the first condition, the knowledge talked about is the possible knowledge and not the actual one.

3. The possibility of the act. For a *mukallaf* to be obliged to conform to his behaviour to a particular pattern of conduct, it is intelligible to stipulate that such a pattern of conduct must be possible to be conformed to his usual behaviour. Based on that, the *mukallaf* can not be commanded to do an impossible act.

The impossibility of an act might be logical or habitual. Logical impossibility is that one which is based upon reason such as doing opposite things at once. An example of it is to sit and stand at the same time. On the other hand, habitual impossibility is that one which can be accepted rationally. Nevertheless it seems odd according to natural laws. An example of it is the impossibility for a human being to fly without an aircraft.

Of the impossible acts that can not be the subject matter of *hukm* is that one which is contrary to the human nature. It is of our nature as humans to feel sad, happy or afraid. So to command the *mukallaf* not to do these things is to command him to do an impossible thing because it is against his nature. However, whenever one comes across some commands that sound contrary to the human nature he must bear in mind that what is commanded actually is not the impossible act rather than another act related to the impossible act mentioned in the command. For example, Allah (swt) says: "So that you do not feel sad for what you have missed and you do not feel happy with what you have been given" (Qur'an, 57: 23). Literally, the *mukallafin* are commanded by this Qur'anic verse not to feel sad or happy when the cause of either occurs. However, what is really intended is to command them not to go beyond the reasonable limits of such feelings whereby sadness would degenerate into despair and happiness would degenerate into pride. Likewise, the Prophet (saw) said: "Do not get angry". In fact, what is commanded is to refrain from the bad consequences of anger such as violence.

Some *Usuliyyin*, however, have held that an impossible act can be the subject matter of *hukm.* They have argued that Allah (swt) commanded some people to believe in Him although he had known that they will not comply with the command as it is understood from the following Qur'anic verse: "As to those who reject faith, it is the same to them whether you warn or you do not warn them, they will not believe " (Qur'an, 2: 6).

In response to this argument, it has been argued that the knowledge of the act that will issue from the *mukallaf* does not deprive him of his ability to choose freely whether to do a certain act or not. So, the act of believing in Allah (swt) is a possible act of the *mukallaf*, however Allah (swt) knows whether *mukallaf* will choose freely to believe in him or not without affecting his freedom of choice.

Al-mahkum fih has been classified into various categories according to the basis on which the classification has been carried out. On the basis of the interest that ensues from its commission or omission, for instance, it has been classified into right of god (*haqq Allah*) and right of man (*haqq al-abd*). The former, as opposed to the latter, is not subject to inheritance, reconciliation or waver.T h e majority of Muslim scholars led by the Hanafis have regarded right of god as that one which is for the interest of the community at large without being exclusive to a particular person. However, right of a man is that one which is for the worldly interest of a definite individual. However, the possibility that the generality and particularity of interests may merge together in one act has caused the addition of two more categories to the already distinguished ones. *Al-mahkum fih* thus has been subdivided in to four categories: First, if the interest is merely general, it is called pure right of god.

The implementation of prescribed punishments *(hudud)* furnishes a good example of this right. Second, if the interest is merely particular, it is called right of man. Contractual rights and proprietary rights are good illustrations of this right. Third, is the combination of the right of God and the right of man, where the former is predominant. This can be exemplified by the prohibition of suicide. Fourth, is the combination of the right of God and the right of man, where the latter is predominant. Right of just retaliation *(qisas)* is a good representative of this right.

On the basis of its enforceability, *al-mahkum fih* has been classified into religious right (*haqq diyani*) and judicial right (*haqq qadayi*). Religious right is what can not be enforced judicially. Therefore its observance relies totally upon the religious commitment of the person obliged by it. A judicial right is what can be judicially enforced. Being so does not mean that it is not religious. It is of course religious, but because of its general collective importance, its observance has not been left to the religious commitment of the person obliged. Therefore, if that commitment fails to generate the necessary observance, such observance would be forcibly generated if the judiciary is set on motion. Hence every judicial right is a religious right and not vice versa. However, a right might be judicial in principle and in practice might not. Offering prayer is a religious right of God in the sense that it can not be judicially enforced in case the person obliged neglects it. On the other hand, the creditor's right to have the debt paid back to him by the debtor is a judicial right in the sense that it can be judicially enforced in case the debtor fails to discharge his obligation. But if the debtor denies the right of the creditor and the latter fails to prove his right before the court, his right would not be enforced and therefore it would get reduced to the status of a religious right in the sense that it depends only on the debtor's religious commitment.

The Legally Competent Person *(Al-mahkum Alayh)*

The conduct govern by the communication of the lawgiver issues from a person who can understand that communication and then behave in accordance with or defiance of what he has understood bearing the responsibility for the consequences of his acts. Thus, the subject of *hukm* (*al-mahkum 'alayh*) must be a person who is adult and sane, that is, legally competent.

It is noticeable that some contemporary Muslim scholars tend to state that the conditions of *al-maahkum alayh* are to have the ability to understand the communication, and to have the capacity (*ahliyyah*). In fact, to have the capacity is to be adult and sane. Being so is not intended for it, but it is stipulated because it indicates the *mukallaf's* ability to understand the communication and act upon his understanding of it. Therefore, the two conditions are thought to be identical and can be reduced to the stipulation of having the capacity alone, and this is what had been commendably done by al-Husari.

Capacity (*al-ahliyyah*) *can be defined as: one's capability of having rights established for him and duties imposed upon him.* Such a capability is not a single status that can be bestowed at once upon man at a particular point of time. It is a multi-layered status that is conferred upon him one by one according to his development in age and reason. Therefore, it has been divided into two types each of which has been further subdivided. They are receptive capacity (*ahliyyat al-wujub*) and creative capacity (*ahliyyat al-ada*).

Receptive capacity has been further subdivided into partial receptive capacity (*ahliyyat al-wujub al-naqisah*) and full receptive capacity (*ahliyyat al-wujub al-kamilah*). Partial receptive capacity is one's capability of having rights without duties or having duties without rights. The capability of having rights without duties is possessed only when the person is an embryo in his mother's womb. He can not be obliged by any kind of obligations, yet he is entitled to such rights as inheritance and bequest. On the other hand, the capability of having duties without rights is possessed by the person after his death. That is because he would be, in case he dies indebted, obliged by his creditors' rights. Some think that man has full receptive capacity after death until his rights towards the others are fulfilled, and his duties towards the others are discharged.

The idea that man can have capacity after death whether partial or full has been correctly rejected. That is because the deceased's rights are inherited by his heirs, whereas his duties are attached to his estate.

Full receptive capacity, on the other hand, is one's capability of having rights and duties. This state starts with one's birth and ends with his death.

Creative capacity is one's capability of having his acts recognized by the *Shari'ah* and, consequently, given rise to their effects. Like the receptive one, it has been further subdivided into partial and full. On the one hand, partial creative capacity is possessed when one attains the age of discretion, that is, the age of seven. In such a state, he is not considered to be obliged by any of the devotional acts such as prayer and fasting. However, if he observes them, they would be valid. But with respect to non-devotional acts, they are classified into three categories, viz. purely beneficial acts, purely harmful acts, and acts which partake in both benefit and harm. Purely beneficial acts yield their effects on the part of the minor such as the acceptance of the donations and bequests made in his favour. Purely harmful acts are considered null and void and consequently they yield no effects on his part. These acts can be exemplified by the making of donations and bequests in the others' favour. With respect to those acts which partake in both such as the conclusion of a sale contract, they are dependent upon the approval of his guardian. Full creative capacity, on the other, is scribed when one attains the age of majority. In this final state, his acts are fully recognized by the *Shari'ah* regardless of their nature.

A Comparative Assessment

According to Islamic jurists, *hukum shar'i* may either be a positive command or a negative command, and the *mukallaf* has to carryout the command ie., to do something or abstain form doing something, as the case may be. We can conveniently call it command or prohibition. If they are supported with definitive proof (*dalil*), it will be either mandatory (*fard*) or prohibitory (*haram*). Hanafi jurists have widened the scope by saying that if the text that conveys the command is definitive in its meaning (*dalalah*) or authenticity (*thubut*) is a *fard* if not, it will be *wajib*. For example, if we can derive one definite command from a Qur'anic verse (*ayah*), it will be a *fard* command. On the contrary, if a Qur'anic verse can be interpreted in such a manners that one definite command cannot definitively emanate from it, the command that is generally inferred from it is known as *wajib* command. A violator (*munkar*) of a *fard* is known as an apostate (*kafir)*; whereas, a violator (*munkar*) of a *wajib* is known as a person who has committed a sin (*fasiq*). We can illustrate it as: a person, who denies performing prayer (*solat*) or giving poors' dues (*zakat*), will be known as a *kafir;* but if a person does not perform *solat fitre*, he will be considered as a *fasiq*. Likewise, if something is asked from a Muslim to be avoided, it is known as *makruh*. Further, some acts may only have recommendatory value (*mandub*); or some other acts may grant option to the *mukallaf*, they are permissible acts (*mubah*). The authors are of the opinion that actually commands can either be positive or negative. Hanafi jurists have also maintained the same, with some further details, which does not make any substantial difference in the jurisprudence of *hukum*, and that can be appreciable.

There is another category of rules, which just determine the legal rules to be internalized. They are neither in the form of command nor are they options. They are known as enactments (*wad*). It can be exemplified as rules prescribing certain conditions (*sabab*) for getting something. The best example of it is the commonly known *hadith* "The killer does not inherit". Based on this, the concepts of *al-hukum al-taklifi* (law of command) and *al-hukum al-wadi* (declaratory law) have been developed.

It has rightly been written that the *ulema* of *usul* have differed with the *fuqaha* to the identification of *hukum shar'i*. For ulema, the text of (Qur'an or *Sunnah*) itself represent command (*hukum*). On the contrary, for *fuqaha*, it is the effect of the text that actually conveys a command (*hukum*). Authors are of the opinion that both, in effect, have conveyed the same thing.

Austin's commands issued by the sovereign can be general or particular; they can be active or tacit. Although Austin has recognized law made by God to His human creatures, law as command of the sovereign dominates. Positive morality for him is the law made by a man for others not in his political capacity. In his theory sovereignty vests in the sovereign, a human being. In effect, his theory visualizes a powerful sovereign, who issues commands, positive or negative supported with sanction. In his theory, there is no scope of any optional law. Thus his theory differs from the Islamic theory of *hukum shar'i* on four grounds: (1) sovereignty in

Islam vests in Allah (swt) and the king, *khalipha* or for that matter any other ruler simply represents Him, as Islamic jurisprudence is based on the sovereign, who is Allah, and vicegerents, who are human being, including the ruler. Thus, commands (*ahkam*) are derived from injunctions contained in or derived from Qur'an and *Sunnah*. Law also can be mad by man based on his endowed reason, but they have to be in conformity with these injunctions. Likewise, man can interpret the law derived from Qur'an and *Sunnah* or can make legal rules based on analogy. (2) In Islam, the violator of any law for which penalty has been prescribed, that penalty is inflicted on him. At the same time, since he has committed a sin, he will be accountable for it in the hereafter. So the sanction is not only the penal sanction. (3) Islam recognizes enabling and optional laws also. (4) Islam does not reject customs. Initially, Islam opposed pagan customs that were encouraging idol worshipping. But now any custom, which are in conformity with Qur'an and *Sunnah,* are acceptable as law.

Bentam's command theory has four categories of commands: command, prohibition, non-command, and non-prohibition. In effect law can be of three types: positive, negative and optional. Classification is closer to the classification of commands in Islam. Bu Bentham's command theory can be distinguished form *hukum shar'i* on the following grounds: (1) As noted above, in Islam, Allah (swt) is the sovereign, and a king, the Parliament, or a dictator exercise their powers within the ambit of the injunctions prescribed in Qur'an and *Sunnah*. Thus, validity of any law made by the king has to be tested on these primary law sources; it will be valid only when it is in conformity with these. This goes against Bentham, as Bentham is of the opinion that 'natural law is the nonsense on the stilt'. He did not believe in 'Is' and 'Ought' relationship. (2) Bentham accepted for constitutional limitations on the sovereign. In Islam, this limitation does not have any value, as God has all powers. A *khalipha* exercises his law-making power within the ambit prescribed by Qur'an and *Sunnah*. In addition to this, Islam does not reject any constitutional limitations. But the constitution itself is not considered to be the supreme law of the country. (3) As noted above Islam does not reject all customs; rather, customs is a source of law.

It will be wrong to say that *hukum shar'i* does not suit to modern democratic states. Authors are of the opinion that it suits to democratic states also. The basic requirements of an Islamic state are that there should be a khalipha (he can be named as a Prime Minister or a President) and a *Shura* (Parliament). Pakistan is an Islamic Republic, and it has a President and a Parliament. Likewise, the Federal Constitution of Malaysia says that Islam is the religion of the state. It has a Yang di-Pertuan Agong (YDPA), a Prime Minister and a Parliament. What actually the Islamic command theory requires is that government will have these two constituents in any form; and more importantly, the government should not violate the express injunctions contained in Qur'an and *Sunnah* by any means. On the contrary, it has been proven above that the Austinian command theory is not suitable to modern states. Bentham's theory is considered to be suitable, but is criticized for rejecting natural law altogether. This is why modern positivists, who are concerned about natural rights of the humankind and who are keen to ensure survival of the man, have worked for revival of natural law in one or the other form.

Conclusion

It is clear from the above discussions that Austin's command theory has been extensively criticized and has rightly been determined unsuitable to the contemporary states. Hart has been conspicuously prominent among his critiques. Bentham's theory, on the contrary, seems to be pragmatic, but it also cannot be suited to a large number of states that laudably believe in independence of judiciary, recognition to judge-made law, acceptance of the minimum content of the natural law, and customs as source of law.

In their command theory, revealed law has no prominence. They totally reject 'Is' and 'Ought' relationship, where the revealed law is considered as a test of validity of man-made laws. This is not suitable to the Muslim world. In these states, whatever is the form of government, revealed laws is the test of man-made laws. If any man-made law is not in conformity with this law, it will be invalid. So, revealed laws have prominence over man-made laws. This is because sovereignty vests into Allah (swt) and the *khalipha* (head of the state) is a vicegerent of Allah (swt). This is already in practice in many Muslim countries, including Pakistan, Iran, Saudi Arabia and Malaysia.

- *References*

RWM Dias, *Jurisprudence* (London: Butterworths, 1985).

HLA Hart, *The Concept of Law* (Oxford: Oxford University Press, 1978).

HLA Hart, Essays in Jurisprudence and Philosophy (Oxford: Clarendon Press, 1983).

Tephen Guest, Positivism Today (Singapore: Darmouth, 1996).

J.G. Riddall, Jurisprudence (London: Butterworths, 1991).

Raymond Wacks, Jurisprudence (London: Blackstone Press Limited, 1987).

G.C. Venkata Subbarao, Jurisprudence and Legal Theory (Lucknow: Eastern Book Company, 1975).

W. Friedmann, Legal Theory (New York: Columbia University Press, 1967).

Abd al-Wahhab Khallaf, *Ilm Usul al- Fiqh* (Cairo: Dar al-Hadith, 2003).

Ahmad Hasan. (n.d.). *The Principles of Islamic Jurisprudence: The Command of the Shari'ah and Juridical Norm* (Islamabad: Islamic Research Institute, International Islamic University Islamabad), Vol. 1.

Sayf al-Din Abi al-Hasan Ali Ibn Abi Ali Ibn Muhammad al-Amadi. (n.d). *al-Ahkam Fi Usul al-Ahkam* (Beriut: Dar al-Kutub al-Alamiyyah).

Badran Abu Al-Aynain Badran, (n.d.). *Usul al-Fiqh al-Islami* (Alexandria: Mu'assasah Shabab al-Jami'ah).

Muhammad Ibn Ismail Al-Bukhari, *Sahih al-Bukhari* (Beirut: Dar al-Kutub al-Ilmiyyah. Kitab al-Adab. Bab al-Hazar Min al-Ghadab, 2003), 3rd Ed., p. 1122.

Abu Hamid Muhammad ibn Muhammad al-Ghazali. (n.d.). *Al-Mustasfa Min Ilm al-Usul* (Beirut: Dar Ihya al-turath al-Arabi).

Ibn Amir al-Haj al-Halabi, *al-Taqrir Wa al-Tahbir* (Beirut: Dar al-Kutub al-Ilmiyyah, 1999).

Ahmad al-Husari, *Al-hukm al- Shar'i Wa masadiruh* (Beirut: Dar Al-jail, 1997).

Mohammad Hashim kamali, *Principles of Islamic jurisprudence* (Kuala lumpur: Ilmiah Publishers Sdn. Bhd, 1998).

Muhammad al-Khudari, *Usul al- Fiqh*. (Cairo: Dar Al- hadith, 2001).

Muwaffaq al-Din Abd Allah Ibn Qudama al-Maqdisi, *Rawdat al Nazir*

Wa Jannat al- Manazir (Makkah: Al-Maktabh Al-Makkiyyah, 1998), Vol. 1.

Mohammed Tahir Haji Mohammad, "Rights and Duties in Shari'ah and Common Law", Ph.D Thesis, International Islamic University Malaysia, 2001.

Fakhr al-Din Muhammad Ibn Umar Ibn al-Husayn al-Razi, *Al-Mahsul Fi Ilm Usul al-Fiqh* (Beirut: Muassasat al-Risalah, 1992).

Muhammad Ibn Isa al-Tirmizi, *Al-Jami al-Sahih* (Beirut: Dar al-Kutub al-Ilmiyyah.Bab al-Azan.Bab La Salat Illa Bifatihat al-Kitab, 2000), Vol. 1.

4

Islamic Commercial Contracts Cases Heard in Civil Courts Under Common Law: A Case Study of Malaysia and England

Norhashimah Mohd. Yasin

Introduction

In Malaysia, matters relating to Islamic commercial law (*fiqh muamalat*) are heard in the country's civil courts due to the division of judicial powers as defined in the Federal Constitution.[1] This is provided for in the Ninth Schedule of the Federal Constitution, which deals with the Federal List and the State List respectively.

Courts dealing with civil and criminal matters come under section 4 of List 1 (Federal List) of the Ninth Schedule. Section 4(e)(i) places "Contract; partnership, agency and other special contracts…" firmly under the civil court system. Furthermore, s7(j) places banking, money-lending, pawn-broking and control of credit squarely under the remit of the Federal Government and therefore matters relating to banking will be heard in the civil courts.

Section 1 of List 2 provides for the cases that fall under the jurisdiction of *Shari'ah* courts when it involves Islamic law and personal and family law of persons professing the religion of Islam. The matters include "succession, testate, and intestate, betrothal, marriage, divorce, dower, maintenance, adoption, legitimacy, guardianship, gifts, partitions and non-non-charitable trusts, *Wakafs*, ...creation and punishment of offences by persons professing the religion of Islam against precepts of the religion except in regard to matters included in the Federal List..."

Islamic banking is governed by Federal-level legislation. Islamic banks are governed by the Islamic Banking Act 1983 (IBA) and Islamic banking conducted by conventional banks is governed by s124 of the Banking and Financial Institutions Act 1989 (BAFIA). The nature and purpose of these two statutes are somewhat different as the IBA was enacted with the intention of Islamic banking in mind while BAFIA was enacted to govern conventional banking. The nature of the dual banking system; a full-fledged Islamic banking system operating in parallel with a sophisticated conventional banking system is the unique feature of Malaysia's financial system. Malaysia is the first country to have a dual banking system model since 1983 with both types of banking working hand in hand utilising the same banking and legal infrastructure.[2]

The purpose of this article is to examine the cases involving Islamic commercial contracts, including Islamic banking as decided by Civil court judges under the Common law jurisdiction. The article is not intended to discuss on the Islamic nature of the contract in terms of its validity, rules and requirements in accordance with classical views as such.[3] Its main idea is to examine the behavioural patterns and techniques the Civil court judges have adopted under the Common law system in Malaysia and her former colonial master, England in deciding the cases related to Islamic commercial contracts accordingly.

The Position in English Courts under Common Law

Islamic commercial cases are very rarely heard in English courts. There only appear to be two cases where the defence counsels attempted to raise the *Shari'ah* related issues deriving from the Islamic commercial contracts. The first case was *Islamic Investment Company of the Gulf (Bahamas) Ltd v Symphony Gems NV and Others*[4] which involved a *Morabaha* contract.[5] The plaintiff was claiming for non-payment for a consignment of gem-stones. The defendant's ground for non-payment was that the stones had not been delivered. However, the plaintiff claimed that the reason for non-delivery was the fault of the defendant.

One of the contentions by the defendant was that the contract was not a valid *Morabaha* and therefore void under *Shari'ah.* The judge, Tomlinson J, accepted this argument but ruled it as irrelevant. He said:

> *"However, it is important to note–indeed, in my judgement, it is absolutely critical to note–that the contract with which I am concerned is governed not by* Shari'ah *law but by English law. Indeed, it is equally critical to note that Dr. Samaan,*[6] *after examining the nature and terms of the contract with which I am concerned, comes to this conclusion: 'I have therefore come to the conclusion that the Agreement in issue does not have the essential characteristics of a* Morabaha *contract.' He then goes on, insofar as he has not already done so, to explain why that is so. Subject only to an argument which Mr. Joseph,*[7] *who has appeared for all three Defendants, has put forward relating to the alleged incapacity of the Claimant company to enter into this agreement in the light of its Memorandum and Articles of Association, it seems to me that it is not of any relevance to the issues which I have to decide what are the essential features of a* Morabaha *contract. The fact is that, as Dr. Samaan states and I have no reason to think is in any way inaccurate, this contract does not have the essential characteristics of a* Morabaha *contract. Furthermore, it is a contract governed by English law. I must simply construe it according to its terms as an Engiish law contract."*[8]

Therefore, in applying English contract law, the court found in favour of the plaintiff (the financier). The main problem was an inherent contradiction in the contract. The preliminary stated:

> *(A) The Purchaser wishes to deal with the Seller for the purpose of purchasing Supplies (as hereinafter defined) under this Agreement in accordance with the Islamic Shari'ah.*
>
> *(B) The Purchaser wishes to request the Seller to purchase the Supplies and sell them to the Purchaser through a Morabaha arrangement and the Seller is willing to make such purchases and sell the Supplies to the Purchaser on the terms and subject to the conditions set out herein.*

However, the main body of the contract contained the following clauses:

25. This agreement and each Purchase Agreement shall be governed by, and shall be construed in accordance with, English law.

26.1 The Purchaser hereby irrevocably agrees for the benefit of the Seller that the courts of England shall have exclusive jurisdiction to hear and determine any suit, action or proceeding, and to settle any disputes, which may arise out of or in connection with this Agreement or any Purchase Agreement and, for such purposes, irrevocably submits to the jurisdiction of such courts.[9]

As a result of the stipulation in clause 25 providing for English law, and clause 26.1 providing for English courts to have jurisdiction, the requirement for the contract to be under *Shari'ah* was deemed to be rendered irrelevant.

This issue also arose in *Shamil Bank of Bahrain v Beximco Pharmaceuticals Ltd and others.*[10] The defendants (the customers) had been given leave to appeal to the English Court of Appeal on one ground, the governing law clause of a supposed '*Morabaha*' contract. The clause in question stated:

Subject to the principles of Glorious Shari'ah, *this agreement shall be governed by and construed in accordance with the laws of England.*[11]

The Court of Appeal had to decide whether the contract was governed by English law and *Shari'ah,* or by English law alone. The High Court judge, Morison J, had already ruled that English law was the sole governing law.[12]

Potter LJ noted that:

"The general reference to principles of Shari'ah *in this case affords no reference to, or identification of, those aspects of* Shari'ah *law which are intended to be incorporated into the contract, let alone the terms in which they are framed. It is plainly insufficient for the defendants to contend that the basic rules of the* Shari'ah *applicable in this case are not controversial. Such 'basic rules' are neither referred to nor identified. Thus the reference to 'the principles of...*Shari'ah*' stand unqualified as a reference to the body of* Shari'ah *law generally. As such, they are inevitably repugnant to the choice of English law as the law of the contract and render the clause self-contradictory and therefore meaningless."*[13]

The Court of Appeal upheld the High Court's judgement and found in favour of the plaintiff bank. However, the Court of Appeal judgement did not rule out the possibility of an English court applying the principles of *fiqh muamalat* to a purported *Shari'ah*-based contract if those relevant aspects of *Shari'ah* could be incorporated into the contract based on the above statement by the Appeal Court judge.

Even if the Court of Appeal had found that it was possible that the contract could be judged according to English law and *Shari'ah*, the court would have declined to do so on the same grounds that the High Court would have declined to do so. As Morison J had said:

> *"Whilst in one sense this court will answer any question posed to it, however difficult, it is improbable in the extreme, that the parties were truly asking this court to get into matters of Islamic religion and orthodoxy.*[14] *This is especially so when the bank has its own Religious Board to monitor the compliance of the bank with the Board's own perception of Islamic principles of law in an international banking context."*[15] .

In other words, the Court was not prepared to judge on *Shari'ah* issues. However, the problem with *Shari'ah*, from the court's point of view, is that it is un-codified, as can be seen in the above statement of Potter LJ. The Court dealt with the 'doctrine of incorporation', under which a different legal code or set of rules can be incorporated into an English contract. The Court cited, as examples, the French Civil Code and the Hague Rules.[16]

English courts are bound by a European Union treaty that only allows a contract to be governed by one national law. This also seems to rule-out a construction such as the contract being heard in an English court, subject to *Shari'ah* as practiced in a particular Muslim country.[17]

The Court of Appeal cited an earlier case heard in the High Court–*Glencore International AG v Metro Trading International Inc.*[18] The issue in this case was the ownership of crude oil in storage tanks in *Fujairah*, United Arab Emirates. The Court had to judge the case according to both English and UAE commercial law to ensure that an English judgement would be valid in the jurisdiction where the oil was physically located. Potter LJ said:

> *"...the judge was concerned with, and heard evidence in relation to, the meaning and scope of the word* 'ghasb'[19] *(misappropriation) as a term used but undefined in Article 1326 of the* Fujairah *Civil Code which was the governing law in the case before him. As such he was*

> *obliged to interpret and apply the term in the dispute before him, with the assistance of rival experts in the law of* Fujairah."[20]

The presiding judge in *Glencore*, Moore-Bick J, was willing to examine the issue at hand from the viewpoint of *Shari'ah*. On the meaning of *ghasb*, he said: "I think that the enquiry must begin with the concept of *ghasb* in Islamic jurisprudence."

The courts in all these English cases utilised the evidence of expert witnesses. However, only in *Glencore* did the court take full notice of these experts. The courts in *Symphony Gems* and *Beximco* disregarded the expect witnesses and in fact regarded their evidence as irrelevant.[21] The difference is that in *Glencore*, the court could also decide on the basis of codified law, the UAE Civil Code 1985[22] and the Mejelle.[23] In the other two cases the courts had no such documentary material to assist them and were solely dependent on the expert witness evidence. Moore-Bick J, had this to say about the expert witnesses, and how he dealt with their evidence:

> *Having made these general comments, I wish to express my gratitude to all the expert witnesses both for the way in which they gave their evidence and for the efforts which they all made to assist me in coming to grips with some difficult questions. Each of them sought to deal with the issues on which he gave evidence fully and fairly and each made a substantial contribution to my understanding of the issues. Where the witnesses were in disagreement I have reached my decision only after giving careful consideration to their different opinions in the context of any relevant legislation and commentaries, preferring the views which seemed to me to be most consistent with a carefully constructed system of the kind which one can discern in the [United Arab Emirates] Civil Code as a whole.*

Malaysian Civil Courts vis-a-vis Islamic Banking Contracts

Given that cases involving *Shari'ah*-based contracts are heard in the civil courts rather than the *Shari'ah* courts, an important issue is whether such Civil courts are competent and capable to hear and adjudicate Shari'ah-related commercial issues.

In Malaysia, the law is based on English Common law principles,[24] so the question arises as to whether there is a place for *Shari'ah* in Malaysian law beyond that stipulated by the Constitution. The leading case in Malaysia on this issue is *Ramah v Laton.*[25]

In this colonial-era case, the Selangor Court of Appeal with a three-man bench of British judges had to decide on the validity of the lower court judgement that allowed expert evidence from two *qadis* regarding a dispute between two wives over their deceased husband's property.

The court held that *Shari'ah* was *lex loci* and not foreign law, and as such, under the legislative provisions of the time,[26] the lower court should have judged the case without needing such evidence to be given:

> *"The question in debate was not, in the view which I take, a question of foreign law at all, but the question was, in the events that had happened, what were the rights of the plaintiff according to the law of this land in the estate of her deceased husband. The local law is a matter of which the Court must take judicial notice. The Court must propound the law, and it is not competent to the Court to allow evidence to be led as to what is the local law."*[27]

However, by a majority decision, the court held that although it should give a judgement on the case, it declined to do so, on the grounds that the judges were not competent to do so. They referred the case back to the lower court with the suggestion that the trial judge refer the case to arbitration[28] under the relevant legislation of the time. The dissenting judge,[29] however, was of the opinion that the court was competent to hear *Shari'ah*-related cases.

Given this background, it may be presumed that Malaysian courts would be somewhat better able and competent to judge cases involving *Shari'ah*-based contracts than their English counterparts. However, this has not generally been the case, and in the early cases involving Islamic banking, the Malaysian courts behaved no differently to the English courts. However, the position has been very inconsistent, as occasionally in recent years, Malaysian Civil courts have shown themselves to be willing to examine the Shariah-issues of the contract within the ambit of Common law.

One case in point is that of *Tahan Steel Corporation Sdn. Bhd. v. Bank Islam Malaysia Bhd.*[30] The plaintiff sought an injunction to prevent the defendant bank enforcing its security until all legal processes had been exhausted, on the grounds that the bank had breached the conditions of the contract, which was one of *Al-Istisna'* (manufacturing sale).[31]

Although the judge, Abdul Malik Ishak J, made his judgement according to Procedural law, he did see fit to briefly look at the Shariah issues. He opened up the possibility of a Malaysian judge referring to *Shari'ah* principles, when he said, with reference to the Central Bank of Malaysia (CBM) website:

> *"...I can take judicial notice of it. Indeed I can take judicial notice of almost anything. Thus, it is permissible for me to take judicial notice of those matters which men of ordinary and average intelligence would be acquainted with...It is also permissible for me to take judicial notice of how certain businesses are carried out."*[32]

He added that: "Generally speaking, I can rely on my own knowledge of the local affairs." When citing the *Beximco* case, he referred to the statement by the trial judge:

> *"With respect, as a Malaysian Judge, I do not agree with the views of Morrison J when his Lordship after relying on Dr. Lau's first expert report said that: '...*Shari'ah *law is made up of conflicting pronouncements and there is a considerable debate as to what is and what is not permissible under it. The situation is complicated by the fact that much of the classical law emerged at a time when many financial concepts simply did not exist.'"*[33]

Abdul Malik J continued:

> *"It must be borne in mind that whenever there is a conflict, reference should be made to the Qur'an (the holy book of Islam) and the* Sunnah *(sayings, teachings and actions of the Prophet Muhammad). Tan Sri Nor Mohamed Yakop, the Second Minister of Finance (as he then was) in his paper entitled Reflections on the Islamic Financial System aptly said: 'If we look at the Islamic financial system, it is natural that we look at the core of Islam itself. Unlike many other religious systems, we see Islam as a* deen, *or as a complete way of life. Beyond basic religious beliefs and practices, Islam shows us how to best conduct ourselves in everyday matters. This code of best conduct is called the* Shari'ah, *and it is the basis of the Islamic financial system.'"*[34]

What Abdul Malik J appears to be saying is that a Malaysian judge can take judicial notice of *Shari'ah*. However, having said that, he was not actually in a position to apply any real *Shari'ah* principles to the contract in the case at hand because, as the issue was the granting of an injunction, conventional procedural law came into play. Nevertheless, in his summing up, he stated that a key factor in disallowing the injunction was the issue of riba. He noted that Bank Islam was an Islamic bank and so was not in a position to charge interest on the debt while civil proceedings were taking place and so was losing money.[35] He stated that:

> "*...I must take cognisance of the fact that the underlying transaction between the plaintiff and the defendant is one of financing under the* Shari'ah *principles. It must be borne in mind that the defendant has not been paid the agreed instalments from 31 January 2002. An Erinford injunction will further impede the ability of the defendant to obtain further sums from the defendant pending the appeal to the Court of Appeal. Here, the defendant as the lender being an institution operating under Islamic banking principles would be made to suffer loss of use of its money by the delay in recovering monies from the plaintiff in the event that this court ultimately decides that the injunction should not have been granted. This loss cannot be compensated by the courts since the defendant in prevented by its strict adherence to Islamic banking principles from taking any penalty interest which would be in the nature of usury.*"[36]

Conflict of Islamic Law and Other Statutes/Laws

So far, all Malaysian cases involving Islamic banking contracts have been in the context of default in payment, with the result that the bank will seek an order for sale of the property charged to it. When this happens, procedural laws such as the National Land Code 1965 and the Rules of High Court 1980 will take precedence. This was decided by the Court of Appeal in *Bank Kerjasama Rakyat Malaysia Bhd v Emcee Corporation Sdn Bhd.*[37] As Abdul Hamid Mohamad JCA stated:

> "*As was mentioned at the beginning of this judgement the facility is an Islamic banking facility.*[38] *But that does not mean that the law applicable in this application is different from the law that is applicable if the facility were given under conventional banking. The charge is a charge under the National Land Code. The remedy available and sought is a remedy provided by the National Land Code. The procedure is provided by the code and the Rules of the High Court 1980. The court adjudicating it is the High Court. So, it is the same law that is applicable, the same order that would be, if made, and the same principles that should be applied in deciding the application. The main source of the applicable law is s256 of the National Land Code.*"[39]

The above principle has been consistently adopted and cited by every case involving a default in payment by a customer of an Islamic financing facility, if property is charged as security.

In fact, the IBA 1983, which is the governing statute on Islamic banking and any matters incidental to it, has overlooked the aspect of conflict between its provisions and other written laws, be they substantive or procedural laws. Section 55 of IBA provides as follows:

> *"An Islamic bank which is incorporated under the Companies Act 1965 shall be subject to the provisions of that Act as well as to the provisions of this Act, save that where there is any conflict or inconsistency between the provisions of that Act and the provisions of this Act the provisions of this Act shall prevail."*

The above section of IBA is obvious that where there is a conflict between IBA and the Companies Act 1965, the former shall prevail. However, what happens if there is a conflict with any other statutes which Islamic banks are also subject to, such as the Contracts Act, NLC, Hire Purchase Act and Sales of Goods Act? Would the Malaysian Civil court apply the legal maxim of "*expressio unius alterius*" which means the "express mention of one thing implies the exclusion of another?" However, from the judgement in the *Emcee* case, the position is that when the case relates to the land (and its security) and the remedy sought for is under the NLC, the law applicable should be the NLC.

Perhaps a lesson could be drawn from Pakistan where their Islamic banking law (s 42 of the *Modaraba* Companies Act and *Mudaraba* (Floatation and Control) Ordinance 1980) cleverly stipulated as follows:

> *"The provisions of this Ordinance shall have effect notwithstanding anything contained in the Companies Act 1913 (VII of 1913) or any other law for the time being in force."*

The above provision overrides all other laws/statutes for the time being in force in Pakistan to give priority to the Islamic banking statute.

Malaysian Court Judgements in Relation to the Contract of *Bai Bithaman Ajil*[40]

Nearly all cases in Malaysian courts have involved the contract of *Bai Bithaman Ajil* (BBA)[41] The issue has always been how much does a customer have to repay the bank in the event of default and whether or not a rebate (*ibra*) can be given in such circumstances.

The first BBA case that Malaysian Civil court had to deal with was *Bank Islam Malaysia Bhd v Adnan bin Omar.*[42] A great deal has been written on this case and it is not proposed to go over this again in any detail.[43] The defendant had defaulted in payment and the bank obtained summary judgement for an order of sale for the property. The bank contended that Adnan had to pay the contracted selling price for the entire period of the contract rather that for the period he had maintained payment. The defendant claimed that he should be entitled to a rebate as would be given for early repayment. The High Court held that the rebate was at the bank's discretion, and as there had been a default, the bank did not have to give one, and so the defendant was liable for the entire amount of the selling price. The reason was that the court made its judgement solely on the basis of the wording of the charge document that stated:

"In the event that the charger shall:

> *(a) fail to pay or default in payment of any one of the monthly instalments under the property sale agreement or other or other monies due and payable to the bank thereunder and under the property sale agreement (for this purpose, failure to pay without demand on the due dates as stipulated in the property sale agreement shall be deemed to be a default); ....*
>
> *Then, and in any of such cases, all monies and liabilities and other dues covenanted to be paid by the charger to the bank and the bank shall forthwith become entitled to recover the same and to exercise the rights and powers upon default under this charge and as provided by the law without any previous notice to or concurrence on the part of the charger."*

As such, the Court of Appeal upheld this decision.[44] *Adnan Omar* was followed by a succession of order-for-sale cases which judged the BBA contract solely in conventional terms.[45]

In *Arab-Malaysian Merchant Bank Bhd v Silver Concept Sdn Bhd*[46] several Shariah issues were raised by the counsel for the defendant which the court took upon itself to address.[47] However, rather like the judge in *Beximco*, the *Silver Concept* judge, Suriyadi J, was not keen on the idea of a civil court applying *Shari'ah* principles, mainly due to disagreements over various issues of *fiqh muamalat*:

> *"In light of the existence of the branches of Sunni and Shia worldwide, with the former comprising no less than four* Mazahib/*schools of thought, what is, and what is not approved by the religion of Islam in relation to the banking business have occasioned the raising of many thorny questions. In practical terms or pragmatic purposes, the existence of those branches and sects cannot be denied. Each equally believes in the righteousness of its principles and belief, perhaps much to the annoyance of the opposing splintered group. For purposes of the matter before me, to lay too much emphasis on semantics and the like, may possibly spell the death knell of the Islamic banking system... The al-Quran as a source is not a problem, as it has remained unchanged since its revelation, and no Muslim of whatever sect will suggest otherwise. The problem is the al-Sunnah. This collection of traditions, sayings and actions has had its fair share of controversy, in the like of their acceptance by branches of followers (sects), generally termed as Mazhabs. The major ones are the Hanafi, Maliki, Shafie, and Hambali... With the procreation of these sects, came the predictable different interpretations of the abovementioned two sources. Certain sects, apart from giving different interpretations have created further discord, by challenging even the very existence and authenticity of some of the* ahadith. *Surely all these differences do not augur well for the ordinary Muslim on the road, especially the non-Arabic speaking Muslim populace. These are only a few of the headaches faced by the legislators and propagators of the Islamic banking system."*[48]

He pointed out that due to this problem, a court could always refer to the *Shari'ah* Advisory Council (SAC) of the Malaysian Central Bank for guidance.[49] The court, in this instance, however, did not make reference to the SAC. Suriyadi J's approach to the case can be defined in his own words:

> *"As it is now, despite being hampered by the paucity of adequate precedents and authority, it is my considered opinion that any transacted Islamic banking business must be presumed to be in order at the outset unless rebutted later (see s 114(e) of the Evidence Act 1950). At its inception, so long as the bank genuinely adheres to the very fundamentals of the al-Quran and authentic* ahadith, *ie the exact demands of the religion of Islam, and the papers on the face of it are in order, that bank may proceed with the relevant banking transaction.*

> *Any slip-shod preparatory work by the bank merely makes the rebuttal easier.*
>
> *In the event any litigation is commenced, it must be appreciated that not every presiding judge is a Muslim, and even if so, may not be sufficiently equipped to deal with matters, which* ulama *(Malay spelling for* luama*) take years to comprehend. Grounded on those reasons, and by the manner of the provisions so enacted any court must accept the matter as being in order at first instance, until challenged. By analogy, in any foreclosure case, if the cause papers are in order, unless there is cause to the contrary as contended by the charger, the order must be given.*
>
> *The rebuttal, when a challenge for purposes of the current case crops up,* inter alia *may come in the form of a statement of disapproval from the in-house Syariah Advisory Body, as set up by the bank. Under the Central Bank of Malaysia (Amendment) Act 2003 new provision of 16B(8), where in any proceedings relating to Islamic banking business etc before any court or arbitrator, any question that arises concerning a Syariah matter, the court may refer such question to the Syariah Advisory Council. The court thus may even refer the matter to that body in the midst of any proceedings."*[50]

Therefore, he made the presumption that the contract was Shariah-compliant unless this could be rebutted by the defendant. His suggestion that the rebuttal could come from the bank's own Shariah Advisory Body mirrors the court's contention in *Beximco* that if the bank's own Shariah advisors state that a contract is Shariah-compliant, then it shall be deemed to be so.

The first Shariah-based ground for challenging the contract is as follows:

> *"The charges created under the Al-Bai Facility and the Al-Wujuh Facility are illegal, null and void, and as such are unenforceable. The following points are notable:*
>
> *(1) the defendant has alleged that the current Al-Wujuh Facility*[51] *was a loan agreement with fixed interest rate payable by the defendant and not a sale's agreement. Likewise that* Al-Bai *Facility had the same fatal flaws. The very fact that the properties were charged accentuated and confirmed that loan status;*[52]
>
> *(2) by deducting eg RM60,000,000 from the gross sum of RM96,225,000 and the splitting up of the so-called gains by 84 months*

(made up of the duration of seven years multiplied by 12 months), the interest sum and percentage could be arrived at. This same formula and fatal effect is equally applicable to the Al-Bai *Facility;*[53]

(3) the agreements were against public policy as they had deceived the public. They being immoral or opposed to public policy as provided for under s 24 of the Contract Act 1950, were therefore unlawful and void;[54] *and*

(4) with the agreements and facilities being illegal, null and void the first and second charges were therefore void."[55]

Suriyadi J rejected these contentions. He stated that BBA involves a sale and a purchase and that the difference between the two constitutes the bank's profit margin. He said: "This manner of contract has never been expressly prohibited by Islam, and is quite well entrenched in Malaysia. It is accepted by Malaysian courts and public at large, and has been given due recognition by the international community."[56]

He took the view that on its face the contract was Shariah-compliant, particularly as all the parties had agreed to all the terms of the contract:

"Having appreciated the available facts, I am satisfied that the papers of the plaintiff were in order in relation to the prerequisites of the contract, and hence the regularity of the Al-Bai Bithaman Ajil facility. All the participating parties had agreed to the type of contract, ie Islamic based, the type and number of facilities, the amount, the mode of payment, period of payment, the profit margin of the plaintiff, the format of the securities, and all the other necessary details."[57]

He rejected any idea that the price difference was equivalent to interest:

"In support of its assertion of the existence of usury, the defendant had ingeniously deducted the cost price of the impugned land from the aggregate sum, and thereafter divided the profit by the number of months needed to complete the agreement. The sum derived, which could be converted and reflected into a certain percentage, in one year was thereafter alleged to be interest.

Notwithstanding the above, I reject any argument that injects the argument that it is not permissible to buy on credit, especially when there is mutual consent. Even Prophet Muhammad had occasion to buy some grain from a Jew to be paid at a specific time, with his coat

> *of mail as security. I am unable to acquiesce to any argument too that, just because a larger sum is agreed to be paid back founded on a buy back concept, with the defendant openly having requested for deferred payment, and with the differential sum resembling interest, the agreement must be void. I am unable to acquiesce to such a suggestion as there is no clear text that prohibits such a transaction entrenched with all those ingredients. Even the followers of the Shafii and Hanafi schools and the majority of Muslim scholars consider it lawful, calling it 'Shifa al ilal fi hokum ziyadat al-thamam li mujarrad al-ajal (translated: The reason for increasing the price due to lapse of time)'* (The Lawful and Prohibited in Islam *by Yusuf al-Qaradawi). I therefore reject the argument of the defendant that, just because the defendant pays more than what was needed to buy the impugned property, such sum (here called profit) must be interest per se."*[58]

He concluded with the observation that once an Islamic contract has been concluded the parties are bound by it:

> *"Parties have agreed before executing the agreements, and without any undue pressure or persuasion, to the preconditions of the Islamic based contract. As mentioned above,*[59] *as parties have agreed to be bound by the* al-aqd *and hence have a conclusive contract (*Uqud*), they are thus bound by the obligation. Both parties are equally bound and must comply with the conditions of the* Uqud *as ordained by Allah at Ch 5:1 of the al-Quran. On that premise the defendant here must comply, and be bound by his willingness to contract into the impugned agreements. He cannot contract out now unless there are cogent reasons to justify that act. Here I found none."*[60]

On the other contention that the bank should give a rebate, the court simply followed the *Adnan Omar* case.

An important thing to note is that the judges in cases where it was alleged that the contract was really un-Islamic took the view that this was simply a ploy to avoid repaying the debt. Suriyadi J opined that:

> *"If times had been good, this litigation would not have been initiated, let alone the transaction be attacked with such vitriolic vehemence as being un-Islamic and void. Likewise if times had been good, come the completion date of the agreements, the defendant would not even have found it necessary to whimper of their so-called 'un-Islamic' ingredients. The defendant cannot deny that it has already received the money by the indirect method of acquiring the impugned land. Unfortunately faced with the current recessionary reality repayment*

became a huge problem for the defendant. Whether unwilling or incapable of complying with the conditions of the facilities given, despite having received the fruits of the agreements, the defendant now strangely protests, and ungraciously attempts to find faults with the transaction."[61]

Abdul Wahab Patail J took a different approach in *Affin Bank Bhd v Zulkifli Abdullah*.[62] The issue, how much the defendant should repay after a BBA default was exactly the same as all previous cases. He considered referring the issue to the National Shariah Advisory Council of the Central Bank, but rejected this after reference to the *Emcee* case.[63]

In addition, Abdul Wahab Patail J decided that as it was purely an interpretation of the contractual terms of the Islamic banking (BBA) contract, reference to SAC was not necessary:

"*Since the question before the court is the interpretation and application of the terms of the contractual documents between the parties and of the decisions of the courts, reference of this case to another forum for a decision would be an indefensible abdication of this court of its function and duty to apply established principles to the question before it.* It is not a question of Shariah law. It is the conclusion of this court, therefore, that there is no need to refer the question to another forum." (emphasis added)[64]

The judge decided not to follow *Adnan Omar* (or *Silver Concept*) on the grounds that:

"The submissions did not address the substance of the term 'sale price' itself and the actual amount due pursuant to it... It cannot, therefore, be said that these cases have specifically established case law that the provider of an Al-Bai Bithaman Ajil facility is entitled to the profit margin for the whole original tenure when the facility is terminated before the end of its tenure."[65]

He noted that although the bank had submitted that, as per *Adnan Omar*, the bank could give a discretionary rebate, "It has not been raised as a relevant dispute in this case." Therefore, as the issue before the court was not really on the 'selling price' and/or 'rebate', there was no need to follow *Adnan Omar*. The main issue at hand is on the question of un-expired tenure and the unearned income as the learned judge stated:

> *"The argument that the bank can give a rebate, and that it is entirely discretionary is, in my view, irrelevant and is not an answer to the question before this court which is whether in the event of early termination of the facility upon default, the bank is entitled to the profit margin on the un-expired tenure and therefore unearned."*[66]

It was contended that the court in *Zulkifli Abdullah* has made a bad judgement[67] as far as Islamic law is concerned. Furthermore, the decision is contrary to the judgement in *Adnan Omar*. However, as far as the doctrine of binding precedents and *stare decisis* which is the corner stone of Common law, it can be said that there is actually no conflict as Abdul Wahab J merely followed a Supreme Court case[68] that allowed the contract itself to be looked into, i.e. to discover the real intention of the contract. In the *Ralamani* case, the Supreme Court stated that: "In our view, the correct approach would be to look at the substance, not just the label which had been attached to the letter. The law will always look beyond the terminology of the document to the actual facts of the situation and it is no longer a question of words but substance."[69] Therefore, Abdul Wahab J examined the substance, rather than the form of the BBA contract at issue. As he said:

> *The substance of the sale price in the Property Sale Agreement in an* Al-Bai Bithaman *Ajil facility, is that it is not a sale price paid by a single payment but it is a series of equal monthly instalments. It is also a substance of the transaction that profit margin is not a profit arising from a sale price arrived at in a bargain, but is based upon the agreed amount and tenure of the facility and the profit rate of the provider. The sale price is then the sum of the provider's purchase price and the profit margin.*
>
> *The essence of the profit rate is that it is based on an agreed real or actual profit of the provider expressed as a percentage, and not an interest rate that is being charged regardless. The profit margin is a function of the bank purchase price, the agreed profit rate on a constant rate of return and monthly rests, and the agreed tenure of the facility. It must be borne in mind that profit margin is calculated with the profit rate applied to the full tenure of the facility during which the instalments are to be made. The sale price is then paid by monthly instalments according to the number of months in the tenure of the facility.*
>
> *That being the case, it follows that* if the customer is required to pay the profit for the full tenure, he is entitled to have the benefit of the full

> tenure. It follows that it would be inconsistent with his right to the full tenure if he could be denied the tenure and yet be required to pay the bank's profit margin for the full tenure. *Furthermore, the sum that is recovered from the facility in the event of default before the end of tenure is applied to other facilities and the bank continues to earn its profit rate on the same sum. To allow the bank to also recover a profit margin for the unexpired tenure of the facility, means the bank is able to earn a profit twice upon the same sum at the same time. That profit margin that continues to be charged on the unexpired part of the tenure cannot be actual profit. It is clearly unearned profit. It contradicts the principle of Al-Bai Bithaman Ajil as to the profit margin that the provider is entitled to. Obviously, if the profit has not been earned it is not profit, and cannot be claimed under the* Al-Bai Bithaman Ajil *facility.* (emphasis added).[70]

Therefore, the bank was held to be claiming for unearned profit, or in other words unjust enrichment. The court then took it upon itself to calculate the amount that the bank was due. He said:

> *"An important feature of the profit margin resulting from it being a part of the sale price is that it must be certain.*
>
> *The profit margin in an* Al-Bai Bithaman Ajil *facility is calculated from: (a) the agreed profit rate; (b) tenure the facility is required and (c) the amount of the facility. The amount of the facility is the bank purchase price. In this case the applicable profit rate at the time was 9% per annum. The tenure was 300 months. The profit margin could be calculated and derived with certainty. Even if the tenure is shortened, the profit margin could be recalculated with equal certainty."*[71]

The judge therefore applied the following calculation:

> *According to the calculations placed before the court for the bank, the bank profit at the agreed profit rate of 9% per annum on RM394,172.06 is RM35,475.49 per annum or RM35,475.49/12 = RM2,956.29 per month or on a 360 day year basis as agreed, RM98.54 per day. Between 1 November 1999 to the date of judgment on 29 December 2005 is a period of 74 months less 2 days. The profit, by simple arithmetic since the payments meantime is not very significant, for 74 months less two days is RM218,767.49. As agreed the bank is also entitled to penalty of RM3,141.44 as on today. Added to the bank purchase price of RM394,172.06 the total due on the date of judgment is RM616.080.99. After crediting the defendant with all the payments he had made of RM33,454.19, the balance due on the date of judgment is RM582.626.80.*

> *The bank is also entitled to profit per day hereafter until full payment at (RM2,956/30) = RM98.54.*[72]

It can be seen that the court treated the contract as though it were a conventional one in the calculation of the daily profit rate. The question is whether the judge merely thought that BBA is like a conventional loan,[73] or whether BBA is really like a conventional loan?[74]

This issue of unearned profit was further explored in *Malayan Banking Bhd v Marilyn Ho Siok Lin*[75] by David Wong Dak Wah JC. He began by stating that he could choose to follow either *Silver Concept* or *Zukiflli Abdullah.*[76]

However, with regards to procedural law, the judge had more flexibility under the Sarawak Land Code (SLC) as compared to the National Land Code (NLC). Unlike in s256 of the NLC where the defendant has to convince the court that there is a 'cause to the contrary', otherwise the court 'shall' make an order-for-sale, s148 of the SLC states "...and the court after hearing the evidence may make such order as in the circumstances seems just.[77]"

The defendant claimed that she should only have to repay the purchase price plus 14 months worth of profit. The defendant's submission stated that: "For the defendant, she in her words contends that though she 'is in default the plaintiff is not entitled in law and *in equity* to claim the said interests of RM495,205.64 after only a period of 14 months since the date of execution of the charge on 31 May 2002 as that interest of RM495,205.64 is for a period of 20 years or 240 months.'" (Emphasis added).

The BBA documents, however, require the entire sale price to be repaid in the event of default.[78] David Wong JC posed the question: "Sale price is defined in both documents to be the sum of RM995,205.64. Faced with such plain language in the aforesaid clauses, does this court have the option to ignore it?"

With reference to the judgment of Denning LJ in *Stockloser v Johnson,*[79] adopted in Malaysia by *K. Umarkanda v E. L. Magness,*[80] David Wong JC found that equity applied to the current case. Given the fact that the current case involved a Shariah-based contract, he stated:

> *"I am fully aware that the BBA documents are drawn up based on Islamic principles and I am applying the common law principle of*

equity in construing the same. This approach is available to me as everyone knows the principle of equity is consistent with Islamic teachings. (emphasis added)"[81]

He further noted that:

> *"Further interaction between Islamic laws and the common law in Malaysia is not something foreign and in fact had been in existence since way back in 1965 (see address at Kolej Universiti Islam Malaysia by the present Chief Justice of Malaysia, YAA Tun Dato' Sri Ahmad Fairuz bin Dato' Sheikh Abdul Halim, on "The Relationship Between Syariah And Civil Law In The Malaysia Legal System: Developments And Future Possibilities" – http://www.kehakiman.gov.my/)."*[82]

David Wong JC stated that his approach was fortified by *Affin Bank v Zulkifli Abdullah*, rather than *AMMB v Silver Concept*. He said:

> *The learned judge [in* Zulkifli*] may have approached the issue purely on construction of the contract basis and came to the conclusion that the real intention of the parties was that the sale price could be recovered only if the purchaser had the full use of the tenure of the facility. The path which the learned judge took to come to his conclusion is creative in view of the clear definition of the sale price in the property sale agreement. However in substance the learned judge had applied the principle of equity in his deliberations in redefining the meaning of "sale price" contained in the property sale agreement. This can be discerned from the words used by his lordship, words like 'unearned profits', 'inconsistent with the borrower's right to the full tenure if he is required to pay the full bank's profit and denied the enjoyment of the full tenure' and '... the bank being able to earn a profit twice upon the same sum at the same time'.* The aforesaid words are words used by the courts when they are referring to the doctrine of unjust enrichment. *Hence I have no hesitation in regarding* Affin *case as an authority for the proposition that it would not be equitable to allow the bank to recover the sale price as defined when the tenure of the facility is terminated prematurely.*[83] (Emphasis added).[84]

He also approved the formula used in the *Zulkifli Abdullah* case in determining the selling price and the rebate to be granted.

Conclusion

There are now many Islamic banks, as well as conventional banks with Islamic divisions, offering products that are purported to be *Shari'ah*-compliant. Problems can arise in the event of any dispute if the jurisdiction is not equipped with a Shariah court that is competent to hear cases involving *fiqh muamalat.* There clearly will be difficulties if the case is heard in the civil court of a non-Muslim country such as the United Kingdom. There will even be difficulties in Muslim countries, if these jurisdictions do not place Islamic banking matters under competent *Shari'ah* courts.

As can be seen in this article, cases involving *Shari'ah*-based contracts heard in English courts under Common law have resulted in the *Shari'ah* aspects of the contracts being completely disregarded. This was despite expert witnesses being called as in *Symphony Gems* and *Beximco*. The reason for this was due to conflict of laws. It was ruled that there can only be one governing law in a contract, and that once English law was held to be the governing law, *Shari'ah* was of no effect. Also, the courts declined any competency to hear *Shari'ah*-related issues and took the views that if the banks' own *Shari'ah* advisors certified that the contract was compliant with *Shari'ah,* then it was deemed to be so.

English courts have left open the possibility of a contract being governed by English law and *Shari'ah*, but only if the relevant part of *fiqh muamalat* is codified and incorporated into the contract. Therefore, there does exist the possibility of using the *Mejelle* as the governing 'rules' of the contract because as codified *Shari'ah* (following Hanafi *fiqh)* this may be acceptable to an English court.

Another possibility is that the commercial law of a country, which is based on Islamic principles, could be incorporated into the contract, such as Jordan or the United Arab Emirates. This possibility derives from the *Glencore* case.

The Malaysian civil courts, which decide according to English common law principles are the competent courts to hear banking cases. When the first cases involving Islamic contracts emerged in the mid-1990s, the courts judged the cases much as an English court would do so, with reference to contract law and conventional banking precedent. However, in recent years, Malaysian judges have begun to take notice of *Shari'ah* principles, particularly as counsels are staring to use them in their contentions, even though they are bound by Common law principles and rules of equity.

So on the one hand Suriyadi J, in *Silver Concept*, held that once there is an *'aqad* (contract) the parties are bound to honour it, and that the profit margin is not the same as interest. On the other hand, Abdul Wahab J, held that the bank was earning a profit twice on the same amount at the same time, which was contrary to an Islamic contract such as BBA.

David Wong JC then extended the principles of *Zulkifli Abdullah* further to hold that if a *Shari'ah* principle is generally the same as a common law principle–such as that of equity–then a Malaysian court can apply it.

For the avoidance of doubt, it could make sense for an Islamic contract issued in Malaysia to incorporate codified *Shari'ah*. However, a recent move by some Malaysian banks is to give their corporate customers the opportunity to have the contract examined by an independent *Shari'ah* advisor of their choice, so that they will then be estopped from claiming later that the contract is un-Islamic.

Despite the fact that Malaysian civil court judges are not expected to be experts in *fiqh muamalat*, and many are in fact non-Muslim, in no case has any reference been made to the Shariah Advisory Council of the Central Bank despite being authorised to do so by law. Most cases involving Islamic commercial contracts in Malaysian Civil courts revolve around procedural matters, and are not directly issues of *Shari'ah* as is supported by Abdul Wahab Patail J in *Zulkifli's* case, i.e. "It is not a question of *Shari'ah* law." This statement reflects the reality that the judges hearing these commercial cases are civil court judges and not *Shari'ah* court judges. This has not however, stopped the judges in some recent cases discussing *Shari'ah* issues. It appears, even without being aware of the fact, that they are following the decision of *Ramah v Laton* that Islamic law is a local law of which the court should take judicial notice.

It can be considered as a positive development that in recent times, Malaysian Civil court judges have taken judicial notice of Islamic commercial matters, even though they could simply ignore it and just apply Common law and the rules of equity completely.

Notes

1. With effect from 31 August 1957–Independence Day.
2. It is not the intention of this article to deal in detail on the aspect of dualism and legal aspects of Islamic banking in Malaysia as it has been

covered elsewhere, see Norhashimah Mohd Yasin, "Legal Aspects of Islamic Banking: Malaysian Experience", Salman Syed Ali & Ausaf Ahmad (ed), Islamic Banking and Finance: Fundamentals and Contemporary Issues, Islamic Development Bank, Jeddah, 2006.

3. There is a great deal of literature written on these aspects in Malaysia which need not to be repeated, see for instance Engku Rabiah Adawiah "Islamic Law Compliance Issues in Sale Based Financing Structures as Practiced in Malaysia", [2003] 3 MLJ, pp. lxii-lxiii., see also Habib Rahman bin Seini Mohideen, "Afffin Bank Bhd v Zulkifli Abdullah–*Shari'ah* Perspective" [2006] 3 MLJ ppi-cl and Mohamad Ismail bin Mohamed Shariff, "The Affin Bank Case: Is Islamic Banking Just Conventional Banking in Green Garb?", [2006] 3 MLJ pp. cli–clxviii.. Refer also to Noor Inayah Yaakub & Hizri Hasshan, "Kekeliruan Terhadap Pembiayaan Bai' Bithaman Ajil di Malaysia (Confusion over Bai' Bithaman Ajil Financing in Malaysia), The Law Review, 2007, pp. 83-99.
4. This is an unreported case heard by the Commercial Court (Queen's Bench Division) on 13 February 2002.
5. In Malaysia, it is spelled as 'Murabahah' which means sale with mark-up.
6. Dr. Yahya al-Samaan, a Saudi Arabian lawyer who was called as an expert witness.
7. Counsel for the defendants.
8. Unreported, heard on 13 February 2002.
9. Quoted in *Symphony Gems*–unreported.
10. [2004] EWCA Civ 19; [2004] 2 All ER Comm 312; [2004] 2 Lloyd's Rep 1. (CA).
11. *Ibid.*, at p. 1.
12. See [2003] EWHC 2118 (Comm); [2003] 2 All ER (Comm) 849. (HC).
13. [2004] EWCA Civ 19; [2004] 2 All ER (Comm) 312, at p.13.
14. In other words, *Shari'ah* is a contentious issue with lots of competing interpretations. Potter LJ felt that: "Finally, so far as the 'principles of ... *Shari'ah*' are concerned, it was the evidence of both experts that there are indeed areas of considerable controversy and difficulty arising not only from the need to translate into propositions of modern law texts which centuries ago were set out as religious and moral codes, but because of the existence of a variety of schools of thought with which the court may have to concern itself in any given case before reaching a conclusion upon the principle or rule in dispute. The

fact that there may be general consensus upon the proscription of *Riba* and the essentials of a valid *Morabaha* agreement does no more than indicate that, if the *Shari'ah* proviso *were* sufficient to incorporate the principles of *Shari'ah* into the parties' agreements, the defendants would have been likely to succeed. However, since I would hold that the proviso is plainly inadequate for that purpose, the validity of the contract and the defendants' obligations thereunder fall to be decided according to English law." See [2004] EWCA Civ at p.14.

15. The view of the Court was that if the Bank's *Shari'ah* advisors said that the contract was *Shari'ah*-compliant, then it should be accepted as such.
16. Governing international shipping.
17. A Malaysian Civil court would not have this particular problem as EU law does not apply in Malaysia.
18. [2000] EWHC 199 (Comm); [2001] 1 All ER (Comm) 103.
19. The issue of '*ghasb*' is dealt with from paragraph 113 to paragraph 138 of the written judgement.
20. The judge added that: "The decision has no relevance to this case." Although it is true that *Glencore* had no bearing on the judgement in *Beximco*, this case does support the indication that an English court would accept a contract as being governed by *Shari'ah* if the relevant *Shari'ah* issue was codified.
21. One can wonder why the latter two courts bothered hearing this expert evidence in the first place if their evidence has no bearing whatsoever!?
22. The UAE Civil Code is derived from the Egyptian Civil Code (based on the French Code) and the Jordanian Civil Code (based on the former Ottoman Civil Code).
23. The Ottoman Civil Code (Mejelle or Majallah al-Ahkam al-'Adliyyah) is codified *Shari'ah* according to Hanafi *fiqh*. It came into force in 1877 and ceased to have legal effect when the Republic of Turkey introduced a new Code in 1926. An official English translation was made in Cyprus in 1901. However, several Arab countries such as Iraq, Syria and Jordan still have Civil Codes based on the *Mejelle*. The latest version of the UAE Civil Code, which came into force in 1985, is partly based on the *Mejelle*, despite the fact (as heard in Glencore, para. 117)) that *Shari'ah* in the UAE is based on the Maliki and Hanbali *mazhabs*. As such UAE judges refer the *Mejelle* as a source of law.
24. The basis of reception of English Common law and rules of equity is a legacy of a British colonial statute, namely the Civil Law Act 1956,

particularly Sections 3 and 5. The writer has ventured into this state of affairs extensively and is not intended to repeat here. See Norhashimah Mohd. Yasin on the sub-topic on "The Application of Civil Law Act 1956" in the article entitled "Islamic Banking in Malaysia: Legal Hiccups and Suggested Remedies", (2001) 9 IIUM Law Journal, at pp. 6-9.

25. (1927) 6 FMSLR 128. The principle of this case was cited with approval in the case of *Fatimah binti Hanis* v *Haji Ismail bin Tamim* [1939] MLJ 134.
26. Since re-enacted as s45 (Opinion of experts) and s57 (Facts of which court must take judicial notice) of the Evidence Act 1950.
27. (1927) 6 FMSLR p. 129.
28. The 'special referee' to be appointed by the trial court was, presumably, a *qadi*.
29. (1927) 6 FMSLR p. 132. Farrer-Manby J noted that: "In the Court of Appeal the preliminary point was taken by counsel for the appellant that at any rate the latter part of the evidence was wrongly admitted since the Courts ought to instruct themselves without evidence of the law within their jurisdiction." He added his dissenting point: "I think the Courts are competent to take evidence on Mohamedan (sic) law... by virtue at least of section 57 of the Evidence Enactment." S57 of the then Enactment and of the current Evidence Act state what a judge can take judicial notice of. This includes "all laws or regulations having the force of law now or heretofore in force in Malaysia" as per the current Evidence Act 1950. He felt that the court should be able to hear evidence on Muslim law if necessary on the ground of custom: "...I do not at present think that it has been made out that these Courts should abandon their established practice for many years of receiving evidence on Mohamedan (sic) law, not only in disputed cases but also almost weekly in the administration of the estates of Mohamedans (sic), where it is the practice for the Kathis [qadis] to certify the proper shares of the beneficiaries in the circumstances of each case."
30. [2004] 6 CLJ 25 & 131.
31. It must be noted that the plaintiff (customer) had already failed to keep up with its repayments before it tried to repudiate the contract.
32. [2004] 6 CLJ p. 26.
33. *Ibid* at p. 30.
34. *Ibid.*
35. He quoted Ayat 275 and 276 from *Surah Al-Baqarah*.
36. [2004] 6 CLJ at p. 136. As such, the judge stated that his main ground

for not granting the injunction was due to public policy because 'lenders' might be reluctant to lend the money to corporate customers, especially under Islamic principles where penalty interest cannot be charged. However, this position had already been resolved by the National *Shari'h* Advisory Council in its Resolution of 14 February 1998 which permits the financier to impose a penalty for late payment. See Central Bank of Malaysia, *Shari'ah* Resolutions in Islamic Finance, Kuala Lumpur, 2007, pp. 37-38.

37. [2003] 1 CLJ 625.

38. Refer to *Bai Bithaman Ajil* (BBA) contract.

39. This principle has been applied in every successive case involving an Islamic contract, where the bank is seeking an order for sale of charged property due to default in payment.

40. In Malaysia, BBA is different from Murabahah mainly in two aspects (i) BBA is used for mid and long term financing while Murabahah is for short term i.e. less than 12 months (ii) BBA is mainly for asset acquisition while Murabahah for working capital. More on this, refer to Norhashimah Mohd. Yasin "Islamic banking Products", *Al-Nahdah*, Vol. 18 Nos 1 & 2 at pp. 34-37. Malaysian Civil court judges have a tendency to regard BBA, as practised by Malaysian banks, as little different to a conventional loan contract. This was demonstrated in the Court of Appeal case *Dato' Hj Nik Mahmud Daud v Bank Islam Malaysia Bhd* [1998] 3 CLJ 605. The defendant had defaulted on the repayment of a BBA contract. He tried to get it voided on the ground that the contract had contravened the Malay Reservation Enactment 1930 (Kelantan), which prohibited a Malay from selling land to a non-Malay (i.e. Bank Islam). The bank won the case but the court agreed with the High Court judge who found there had been no real sale and purchase. Ownership had not been transferred. He had said: "...it was never the intention of the parties, in as much as it can ever be said to be within their contemplation, to involve any transfer of proprietorship. It so happened that the execution of the Property Purchase Agreement and the Property Sale Agreement constituted part of the process required by the Islamic banking procedure before a party can avail itself of the financial facilities provided by the defendant. Hence, that would account for the contemporaneous execution of the two agreements; and in fact, it would be observed that the Property Purchase Agreement would be rendered otiose and bereft of any consequential value the moment the Property Sale Agreement was signed."

41. BBA is similar to the contract known as bai' muajjal or bai' muazzal in South Asia. In fact, many cases involving BBA contracts are judged

along the conventional principles with Common law as its guiding principles.

42. [1994] 3 CLJ 735 (Current Law Journal) High Court.
43. For example, see Norhashimah Mohd. Yasin, "Islamic Banking: Case Commentaries Involving *al-Bai Bithaman Ajil*" [1997] 3 MLJ cxcii,; Norhashimah Mohd. Yasin, "Financing Aspects of *Al-Bay'Bithaman Ajil*" (BBA) Contracts" [1997] 3 CLJ Supp, I; KL. By the same author, "Bay' Bithaman Ajil (BBA): Sale or Loan Contract?, and Appeal Court Decision on Al-Bay' Bithaman Ajil (BBA): Misunderstanding and/or True State of Affairs?", in, Syed Ahmad Idid (Ed) *Judicial Decisions Affecting Bankers and Financiers* (KL: Malayan Law Journal, 2003).
44. Unfortunately, there was no written judgement from the Court of Appeal so it is impossible to establish the court's *ratio decidendi* for upholding the judgement of the lower court.
45. Such as *Bank Islam Malaysia Bhd v Shamsuddin bin Haji Ahmad* [1999] 1 LNS 275 and *Bank Islam Malaysia Bhd v Pasaraya Peladang Sdn Bhd* [2004] 7 MLJ 355.
46. [2005] 5 MLJ 210.
47. There were eight grounds, of which two were *Shari'ah*-related issues. The defendant was trying to find a 'cause to the contrary' (s 256(3)) to make s 256 (Application to court for order for sale) of the National Land Code inapplicable.
48. [2005] 5 MLJ p. 218.
49. Under s16B (added by a 2003 amendment) of the Central Bank of Malaysia Act 1958. Until now, no reference has been made by any court to the SAC.
50. [2005] 5 MLJ pp. 217-218.
51. The bank's name for a revolving Islamic account.
52. It has often been alleged that BBA is a '*hilah*' (legal trick) and similar to an interest-bearing loan. However, although the SAC of the Central Bank has regarded BBA as an approved *Shari'ah* contract, the practice by banks may be open to dispute and controversy.
53. This is exactly what the courts in *Zulkifli Abdullah* and *Marilyn Ho* have done as will be seen later in this article.
54. This is a claim of misrepresentation, that the contract is not really Islamic.
55. [2005] 5 MLJ pp. 220-221.
56. [2005] 5 MLJ p. 223.

57. *Ibid.*
58. *Ibid* at pp. 223-224.
59. "Under the Islamic Law of Contract, the Arabic word for contract is al-aqd, which literally means an obligation or tie. It is an act of sealing a bargain (*Shariah: The Islamic Law* by Abdur Rahman I Doi p. 354). After the offer and acceptance has been concluded, the obligation that arises out of that conclusive contract is called '*Uqud*', thereafter to be fulfilled or complied with (Qur'an , 5:1)."at [2005] 5 MLJ at p. 222.
60. [2005] 5 MLJ p. 227.
61. *Ibid* at p. 223. Likewise, Morison J in *Beximco* had said: "So far as the bank was concerned, that is likely to have been sufficient for its own regulatory purposes but there is no suggestion that the defendants were in any way concerned about the principles of Sharia'a law either at the time the agreement was made or at any time before the proceedings were started."
62. [2006] 1 CLJ 438.
63. *Ibid* at p. 447.
64. *Ibid* at p. 448.
65. *Ibid.*
66. *Ibid* at p. 451.
67. See footnote no. 3.
68. *Malayan Banking Bhd v PK Ralamani* [1994] 2 CLJ 25.
69. *Ibid* at p. 449.
70. [2006] 1 CLJ p. 449-450.
71. *Ibid* p. 451. Interestingly, the defendant in Silver Concept argued by applying this demonstrated that BBA is similar to an interest-bearing loan contract! This in fact affirms the writer's earlier contention that BBA as practiced in Malaysia resembles a loan contract to all intents and purposes, see the article entitled "-Bay' Bithaman Ajil (BBA): Sale or Loan Contracts? in Syed Ahmad Idid (ed), Judicial Decisions Affecting Bankers and Financiers, Malayan Law Journal, 2003."
72. [2006] 1 CLJ 452.
73. Abdul Wahab Patail J, in an obiter, criticised BBA and compared it unfavourably with a conventional contract, at least in the case of default: "When the gratification of being able to satisfy the pious desire to avoid financing containing the elements of Riba gives way to the sorrow of default before the end of tenure of an Al-Bai Bithaman Ajil facility, the revelation that even after the subject security had been auctioned at full market value there remains still a very substantial

sum still owing to the bank, comes as a startling surprise. All the more shocking when it is further realised that a borrower under a *Riba*-ridden loan is far better off."

74. For more on this issue see Norhashimah Mohd. Yasin, "Appeal Court Decision on Al-Bay' *Bithaman Ajil* (BBA): Misunderstanding and/or True State of Affairs?", in, Syed Ahmad Idid (Ed), *Judicial Decisions Affecting Bankers and Financiers* (KL: Malayan Law Journal, 2003).
75. [2006] 3 CLJ 796.
76. At the outset, he noted that he would still have to follow the *Emcee* case and apply the Rules of High Court 1980 and, in this case, s148 of the Sarawak Land Code.
77. [2006] 3 CLJ p. 818.
78. In the charge annex and the Property Sale Agreement.
79. [1954] 1 QB 476, [1954] 1 All ER 630.
80. [1984] 2 CLJ 23.
81. [2006] 3 CLJ 821. Ironically he referred to the judgement in *Silver Concept*: "Stripped of all the heavy Arabic sounding words, any law student will feel less intimidated by any Islamic contractual transactions, as the fundamentals are not too dissimilar with most common-law contract. The latter and the Islamic contractual transactions in fact are not too dissimilar in their treatment too to all contracts, even those that are a bit dodgy e.g. those tainted by fraud, misrepresentation, inducement etc."
82. *Ibid* p. 822. As mentioned earlier, the interaction between *Shari'ah* and Common law goes back at least to the time of *Ramah v Laton*.
83. He also said that the judgement was based on public interest, as someone who defaults on a BBA facility should not be in a worst position that a person with a conventional loan.
84. [2006] 3 CLJ 822.

5

Judicial Precedents: An Expository Study of Civil Judicial System and *Shari 'Ah* Court System

Abdul Haseeb Ansari

Introduction

In the common law system, judicial precedents have very high value. Based on the doctrine of *stare decisis*, decisions of higher courts are considered to be binding on lower courts. Initially, it was so rigidly applied that in the British legal system even House of Lords could not change its own decisions. Later on in order to do away with this hardship, the doctrine of prospective overruling was developed and practices. The position more or less is the same in other jurisdictions based on common law system, like India, Malaysia and Pakistan. The development of judge-made law in England got impetus from the change of a deep-rooted perception of the British courts that judges simply interpret the law; they do not make it. This was followed in other countries also. This is why in Malaysia judges like Justice Harun Hashim and jurists like Prof Ahmad Ibrahim emphasized on developing common law that is appropriate for the country, instead of following the British common law. This seems to have achieved considerable success.

In the traditional *shari'ah,* the concept of judicial decisions of higher courts to be binding on lower courts was not acceptable; all cases had to be decided on the basis of their own merits and previous decisions were considered merely as a source of guidance for future decisions. In some countries, including Malaysia and Saudi Arabia, this position is still being maintained. On the contrary, in Pakistan, where *shari'ah* courts and civil law courts are fully integrated, the doctrines of judicial precedents and *stare decisis* are followed. In view of this, a question arises as to whether these doctrines should have that amount of sanctity in the *Shari'ah* court system, as they have in the civil court system of England or Pakistan.

The paper discusses this issue and various other issues pertaining to the scope and dimensions of applicability of the doctrines of judicial precedent and *stare decisis*.

Judicial Precedent in Civil Law

In the British legal system, judicial precedents have always been considered as an important source of law. The whole gamut of common law of England is based on judicial delineation of imminent judges on various intricate issues which could not properly be answered by enacted laws, and also because enacted laws did not cover the whole milieu of human behaviors and human relations. Salmond appropriately writes that in English law the great body of common or unwritten law is almost entirely the product of decided cases, accumulated in an immense series of reports extending backwards with scarcely a break to the reign of the Edward the First at the close of the thirteenth century. This happened so in spite of the orthodox and narrow view of Savigny and Stobbey that judicial decisions are merely evidence of custom and of the law derived therefrom. According to them, a court can depart from its formal practice and no court is bound to practice of another. Departure from a practice is not only permitted but also required if there are better reason(s) for a different treatment of the question of law. Keeton rejected this view and said that judicial decisions were good authority of law. Thibaut, who was supporter of codification of law, pleaded that if in any court a rule has been frequently and constantly been followed as law and no rule has been made against it, it should be adopted as a rule of law. Similar view has been expressed by Balckstone in his *Commentaries on the Law of England*. He writes: "For it is an established rule to abide by former precedents, where the same points come again in litigation; as well as to keep the scale of justice even and steady and not liable to waiver with every new judge's opinion, as also because in the case being solemnly declared and determined, what before was written, and perhaps different, has now become a permanent rule, which it is not in the breast of any subsequent judge to alter or vary from, according to his private sentiments." The sanctity of judicial decisions remained almost the same in other commonwealth countries. In these countries, judicial decisions are considered to be one of the sources of law, along with statutory law and customary law. Initially, they relied on the common law developed by the British courts, but some of them, significantly India, developed their own common law suited to their socio-economic conditions. In Malaysia also, jurists, notably Prof. Ahmad Ibrahim, and judges, notably Justice Harun Hashim, stressed on developing common law suited to the conditions of the country. Due to this now the applicability of the British common law is not relied upon in many cases.

This is notable here that neither Roman law, as one of the justinian constitutions specifically provided that no judge or arbitrator is to consider himself bound by wrong juristic opinions; for if an erroneous decision is given effect, it will corrupt future judgments of other judges. It is also notable that most of the jurisdictions, as civil law countries, only followed written law (enacted law) as the source of law and gave less importance to judge-made law. Notably, Article 5 of the French Civil Code specifically rules that judges are forbidden, when giving judgment in the cases, which are brought before them, to lay down general rules of conduct or decide a case by holding it was governed by previous decision. Initially, as a matter of rule the continental practice has been that judicial decisions were of persuasive value. According to Lipstein, the importance of reported decisions has, however, been increasing in France and Germany for some time, and as a matter of degree the courts of these countries tend to attach greater weight to their own previous decisions than to the views of text-writes.

The position of judicial precedents in the United States, where judiciary commands relatively more power than the courts of Great Britain, is also of great importance. There also, judicial decisions are considered to be the most potent source of law (the American

Realist Movement may be recalled). Justice Cardozo is one of the supporters of the adherence to judicial precedents, but his approach is not strict one. He wants it to be relaxed in certain situations, where it is necessary not to adhere to the existing precedent. In *The Nature of the Judicial Precedents* he writes: "In these days, in the United States, there is a great deal of discussion whether the rule of adherence to precedents ought to be abandoned...I think adherence should be the rule and not the exception. I have already have occasion to dwell upon some of the considerations that sustain it. To these, I may add that the labour of judges would be increased almost to the breaking point and every past decision could be responded in every case, and one could not lay one's own course of bricks to secure the foundation of the courses laid by others who had gone before him. Perhaps the constitution of my own court has accentuated to this belief. We have had ten judges, of whom only seven sit at a time. It happens again and again, where the question is a close one that a case which one seeks is decided one way might be decided another way, the next if it were then heard for the first time. The situation would, however, be intolerable if the weekly changes in composition of court were accompanied by changes in its rulings. In such circumstances there is nothing to do except to stand by the errors of our brethren of the week before, whether we relish them or not. But I am ready to concede that the rule to adherence to precedent, though it ought not to be abandoned, ought to be in some degree relaxed. I think when a rule, after it has been duly tested by experience, has been found to be inconsistent with the sense of justice or with the social welfare, there should be less hesitation in frank avowal and frank abandonment. We have to do this sometimes in the field of constitutional law. Perhaps we should do so often in fields of private law where considerations of social utility are not so aggressive and insistent. There should be greater readiness to abandon an untenable position when the rule to be discarded may not reasonably be supposed to have determined the conduct of the litigants, and particularly when in its origin it was the product of institutions or conditions, which have gained a new significance or development with the progress of the year."

The doctrine of judicial precedent has developed over many years. It has passed through fierce debates. Some, including

Holdsworth, gave less importance to it. According to them, a precedent is reported, may be cited, and will probably be followed in subsequent judgments. Some others, including Goodhart, were of the opinion that a precedent not only has great authority but must (in certain circumstances) be followed. Certain circumstances here would refer to 'same facts and circumstances'. It will be appropriate here to say that in such countries where judicial precedents are taken in its strict sense, they have to be applied, unless there are strong probabilities that their application might result in injustice. In other countries, where it is loosely taken, they should have persuasive value depending on the level of courts, and number of judges. If a judgment has been given by a big bench or full bench of the apex court of the country, it should have a greater degree of persuasion.

There is a fear, which is rightly so, that if the doctrine of judicial precedent is strictly followed, there are chances that an erroneous decision, which yields injustice, might be followed and that will be against the very idea of having a justice system. This can be rectified by the legislature by annulling the effect of the judgment or by application of the doctrine of prospective overruling or distinguishing the subsequent case from the previous case. The first two are better solutions because in the circumstances when the fact and situations are similar to distinguish the subsequent case is not possible. Salmond notes that "overruling is not in itself an adequate solution, for it is possible only for a higher court and involves the litigants in considerable expense". How about the situation where no case comes for a long time and legislature does not take notice of the erroneous decision? In these situations there will be no choice but to follow the erroneous judgment. The author is of the opinion that cognizance taken by the legislature and annulling the effect of the judgment by necessary enactment is a better choice. The task can be easy if erroneous judgments are highlighted by experts of law or by a judge in a subsequent case. In India, for example, there is Law Commission. It has been constituted to advise the legislature from time to time about possible changes to be brought about in the exiting laws. It has pointed out from time to time many erroneous judgments and law made by the Parliament or the State Assembly has thus annulled them. However, both the options must be open.

Judicial Precedents: Advantages and Disadvantages; Authoritative and Persuasive

In the British legal system, where the doctrine of judicial precedent was so deep rooted that precedents were considered to be constitutive and they could not be abrogated at all. Even the House of Lords could not change any principle developed or relied upon in any case. So as to break this hardship, the doctrine of prospective overruling was developed and followed as and when the principle was considered not to impart justice or the principle relied upon was considered to be erroneous. This position is still maintained, but overruling can be done with prospective effect only by a bigger bench of the same higher court or a superior court by giving sufficient reasons, which is the common practice. In other words, the right of prospective overruling cannot be arbitrarily exercised. This position is still maintained in many commonwealth countries. Thus, if there is a settled rule of law established by higher courts, by virtue of the doctrine of *stare decisis* and hierarchy of the courts of the country, it has to be followed by lower courts, even if the judge approves it or not. This is also warranted because expediency demands that the uniformity and certainty in law has to be maintained, so that law can easily be known by the people, in particular by litigants. If a principle of law needed to be applied on a given facts of a case and if it has to be found from the gamut of conflicting decisions, the task to find the appropriate principle will be next to impossible. Justice and fairness requires that law should be appropriate and easily comprehendible. Multiplicity of opinions on the same question of law will simply lead to confusion, and thus in many cases justice cannot be imparted. The added advantage of strict application of the doctrine of judicial precedent is that it shows respect to senior, experienced and relatively mature judges; it also brigs about a conducive atmosphere for governing human relations and human behaviors and a healthy social development. Various jurists have specifically outlined these advantages. Some of them, as quoted by Mahajan in his book entitled *Jurisprudence & Legal Theory,* are as under:

Jessel, M.R.: "If I find a long course of decisions by inferior courts acquiesced which has become part of the settled law, I do not think that it is the province of the appeal court after a long course of time to interfere, because most contracts are regulated by those decisions. There is another consideration that always has weight with me. When the law is settled it gets into the text-books which are a very practicable guide to practitioners...Where a series of decisions of impoverisher courts has put a construction on an Act of Parliament and thus have made a law which men follow in their daily dealings, it has been held, even by House of Lords, that it is better to adhere to the course of decision than to reverse them, because of the mischief which would result from such a proceeding. Of course, that requires two things, antiquity of decisions and practice of mankind in conducting their affairs."

This is notable that Jessel has emphasized on following the rules that have been settled and that have been internalized by the people. He says it is better to adhere to them. It means any settled principle of law can be changed only when it is warranted for better justice. In this case, there has to be sufficient reason(s) for the reversal; otherwise, it will be an unfair act on the part of the appellate court. What Jessel has said is generally practiced in almost all countries, where the doctrine of judicial precedent is adhered.

Lord Loreburn: "I think this case falls within the rule that it is not necessary or advisable to disturb a fixed practice which has been long observed in regard to the disposition of property, even though it may have been disapproved at times by individual judges, where no real point of principle being violated"

Loreburn has thus said the same thing on what Jessel has emphasized. According to him, a settled rule of law has to be followed, where no real point of principle is violated.

Lord Buckmaster: "Firstly, the construction of a statute of doubtful meaning, once laid down and accepted for a long period of time, ought not be altered, unless your Lordships could say positively that it was wrong and productive of inconvenience. Secondly, upon which title to property depends or which by establishing principles of construction or otherwise form the basis of contracts ought to receive the same protection. Thirdly, decisions that affect the general conduct of affairs so that their alteration would mean that taxes had been unlawfully imposed or exemption obtained, payments needlessly made, or the position of public materially affected ought in the same way to continue."

Lord Buckmaster has also said almost the same thing using different words and giving some practical examples. It is submitted that in the situations that he has mentioned or where social morality has to be changed with the change of the general practice of the people and it is so demanded by justice, principles adhered to even for a long time can be altered or totally changed. So is the case where interpretation of any provision of a statute was wrong and because of that justice as it should have been could not be imparted.

Julius Stone: "Precedent had played and will continue to play a most important part in common law judicial achievement. In the first place, precedents present for the instant case a rapid if incomplete review of social contacts comparable to the present, and of rule thought suitable for those contexts by other minds after careful inquiry. In the second place, precedents serve to indicate what kind of result will be reached if a particular premises or category is chosen for application in the instant case, and permit comparison with the results if some other premises or category is adopted, either drawn from other cases or judicially invented. In *Haseldine* v. *Daw* [1941] 2 KB 343, the common carrier cases gave the court a ready view of the result for the lift passenger if that analogy were followed, as well as of the context in which courts in the past had regarded such results for an injured plaintiff. The case on occupiers of premises afforded another glimpse of other results deemed just in another context. But the court has still to make up its mind that it wished to reach one or other result, or some results, quite different from either, in the context that was actually before it in *Haseldine* v. *Daw*."

It is notable that Julius Stone has conveyed the same importance of an established judicial practice as has been said by the author above. He has strengthened this view when he says, "A good judge is one who is the master, not the slave, of the cases."

We have noted above the position of binding judicial precedents. There are certain situations where precedents are not binding, that have mere persuasive value. The judges are under no obligation to follow them. But when they decide to follow them, they may assign them the value, as they seem fit. These situations are:

(a) *Obitor Dicta*: According to Salmond, they are generally understood as statement of law which go beyond the occasion, and lay down a rule which is irrelevant to the purpose in hand, or is stated by way of analogy merely, or is regarded by a later court as unduly wide. A judicial dicta, thus, is other than the *ratio decidendi* of the case, eg, the principle on which the decision of the case is relied upon. This is, in fact, additional and has nothing to do with the decision of the case. Even if it is deleted from the case, the decision of the case remains unaffected. For example, in a case, Justice Hidayatullah, as he then was, of the Supreme Court of India traced the history of the word 'Hindu', which was not necessary for deciding the case. There are situations where a *dicta* has greater value. These situations are: when the apex court of the country or an eminent judge has given it. In both of these situations, although lower courts are not bound by it, but they have to assign much value to it.

(b) Foreign Judgments: In the British legal system, foreign judgments, especially of United States of America, Canada and Australia had been of great importance; they had persuasive force. Even now, they are considered to be of great importance. This has been the practice in many countries, including Malaysia, that often foreign judgments, especially of British judges, are relied upon by the courts. In Malaysia, initially, the courts gave more importance to decisions given by the British courts. This trend has so far been considerably reduced, as they strive to develop common law suited to the conditions of the country. However, in some cases even now courts rely upon foreign judgments, notably decided by British and Indian courts. On the contrary, Indian courts also quite often quote judgments of foreign courts; but have fast developed common law suitable to Indian conditions.

(c) Judgments of Privy Council: We know that from commonwealth countries final appeals had to be made to the Privy Council. British courts have shown respect to judgments of Privy Council, but have refused to assign binding force to them. However, the decisions of the Privy Council bind the courts of the country from where the appeals originated. In other countries, decisions will have only persuasive value. This is because for the country from where appeals were made to the

Privy Council, it acted as the apex court of the country and the courts of that country will be bound by its decisions by virtue of the doctrine of the *stare decisis.* But when this system is abolished, its decisions henceforth will not have any binding force; they will merely have persuasive value. So far previous decisions are concerned, they are binding, but there is a controversy about overruling the decision where the Privy Council erred. The author is of the opinion that the new apex court of the country, for example the Supreme Court of Malaysia (before it was abolished and Federal Court was constituted), the Federal Court, but not the Court of Appeal, should have the authority to overrule any of the erroneous decisions of the Privy Council. .

Circumstances That Destroy or Weken The Binding Force of Precedent

We have noted above that a decision loses its force when it is abrogated by the legislature by making legislation against it. So is the case when a judgment is overruled or reversed. These and some other situations that weaken or destroy the binding force of precedent are as follows:

(a) Abrogated Decisions: A decision stands to be abrogated when a statute or a statutory rule inconsistent with it is subsequently enacted. Overruling or reversal of case by a higher court has the same effect. Since overruling is done by a superior authority, the courts become bound with the case that has overruled the previous case. This is because when a case is overruled, it looses its existence (it stands abrogated). So as to do away with possible complications with the following of the overruled case, the new case has only prospective operation. For this reason, it is known as the doctrine of prospective overruling. In England, based on *Elder* v. *Patterson* [1924] AC 522, House of Lords could not overrule its own judgment. The position is changed now. It started changing from *London Transport Executive* v. *Betts* [1959] AC 213. In this case Lord Denning in his dissenting judgment considered that the House of Lords could disregard its prior judgment. In *Scruttons Ltd* v. *Midland Silicones Ltd* [1962] AC 446, the House of Lords by majority of four to one favoured this. In this case, two of the majority distinguished the prior case on its special facts and based their decision on the obscurity of the *ratio decidendi* in that case. Two of their Lordships, however, considered that they were free to question previous decisions of their own House if out of line with other authorities or established principles. In India also, the Supreme Court of India can overrule its own judgment. For this, *Golak Nath* case (AIR 1967 SC 1643) may be referred. Article 141 of the Constitution of India says that the law declared by the Supreme Court of India shall be binding on 'all courts'. The expression 'all courts' is wide enough to cover the Supreme Court also, but the Supreme Court ruled in *Bengal Immunity* case (AIR 1953 SC 661) that the expression did not include the Supreme Court. So is the case in Malaysia.

The present Malaysian Federal Court can overrule its own decision (see infra). The Privy Council never considered it to be bound by its own decision (the following cases may be referred: *Read* v. *Bishop of London* [1892] AC 644; *Attorney General* v. *Reynolds* [1979] 3 All ER 129. In civil matters, Federal Court considered itself not to be bound with the decision given by its predecessor Supreme Court. But the position is opposite in criminal matters. However, a number of criminal and civil cases establish that the Federal Court was not bound with its own previous decisions The following cases may be referred: *Central Securities* v. *Haron bin Mohamed Zaid* [1980] 1 MLJ 304; *Oie Hee Koi* v. *Public Prosecutor* [1966] 2 MLJ 183. The present Federal Court is also not bound by its own decision. For this, *Dalip Bhagwan Singh* v. *Public Prosecutor* [1998] 1 MLJ 65 may be referred. However, the Federal Court in civil matters is not bound with the decision of its predecessor Supreme Court. For this, the following cases may be referred: *Malaysian National Insurance* v. *Lim Tiok* [1997] 2 MLJ 165; *Tan Chik bin Ibrahim* v. *Safety Life and General Insurance* [1987] 1 MLJ 217. The position with respect to criminal matters is different. Cases including *Tan Boon Kian* v. *Public Prosecutor* [1995] 3 MLJ 5140 support this. The position of the Court of Appeal is different. It is bound by its own decisions. The following cases may be referred: *Kesultanan Pahang* v. *Sathask Reality* [1997] 2 MLJ 701; *Kwong Yik Bank* v. *Ansonia Management*

Associates [1999] 1 AMR 377. This seems to be logical. An overruling can be express or implied.

(b) Affirmation or Reversal on a Different Ground: If a case has been decided by the lower court on ground A, but the higher court decides it on ground B, which is entirely different than the ground A, what will be the position of the judgment? Will it be considered to have lost its value? Jessel, MR is of the opinion that the whole case of the lower court will loose its value and thus will not be binding on other courts as a precedent. Salmond is of the opinion that such a case is not necessarily deprived of its significance as a judicial determination of law. It is deprived of any absolute binding force it might otherwise have had; but it remains an authority that may be followed by a court that thinks the particular point to have been rightly decided. The author is of the opinion that Jessel, MR is at right footing, as when a case is decided by a higher court on different ground(s), it losses its value as a precedent.

(c) Ignorance of Statute: Any judgment given ignoring any statutory rule or rules of a delighted legislation, is considered to be a decision *per incurium*, which will not have force to bind the courts. Existence of the rule may or may not be in the knowledge of the court. However, mere fact that the earlier court misconstrued a statute, or ignored a rule of construction is no ground for impugning the authority of the precedent. A precedent on the construction of a statute is as much binding as any other, and the fact that it was mistaken in its reasoning does not destroy its binding force.

(d) Inconsistency with Earlier Decisions: When a court in its decision has overlooked an earlier decision of a higher court, the decision will be of no value as a precedent, as it is also considered to be a decision *per incurium*.

(e) Inconsistency between Earlier Decisions of the Same Rank: In such a situation, the court is not bound by its own previous decisions. This rule is being followed by both the Court of Appeal and the House of Lords. Salmond explains this rule by writing "the rule is that where there are previous inconstant decisions of its own, the court is free to follow either. It can follow the earlier, but equally if it thinks fit it can follow the later...It will be seen, therefore, that the binding force of precedent both to the category of abrogation by subsequent facts and to the category of what is here called inherent vice. The earlier case can be disregarded because of the subsequent inconsistent decision on the same level of authority, and the later case can be disregarded because of its inherent vice of ignoring the earlier case."

(f) Precedents *Sub Silentio* or Not Fully Argued: When a particular point of law involved in is not perceived by the court or if a case has not fully been argued, the case will not have binding effect as a precedent. This has been exemplified by Salmond in the following words: "A decision passes *sub silentio*, in the technical sense that has come to be attached to that phrase, when the particular point of law involved in that decision is not perceived by the court or present to its mind. The court may consciously decide in favour of one party because of point A, which he considers and pronounces upon. It may be shown, however, that logically the court should not have decided in favour of the particular party unless it also decided point B in his favour; but point B was not argued or considered by the court. In such circumstances, although point B was logically involved in the facts and although the case had specific outcome, the decision is not an authority on point B. Point B is said to pas *sub silentio*." A precedent is not destroyed because it was badly argued, inadequately considered, and fallaciously reasoned. Thus, a rather arbitrary line has to be drawn between total absence of argument on a particular point, which vitiates the precedent, and inadequate argument, which is a ground for impugning the precedent only if it is absolutely binding and indistinguishable. There appears to be an exception if the court is deciding the precedent expressly intimated that the matter had not been fully argued or considered. This view has been supported by the Indian Supreme Court in *Balkrishna Rao* v. *Haji Abdullah Sait* (1980) 1 SCC 321, when the court says that the binding force of a precedent does not depend on whether a particular argument was considered there in or not, provided the point with reference to which an argument was subsequently advanced was actually decided by the Supreme Court.

(g) Erroneous Decisions: A decision will stand to be erroneous if it is founded on a wrong principle or conflicts with a fundamental principle of common law. Such a decision has to be ignored. Salmond is of the opinion that perfection may be sacrificed for certainty. It means when for a long time a decision has been relied upon and practiced by the people, it should remain in practice. However, this decision may be overruled, if the court thinks that the correct law should be practiced.

Circumstances That Increase or Decrease The Authority of Precents

In certain circumstances, the authority of precedents increases. The level of the court, the number of judges constituting the bench, the eminence of the judges, unanimous judgments, and the eminence of the lawyers are important factors that augment the value of precedents. Likewise, if precedents are followed for a longer duration of time, they are considered to be established as precedents. The courts give them more value. It does not mean that such judgments cannot be overruled or annulled by appropriate legislations. But as we have noted above, overruling by courts and abrogation by legislation have prospective effects. Judgments that are ignored in subsequent decisions, their authority diminish.

On the contrary, where the bench is relatively small, judges constituting the bench are not that eminent, judgment has dissenting opinions, judges have reached to the same conclusion by applying or relying upon different legal principles, or the case was argued by not an eminent lawyer at the Bar, the value of judgments is considered to be not that high and, thus, they are considered to be weak precedents. If a case is overruled or annulled by the legislature, it looses its sanctity as a precedent.

Stare Decisis in Malaysia (Civil Courts)

The Doctrines of judicial precedent and *Stare Decisis* are applied in the same manner as followed by the British courts. The application of the second doctrine in Malaysia is complex because of the reorganization of the judicial structure three times. However, Malaysian Judges have avowed the application of the doctrine in several cases. Notable among them are: *Public Prosecutor* v. *Datuk Tan Cheng Swee* [1980] 2 MLJ 276; *Kumpulan Perangsan Selangor*

v. *Zaid bin Haji Mohd Nob* [1999] 1 MLJ 789; *Cooperative Central Bank Limited* v. *Feyen Development* [1997] 2 MLJ 829; and *Dato Sang Heng Seng* v. *Tan Kim Hor & Another* [2006] 1 CLJ 577 (FC). In *Dato Sang Heng Seng*, Steven Shim CJ (Sabah and Sarawak) held, "Court of Appeal is bound by the doctrine of *stare decisis*... Judicial hierarchy must be observed in the interests of finality and certainty in the law and for orderly development of legal rules as well as for the courts and lawyers to regulate their affairs. Failure to observe judicial precedents would create chaos and misapprehension in the judicial system." (see paragraphs 2 and 3 of the case) Abdul Hamid FCJ observed that the judgments of the Federal Court were binding on Court of Appeal. Whether the Court of Appeal agrees with them or not, it was incumbent upon it to apply that. However, if the Court of Appeal for good reasons for disagreeing with previous judgments, it could point out those reasons for the Federal Court to review them. But the review, if were to be done, it should be done by the Federal Court. Until the required review is not done, the decision would remain binding on the Court of Appeal. This is required by the doctrine of *stare decisis* (see paragraphs 20, 23 and 24 of the case). This may, however, be noted that the Federal Court in *Dalip Bhagwan Singh* v. *Public Prosecutor* [1998] 4 MLJ 1, developed 2 principles: 1. In case of two conflicting decisions of the Court of Appeal, courts lower in the hierarchy may choose to follow either of the decisions irrespective whether it is the earlier or later decision, for the dates do not matter to the Court of Appeal itself; 2. In case of the two conflicting decisions of the Federal Court, all courts below must choose to follow the later decision because the later decision represents the existing state of the law and therefore prevails over the earlier decision. The author is of the opinion that it is better if uniformity is maintained.

Ratio Decidendi

Meaning

As opposed to obiter dicta, *ratio decidendi* is a principle/rule of law acted on by the court in deciding the case. It thus refers the proposition of law for which a case is the authority. In *Bridges* v. *Hawkesworth* (1851) 21 LJQB 75, where a customer found some money on the floor of the shop, the court applied 'finders-keepers' principle and decided the case in favour of the finder of the money. Contrary to this, in *South Staffordshire Water Company* v. *Sharman* (1896) 2 QB 44, where the defendant found two gold rings in the pool of mud owned and occupied by the plaintiff, court did not apply this principle and ruled that the principle would be applicable only when something is found at any public place. Since the money in the first case was found in the area of the shop, where customers were allowed to come, was the public place and thus the principle was applicable. In this case position was different. From these two cases we can know the situation where the principle will be applicable, and where it will not be applicable i. e., the total picture of the applicability of the law. However, each case has its own ratio. We can also infer from these cases that tater cases may widen, restrict, or explain a legal principle applied in earlier case(s), or may distinguish from it. So, for understanding the legal position at a point of time, all cases related to the basic principle will have to be considered together.

Methods to Determine Ratio

It seems that it is easy to determine the ratio of a case. But practically speaking, in many cases, it becomes difficult to find it. For example, where the court has simply given order with a brief reasoning, or the case has lengthy and complicated facts and the court has discussed the case in its judgment in many directions; or as it was in *Donogue* v. *Stevension* [1932] AC 562, where the parties agree to a tort committed and the court simply determined the quantum of the damages to find the ratio is a difficult task. In spite of these difficulties, jurists have attempted to develop certain rules for determining *ratio decidendi* and that can successfully be applied in many cases.

The first popular method is commonly known as 'reversal method', which has been developed by Wambaugh. He suggests that if we reverse the proposition of law put forward by the judge and if with the reversal of it the actual decision of the case also changes, the principle is the *ratio* of the case. On the contrary, if it does not affect the decision, it cannot be the *ratio* of the case. For example, in the *Bridges* case, the legal proposition applied is 'finders-keepers'. This is the *ratio* of the case because if we reverse it, the decision of the case will also change. In the *Staffordshire* case, the legal proposition is 'finder is the keeper, provided he finds something on a public place'. This is the *ratio* of this case because if we reverse this, the decision of the case will also change. This method seems to be simple for determining *ratio decidendi* in a given case. It is applicable even in a case where the lawyer arguing the case has relied on more than one principles but the court accepts only one of them and decides the case accordingly. Likewise, the court can rely on more than one principles and reversal of each one of them changes the decision, each one of them will be considered as the *ratio* of the case. But the method fails in cases where there are a lot of legal propositions relied by the court and reversal of one of them separately does not affect the decision. This method also does not work where court has not given any proposition of law.

Another method is the 'facts and decision' method. In this method, for determining the *ratio* of the case, the relevant facts of the case as ascertained by the court and the decision on it are taken into consideration. This method has been suggested by Dr. Goodhart. In spite of the fact that this method can be applied in relatively large number of cases, the practice adopted by the courts around the word is quite different. Salmond writes, "...Courts seem to pay more attention to the judge's own formulation of rule of law than Dr. Goodhart's test would allow. The courts look at this, it seems, not just to discover the material facts but to discover the rule which the judge thought himself to be applying. On the other hand, it is true that any such rule must be evaluated in the light of the facts considered by the court to be material." This method also fails in many situations. Some of them are: 1.Where the facts are hypothetical, or parties have already agreed to a fact and the court has simply to give its order. For example in *Donogue* v. *Stevensin* [1932] AC 562, the court had nothing to do about the facts for establishing a case of negligence; it had to determine the amount of damages, which the defendant had to pay. 2. Court may give ruling on law irrespective of the facts of the case remains A or B. 3. Court first determines the law then looks into the facts of the case and finally rules that the principle will not be applicable in the case. This was the situation in *Hedley Byrn & Co. Ltd.* V. *Heller & and Partners Ltd.* [1964] AC 465. In this case, the court ruled that if a person gives advice to another in the course of business or professional affairs in such circumstances that a reasonable man would know that this advice is being relied on, then there is a duty, even in absence of any contractual relationship, to take reasonable care that the advice is good. Then the court said that the principle would not be applicable in this case, as the defendant had exonerated himself from the liability. 4. There are cases where several points are raised in a court and the court decides one point in favour of one party and the other point in favour of the other party and gives judgment in favour of one of the parties. In this case, the point decided in favour of the party who lost the case is said not to be part of the *ratio* of the case. Nevertheless, this remains a controversial situation.

Do Judges Make Law?

Proponents of the historical school are of the opinion that the source of law is customs. The role of judges is to find them and base their decisions on them. Also an appropriate law-making authority, the sovereign or any subordinate authority, makes law. It has been stressed by British judges quite often that they decide on the basis of laws and customs; they are simply to interpret the law, not to make the law. But this perception changed. Based on this, there exist two theories: one, judges declare the law; second, they are lawmakers also. It will be appropriate to critically examine these theories.

Declaratory Theory

Blackstone has been one of the biggest supporters of the declaratory theory. In its support, he writes, "A judge is sworn to determine, not according to his own private judgment, but according to the known laws and customs of the land; not delegated to pronounce a new law, but to maintain and explain the old one *jus dicere et non jus dare*." Thus, the function of the judge, according to him, is expository in nature. His job is to find the law, to apply it on the given issues, and to get the result. They are interpreters of the law, and not law-makers. As stated above, this is the old view and all Great British judges in the olden days were supportive to this view. Lord Esher, thus, in *Willis* v. *Baddeley*, (1820) 2 QB 324, ruled, "There is no such thing as judge-made law, for the judges do not make the law, though they frequently apply the law to circumstances as to which it has not previously been authoritatively laid down that such law is applicable." Mathew Hale's view also supports this view. He writes in *History of Common Law*, "...the decisions of courts of justice...do not make a law properly so called, for that only the King and Parliament can do so; yet they have great authority in expounding what the law is;...And though such decisions are less than a law, yet they are a greater evidence thereof, than the opinion of any private person, as such, whatsoever."

Bentham and Austin have been critical to this notion. Bentham considers the orthodox view "as a willful falsehood having for its object the stealing of legislative power by and for hands which could not or does not, openly claim it". Austin has also inveighed saying "the childish fiction employed by our judges, that ...common law is not made by them, but is a miraculous something made by nobody, existing, from entirety and merely declared from time to time." However, for them, judge-made law is a kind of subordinate legislation, as judges work under the authority of the sovereign. So, their idea is solely based on the notion of supremacy of the sovereign, and not on judicial independence. Some of the American jurists have also been critical to this notion. Munroe Smith in *A General View of European Legal History* also expressed similar view. We writes, "The fact that English common law has never had any existence except in decisions; that by decisions it has been developed in historical times from sanctity beginning into a great and complex system; that by decisions its rules have continually been modified and frequently overruled, these facts have been more cogent to the average mind than any official theory." On the contrary, Carter in *Law, Its Origin, Growth and Function* writes, "If what the judges did was to declare a law not before existing the subjection by them of one of the parties to liability for an infraction of the law, in a transaction occurring before the existence of the law, would be an indefensible outrage. Anyone who undertakes to support Austin's theory encounters here an ugly dilemma; the law by which a judge makes a decision either existed at the time of the transaction involved in the case, or it did not, and was made by the judge; if it did exist, the judge did not make it – if it did not exist at the same time of the transaction, then what the judge has done and the sovereign ratified is to compel a man to suffer for the violation of a law committed before the law was made. No theory of law can stand which involves such a consequence." Venkata Subbarao in *Jurisprudence and Legal Theory* has come out with a marvelous criticism of Carter in the following words: "To suppose as Dr Carter does, that all judicial decisions are and must merely be declaratory of existing law involves the assumption that law is of infinite range and provides for every conceivable case before hand." But Bacon said long ago, "The narrow compass of human wisdom cannot take in all the cases which time may discover". There frequently arise novel cases or cases of first impression which the judge has to decide without the assistance of any pre-determined legal rule. The principles laid down by judges in such cases are bound to be a distinct contribution to the existing law. Dr. Carter does not concede this. It is notable that there might be certain situations where judges do not find any appropriate law to decide, but as they have to decide the cases, they decide on the basis of their own hidden reason keeping in view the basic requirements of justice. Many cases are decided on the basis of the equitable principle - justice, equity and good conscience - as there are no appropriate legal or customary rules to decide. These cases can easily be traced in case reports. The cases like *Rayland* v. *Fletcher* (1868) LR 3 HL 330 and *Heldley Byrne* and many more are considered as epoch-making judgments, which have either been innovative or have given such directions to the law that were not anticipated by legislatures. Salmond has expressed the similar view. He writes, "...It is clear that judges do more at times than apply existing rules: sometimes they widen and extend a rule of law; sometimes they devise a rule by analogy; and sometimes they create an entirely new principle. Courts then have the power to developing the law at the same time that they administer it."

Judges Do Make Law

We have noted above that the declaratory theory is not so convincing and it is considered to be outdated. Presently, it is widely accepted that judges have plenty of occasions to make law. Diecy and Gray have been great supporters of the notion that judges do make law. Dicey in *Law and Opinion in England*, thus, observes, "As all lawyers are aware, a large part, as many would add, the best part of law of England is judge-made law – that is to say, consists of rules to be collected from the judgments of the courts. This portion of law has not been created by Acts of Parliament and is not recoded in the statute book. It is the work of the courts; it is recorded in reports; it is, in short, the fruit of judicial legislation." Prof. Gray has been a stanch supporter of the view that judges make law. He recognized the productive role of judges in the law-making process as law-makers and interpreters of the law. He writes in *Nature and Source of Law*, "...*a fortiory,* whatever hath an absolute authority not only to interpret the law, but to say, what the law is, is truly the law giver." We have already noted criticism of Salmond on the declaratory theory. In support of the notion that judges make law, he writes, "The great body of common or unwritten law is almost entirely the product of decided cases, accumulated in an immense series of reports...Orthodox theory indeed long professed to regard the common law as customary law, and judicial decisions as merely evidence of custom and of the law derived therefrom. This was never much better that an admitted fiction. In practice, if not in theory, the common law of England has been created by decisions of English judges...In England the Bench has always given law to the Bar..." Lord Denning, who has contributed a lot through his epoch-making decisions in development of the common law of England, remarks, "The truth is that the law is uncertain. It does not cover all the situations that may arise. Time and again practitioners and judges are faced with new situations where the decision may go either way. No one can say what the law is until courts decide it. The judges do every day make law, though it is almost necessary to say so. If the truth is recognized, then we may hope to escape from the dead hand of the past and consciously mould new principles to meet the needs of the present." Lord Denning has said so and has proved it to be true though his large number of noteworthy judgments, which have evolved entirely new principles or have given new directions to various legal practices.

Based on the discussions on the above two theories, we can say that on many occasions judges make law. They do so when no enacted or customary rule exists on which they can rely upon. They also do so through interpretations. It does not mean that they usurp or encroach upon the legislative power of the Federal or state legislative body, as the case may be. They do not enjoy unrestricted power to make law, as the law-making power rests with the legislature. Allen in *Law in The Making* writes, "The judge cannot, however much he may wish to do so, sweep away the prevailing rule of law and substitute something else into practice. In this sense it is no 'childish-fiction' to say that he does not and cannot make law. The legislature, on the other hand, has an entirely different prerogative. It is not confined to law in the present or past, but may do so it wills with the future. It can make new law in a sense that is quite precluded to the judge. It legislates where the judge interprets. The legislature can at any time project into the future a rule of law which has never existed in England; the courts can do nothing of this kind." They cannot, thus, overrule any legislated rule; they cannot widen or restrict the scope of any legislated rule if there is no scope to do so. Likewise, authoritative presidents also delimit the power of judges. In spite of this, judges have plenty of scope to legislate. Some of them are: 1. They can widen the scope of any inclusive definition within the limits determined by the law; 2. They can make any rule clear to reflect the true spirit of the legislation; 3. They can remove paradoxical situations in any statute. 4. They can fill in the blank in any statutory provision. 5. If there is no law to apply, they decide the case on the basis of equitable principle agreed upon by them. 6. They can distinguish or explain any judicial precedent; and 7. Sometimes, they can develop entirely new principles. These principles are innovative. Justice Krishna Iyer and Justice P. N. Bhagwati of the Indian Supreme Court have done so. We can conclude saying that the primary function of judges is to interpret the law. They are not law-making authorities of the state. However, they can make law through interpreting legislated law or customary law. They, as a guardian of morality, can declare any social practice as immoral and can declare it to be illegal to be practiced. On many occasions, on the other hand, their job is expository i.e., they merely declare the rules of law and base their decisions on them.

Judicial Precedent in *Shari'ah* and State Practice

Shari'ah Position

Qadi

Under the *shari'ah*, it is the duty of the head of the state to administer justice between litigants. This function of the state is tc be exercised by *qadi* appointed by the state having full qualifications required by the law in order to hold and discharge judicial functions (Refer to: Ibne Abedine (Muhammad Amin), *Radd ul-Muhtar*, vol. iv, p. 207; Al-Marghinani, *Hidayah*, vol. ii, p. 612). The status and function of the *qadi* is sacred; and he has been ordained to do *'adl* (justice). The Qur'an clearly says, "...and he has to set up a balance (of justice), in order that he may not transgress (due) balance. So establish weight with justice and fall not short in the balance." (Lv: 7-9). It further says, "We sent afore time Our apostles with clear signs and sent down with them the Book and the Balance (of right and wrong), that men may stand forth with justice..." (xLii:7). Thus, in *shar'ah*, justice has to be imparted in the name of Allah within the boundaries of Qur'an and *Sunnah* (Prophetic traditions); it is a devotional act to be imparted as a religious duty. It is, therefore, a big religious responsibility on the *qadi*. Although on the qualification of a *qadi* there exists dispute between *Sahfais* and *Hanafis*, for these reasons, the author feels that the person who is appointed to undertake the responsibility to act as a *qadi* must be a competent person. Among all qualifications, the important one is that he must be well versed in *shari'ah*. It is, therefore, a duty of the state to appoint a competent person, who has confidence in his ability to discharge his duties impartially, to the office. It is therefore warranted that a *qadi* should be up-to-date in all aspects of *shari'ah* and must follow *taqwa* in his acts of human relations and human behaviours.

Hierarchy of Courts

Initially, the Caliph exercised the judicial function. There were no levels of courts, like trail courts and appellate courts. Judicial functions were exercised by the Prophet (saw) himself: after his demise, the job was done by the *Khulafa Rashedeen*. Decisions given by them were executed without any delay, for the sake of speedy justice and as there were no appeals (*murafa'a*) against them, as there did not exist *mahakim isti'af* (appellate courts) and *mahakim tamyiz* (causation court). Thus, there was no question of reversal of any decision by any superior court. For futher details, Mohammad Iqbal Siddiqui, *The Penal Law of Islam*, p.183; Hashim Kamali, "Appellate Review and Judicial Independence in Islam", in

Chibli Mallat (ed.) *Islam and Public Law*, p. 49 may be referred. For non-existence of appellate courts, Ibn Hazam al-Zahiri gives reasons that all decisions in *shari'ah* are declaratory in character. Thus, a *qadi* merely declares the application of law in a given situation...When he declares the ruling (*hukm*), he intends it to be applicable in a particular dispute, then it must be implemented. For, it is incorrect in principle to set aside the ruling when a competent judge has verified its application. For further details, Abu Muhammad Ali bin Hazm, *Al-Muhalla*, p. 422 may be referred. If we strictly adhere to these authorities, we can say that there cannot be provision of appeal courts in an Islamic judicial system. But this view has been contradicted by some other authorities. According to Fathi Uthman there can be circumstances in which judicial decisions are liable to be reversed. This view has been supported by Ghulam Murtaza Azad for the reason that for removing errors that may lead to evil and injustice which are not at all warranted. The following may be referred: Fathih Uthman, *Al-Fikir al-Qanun al-Islami: Bayn Usul al-Shari'a wa Turath al-Fiqh*, 314; Ghulam Murtaza Azad, *Judicial System of Islam*, p. 100. Khaliph Umar b. Khattab did not deny review of *qadis'* decisions in two cases, as they were not based on interpretation of Qura'an or *Sunnah*; rather, they were based on the personal reasoning (*ijtehad*) of the *qadis*. This has been reported by Abu Muhammad Abdullah b. Qudama al-Muqdisi in *Al-Mughni*, Ed.1, p. 34. It means the possibility of appellate review and reversal of decisions of lower courts cannot totally be denied. It is also clear from the letter written by Umer b. al-Khattab to Musa al-Ashari (see *infra*) that judicial review is possible by the same *qadi*. According to the author, the second view is closer to imparting justice; moreover, it is imperatively warranted when a state is big; as in that state, only through appellate courts certainty in *shari'ah* matters can be maintained.

With the expansion of the territory and development of law, the job was delegated to competent persons to act as *qadis*. They had territorial, specific and concurrent jurisdictions. They performed their duties independently. When the Muslim state further expanded, the judicial system was reorganized and different levels of courts were constituted. Administration of the judicial system was within the power of a *qadi al-qudat* (chief *qadi*), who can be considered as chief judge of the country. For example, Abu Yusuf was appointed as a chief *qadi* by Harun al-Rashid and Abdullah b. Husain b. Abi al-Shawarbi was appointed to the office by M'izz al-Dawlah. The whole system in judicial matters worked independently without any interference by the Governor. The chief *qadi* of the country had the power to appoint chief *qadis* of the states and *qadis* for all cities.

Doctrine of Judicial Precedent

As stated above, the job of a *qadi* was to impart justice among litigants without any fear or favour and base decisions of facts and evidence produced before him. The system can be considered to be a combination of adversarial system and inquisitorial system of today, as in many cases for imparting justice, *qadi*s had to investigate for finding the truth so that they could impart justice. However, their functions were not interfered by the executive head of the state, Caliph or Governor. In order to know the complete picture of jurisdictional and functional aspects of *qadis,* the directives issued by Caliph Umer to *qadi* Ali Musa al-Ashari, which is opt quoted, are worth referring (Refer to Ibn Khaldun, *Muqaddimah*, Ed. 5, vol. I, pp. 453-454).

The part of the text of the letter that is relevant from the point of view of judicial precedent is as follows: "...If you gave judgment yesterday and today, upon reconsideration, come to the correct opinion, you should not feel prevented by your first judgment from retracting: for justice is primeval, and it is better to retract than to persist in worthlessness...Use your brain about matters that perplex you and to which neither the Qur'an nor the *Sunnah* seems to apply. Study similar cases and evaluate the situation through analogy with those similar cases..."

This letter does not support the doctrines of judicial precedent and *stare decisis*. *Qadi*s were supposed to decide all cases on their merits. They have not to be prevented by their previous decisions. It means they were not bound by their previous decisions. However, they were allowed to take guidance from them. Based on it, it can be said that the same situation should prevail even when several levels of courts are established. This is notable that *Sunnah* of the Prophet (saw), which included his decisions also, had to be followed, as they are based on divine wisdom and thus have the characteristics of universality, immutability and eternity. Now, the *Sunnah* of the Prophet (saw) are binding, and decisions given by *Sahaba* (ra) (his companions) do not have binding force, but they have very high degree of persuasive force, as the Prophet (saw) told to the people that after his demise follow his allies. *Qadis* can hardly differ from them. This notion gets from the following two *ahadith*: 1. On one occasion, Prophet (saw) said, "My companions are like stars. If you follow any of them, you get *hidayah* (right path, good guidance)." [Khatib Baghdadi, *Kifayah*, p. 48]. 2. On the other occasion he (saw) said, "You hold steadfastly my practices and distinctiveness of *khulapha Rashdeen*." [Tirmizi, *Sunan*, vol. 5, p. 45, *hadith* no. 2676.]

We can, thus, infer that the classical practice does not subscribe to the doctrine of judicial precedent. However, decisions of higher courts may have a considerable degree of persuasive force. Decisions given by the Prophet (saw) and his companions have special value in the Islamic court system.

Based on above discussions, we can conclude that according to *shari'ah* there can be hierarchy of courts, decisions of higher courts will not be binding on lower courts. Nevertheless, they will have persuasive value and they can be considered for deciding later cases. It is also clear that decisions of courts, even decisions of the apex *shari'ah* court will not have the sanctity of *fatawa*, as *fatwa* can be given by a *mufti* or a group of *muftis*. At this point, a question arises: should we maintain that position? The answer can be given only after an expository study of some of the countries that have *shari'ah* court system or a mixed system of both civil courts and *shari'ah* courts.

State Practice

Malaysian Position

In Malaysia, the court system has three sets of courts: civil courts, *syariah* courts and native courts of Sabah and Sarawak. Article 121-131 of the Federal Constitution deal with the judicial system to administer civil law in the country, which comprises of Federal Court, Court of Appeal and High Courts. In addition to these, there are District Courts (Inferior courts). We have noted above that the Doctrine of Judicial Precedent applies in the country. *Syariah* courts of states and of Federal Territory have been created under entry 1 of the State List and entry 6(e) of the Federal List of the Ninth Schedule of the Federal Constitution. Native courts have been brought into existence in Sabah and Sarawak under entry 13 of the State List. It has been said in *Sukma Darmawan Sasmitaat Majid* v. *Ketua Pengarah Penjara Malaysia and Anor* [1999] 2 MLJ 241 (F C) that the three sets of courts are parallel i.e., one court system cannot interfere in other court systems. It means civil courts of the country cannot interfere into the jurisdiction and working of *syariah* courts of the country. This has further been accentuated by Article 121 (1A) of the Constitution, which clearly sates that Courts referred to in Clause (1) shall have no jurisdiction in respect of the *syariah* courts. This is because the Constitution does not warrant any interference of the Federal Government or its courts in *syariah* matters, including the *syariah* courts system, because they are state matters and states want to maintain their autonomy in these matters (Reid Commission Report may be referred). This has also been the attitude of the civil courts that even where they found the decision of the *syariah* courts to be wrong, they did not interfere with the decision given by the *syariah* courts. The following two cases prove this fact: *Ng Siew Pian* v. *Abd wahid bin Abu Hassan* [1992] 1 MLJ 425; *Kamariah Ali* v. *Kerajaan Negri Kelantan, Malaysia* [2002] 3 CLJ 766 (C A). On the contrary, with few exceptions, *syariah* courts have not given heed to civil courts' decisions. The following cases may be referred: *Jumaaton dan satu lagi* v. *Raja Hizaruddine* [1998] 6 MLJ 554; *Tengku Abdul Kadir* v. *Majlis Agama Islam, Kelantan* (1995) (*Syariah* Court of Appeal) 9:1 JH 34. In the second case the court refused to differ from the civil court's decision on the ground of *res judicata* and public interest in maintaining consistency in judicial decisions. For a detailed account on this issue, Farid Sufian Shuaib, *Powers and Jurisdiction of Syariah Courts in Malaysia* (MLJ, Malaysia: 2003) may be referred.

All states and Fedearl Territory have their separate sets of *syariah* court system. There are, thus, hierarchy of *Syariah* Court of Appeal, *Syariah* High Court and *Syariah* District Courts. In every state, *Syariah* District Courts are bound by administrative orders issued by the *Syariah* High Court of the state. But in judicial matters, all *syariah* courts are independent. It means courts while deciding any question of law may consider *ratio decidendi* of previous cases of any level, but they are not bound with them. Each case is supposed to be decided on its own merit. In short, the doctrine of judicial precedent is not applicable in the *syariah* court system of the country e.g., the *syariah* courts maintain the classical *shari'ah* law position. This has clearly been stated by *Syariah* High Court of Selangore *in Pendkwa syari'i Lwn Fahyun Hanim, Noni Mohamad and Sharina Shaari, Jurnal Syariah*, 8:1 [2000] 137, at p. 148, in the following words: "*Sukacita ingin saya menjelaskan di mana Penguam Syari'I cuba mengaikan atau merujuk kepada kes-kes Mahakmah Awam juga kes-kes yang terdapat di Jurnal Hukum. Untuk makluman dan perhatian khususnya kepada Peguam Syari'I, Mahakmah syariah tidak terikat dengan keputusan Mahakmah Awam atau Sivil yang merupakan doctrin duluan. Begutu juga kes-kes Mahakmah Syariah tidak mengikat kepada mana-mana Mahakmah Syariah yang lain atau degan perkataan yang lain doctrin duluan mengikat tidak di di Mahakmah Syariah.*" In short, it means the *syariah* courts are not bound by decisions of the civil courts. Similarly, they are not bound by the earlier *syariah* courts' decisions.

Sisters in Islam, an NGO, submitted a memorandum to the Government of Malaysia in March 1997. They proposed: 1. *Syariah* courts should adopt the system of binding precedent similar to that practiced by the civil courts in the country. This, according to them, would ensure that the *syariah* courts of the first instance would be bound by the decisions of the *Syariah* High Court, and decisions of the *Syariah* Court of Appeal would have binding effect on both *Syariah* High Courts and *Syariah* District Courts. 2. A Federal *Syariah* Judicial System should be established. According to them, the establishment of a single Federal Syariah Judiciary Administering one set of Islamic Family Law will do away with the possibility of multiplicity of opinions on one question of law. (see *www.sisters* in Islam.org.my/memo/040197.htm) The author is of the opinion that for the sake of uniformity and certainty of Islamic law within a state, the doctrine of judicial precedent should be followed by the *syariah* court system of the states. This will serve the public interest in a better way. There is no prohibition by Qur'an and *Sunnah* for it also. To have a Federal *Syariah* Judicial System applicable to all states will be an ideal situation. There is possibility that the Federal Government of the country can enact a law for sake of uniformity in law under Article 76 (1) (b) of the Federal Constitution, but there is all probability that states will not agree for it. And unless they ratify the law, it will not be applicable in states. We have already noted this above that *syariah* court system is a state subject and according to the Reid Commission states value very much their autonomous powers regarding Islamic matters. This seems to be true. For a detailed account, refer to Farid Sufian Shuaib, *Poweres and Jurisdiction of Syariah Courts in Malaysia*, pp. 22-23. The idea of establishing a Federal *Syariah* Court, which was mooted by the Federal Government few years ago, is also a wonderful proposal. The decisions of this court if made to be binding on state *syariah* courts will bring about certainty in family law and other Islamic law of the state from where the case in appeal will come to this apex court. But for the same reason it is also not feasible.

Recently, a proposal to have a grand mufti in the country was mooted by Dr. Syed Ali Tawfiq Al-Attas, director general of the Institute of Islamic Understanding Malaysia (Ikim). He said that Malaysia needed a grand mufti to prevent the teachings of the religion from being distorted. He suggested that a grand mufti can be appointed by the Yang de-Pertuan Agong, who is the head of Islam in the country. He suggested this for having an authoritative figure to unite differing views among religious scholars on certain issues, which might cause confusion among believers. He further supported his proposal by saying that a grand mufti would also ensure proper role to be played by enforcement agencies in developing the faith of believers. The idea might be inspired by the institution of the grand muftis of Egypt, Jordan and Australia and their role in their respective countries. The idea is quite good, and the reasons appended to it are also quite convincing. *Fatawa* given by the proposed grand mufti will certainly bring about uniformity on many differing religious issues. If legally accepted so, they can be made as the law of the country and can appropriately be precedents to be followed by the *Syariah* courts of the country also. But as stated above that Islam is a state subject with rulers as the depositories, the situation is Malaysia is different. To this effect, the

Deputy Prime Minister Datuk Seri Najib Razak has rightly said that the idea of having a grand mufti in the country is constitutionally not feasible, as the federal Constitution does not allow for it. He further said, "It will be difficult. It would not be possible to implement this suggestion, based on what we have in our constitution. The exclusive right to decide on Islam is with the ruler of each sate." (see *New Straits Times*, December 30, 2006)

Position in Pakistan

Pakistan has an integrated judicial system, where courts are competent to decide on civil matters as well as matters pertaining to *Shari'ah*. For example, Criminal Courts have jurisdiction to hear cases pertaining to *Hudud*. Decisions of the Criminal Courts are appellable to the Federal *Shariat* Court. The Federal *Shariat* Court, which has 8 Muslim judges with 3 Ulema well versed in Islamic law, and which is, in fact, part of the Supreme Court, on its own motion or through petition by a citizen or a government (Federal or Provincial), may examine and determine as to whether or not a certain provision of law is repugnant to the injunctions of Islam. Appeal against its decision lies to the *Shariat* Appellate Bench of the Supreme Court, consisting three Muslim judges of the Supreme Court and not more than 2 *Ulema*, appointed by the President. If a certain provision of law is declared to be repugnant to the injunction of Islam, the government is required to take necessary steps to amend the law so as to bring it in conformity of Qur'an and *Sunnah*. By virtue of Article 203G of the Constitution decisions of the Court are binding on High Courts as well as the subordinate judiciary. Refer to *The judicial System of Pakistan, a* write up prepared by the Secretary, Law and Justice Commission of Pakistan and Registrar of the Supreme Court of Pakistan at: *http://www.Ljcp.gov.pk/menu%20items/item-16/the%20judicial%* 20system% 20of%20pak.htm. visited on 4 January 2007)

We have noted above that the decisions of Federal *Shariat* Court are binding on High Courts and subordinate judiciary. Likewise, Article 189 of the Constitution makes decisions of the Supreme Court binding on all other courts. This proves that the doctrines of judicial precedent and *stare decisis* are practiced in the judicial system of Pakistan. Decisions on *Sahri'ah* are no exceptions. Rather, the decisions of the Federal *Shariat* Court, if not revered by the *Shariat* Appellate Bench of the Supreme Court, have the sanctity of a *fatawa* and the Legislature is required to make necessary changes in the law to bring it in conformity with Qur'an and *Sunnah*.

Position in Saudi Arabia

The judicial system of Saudi Arabia is mainly based on *shari'ah*. There is hierarchy of *shari'ah* courts. Decisions of *shari'ah courts* are solely based on *shari'ah* principles and presided over by experts of Islamic law. In addition to this, the judicial code of the country stipulates that specialized courts–secular tribunals–may be established by passing Royal Decree. There are some secular tribunals outside the *shari'ah* court system to deal with generally cases of violations of administrative rules. They have been established under different ministries. The Grievances Board operates under the authority of the Bureau of Presidency of the Council of Ministers. The Home Ministry is in charge of the special police who enforce motor vehicle regulations. Likewise, the Ministry of Commerce supervises arbitration and Appeal Boards established to settle commercial disputes, especially those involving foreign business transactions. The Ministry of Labour and Social Affairs enforces labour law through special labour committees established by it. It is notable here that in most of the cases decisions given by these tribunals are considered to be final, but in exceptional cases the Minister concerned can review them and decide on its own merit. However, previous cases are considered while deciding later cases; and the verdicts of Ministers on certain legal issues have very high degree of persuasive force. They can only be distinguished when facts are different and justice cannot be imparted by following them.

In Saudi Arabia, *shari'ah* court system includes summery courts, general courts of first instance and appeal courts. Summery courts have jurisdiction to decide over minor civil and criminal matters, and general courts of first instance is entitled to try all cases beyond the jurisdiction of summery courts. Summery courts are presided over by one *qadi*; contrary to this, with respect to serious crimes like murder, major theft and sexual misconducts general courts of first instance is supported with three *qadis*. Decision of both types of courts are appeallable to the appeal court, which is known as *shari'ah* appeals court. This court has three departments to deal with three different types of suits: penal suits, personal status suits and other types of suits. The Minister of Justice acts as the *de facto* Chief Justice. He is supported by the Supreme Judicial Council, a body of 11 leading *ulama* of the country, presided over by him. The supreme Judicial Council acts as courts and reviews all decisions referred to it by the Minister of Justice. In addition to this, it expresses legal opinions on question of law referred to it, and approves all sentences of death, amputation of fingers and hands, and stoning to death. The king is at the pinnacle of the judicial system, functioning as final court of appeal and as a source of clemency.

In the Saudi Arabian judicial system, the concept of judicial precedent does not exist. All cases at all levels are decided on their own merits. For the sake of ensuring justice, courts are free to distinguish from any previous case. However, cases decided by higher courts have more sanctity and thus have relatively high degree of persuasion force.

Based on the above expository study of state practices, we can conclude that there is no uniformity, as in Malaysia and Saudi Arabia the classical position is being maintained by the *shari'ah* courts, and in Pakistan both doctrine of *satre decisis* and doctrine of judicial precedent are being followed. In Malaysia, they are being followed in the civil courts system only. The suggestions to have a *Federal Syariah Court* is not viable, as *shari'ah* is a state subject and it seems that states will not be able to give this jurisdiction to the Federal Government.

CONCLUSION

Based on above discussions, we can conclude that the judicial systems of common law countries prove that doctrines of *stare decisis* and judicial precedent are useful tools in imparting justice. The hardship, that they had, has already been removed by a new doctrine of prospective overruling. Erroneous decisions can also be annulled by Acts of the legislature or decrees of the king as the case may be. We have noted that continental practice is different, because civil law system is followed there. In spite of this fact, decisions of higher courts, especially of the apex court of the country has a great degree of persuasion. The author is of the opinion that in these countries the present position should be altered by giving more value to decisions of higher courts.

It is true that both the methods of determining *ratio decidendi* are useful. But they are not free from criticisms. In view of this, the author is of the opinion that efforts should be made to find any other suitable method.

It has been exemplified in the above discussions that judges make law. They make law via interpretations. Although this notion is very weak in civil law countries, there also through judicial interpretations, statutory law immensely takes definite shape.

On the basis of the practices in three Islamic countries discussed above, it can be said that with respect to judicial system and following of the doctrine of judicial precedent, there is no uniformity. In Pakistan, the doctrine is followed because there is an integrated judicial system and the Constitution expressly provides that decisions of the Supreme Court are binding on all courts of Pakistan. Decisions of High Courts are binding on lower courts. This situation is there because Pakistan belongs to common law countries and in these countries the doctrine of judicial precedents has high value. But the position in Malaysia is slightly different. The doctrine in followed in the civil court system; it does not apply in the *shar'ah* court system. It is being argued there that the doctrine of judicial precedent should be made applicable in the *shari'ah* court system as well. The author is of the opinion that if states of the Malaysian Federal System decide to apply the doctrine, it can be applied. There is no harm in it. It will rather bring about uniformity in approach on disputed questions of law. It is rather warranted. There is no feasibility to have a Federal Court of Appeal, as this will be possible only when states authorize under Article 76(1)(c) of the Federal Constitution to the Federal Legislature to legislate, which is far from reality. In Saudi Arabia and other such countries, where *shari'ah* is the main stream of the judicial system and other judicial tribunals which have jurisdiction to deal with some civil law matters only, just supplement it, for the given reasons, should also follow the doctrines of *stare decisis* and judicial precedent, as there is no express prohibition in *shari'ah* on them. In Islam, justice is the sacred trust from Allah (swt) and it has to be imparted without any fear or favour. When we follow these doctrines, we can impart justice in a better way. It should be made clear here that in a country like Malaysia, where there are two streams of judicial systems, these doctrines should be observed separately: decisions of higher civil courts should not be binding on *shari'ah* courts.

References

Al-Marghinani, *Hidayah* (Bairut: Al-Maktabah al-Islamiyah, 1987), vol. ii.

Anwar Ahmad Qadri, *Islamic Jurisprudence in the Modern World* (Delhi: Taj Company, 1986).

A. T. Von Mehren, *The Civil Law System: Cases and Materials* (London: Prentice-Hall, 1957).

Ibne Abedin (Muhammad Amin), *Radd ul-Muhtar* (Bairut: Darul Fikr, 1386 H) vol. iv.

Ibn Khaldun, *Muqaddamah* (Bairut: Darul Qalam, 1984), Ed. 5, vol. i.

Abu Muhammad Ali bin Hazm, Al-Muhalla (Cairo: Dar al-Fikr, 1351 H).

Abu Muhammad Abdullah b. Qudama al-Muqdisi, *Al-Mughni* (Bairut: Daral Fikr, 1405 H), Ed. 1.

C. Morris, *The Justification of the Law* (Pennsylvania: University of Pennsylvania Press, 1971). G. W. Paton, *A Text Book of Jurisprudence* (London: Oxford University Press, 1972).

C. K. Allen, Law in the Making (London: Oxford University Press, 1964).

Dennis Lloyd, *Introduction to Jurisprudence* (London: Sweet and Maxwell, 1994), Ed. 6 by M.D.A. Freeman.

Farid Sufian Shuaib, *Powers and Jurisdiction of Syariah Courts in Malaysia*, (Kuala Lumpur: MLJ, 2003).

Fathih Uthman, *Al-Fikir aḷ-Qanun al-Islami: Bayn Ususl al-Shari'ah wa Turuth al-Fiqh* (Cairo: Dar al-Fikr).

G. C. Venkata Subbarao, *Jurisprudence and Legal Theory* (Lucknow: Eastern Book Company, 1975).

G. W. Paton, *A Text Book of Jurisprudence* (London: Oxford University Press, 1972).

Ghulam Murtaza Azad, *Judicial System of Islam* (Islamabad: Islamic Research Institute, IIU, 1987).

J. W. Salmond, *Jurisprudence* (London: Sweet and Maxwell, 1966), Ed. 5 by P. J. Fitzgerald.

Khatib Baghdadi, *Kifayah* (Medina: Al-Maktab al-Islamiyyah, 1974).

Mohammad Hashim Kamali, *Principles of Islamic Jurisprudence* (Kuala Lumpur: Ilmiah Publishers, 1989).

Mohammad Hashim Kamali, "Appellate Review and Judicial Independence in Islam", in Chibli Mallat (ed.) *Islam and Public Law* (London: Grahm and Tortman, 1993).

Mohammad Iqbal Siddiqui, *The Penal Law of Islam* (Lahore: Qazi Publications, 1979).

Tirmizi, *Sunan* (Bairut: Dar Ihyaa al-Turath al-Arabi) vol. v.

V. D. Mahajan, *Jurisprudence and Legal Theory* (Lucknow: Eastern Book Company, 1987), Ed. 5.

6

Drugs Misuse In Malaysia: Past and Present

Abdul Rani Bin Kamarudin

The History of Commercialization of Drug in South-East Asia

Drug use in Malaysia (then Malaya) dates back to the early nineteenth century with the British presence in the Far East including Malaya.[1] Opium was then an important commodity, the British Company forcefully used in exchange for goods such as spices etc from the Malay Archipelago to be used for purchasing tea from China. The British in India were becoming masters of an empire, and to pay for that empire, they were turning with more and more urgency to the profits of their trade with China, largely tea trade to London. China's enormous population offered the British, unlimited possibilities for its commercial expansion. Chinese junks had before 1819 collected a variety of products from Siam (Thailand), the Malay Peninsula, and the archipelago: rattans, pepper, mother-of-pearl, tins, birds' nest, and betel-nut from Malaya; tin from Bangka island; occasionally, rice from Manilla; and coral, amber, and sandalwood from the Moluccas and Micronesia.[2] To find goods to sell to the Chinese (China) in exchange-pepper and tin in particular–the British moved into South-East Asia.[3] Singapore[4] served as a depot for British goods, principally textiles, metals, Indian opium, and piece-goods for distribution in the Malay Peninsula, Borneo and Sulu; pepper, gold, and tin from Pahang and Trengganu; tin from Perak and Selangor;

and spices, dragon's blood, sago, betel, coffee, and camphor from Sumatra.[5] Based on a contemporary account by H.M. Elmore, Professor Parkinson described the patterns of trade prevailing in early 19th century South and South-East-Asia:

> *These* opium ships *(my emphasis)...from Bengal..[touched] Junk Ceylon (ujung salang: Phuket), Penang, Selangore, Malacca, Lingin, Pelembang, and ... Batavia... At all these ports of call the ships would get rid of her cargo, taking tin, ivory and [Mexican] dollars in exchange. Any cargo left over was then disposed of on the West Coast of Borneo, for gold, and the ship would then collect more tin, and pepper, and proceeds to the Straits of Banca to meet the Company's ships, due there about August. These would take on board much of the tin and pepper, on payment of freight, giving a loan of dollars in exchange. Paying in specie, the ship was then to buy more tin, pepper, rattans, wax and betel-nuts, and then follow the China ships towards the end of September. It was necessary to discharge and load the return cargo with extraordinary speed in order to sail again in November and reach Calcutta in the following month, ready to begin the voyage again.*[6]

The crucial role of opium in the British imperial edifice was underlined as follows:

> *From the* opium trade *(my emphasis) the Honourable Company has derived for years an immense revenue and through them the British Government and nation have also reaped an incalculable amount of political and financial advantage. The turn of the balance of trade between Great Britain and China in favour of the former has enabled India to increase tenfold her consumption of British manufactures, contributed directly to support the vast fabric of British dominion in the East, to defray the expenses of His Majesty's establishment in India, and by the operation of exchanges and remittances in teas, to pour in abundant revenue into the British Exchequer and benefit the nation to an extent of £6 million yearly without impoverishing India.*[7]

How Drugs Began To Be Misused In Malaysia

Malaya, as it was then known, was being carved-out of the rugged terrain and jungles in the early 19th century. In opening up the country and developing its tin mines, rubber and pepper estates, the British brought huge numbers of Chinese and Indian workers into Malaya to work in the tin mines, rubber plantations and pepper estates respectively.[8] The Chinese were the first people who introduced into the country the habit of opium smoking. Employment in the new country brought them enough money to spare. There was some period of leisure after a grueling day's work, but there were no amenities with which they could occupy themselves. Most of them had left their families behind in the mother country. Opium smoking thus became one of the habits. Some smoked it as a medicine, to cure aches and pains and ward off diseases (opium was believed to have a beneficial effect upon tuberculosis of the lungs, diarrhea, and malaria). At the time, it was not considered harmful and there was no restriction or taboos as to its use. It has been recorded that opium consumption among some of the Chinese in Singapore and the Straits Settlements was evident since 1867.[9] The use of morphine was also prevalent during that period of time. Supply involved illegalities because the importation and exportation of deleterious drugs like morphine and cocaine for example, would require the written permission of the State Surgeon or in his absence the Government Medical Officer.[10] There was no way of ascertaining how widespread the misuse of morphine then, since the government did not control it in the way it controlled opium. In addition to this problem, there was also indication that Indian immigrant particularly the dockworkers, used cannabis.[11] The use of drugs among the natives, however, was initially rare.[12]

Early Legislations in Regulating Drugs Use

In 1910, the British Government took over the importation, sale and distribution of opium. The Government licensed all retail shops, while mine owners and other large employers of Chinese labour imported their own opium, converted it into *chandu,* and dispensed it to their own employees. After many years, the government, in some states, collected their own taxes on opium, and while that policy did not make the slightest difference to consumers, it enabled the government to calculate this source of revenue for each successive period of three years.[13] The Geneva Convention on Drugs, held on 19th day of February 1925, prompted the British to impose restrictions on the sale and consumption of opium. Registered opium smokers or authorised consumers however continued to 'enjoy' this privilege. By 1929, the Federated Malay States had 52,313 registered opium users. A further restriction was imposed in 1934, as a result of a treaty signed in Bangkok on the use of opium. Only those, who had doctor's recommendation, were allowed to use it.[14] By 1941, there were 75,000 opium users; and it was estimated that the number of those, who were not registered, might well be double. After the World War two, the British prohibited the unauthorised use of opium. On the 1st day of November 1943, Tan Cheng Lock wrote:

> *Throughout the history of Malaya during perhaps the last one hundred years or more a very substantial portion of its revenue was derived from the opium consumed by the Chinese population of the country. The pernicious habit of opium smoking should be completely done away with, and more drastic step should be taken to eradicate the evil, which has caused a marked deterioration in the character and physique of the Chinese who indulge in it...*[15]

In order to prohibit the possession, use, manufacture, sale, and importation of dangerous drugs, the Dangerous Drugs Ordinance of 1952 was promulgated by the High Commissioner with the consent of the Rulers in Council of the Federation of Malaya.[16]

The Early Causes for the Outbreak in Drug Misuse

Opium abuse continued, but mainly amongst men in their late fifties, particularly old Chinese males. The attitude at the time seemed to have been that the death of these older generations would end the drug addiction problem. The combination of the "hippy culture" and the consequences of the Vietnam War in the late 1960 and early 1970 saw a change in the pattern of drug use in Malaysia. The drug-taking habits of the American soldiers, who were in Malaysia for "rest and recreation", influenced Malaysian youths. Youths of all races began abusing drug at a wider range. Cannabis was an all-time favourite with this group, which moved on to the abuse of heroin, *morphine* and other dangerous drugs. Psychotropic substances like *methaqualone*, *amphetamine*, *barbiturate* and others were also abused. The American withdrawal from Vietnam made the drug syndicates realized that there would be a reduction in the demand for drugs. The syndicates, therefore, began to expand their network of drug trafficking activities to South-East Asian countries. Malaysia unwittingly was used as a transit for the `exportation' of drugs for new markets in Asia and Western countries. Though, Malaysia is not a drug `producing country', it is nevertheless beset by the drug menace. The notorious `Golden Triangle' area that comprised the common borders of Burma, Thailand and Laos is a drug-cultivation region. The drug abuse scenario in South-East Asia changed, and the rate of drug addiction increased dramatically in the late 1960s. There was an explosion of what had been originally a contained habit of opium smoking by the Chinese immigrants, and later cannabis smoking by the Indian immigrants for `therapeutic purpose'. Addicts were no longer confined to the traditional group (elderly Chinese opium addicts), and drug abuse among all racial and age groups was on the increase. Youths particularly were the most at risk and more and more types of drugs were available illicitly. [17]

When Malaysia attained its independence in 1957 from the British, it thus inherited that burden of checking the scourge caused by the abuse and misuse of drugs. Given that the nation was still young, no serious efforts were actually made to address the problems. The immediate threat from communists ended on 30th July 1960 when the state of emergency was ended, but the security of the Federation was still very much in issue.[18] In fact, it was only in 24th December 1989 that terrorism from the Malayan Communist Party ceased altogether.[19] Communal tension that resulted in racial riots on 13th May 1969 led to another state of emergency. The Parliament that was dissolved on 20th March 1969 did not reconvene until 1972. Hence, the prevailing drug problems unsurprisingly continued quite unabated until the early to mid seventies. The notion that the drug problems, typically associated with the older generation who were mostly Chinese, would gradually dissipate with the passage of time did not become a reality. On the other hand, youths of all ages had already started to take drugs in 1960. It was in 1973 that tough steps were taken by increasing the penalties for various offences under the Act. The efforts continued to gain momentum in 1975 with the introduction of treatment and rehabilitation facilities and the inclusion of trafficking as an offence. Nevertheless, for whatever reasons, the response of the Malaysian Government in curbing the drug menace can be said to be pathetic or "too little too late".

The Gravity of Drugs Misuse

On the 19th of February 1983, the drug menace was declared to be the main threat to national security. The declaration was made because drug addiction would have reached epidemic proportions if a tough stand was not taken to address the menace. 65% of the addicts were young men between the age of 20 and 29. They represented the backbone and hope of the nation's future. The adverse effect on the uncontrolled drug addiction and trafficking would threaten the socio-economic well being, spiritual and natural culture of the nation's population, hence undermining national resilient and national security.[20] The then Home Affairs Minster, Dato Musa Hitam when tabling the Dangerous Drugs (Amendment) Act A553/83 before the House of Representatives on 24th March 1983, spoke of the growing seriousness of the drug problem that threatened and had threatened national security and integrity - it was not merely a social problem. The Prime Minister, Dato Seri Dr Mahathir Mohammed (as he then was), on the 10th of September 1983, following a Cabinet decision signed the National Security Council Directive number 13.[21]

The Current Dangerous Drugs Law

The Dangerous Drugs Act 1952 (previously known as the Dangerous Drugs Ordinance 1952)[22] is the foremost statute in Malaysia on drugs control, covering penal, procedural and evidential matters, as well as regulating the importation, exportation, manufacture, sale and use, possession, cultivation, the use of premises of certain dangerous drugs and substances mention in the schedule to the Act. Malaysia's other major statutes on drugs are; Poisons Act 1952, Drug Dependants (Treatment and Rehabilitation) Act 1983; Dangerous Drugs (Special Preventive Measures) Act 1985; and Dangerous Drugs (Forfeiture of Property) Act 1988.

The Dangerous Drugs (Special Preventive Measures) Act 1985, the Dangerous Drugs (Forfeiture of Property) Act 1988, and the Poisons Act 1952 would not be discussed due to the extreme length of time required if they are to be duly discussed. Suffice to just say that the Dangerous Drugs (Special Preventive Measures) Act 1985 is an Act designed primarily for detaining or restricting preventively any person (drug traffickers) where there are grounds to believe that they are involved in drug trafficking activities: It is akin to the Internal Security Act 1960. The Dangerous Drugs (Forfeiture of Property) Act 1988 deals with the procedure of forfeiting the illegal proceeds of drug trafficking, prohibiting the use of property for drug trafficking activities and money laundering of the illegal proceeds of drug trafficking. The Poison Act 1952, on the other hand, regulates the importation, possession, manufacture, compounding, storage, transport, sale and use of poisons. It regulates the use of drugs that are not covered under the First Schedule of the Dangerous Drugs Act 1952. The types of poisons that fall under the control of the Poison Act include substances used for industrial, medical and agricultural purposes. Certain poisons are categorised as psychotropic substances and its supply, possession or administration, as the case may be, are done through medical practitioner, veterinarians, and dentists. Members of a local authority or public authority, members of the governing body of a public hospital, registered medical practitioners, registered dentists, registered nurses ad midwives and registered pharmacists, chemists and wholesalers and retailers of poisons licensed under the Poisons Act 1952 are also exempted to a similar extent.[23] Similar category of persons or bodies are also authorised or licensed under the Dangerous Drugs Act 1952, to deal, administer, possessed or supply controlled drugs.[24] The Minister of Health is empowered to withdraw the authorisation given to person in the medical profession where such license or authorisation was acted upon irresponsibly.[25] The Dangerous Drugs (Hospital, etc.) (General Exemption) Order, 1952, exempts public hospital, public infirmary, public clinic, public mental hospital or public sanatorium supported by any public authority, public funds, charity or voluntary subscription where dangerous drugs are dispensed by a registered pharmacist, or in his absence, by a registered medical practitioner. That Order also provides provisions for the safe custody, handling and records of the dangerous drugs in question.[26] With respect to the Drug Dependants (Treatment and Rehabilitation) Act 1983, the treatment and rehabilitation policy is discussed rather than the legal aspect of the Act.

Dangerous Drugs Act 1952

The Dangerous Drugs Act 1952 is the foremost statute in Malaysia on drugs control, covering penal, procedural and evidential matters, as well as regulating the importation, exportation, manufacture, sale and use of opium and of certain other dangerous drugs and substances. The Act even provides for the mandatory death penalty to convicted drug traffickers, while the offence of cultivation and production is punishable with life imprisonment.[27] An offence under the Act is generally unbailable and seizable (arrest without a warrant) in that the police may arrest without a warrant any person, if they have reasonable suspicion that he or she is concerned in the commission of any offence under the Act. The punishment under the Act is undeniably deterrent in nature in the sense that the punishment is more punitive in relation to the offence (see Table 1).

Procedures and Evidence

In 1983, drug enforcement officers were given added power under the Dangerous Drugs Act 1952, by the introduction of section 27A to intercept (with the consent of the Public Prosecutor) communications; the evidence so obtained shall be admissible at a criminal trial.[28] The Dangerous Drugs Act 1952 is in reality designed to facilitate investigations and conviction. The admissibility of the evidence obtained by interception of communication, the credibility of the evidence of an agent provocateur, the protection that is accorded to an informer, the use of presumptions, and the fact that most offences under the Act are unbailable (not non-bailable), were all aimed towards combating the drug menace. (See Table 2)

Trafficking

Trafficking was made in 1975 as an offence under section 39B of the Dangerous Drugs Act 1952, but then the punishment was life imprisonment and or whipping or death. Trafficking was introduced in 1975 as an offence under section 39B of the Dangerous Drugs Act 1952, which is punishable by death, or life imprisonment and whipping. It is an offence to traffic or offer to traffic in dangerous drugs, including any act preparatory thereto. Due to the gravity of

Table 1

Types of Offences under the Dangerous Drugs Act, 1952

Note: not less than (>), not exceeding (<); Amd= Amendment; Add= Addition

Type of Offence	*Section*	*Type of Drugs/ Matters*	*Punishments*
Importation	4(1)	Raw opium, coca leaves, poppy straw and cannabis	3-5 years imprisonment
	9(1)(a)	Prepared opium	<5 years imprisonment or <RM 20,000 fine or both.
	12(1)(a)	Other dangerous drugs (Part iii, iv and v of First Schedule)	<5 years imprisonment or <RM 20,000 fine or both.
	20	Dangerous drugs - breach of the terms and conditions of authorisation	3-5 years imprisonment
	38(1)	Dangerous drugs through ship or aircraft	<RM 10,000 fine (Detention of ship and aircraft or <RM 10,000 is furnished as security).
Exportation	5(1)	Raw opium, coca leaves, poppy straw and cannabis	3-5 years imprisonment
	9(1)(a)	Prepared opium	<5 years imprisonment or <RM 20,000 fine or both.
	12(1)(b)	Other dangerous drugs (Part iii, and iv of First Schedule)	<5 years imprisonment or <RM 20,000 fine or both.
	19	Dangerous drugs – breach of the terms and conditions of authorisation	3-5 years imprisonment
	38(1)	Dangerous drugs through ship or aircraft	<RM 10,000 fine (Detention of ship and aircraft or <RM 10,000 is furnished as security).

contd. table

Type of Offence	*Section*	*Type of Drugs/ Matters*	*Punishments*
Possession	6	Raw opium, coca leaves, poppy straw and cannabis or the respective seeds of the plants	<5 years imprisonment or <RM 20,000 fine or both.
	9(1)(b)	Prepared opium	<5 years imprisonment or <RM 20,000 fine or both.
	10(2)(a)	Pipe or other utensils for smoking prepared opium, or for the preparation of opium for smoking, consumption or otherwise	<$2,000 fine or <1 yr imprisonment (FM 30/52); <RM 5,000 fine or <2 years imprisonment or both. (Am: A112/72)
	12(2)	Other Dangerous Drugs (Part iii, iv & v of First schedule	<RM 20,000 fine or <5 years imprisonment or both.
	39(A)(1)	Prescribed amount of certain dangerous drugs (2<5g heroin or morphine or monoacetylmorphine [or mixture of any of them]; 5<15g cocaine; 20<50g cannabis or cannabis resin [or mixed]; 100<250g raw & prepared opium [or mixture of any of them]; 250<750g coca leaves	2-5 years imprisonment and 3-9 strokes of whipping
	39A(2)	Prescribed amount of certain dangerous drugs (5g> heroin or morphine or monoacetylmorphine [or mixture of any of them]; 15g> cocaine; 50g> cannabis or cannabis resin [or mixed]; 250g> raw opium or prepared opium [or mixed]; 750> coca leaves	>5 years imprisonment to imprisonment for life, and >10 strokes of whipping
Trafficking	39B(1)	Traffic or offer to traffic or any act preparatory thereto	Death penalty – 39B(2)
Planting or Cultivating	6B(1)	Any plant where raw opium, coca leaves poppy-straw or cannabis may be obtained directly or indirectly	Imprisonment for life and >6 strokes of whipping.
Manufacture/ sale/ distribution	16(1)	Dangerous drugs (Part iii, iv & v of First Schedule)	General penalty: section 39 (<RM 5,000 or <2 years imprisonment or both)

table contd.

Type of Offence	*Section*	*Type of Drugs/ Matters*	*Punishments*
	9(c)	Prepared opium	<RM20, 000 or <5 yrs imprisonment or both
Consume	10(2)(b)	Prepared opium	<RM 5,000 fine or <2 years imprisonment or both
Administration on others	14(1)	Dangerous drugs (Part iii & iv of the First Schedule)	<RM 10,000 fine or <3 years imprisonment or both
Self-administration	15(a)	Dangerous Drugs (Part iii & iv of the First Schedule)	<RM 5,000 fine or <2 years imprisonment or both
Premises	10(1)	Owner/occupier permits its use; or is concerned in its management, for making or sale or smoking or consumption or otherwise of prepared opium	<$5,000 fine or <2yrs imprisonment or both (FM30/52); <RM 10,000 fine or <3 years imprisonment or both (Amd: A112/ 72)
	13	Occupier keeping or using it for unlawful administration of dangerous drugs (Part iii & iv of First Schedule); owner or occupier permits its use to other person for purposes of administration on a hûman being or for smoking, consuming or otherwise of the same	<RM 10,000 fine or <5 years imprisonment or both
	15	Being in any premises kept or used for any purposes specified in section 13	<RM 5,000 fine or <2 years imprisonment or both
Trading	17	Products with phenanthrene alkaloids of opium or ecgonine alkaloids of coca leaf	<RM 10,000 fine or <5 years imprisonment or both

table contd.

Type of Offence	*Section*	*Type of Drugs/ Matters*	*Punishments*
Transit	21(1)	Dangerous drugs without first having authorisation from the respective export and import authority	<RM 20,000 fine or <5 years imprisonment or both
	22(1)	Moving of dangerous drugs from the conveyance or moving of the same after removal from the conveyance without a removal licence	<RM20, 000 fine or <5 years imprisonment or both
	23(1)	Tampering of dangerous drugs and undermining the packaging	<RM20, 000 fine or <5 years imprisonment or both
	24(1)	Causing or procuring the diversion of dangerous drugs to any destination other than its original consigned destination	<RM20, 000 fine or <5 years imprisonment or both
General	28	Obstructing an inspection, entry and or search of premises or conveyance, or seizure of anything for which there is reasonable ground for suspecting that an offence under the Act has been or is being committed	<RM 2,000 fine or <1 year imprisonment or both
	32	Making false declaration for purposes of obtaining a licence/permit under the Act	<RM 2,000 fine or <1 year imprisonment or both
	33	Abetting and attempting the commission of an offence under the Act or act preparatory thereto	As provided for such offence
	34	Abetting in Malaysia the commission of an offence abroad or act preparatory thereto of correspondingly law that would constituted an offence if committed in Malaysia	As provided for such offence
	35	Liability of every officers/person concerned in the management of the company; liability of principal for acts committed by his agents or servants in the course of his employment, and the liability of the servant and agent themselves	As provided for such offence

Table 2
Amendments to Procedures and Evidence

Section	*Procedure*
3C (2)	- Seizure and forfeiture of dangerous drugs and goods used in the offence (Add: Act 64/ 1966); - Seizure and forfeiture of all conveyances used in the commission of drug offences irrespective of knowledge, consent or connivance (Amd: A194/1973)
37A	- Procedural admissibility of statements made under the Act at trial (Add:293/75); - Procedural admissibility of statements made under the Criminal Procedure Code to be admissible under the Dangerous Drugs Act 1952 (Amd: 553/83)
41A	Abolish jury trial and preliminary inquiry in the High Court. Trial is by a judge sitting alone. (Add 426/78)
41	- Amendments giving Sessions Court jurisdiction to try all drug offences except for trafficking cases that carry the death penalty (Amd. Act 426/78) - Amendment to give Magistrate like jurisdiction with custodial sentence limited to 5 years (Amd. Act 553/83)
41B	Certain drug offences were made unbailable (Add: 426/78)
31A	Medical examination of arrested person (Add 553/83)
31B	Further detention (up to 15 days) of suspected offender where investigation could not be completed within 24 hours. (Add: 553/83)
27A	Intercept any postal article or telegraphic message or telephonic conversations (Add: 553/83)
31	Offences under the Act are deemed seizable and arrest could be effected without a warrant (Amd: Act 553/83)
40A (1)	Agent provocateur shall not be presumed unworthy of credit (Add: 390/ 77) and (Am:596/84)
40A(2)	Statements made to agent provocateur who is a police officer by person subsequently charged to be admissible (Add:Act 596/84)
27A Add:553/83	Power to intercept communication and the admissibility of such evidence at trial (Add: 553/83)

the charge, prosecution under the section requires the consent of the Public Prosecutor.[30] In 1983, the Malaysian government, contemporaneously with its declaration that drug misuse is a threat to its national security, amended section 39B of the Dangerous Drugs Act 1952, making the death penalty the only punishment for trafficking. The government when moving the Bill noted that life imprisonment and whipping were not an effective deterrent against drug trafficking activities, which were increasing between 1980 and 1983. The government took note that the drug menace had spread wide and affected people of all races and ages. It leads to moral decadence, loss of self-respect, crimes and drug-related crimes. To the government, drug traffickers were nothing more than heinous human beings who commit murder and long-term torture. The drug traffickers were considered as traders of death, destruction and misery. Their acts were regarded as acts of treason, and hence could not be pardoned or sympathized.[31]

Possession

In 1973, a new section 39A was added in the Dangerous Drugs Act 1952, prescribing a minimum three years to a maximum of fourteen years imprisonment for unauthorized import or export of dangerous drugs, namely morphine or heroin of 5 grammes or more in weight.[32] Additional punishment of whipping of not less than six strokes was added to section 39A in 1975. Section 39A was substituted in 1983 for offences under the Act where the subject matter is heroin or morphine of 5 grammes or more in weight, or prepared opium or raw opium weighing 250 grammes or more in weight. Imprisonment is between 5 years to life with whipping of not less than six strokes.[33]

In 1986, section 39A was refined and restated as section 39A(2) for offences under the Act where the amount of prohibited drugs in possession is material. Complementarily, section 39A(1) was introduced, and is meant for offences where the quantities of prohibited dangerous drugs in possession are less or nominal, and which do not warrant the same kind of treatment or punishment provided by section 39A(2). For section 39A(1), the punishment is less severe with imprisonment from two to five years and mandatory whipping from three to nine strokes.[34] Whether the offender will be sentenced under 39A(1) or 39A(2) will depend on the amount of dangerous drugs involved.

Presumptions of Trafficking

Section 36 to 37A of the Dangerous Drugs Act 1952 relate to evidence. The burden of proof that one has a licence, authorisation, exception or defence lies on him.[35] The use of presumption to aid proof is basically in section 37. Section 37(d) presumes (until proven otherwise) that a person, who has dangerous drugs in his custody or control, has possession and knows the nature of such drug. If the prosecution proves that the defendant has custody or control of the dangerous drugs, the onus is then on the accused to rebut the presumption on the balance of probabilities that he was not in possession of the dangerous drugs or that he did not know the nature of such drug.[36]

The presumption that a person in unlawful possession of certain quantities of controlled drug is trafficking in it was introduced in 1977 as section 37(da). If the accused succeeded in rebutting section 37(d), it follows that the presumption of trafficking (where the possession is of certain quantities) under section 37(da) does not apply. It also follows that if he failed in rebutting section 37(d) but succeeded on section 37(da), the proper sentence for him, if he is convicted for possession will be under section 39A, unless the prosecution proves (persuasive burden) to the contrary. Even where the defendant failed to rebut both presumption under section 37(d) and (da), the presumption of trafficking does not become irrebuttable, as the court is obliged (albeit awkwardly) as a separate exercise to consider whether the evidence of the defence as a whole has rebutted the presumption of trafficking under section 37(da).[37]

The quantities of controlled drugs required to attract the presumption of trafficking were reduced a number of times to ensure that a drug addict who possessed more controlled drug than he needs for his own personal consumption, must necessarily be presumed to be trafficking in it. Other types of drugs were added to the lists in the schedule from time to time. The Malaysian government from her experience found the amount required to trigger the presumption of trafficking was too high in the light of the prevailing circumstances. The Dangerous Drugs (Amendment) Act 553/83 assumed that a gram of heroin could make 100 to 200 hundred injections whilst an addict normally required about 4 to 5 injections in a day. It was further emphasised that a straw or tube of heroin weighs between 0.05 to 0.06 grammes and an addict never did possess more than 10 tubes or straws for his personal consumption unless for purposes of illicit trafficking. Thus, a heroin addict would at the most only need between 5 to 10 grammes for personal use. Likewise, a similar calculation was possible in cases of others. Therefore, reducing the weight from 100 grammes to 15 grammes for example to attract the presumption of trafficking was justified to redress the known defects in the law towards combating the drug menace.[38] (See Table 3).

Table 3
Presumption of Trafficking

Section	*Matters: Presumption of trafficking*
37(da)	100g or more in weight of heroin or morphine;
Add: 390/77	1,000g or more in weight of prepared opium;
	5kg or more in weight of raw opium;
	200g or more in weight of cannabis or cannabis resin (Add:390/77);
	15g or more in weight of heroin (Am 553/83);
	15g or more in weight of morphine (Am 553/83);
	15g or more in weight of heroin and morphine (Am 553/83);
	1,000g or more in weight of prepared opium (Am 390/77);
	1,000g or more in weight of raw opium (Am 553/83);
	200g or more in weight of cannabis or cannabis resin (Am 390/77)
	15g or more in weight of heroin (Am 553/83);
	15g or more in weight of morphine (Am 553/83);
	15g or more in weight of monoacetylmorphines (Am: 596/84);
	15g or more in weight of heroin, morphine and monoacetylmorphines or from any of those two (Am:596/84);
	1,000g or more in weight of prepared opium (Am 390/77);
	1,000g or more in weight of raw opium (Am 553/83);
	1,000g or more in weight of prepared opium and raw opium (Am: 596/84);
	200g or more in weight of cannabis;
	200g or more in weight of cannabis resin; or
	200g or more in weight of cannabis and cannabis resin (Am:596/84);
	40g or more in weight of cocaine (Am:659/86); or
	2,000g or more in weight of coca leaves (Am 659/86)

Treatment and Rehabilitation of Drug Dependants

Since 1977, the treatment and rehabilitation concept practised in Malaysia has been the 'cold-turkey' approach i.e. without the use of substitute drugs. Its strategy is to rehabilitate drug dependants to be effective members of society, by severing their dependency on illicit drugs and preventing recidivism. Hence, it works towards sustaining the attitudinal and behavioural change of the recovering addicts to remain free from illicit drugs. Treatment and rehabilitation in

Malaysia through opiate maintenance was stopped in 1977, because it does not eradicate dependence and could be abused. A drug dependant may have built up remarkable tolerance, hence needed a higher dosage leading to increased health risks from overdose and respiratory problems. Furthermore, it could also lead the patient to find other drugs, the moment the effects of substitute drugs lose their effect (it may well be due to smaller dosage of the *methadone* itself). There is also no guarantee especially of drug addicts undergoing outpatient maintenance treatment would abstain from taking drugs illicitly. Similarly, providing needles and syringes to addicts is not a guarantee that the same will not be shared or used more than once. Such a policy would also convey a wrong signal as to drug taking. Moreover, such a move is incompatible with Malaysia's policy of lifestyle free from drugs.[39] Further, maintenance on *methadone* would also not work with non-opiate misusers (e.g. *cocaine*) or multi-drug misusers making in-patient detoxification seems the only solution.

The move to reconsider the cold turkey method to maintenance on drug prescription (such as *methadone*, *subutex*) was because the current treatment and rehabilitation of drug dependants was considered a failure, and Prime Minister Datuk Abdullah Ahmad Badawi was unhappy that the relapse rate is almost as high as 90%.[40] Treatment and rehabilitation centres have been in Malaysia for quite a long period of time, but yet the relapse rate at times were 75 percent,[41] and may even be higher i.e. 85%.[42] It is now conceded that 75 to 80% of drug dependants relapse after their discharge from rehabilitation centres. There are now an estimated of 293,000 identified drug addicts in the age between 21 and 29 years old despite an awesome budget of RM200 million spent in 2005 on treatment and rehabilitation, and RM 92 million in just the first 4 months of 2006.[43] Datuk Wira Abu Seman, the deputy minister of Federal Territories said that the campaign against drug misuse for the past 20 years amounting to RM 1.3 billion failed to achieve its goal due chiefly to society 'dumping' the problem to the government alone.[44]

The government has turned around its policy almost 360 degrees to not only treat addicts on maintenance on drug therapy prescription but also to supply needles and condoms to drug dependants to control the spread of HIV. The deputy Prime

Minister, Datuk Najib Tun Razak, when opening the 30th National PEMADAM (non-governmental organization on anti drugs misuse) annual general assembly in Perak Darul Redzuan on 25th June 2005 said that harm reduction is a drastic step necessitated under dire conditions and is allowed under Islamic law. He said that there were 64, 000 people infected with HIV and that if drastic actions were not taken, an estimated 200,000 to 300, 000 people would be infected in the next two or three years.[45] The health minister, Chua Soi Lek on 4th September 2005 said that treatment and rehabilitation based on harm reduction *vis a vis* giving of free needles and condoms which was supposed to commence in October 2005 was rescheduled to January 2006 to lay down more systematic rules, training of staff and implementation. However, prescribing problematic drug dependants drug prescription on *methadone* took off as plan in October 2005. This method of treatment and rehabilitation was done in few major cities and would be monitored after six months, and if proven successful, it would be implemented nationwide.[46] The deputy health minister Datuk Dr Abdul Latiff Ahmad also said that drug addicts who have voluntarily undergone replacement therapy treatment with *methadone* can continue doing so for the rest of their lives. The therapy treatment on *methadone* was to help addicts get back to society. There were 1,200 drug addicts who had undergone for the treatment nationwide since October 2005 with 18 centres involved in government hospitals, health clinics and selected private clinics. This maintenance on *methadone* drug prescription scheme is expected to cater for 15,000 drug addicts by 2010. The deputy health minister also said that based on the National Anti Narcotics Agency, there were some 130,000 registered drug addicts in the country.[47] Off course, doctors given permission by the Ministry of Health to lawfully prescribe drug dependants on drug maintenance such as *subutex* and *methadone* should not act irresponsibly by selling to non- drug dependants.[48]

It is a fact now conceded by the Malaysian government that many and probably most drug dependent individuals take a long time to learn to live without drugs. In other words, subtle physiological and psychological changes may last long after drug withdrawal, predisposing the individual to relapse.[49] Detoxifying is the first part of the treatment and not really that difficult to accomplish, but preventing relapse or recidivism is the main problem. This relapsing condition is even acknowledged by local drug expert Dr Mahmud Mazlan that the craving for the drugs seems to be permanent, and a former drug addict may easily get tempted into taking again drugs even though he may have been free of drugs for 100 years: Drug taking, he warned, even on couple of occasions is a one way ticket to hell. He claims that drug dependence undergoing maintenance treatment on drug *Buprenorphine* prescription achieved 65% success between 6 to 12 months compared to the cold turkey method success rate of 20%. More importantly, the drug dependants are able to work and be with family members.[50] Maintenance on drug prescription as a pragmatic an effective mode of treatment and rehabilitation of drug dependence cum harm reduction is also shared by lecturer, Dr Rusli Ismail of Molecule Medication Research Institute, Universiti Sains Malaysia, Kelantan.[51] Prof Dr James Scorzelli of the Department of counselling and Applied Educational Research, Northeastern University, Boston said;

> *...Relapse is a normal part of the disease process and can be expected since it may take many relapses before a person will be able to maintain sobriety. ...high relapse rate should be expected because addiction is a disease. Another view which I adhere to, is that addiction is a learning process.*[52]

Conclusion

The Malaysia zero-tolerance policy on drugs is justified legally and morally, and is inevitable if the society is to thrive. The social, economic and health costs of allowing the drug problems to grow unabated would be too formidable for any developing country like Malaysia to bear. The law reflects the sentiment of the people that drugs are evil and call for tough measures; drug taking as a sub-culture cannot be allowed to take root in Malaysia's society. That is understandable given the long history of drug usage in Malaysia (Malaya). The Dangerous Drugs Act 1952 provides part of the tools needed to crack down on the availability of illicit drugs. Enforcement should also suppress and disrupt demand for drugs, by making street markets more hazardous and less predictable places for both users and dealers. That way 'heavy' users, user-dealers and novice users are deterred, thus producing a preventive effect. Enforcement could make an impact by making it difficult for anyone who wishes to get illicit drugs. Communities need to be protected as well from drug-related anti-social and criminal behaviour by reducing the damage that drug addicts cause to communities, and the enormous pressure it places upon local policing and criminal justice services, social care and health budgets.

It can be seen particularly for Malaysia that legalising and decriminalising drugs misuse is not seen to be an answer to the drug problem. The risk is thought too great, as the use of soft drugs could be the first step towards dependency or chronic dependency on hard drugs. The Malaysian government's approach that the drug problem has to be treated as a threat to its national security has had positive result in that the Malaysian public now perceives drug taking as wrong, whatever the circumstances. Even then, drug misuse is to this day still menacing the Malaysian society. The Prime Minister Datuk Seri Dr Mahathir (as he then was) said in May 2003 that inculcation of good values and proper education is the key to success in eradicating drug misuse in the younger generation, and severe punishment alone could not possibly wiped out the drug menace in the society. He emphasized that parents too must inculcate in their children the heinous nature of narcotic drugs if misused or unlawfully used.[53]

Permissibilty of Use of Drugs Under *Shariah*

Islamic religion enjoins mankind to take in any thing that is not harmful to him. A plethora of verses of the holy Quran explicitly discussed about what is consumable for its harm-free and what should be abstained from for its harmfulness. Allah SWT mentioned in various verses of the holy quran of which some of them are as follows;

1. In surah Al-baqarah 2:168

   "O ye people! Eat of what is on earth, Lawful and good; and do not follow the footsteps of the evil one, for he is to you an avowed enemy".
2. In Quran 7:32

   "Say: Who hath forbidden the beautiful (gifts) of Allah, which He hath produced for His servants, and the things, clean and pure, (which He hath provided) for sustenance? Say: They are, in the life of this world, for those who believe, (and) purely for them on the Day of Judgment. Thus do We explain the signs in detail for those who understand".

3. In Quran 5:90
"O ye who believe! Intoxicants and gambling, (dedication of) stones, and (divination by) arrows, are an abomination,-of Satan's handwork: eschew such (abomination), that ye may prosper."

The Position of Islam in Curing with Haram

It is imperative to reiterate that Islam does not only legalize treatment of diseases but also urges and enjoins on it. This assertion can be well buttressed by both practical and theoretical prophetic traditions. Example of the practical; 1-Hadith, that Angel Jibril came to the Prophet while he was sick and said," May be your body has some complaint"? Then he (JIBRIL) did "Ruqyah" for him.[54]

Examples of the theoretical proofs are; 1-The Prophet (PBUH) was reported to have said, "you should seek for treatment but do not treat yourself with haram"[55] 2-In another hadith, the Prophet (PBUH) said fire is from the hotness of 'Jahannam' when any of you find that, he should chill it with water.[56]

Procurement of Cure by Using Alcohol and Dangerous Drugs

The early Muslim scholars did not mention hard drugs in their discussions on various intoxicants. All one can find in their inked-intellectual heritage is alcoholic drinks and other intoxicants made from "grapes" and other beverages. Their non discussion of hard drugs which are rather called in Arabic "Al-mukhaddirat" (nacortics) is subject to its non existence in their own time. But, they extensively discussed the prohibition of alcohol in curing diseases based on the hadith of the Prophet (PBUH) that are expressively against that. Viz;1-In his prohibiting the use of alcohol in the procurement of cure, the Prophet (PBUH) said "it (alcohol) is a disease and not a cure"[57]. 2-Another hadith, the prophet (PBUH) said "ALLAH did not put cure in what He has made unlawful to you[58]."

Drugs Misuse and the *Shariah*

As the focal of these paper is about knowing the stance of Islamic law regarding drugs misuse, it will augur well to give a brief historical background of the know-about of dangerous drugs which are termed as "Al-mukhaddirat" in the Muslim world. Thus, Ibnu Taimiyyah submitted that "Al-mukhaddirat" (narcotics) first came into existence in the Muslim world in the late sixth century of Hijrah calendar. He also stated that it became known to the Muslim with the" Tatarian" invasion,[59] this, as clarified by Al-imam Al-dhahbi, a renowned Muslim historian, took place in the year 606 of hijrah.[60] Which ever the exact date of its emergence in the Muslim world, the undisputable claim is that, it was neither known to the early jurists nor exists in their era as implied by the statements of the aforementioned scholars. Be that as it may, some of these jurists have presumed it to be alcohol by making Qiyas (analogy) of dangerous drugs to "Al-khamr" having found that it has the same ratio decidendi with "Al-khamr" and they declared the consumer to be liable for *shariah* penalty akin to that of consumer of Al-khamru. While some have a dissenting opinion and opined that ta'zir (reprimanding) will suffice[61].

However, these forbidden substances enjoy legal aids at times by taking shelter under the canopy of "Dharurah"(necessity). In order not to digress, the paper will be limited to the applicability of "Al-dharurah"in the aspect of drugs only and not in "Al-khamr". Also, the paper will only focus on the circumstantial phenomenon that may invoke application of "Dharurah" (necessity) to act as a bona fide ground in the use of drugs.

Al-dharurah" as A Bona Fide Ground For Taking Drugs

The Ulama' have always cited the popular Islamic legal maxim "Al-dharuratu tubihu al-mahdhurat"[62]. Meaning, Dharurah (necessity) legalizes what is banned. To this effect, the contemporary scholars have permitted the use of hard drugs for only the purpose of "dharurah" with the condition that it is used under the prescription and supervision of a competent doctor.[63] They supported this with the following verse of the Holy Qur'an in surah Al-baqarah 2: 173.

> *He hath only forbidden you dead meat, and blood, and the flesh of swine, and that on which any other name hath been invoked besides that of Allah. But if one is forced by necessity, without willful disobedience, nor transgressing due limits,-then is he guiltless. For Allah is Oft-forgiving Most Merciful.*

In academic research conducted by the directorate of academic research fatwa (calling and guidance) in the Kingdom of Saudi Arabia from 25th-30th Shawwal 1394AH they declared that opium is one of the most dangerous drugs and they concluded that it is haram to take it for recreation, but permissible for medical usage subject to prescription of a sincere doctor.[64]

In addition, Prof. Dr. Wahabah Al-zuhaili, mentioned in his book, Alfiqh Al-Islami waad-dilatuhu, it is unlawful to take all types of hard drugs because of its harmfulness to the body and the sense organ citing an example with narcotic, opium and hashish (cannabis) and the like. He cited an authority of hadith reported by Umu Salmah may Allah be pleased with her who said "the prophet (PBUH) prohibited every thing that causes intoxication and slackness"[65]. "But it is permissible to take drugs that contain alcohol for the reason of "dharurah" or need, with the condition that a substitute (that is legal) is not available". "It is permissible to use drugs in surgical operation, pain relief through injection, drinking or swallowing."[66]

More interesting, Imam Al-Nawawi confirmed in his famous book, our companions-Shafii school of thought-said, "it is lawful to take drugs for anesthetization for necessity", he further said, "if there was a need to amputate ones hand that is rust-eaten, and needed to take anesthetization, two phases in the madh-hab, the authentic one is lawfulness".[67]

Notes

1. Read the thesis–Kamarudin, A. R. (2002), *Legal Aspects of the Control and Prevention of Dangerous Drugs Misuse: Comparative Study of Malaysian and English Laws*, in chapter 2: *Historical Perspective* & chapter 3: *Drugs Misuse in Malaysia*, for the details of British involvement in the Far East in the distribution of opium.
2. Desai, D.R. Sar. (1977) *British Trade And Expansion in South East Asia 1830-1914*, at pg. 26-27 & 30, Allied Publishers Private Limited, India; Tarling, N. (1962) *Anglo-Dutch Rivalry in the Malay World 1780–1824*, at pg 3, Cambridge University Press/University of Queensland Press.
3. Tregonning K.G. (1965) *Malaysia*, at pg 15, Angus & Robertson– for Australian International Affairs, London.
4. Sir Thomas Stamford Raffles claimed he founded Singapore on the 6th of February 1819. In June 1823, he left Singapore for good and arrived

in England in 1824. He died at his house at High Wood, near Hendon on Wednesday, 5th July 1826-see John Bastin, *Sir Thomas Stamford Raffles*, at pg.14, published by The Ocean Steam Ship Company Ltd, Liverpool, 1969.

5. Desai (1977) *British Trade And Expansion in South East Asia 1830-1914*, at pg. 43.

6. C. Northcote Parkinson (1937) *Trade in the Eastern Seas, 1793-1813*, at pg. 350-351, quoted by Desai (1977) *British Trade And Expansion in South East Asia 1830-1914, at* pg. 30; Holden Furber (1948) *John Company at Work*, in chap. 5: The Country' Trade of India, quoted by D.G.E.Hall (1955) *A History of South-East Asia*, at pg. 424, London, Macmillan & Co. Ltd.

7. Great Britain, House of Commons, *The Means of Improving and Maintaining the Foreign Trade*, Parliamentary Papers, C.746, VI, (1821), p. 280 - quoted in Desai (1977) *British Trade And Expansion in South East Asia 1830-1914*, at pg. 29; This revenue rose from £39 837 in 1773-4 to £78 300 in 1783-4, and in 1793 reached a quarter of a million sterling which went some way to balance the silver sent to China to pay for silk and tea; See Beeching, J. (1975) *The Chinese Opium Wars,* at pg. 26, Hutchinson & Co. (Publishers) Ltd, London; Brian Harrison (1995) *South-East Asia - A Short History*, at pg. 151, Macmillan & Co., Ltd, London.

8. Malaysia attained independence on the 31st day of August 1957 from the British.

9. Tong, Teck Ing (1975) "Opium in the Straits Settlements -1867-1909," quoted by Syed M.Haq (1990) *Three Decades of Drugs Abuse on The Malaysian Scene*, at pg 10, Universiti Kebangsaan Malaysia, Bangi.

10. See (i) section 4 of Deleterious Drugs Enactment, 1907 (Enactment No. 22 of 1907), Federated Malay States–State of Selangor. Published in the Selangor Government Gazette of 20th December, 1907, No. 31, vol. XVIII, Notification No. 908; (ii) Section 5 and 6 of Deleterious Drugs Enactment No.15 of 1938 (Government of Kelantan); (iii) Section 5 and 13 of Deleterious Drugs Enactment No. 16 of 1928 (Chapter 183)–Federated Malay States as amended by the Deleterious Drugs (Amendment) Enactment No.36 of 1936 (Federated Malay States).

11. Central Narcotics Bureau, Malaysia (1977), *The Drug abuse Problem in Malaysia*, pg. 2 and 3.

12. Rule 7 to the Chandu Shops Enactment, 1906-26th February, 1906 (Selangor Govt. Gazette of 2nd March, 1906, No. 5, Vol. XVII, Notification No. 119); Rule 7 of the Chandu Shops Enactment, 1906 -

24th April 1906 (Perak); Rule 7 of the Chandu Shops Enactment, 1906 -13th May, 1906 (Pahang): - The preceding Enactments for example permitted only an adult male Chinese into the chandu smoking shop. Section 11(i) (e) (1) & 14 of The Opium and Chandu Enactment 1919 (Enactment No. 19 of 1919 - as amended by Enactment No. 4 of 1920) states that a licence holder of a chandu smoking shop was not allowed to sell or offer for sale or delivers any chandu except to male chinese of not less than 21 years of age-Johore Govt. Gazette, 15th December, 1919. Rule 12 of The Opium and Chandu Enactment 1919 as amended by Enactment 1 of 1929 (Johore Govt.Gazette, 29th May, 1929, Notification No.308) states that no person other than an adult Chinese shall be registered as a registered smoker. Section 15(h) & 18 of The Opium And Chandu Enactment, 1931 (Enactment No. 10 of 1931) - Johore Government Gazette of 16th September, 1931as Notification 578 - prohibited the employee in a Government chandu shop from permitting or allowing any person other than an adult male Chinese to enter any Government chandu smoking shop, and unless so authorised, any person other than an adult male chinese who entered the Government chandu smoking shop shall be guilty of an offence. Rules No. 7 of the Chandu Shops Enactment, 1906 (Enactment No. 4 of 1906)-23rd February 1906 (Negeri Sembilan Govt. Gazette of 23rd February, 1906, No. 5, Vol. Xl, Notifications No. 59) prohibited the licensee of licensed premises from permitting any person into the smoking shop other than adult male Chinese. The Opium And Chandu Enactment, 1931 (Cap134) as amended by Enactment No.5 of 1931 & Enactment No. 36 of 1934 defined registered smoker as any adult Chinese registered under this Enactment or Rules made thereunder as a consumer of chandu.

13. Sir Frank Swettenham (1948) *British Malaya: An Account of The Origin and Progress of British Influence in Malaya*, at pg 255, George Allen & Unwin Ltd., London.

14. See for example, (a) Rule 2 & 3 of the Opium And Chandu Enactment (Cap 134 of the Revised Edition)-Federated Malay States Government Gazette of 21st August, 1936, No.19, Vol.XXVIII, Notification No.3603, (b) The Chandu Enactment, 1347 of Kedah-Notification 2048 in Gazette 24th March, 1934, No. 36, Vol. 10, whereby the Registers of Chandu smokers, introduced under the Rules for the Registration of Chandu Consumers published as Gazette Notification 398, 23rd November, 1929 and subsequently amended from time to time was finally closed on 31st December, 1934, except for persons who were certified by a medical practitioner duly registered in accordance with the provisions of the Medical Practitioners

Enactment, 1336, to require chandu for reasons of health, (c) The Opium And Chandu Enactment, 1931 (Johore Govt. Gazette, 28th February, 1934, as Notification No. 176), whereby the Registers for Chandu Smokers kept under the Rules in Gazette Notification No. 792 of 25th November, 1931 was closed finally on the 31st December, 1934, except for a persons who were certified by a registered medical practitioner to require chandu for reasons of health, (d) The Registers of Chandu smokers introduced under the authority of the rules for the registration of chandu smokers, published as Notification No. 525 in the Gazette of 28th January, 1929 and amended from time to time, was finally closed on the 31st December, 1934, except for persons who were certified by a registered medical practitioner to require chandu for reasons of health-The Opium And Chandu Enactment, 1931 (Federated Malay States Government Gazette of 29th December, 1933, No. 27, Vol. XXV, Notification No.9315, (e) The Opium And Chandu Enactment (Cap 134)-rule 4(g) Chandu Rules, 1939 (Supplement to the Government Gazettes of the Federated Malay States and each of the States of Perak, Selangor, Negeri Sembilan and Pahang of 30th June, 1939, No. 14, Vol. XXXI, Notification No. 3073) where a certificate from a Government Medical officer that he requires chandu for reasons of health was required to enable him to be registered as a chandu smoker.

15. Tan Cheng Lock (1947) *Malayan Problems, from a Chinese Point of View*, pg. 36-quoted by Mimi Kamariah Majid (1995) *Dangerous Drugs Laws*, at pg. 1; Trocki (1990) *Opium and Empire: Chinese Society in Colonial Singapore, 1800-1910,* at pg. 183.
16. F.M. Ordinance No. 30/1952 w.e.f. 1.11.1952 (L.N. 544/52). It repealed previous ordinances and enactments on drug control laws. See also Malaysia's Sale of Food and Drugs Act 1952, and the Poison Act, 1952.
17. Central Narcotics Bureau, Malaysia (1977), pg 2–4; Syed M. Haq (1990), pg 10–12; National Narcotics Agency (1998), *Laporan Dadah 1997*, pg 4–5, & (1996), *Narcotics Report 1996*, pg 1–2; Anti Narcotics Task Force (1995) *Narcotics Report 1995*, pg 1–2, & (1994), *Narcotics Report 1994*, pg 1.
18. House of Representatives, Parliamentary Debate, 21st June 1960; A state of emergency was declared on 12th January 1949 under the Emergency Regulations Ordinance 1948 [7th July 1948-Federation of Malaya Government Gazette, No. 12 of 1948]. It was repealed (Act A25/1963) when the emergency ended [Legal Notification 185/1960].
19. The Bangkok Accord between Malaysia, the CPM and Thailand on

24th December 1989; Berita Harian Online (1999), 8th August 1999, *Rahim Noor Letak Jawatan*.

20. National Narcotics Agency, *Laporan Dadah, 1997*, at pg 12, Ministry of Home Affairs, Malaysia; National Narcotics Agency (1997) *Kenali Dan Perangi Dadah*, at pg 48, Ministry of Home Affairs, Malaysia; National Narcotics Agency, *Narcotics Report 1996*, at pg 7, Ministry of Home Affairs, Malaysia; Anti Narcotics Task Force, *Narcotics Report 1995*, at pg 9, Ministry of Home Affairs, Malaysia; Anti Narcotics Task Force, *Narcotics Report 1994*, at pg 5, Ministry of Home Affairs, Malaysia.
21. Anti Narcotics Task Force, *Narcotics Report 1995*, at pg 4–5, Ministry of Home Affairs, Malaysia; Anti Narcotics Task Force, *Narcotics Report 1994*, at pg 2–4, National Security Council, Prime Minister's Department, Malaysia.
22. F. M. Ordinance 30/1952. w.e.f. 1.11.1952 [L.N.544/52]. The Ordinance was revised in 1980 (Act A491/80) and henceforth assumed the name Dangerous Drugs Act 1952 (Act 234). The Act was extended to Sabah and Sarawak vide P. U. (A) 157/1978.
23. Section 7, 8, 12, 15, 18, 19, 20, 21, 22 & 23 of the Poison Act 1952-Malaysia.
24. Section 6B(2), 7(1), 9(1)(b), 12(2), 14, 15(a), 16 and 47 Dangerous Drugs Act 1952; See also Regulation5, 6, 7 and 8, Dangerous Drugs Regulations, 1952.
25. Regulation 10 of the Dangerous Drugs Regulations, 1952.
26. L.N. 556 of 1952.
27. See section 39B and 6B of the Dangerous Drugs Act 1952.
28. Dangerous Drugs (Amendment) Act A553/83.
29. Section 39B(3), Dangerous Drugs Act 1952: Dangerous Drugs (Amendment) Act A293/75 (no. 1).
30. Section 39B(3), Dangerous Drugs Act 1952: Dangerous Drugs (Amendment) Act A293/75 (no. 1).
31. Read the House of Representatives (Parliamentary Debate), 2nd and 3rd Reading of the Dangerous Drugs (Amendment) Act, 24th March 1983, pg. 7404-7460.
32. Dangerous Drugs (Amendment) Act A194/73.
33. Dangerous Drugs (Amendment) Act A553/83.
34. Dangerous Drugs (Amendment) Act A659/86.
35. Section 36, Dangerous Drugs Act 1952; See also section 105 and 106, Malaysian Evidence Act.

36. *PP v. Yuvaraj* [1970] AC 913.
37. *Mohamad Radhi bin Yaacob v. Public Prosecutor* [1991] 3 MLJ 169, at pg 172–Supreme Court.
38. House of Representatives, Parliamentary Debate, 2nd & 3rd reading of the Drugs Dependants (Treatment & Rehabilitation) Act 1983 Bill, 25th March 1983, at pg 7552-7588.
39. National Narcotics Agency (1997) *Kenali Dan Perangi Dadah*, at pg 27, 63–67; See also Hough, M. (1996) *Drugs Misuse and the Criminal Justice System: A Review of the Literature*, Home Office Drugs Prevention Initiative, Paper 15 at pg 2 of 3 of Executive Summary, and pg 3 of 11 of chapter 4: Communities Penalties.
40. Berita Harian, *Malaysia Timbang Kaedah Baru Pulih Penagih*, at pg 1, 21st January 2004.
41. Berita Harian Online, *Mahkamah berhak tentukan Hukuman*, Wednesday, 6th January 1998; Singapore Straits Times, *Spruce up offices to curb drug abuse*, August 29, 1999: *http://straitstimes.asia1.com.sg/reg/mal4 0829.html*; Singapore Strait Times, *400,000 workers lost to drug abuse: KL*, August 30, 1999: *http://straitstimes.asia1.com.sg/reg/mal9 0830.html*
42. Parliamentary Debate, House of Representatives, *Melanjutkan Tempoh Kuat kuasa Akta Dadah Berbahaya (Langkah-Langkah Pencegahan Khas) 1985*, 25th April 2000, pg 39 - 89 at pg 78 82–the Deputy Home Affairs Minister disputed the survey by PEMADAM on 2, 400 residents that the relapse rate is 85%.
43. Berita Harian (Rohana Mohd Nawi reporting) Tuesday, 27th Jun 2006, at pg 17, *Hanya 25 Peratus Pelatih Pusat Serenti DiPulihkan*, in interview with Deputy Minister of Internal Security, Datuk Mohd Johari Baharun, after the launching of the International Anti Narcotics and State Anti Narcotics Carnival in Kota Baru, Kelantan.
44. Utusan Malaysia (Norizan Abdul Muhid reporting), *Kempen Anti Dadah Gagal, Kerajaan Rugi RM 1.3 Billion*, at pg 30, Tuesday 27th June 2006.
45. The Star Newspaper, *Islamic Way for Needle, Condom Programme*, at pg 2, Monday 27th June 2005.
46. Utusan Malaysia (by Sadatul Mahiran Rosli), *Jarum, Kondom Percuma Mulai Januari*, at pg 1 & 4, Monday, 5th September 2005.
47. The Star Newspaper, *Lifelong Meth Treatment for Addicts*, Friday, 10th February 2006, at pg 21.
48. New Straits Times, *New Programme to Help Addicts Kick the Habit*, at

pg 13,Tuesday, 25th May 2004; Berita Harian, *Perangi Gejala Dadah Usaha Berterusan*, at pg 17, Tuesday 27th June 2006.

49. See Bucknell and Ghodse (1991) *Misuse of Drugs*, at pg 71, Waterlow Publishers. London.
50. Laporan Shafinaz Sheik Maznan, *Ketagihan Dadah Ubah Fungsi Otak* dengan pakar penagihan dan psikiatri, Dr Mahmud Mazlan, Mingguan Malaysia, at pg 27, Ahad, 1hb Februari 2004.
51. Rusli Ismail, *Tukar Paradigma Tangani Dadah*, Utusan Melaysia, at pg 6, Thursday, 9th December 2004.
52. Scorzeli, James F. (2006) *Relapse Prevention: Strategies and Techniques*, at pg 3-4, a paper presented in the International Counselling Symposium on Drug Prevention and Rehabilitation 2006, 5th-7th September 2006, organised by Islamic College University of Malaysia in collaboration with the Ministry of Higher Education of Malaysia & the National Anti Drug Agency of Malaysia, in Crown Princess Hotel, Kuala Lumpur, Malaysia.
53. New Straitstimes, *Dr Mahathir on the Only Way to Rid the Country of Drug Scourge*, at pg 2, 20th May 2003.
54. See kanzu Al-ummal. V. 10 P: 112.
55. Majma' Al-zawa-id v. 5 p: 169.
56. see Majma' Al-zawa-id v. 10 p: 63.
57. see Sahih Al- bukhari.
58. see Sahih Ibni Al-hibban.
59. Al-siyasatu Al-shar' iyyah by Ibn Taimiyyah p: 128.
60. Duwal Al-Islam by Al-dhahbi v. 2 pp: 11,13,23,28,112. Also see Al-fatawa Al-kubrah by Ibnu Taimiyyah. v. 4 pp. 263, 264.
61. sse tab-yinu al-haqa-iq sharh kanzu al-daqa-iq v.p:196 also Al-siyaatu al-shar-iyyah by ibnu Taimiyyah p: 108.
62. See Al- asbah wanazair by Ibnu Nujaim p: 94.
63. See Islamiyyat Al-mukhaddirat waba-u Al-shuub by Dr. Fu'ad Ali Mukhaimir p: 106.
64. Mushkilatu Al-muskirat wa al-mukhaddirat by Dr.Muhammed Ali Al-Bari p: 20.
65. Abu Daud and Imam Ahmad bin Hanbal.
66. Al-fiqh Al-Islami wa-addilatu by Prof.Dr. Wahabah Al-zuhaili v. p: 2626.
67. Al-majmu' Li Al-nawawi v. p: 7.

7

Islamic Law and Modernity Conflict and Reconciliation

Hikmatullah Babu Sahib

Introduction

Recent years have witnessed increased enquiries into Islam and its laws. Questions have been raised about the rationality, applicability and compatibility of Islamic law vis-a-vis modernity. Equally remarkable is the emerging Islam-consciousness and readiness of some Muslim women to challenge the male dominated religious orthodoxy and their authorities. What is saddening, however, is that many a time these challenges have turned out little more than ugly, often scathing and generally irrational condemnation of Muslim scholars. The challenges to and criticism of Muslim scholars speak volumes about the misunderstanding of the true nature of both Islamic Law and Modernity. In a bid to understand the relationship between these two concepts, people seem to have unwittingly fallen into the trap of needlessly categorizing Muslim scholars as fundamentalists and liberals; fanatics and moderates; religionists and secularists. Such classifications do not help resolve the confusion in the Muslim mind over the significance of those two concepts and their relations with one another. Some educated Muslims feel that Islamic Laws are to be interpreted in the light of modernity, whereas some academicians stress that rather modernity has to be treated in the light of Islamic Law. Essentially, Islamic Law demands of Muslims to maintain its sanctity in every situation whatsoever, while some sections of the Muslim society want to see practical relevance of Islamic law to the changed situation. Those favoring the dominance of Islamic law in all situations are generally categorized as fanatics, fundamentalists, and orthodox according to the degree of their wanting to preserve the law regardless of any changing circumstances. As for those who call for the modernization of Islamic law, they have in turn earned on epithets like modernists, reformists and liberals according to the degree of dilution of Islamic Law they sought in the chemical solution of modernity. The fundamental dispute thus rotates around the two central realities, i.e.: Islamic law and modernity. Are they compatible or are they mutually exclusive? This article attempts to analyze the nature of the relationship between the above-mentioned two phenomena.

Defining Modernity

Defining modernity is a monumental task. This term has been used in so many ways and often used interchangeably, at times justifiably with a score of other related terms such as modernization, humanization, secularization, development, progress, modernism, humanism and secularism. Any attempt to distinguish the term modernity from these terms necessitates an understanding of lexicologically related terms such as: [a] modern, [b] modernization, and [c] modernism. The term modernity basically signifies the quality of using or willing to use very recent methods, ideas, fashion or ways of thinking[1]. Explaining the differences between these terms J. F. Wilson observes that the term 'modern' is "a correlative term: it implies what is new as opposed to what is ancient, what is innovative as opposed to what is tradition or handed down"[2]. This term is almost always taken to mean the present age. But the term "modernization" is different from the term "modern". According to Wilson, modernization is "a programmatic remaking of the political and economic aspects of society in support of the new"[3]. Thus the process of modernization remakes or reforms the traditional character of the political and economic institutions of a given culture based on the affirmation of new discoveries or innovations. In Wilson's scheme of definitions the term modernization is strictly applied only to politics and economics. As regards the term "modernism", it is linked to religious traditions. Prof. Berger defines modernization as the "growth and diffusion of a set of institutions rooted in the transformation of the economy by means of technology"[4]. As such he believes that a "modern society" does not exist, but "there are only societies more or less advanced in a continuum of modernization"[5]. Technology alone may not be considered as the hallmark of modernity. Bellah suggests viewing modernization as a "moral and religious problem"[6]. He says:

> *"Success" in modernization is always relative and transient because modernization itself is so endlessly subversive of every fixed position, no matter how great an achievement it may have been originally. There are no grounds for complacency that any society has in any final sense "solved" the problems of meaning and modernization"*[7].

It seems modernization poses a challenge to religion. But many traditionalists consider "modernism" to be the far greater challenge to their religious heritage. The term "modernism" may be defined as a "conscientious effort on the part of the participant to enlighten a particular religious tradition by accommodating or adapting to cultural or intellectual innovations of the day". The term "modernity" differs from the term "modernism". Modernity implies an intention or desire to change rather than a firm commitment to change. Modernity does not exert any pressure on religious or cultural traditions to change. Modernity may rather incorporate traditional aspects just as traditions may adopt modern concepts. Both of them "infiltrate and transform each other"[8]. Yet differences may occur between them. These differences may be caused by various interpretations of modernity. Some interpretations equate modernity with rationality and enlightenment.[9] One may not agree to this interpretation. There may be a clear conflict between modernity and rationality. A spectacular example of such a conflict is the modern practice and recognition of same sex marriage. Modernity permits same sex marriage and does not consider it as a negative affair. Is it rational to allow lesbianism and homosexuality? Only a pervert will ever consider these socially abominable practices as reasonable. Modernity appears dynamic, forward-looking, and progressive, on the one hand and is the breeding base of the new problems it brings in the name of novel achievements, on the other. Not every achievement caused by modernity may ensure the progress of society. Social progress is matched by social pathology[10]. But modernity may, at times, ignore social realities and necessities. Islamic law seeks to govern Muslims, individually as well as socially. Can there, therefore, be any possibility of adjustment between modernity and the Islamic law? Can Islamic Law totally ignore modernity?

Law and Modernity

Describing the challenges posed by modernity, Eagleton observes:

> *Being courageous was necessary part of being a warrior in the ancient sagas, whereas being brave is not necessarily part of what it means to be a soldier today. A cowardly officer is still for us an officer, at least until he is cashiered, whereas a cowardly leader for certain pre-modern societies would have been no kind cf leader at all. For them, certain virtues were essential to performing certain social roles, which is not always true of us today*[11].

This means there may be some clashes between social values and modernity as cherished by the modern world. Some modernists may look at Islamic law as incomplete and inadequate. Some of them may curiously find modern European and international law as complete and legitimate legal systems in all respects.

> *It was on these Western traditions of individualism, humanism, and rationalism and on legal principles protecting individual rights that twentieth-century international law of human rights ultimately rests.*

It is well known that the phenomena of individualism, humanism, and rationalism are all by-products of modernity. The laws are, however expected to conform to these philosophies. Many in the West feel that Islamic law is antiquated. There is, then, a need for complete reorientation of Islamic law so as to conform to the three main principles of modernity: individualism, humanism, and rationalism. Islamic law here obviously, stands misunderstood. It is not studied properly by the west. Islamic law respects human individuals but not at the expense of society. It advocates humanity in its provisions but avoids making man the deity. It obviously is based on a rational approach; its principles are all enlighteningly rational. One should not contest the idea that the modern western law consists of excesses, which ultimately hurt both the individual and the society. These excesses in Western traditions however, can easily be surmounted by Islamic law which sets a limit to absolute individual freedoms by linking human rights to those of God. Thus man, as Islam sees it, essentially moves within the orbit set by God. But, many feel that Muslims' over-insistence on following past solutions to new problems has put unnecessary restriction on human creativity. This is yet another misconception of Islamic law. An objective study of Islamic law may help one understand its true nature.

What is Islamic Law?

Many people are not sure what they really mean by Islamic Law. Does it refer to *shari'ah* or *fiqh*. An understanding of their difference is essential in defining the role of Islamic Law in modernity. *Shari'ah* signifies the absolute and immutable divine law. This law can in no way accommodate changes whatsoever. Time and space do not play any role in its formation and reformation. It rather seeks to change the human settings. The details of the *Shari'ah* are available in the *Qur'an* and the *sunnah*. *Fiqh* refers to the interpretations of the *shara'i* provisions by scholars in accordance with their time-space realities.

The *shari'ah* came down to man in fragments and stages, as the need arose. Man is short-lived and is geographically, historically and linguistically dispersed. Therefore, the Messengers of God who were given the *Shari'ah* had to be many and geographically, historically and linguistically dispersed. Some of the messages concerning *Shari'ah* were meant only for particular people and some were of universal nature. Some of those Messengers worked simultaneously but amidst different people at different places. Some of them were raised amidst the self-same people at different times. This is evident from human history.

Divine Guidance for man, i.e. religion, has to continue unceasingly as long as he enjoys the freedom of choice and action. And it has to be ever progressing and ever developing in its refinement because mankind is ever progressing and developing in the refinement of its culture and civilization. The need of further refinement of human thought and culture entailed communication among various communities and nations. And with the dawn of the era of ease, convenience and improvement in the facilities of communication, the age of seclusion of communities, tribes and nations became out of times. Therefore, the need for sending down the revealed messages exclusively to particular tribes, communities or nations became obsolete.

This brought forth the need for one single and final universal Divine Message, i.e. revealed religion, for the entire humanity. Therefore, the Divine Wisdom chose to finalize the appearance of Messengers and Prophets and their messages by sending a Final Messenger with a Final Message for the entire mankind for all the further time until the Last Day. Now any Divine Message or religion, in order for it to be final, universal and lasting, has to be comprehensive and flexible and it should abrogate, wholly or partially, the earlier messages, which were meant to guide only particular geographical, historical or ethnic tribes or communities. Only those parts thereof should be maintained that are more general and relevant to all. Islam is such a Divine message or Guidance which meets all these requirements in their entirety and claims to be the Universal hence the Final Message to the whole of mankind, and its Final Prophet (s.a.w.), who received it also claimed, in no ambiguous terms, that he was the Last of the Divine Messengers; and that he had been sent for the guidance of the whole of mankind.[12] The Divinely Revealed religion cannot be in an endless flux. Sooner or later it must come to an end. When it must come to an end it must also have its perfection. When it has reached its perfection it must also declare the inapplicability of the forms of religions existent before it. The only certain thing in this regard is the continuation of that perfection. When the Divinely Revealed Religion reached its perfection through the Prophet Muhammad (s.a.w.), the continuity of *that* perfection was ensured by the Companions, their followers, the followers' followers and the successive generations of the *'ulama'* or scholars who stand as the standard bearers of that continuity of the perfection.

Islam represents the perfection of the Divine Message. Its teachings are essentially contained in the *Qur'an* and the *Sunnah*. The *Qur'an* is the word of Allah and the *Sunnah* is its methodological and practical interpretation as available today in the form of Prophet Muhammad's (s.a.w.) recorded sayings, doings, and tacit approvals. Muslim scholars including jurists, in an effort to come up with Islamically acceptable solution to the new problems and issues, deliberated over the available principles and rulings in the *Qur'an* and the *Sunnah*. This kind of contribution towards Islamic law is known as *fiqh*. The *Qur'an* and *Sunnah* stand as originally Divinely revealed, whereas the *fiqh* represents human endeavor. The *fiqh* dimension of Islamic law may or may not be universally valid. The differences among jurists are not differences on the *Qur'an* and or the *Sunnah* but are caused by the various angles with which the jurists look at the issues concerned.

The basic doctrine of Islam is composed of two components, unity of God and unity of mankind. Both these components are interdependent. Unity of God is realized only when mankind is conscious of its position. Likewise, unity of mankind will remain elusive as long as man does not accept the Oneness of the Supreme Authority. The realization of these two objectives leads to harmony in human society. Muslim scholars who shoulder the sacred responsibility of guiding society towards its betterment never slacken in their task. They laid the foundation of mainly two theories and principles so as to maintain the sanctity of Islamic law: (1) *usul al-din* (doctrinal theory), and (2) *usul al-fiqh* (legal theory). It was explained by scholars that any effort to derive any legal ruling from the original sources (the *Qur'an* and the *Sunnah*) should be based on the above-mentioned two theories; and that an effort to derive any ruling from them without basing it on the above two theories will be unacceptable. A systematic school of law has to have a philosophy as its basis without which there will be no cohesion in its laws. Islamic law is based on *usul al-fiqh* (legal theories), which is based on *usul al-din* (doctrinal theory). Islamic law is not appreciable if it is based on *usul al-fiqh*, which contradicts any principle of *usul al-din*. That is why the differences among scholars are neither related to *usul al-din* nor to *usul al-fiqh*. Differences occur only in their application of *usul al-fiqh* to their understanding of the basic principles laid down in the *Qur'an* and *Sunnah*. Due to these differences there have emerged various schools of *fiqh* (jurisprudence).

Presently, the Muslims have adopted mainly five schools of Islamic law. The existence of these schools of law does not represent the existence of five completely different sets of Islamic law. They are all within the parameter of *usul al-din* and *usul a-fiqh.* The words of the *Qur'an* and the reports of the *Sunnah* provide room for such differences. If one look at these legal differences of scholars objectively, one may not necessarily find them contradictory to each other but rather they are applicable in different situations. This attribute of Islamic law only proves the flexibility of the law as contained in the *Qur'an* and the *sunnah.* It is this flexibility of Islamic law which saves it from being rigid. These schools of Islamic law are based on certain doctrinal constants and certain jurisprudential constants on which all of them agreed and they only differed in respect of the jurisprudential variables. These variables provide for a needful diversity within the essential unity of the *shari'ah.* These variables are based on the *quwwah* (strength) and *da'f* (weakness) of the *mukallafs* (morally responsible beings i.e. men) in respect of their *iman* (belief), *islam* (action) and *ihsan* (perfection), and their physical capability, at all different times of their life. Islamic law is also based on two sets of laws: *amr* (injunctions) and *nahy* (prohibitions), and on the two grades of *takhfif* (softening) and *tashdid* (hardening). Those who are strong have been addressed with the hardening of the law and those who are weak are addressed with the softening of the law. Both the groups of people will be considered to have obeyed the one and the same *shari'ah* from their lord. Therefore, in deducing any particular law from the sources the criteria of the schools of law rotate between the two sides of the balance, the hard and the soft on the basis of the strength and weakness of the people to whom the law is addressed. It is on this balance that each school of law reaches its jurisprudential concord in respect of the jurisprudential variables.

The Islamic jurists (*fuqaha'*) did not have any reservation against learning from or teaching to one another Islamic jurisprudence, despite the differences in their respective schools of law. These schools of *fiqh* have, accordingly not necessitated the setting up of distinct churches in Islam, contradicting each other. Muslims are rather free to chose and practice the guidelines provided by any school of law at any given time and space. For instance, in their *salat*, they can stand behind and follow any *imam* (prayer leader) hailing from any school of *fiqh.*

Despite such amity within the structure of Islam, Uninitiated Muslims have unwittingly fallen prey to their own imperfections and engaged in sectarian sentiments. This is one of the major challenges Islamic Law is facing today. *Fiqhi* (legal) bias is chiefly caused by the approach that the *shari'ah* and *fiqh* are both the same hence both of them equally sacrosanct. *Fiqh*, as has been discussed above, consists of the rules deduced by *'ulama'* from the *Qur'an* and *sunnah* to regulate the conduct of the Muslims in their multifarious avocations. Thus, it is to a considerable degree man-made. It can change and ought to change if the circumstances change or a new insight is acquired by man in respect of his life or in that of the divine commands. Therefore, the deductions made in *fiqh* through the process of *ijtihad* are not eternal. Some scholars, for example, have declared transplant of human heart and the cornea of the eyes as *divinely* prohibited[13]; some even prohibited the use of loud-speakers in the *masjid*. These opinions of some scholars have lost their validity due to changes brought about by modernity. Thus it would be unwise on the part of Muslims to adhere to the juridical decrees that have turned obsolete and stand outdated.

Modernity and Islamic Law: Conflict and Reconciliation

It has been charged that Muslim scholars have closed the door of *ijtihad* (reasoning and deliberation). This closure must be taken in the sense that the gate was closed for those who are not qualified to exercise *ijtihad*. It is unthinkable for the door to be closed because Islam has to remain a living faith[14]. Muslim scholars must be actively involved in scrutinizing new issues and challenges posed by modernity to Islamic law and exploring the boundaries of accommodation between them. For that matter, *fiqh* has to undergo changes and absorb the shock of surprises[15]. To achieve this goal there is a need to consider the differences of the various schools of law as differences of interpretations and not as conflicts.

Amin Ahsan Islahi while talking about the dynamism of Islamic law advances several examples from the daily affairs of life so as to show that there is sufficient room for adjustment between the fundamental Islamic principles as enshrined in the *shari'ah* and the *fiqh* that is ever progressive. Some of those examples are given here below.[16]

The dietary habits of Muslims are governed by certain fundamental principles in the *Qur'an* and *Sunnah*. But there are no restrictions on the ways and means to prepare, develop, and preserve food. Likewise, the dress code of man is a very important issue. The *shari'ah* has simply given some broad basic rules of dressing. As for its detailed description, it has left man free to design and trim the raiment in accordance with the changing taste and needs. Marriage is another crucial matter in human life. The *Qur'an* and *Sunnah* have laid down some fundamental rules on it. As long as these rules are observed, there is no problem for man to solemnize, celebrate and enjoy the marriage. Political life of man too has been guided by the *shari'ah* through some basic values. It grants man freedom to choose the system of government as per the changing needs of the time.

As has been said very briefly above, the *fiqh* needs *ijtihad*. It is this attribute, which makes Islamic law very progressive and dynamic whereby it can be adjusted and readjusted in any given situation whatsoever. Amin Ahsan Islahi considers *ijtihad* the cornerstone of Islamic law. The vast treasure of Islamic law stands as an evidence to its progressive nature. For this matter, *ijtihad* has always played a very crucial role. In modern times too, *ijtihad* is to be exercised so as to let Islamic law keep abreast with the changing scenario.[17]

There are many areas of conflict between Islamic Law and Modernity. However, the popularly contentious issues are related to the *shara'i* status of women and to Islamic banking. The following discussion, therefore, will focus on these two issues.

The *Shara'i* Status of Women

Under the rubric of women's status in Islam, such issues as marriage and divorce, testimony, and the impact of *qawamah* (legal guardianship) are considered among the deeply contentious. Modernist Muslim scholars like Abdallahi an-Na'im and the likes are of the view that some of the explicit Qur'anic revelations inspire the classical jurists with a variety of discriminatory laws, practices and even attitudes against women. For instance, the Qur'anic verse 4:34 ("*Men stand superior to women*") is considered as discriminatory. According to an-Na'im, the reason for this superiority of man to woman is due to his material and financial support of women[18]. Even though the verse (4:34) has been rendered variously to mean men's absolute control[19] or a degree of men's excellence over women[20], the underlying message distinguishes a division of roles premised upon the gender that offers men a degree above women. An-Na'im feels that this verse is discriminatory since it only sanctions the exercise of authority by men over women but never the reverse, because "men as a group are the guardians of and superior to women as a group, and the men of a particular family are the guardians of and superior to the women of that family"[21]. As a result the notion of women holding authority over men is legally denied by disqualifying women from holding general public office[22], including the office of judiciary, which the Hanafites allow only in civil cases[23]. But an-Na'im is of the opinion that this verse enforces the notion of the inferiority of women "that are ingrained in the attitudes and mentality of both men and women from early childhood"[24]. He suggests that this verse needs to be understood in its historical context but at the same time it needs to be re-interpreted in the light of modern society.

The statements by conservative modernists like Tabandeh and Mawdudi suggest a degree of psychological and intellectual inferiority of women. Tabandeh in his commentary on Universal Declaration of Human Rights says that "women are deficient in the intelligence needed for tackling big and important matters; they are prone to making mistakes and lack long-term perspective. For this reason, they must be excluded from politics"[25]. Mawdudi also expresses similar negativism when he says: "Women lack firmness, authority, strong willpower, and the ability to render unbiased, objective judgment"[26]. These comments certainly deride women's ability, which has no textual supports[27]. The rendition of the term *qawwam* may not necessarily always mean caretaker, keeper, custodian or guardian of women. These imports connote certain degree of negativity. The word may comfortably be rendered as "(jealously) guarding to uphold the honor and dignity of women" or as "protectors of women's honor and dignity" because of their preciousness and not due to any inherent weaknesses of women. It may be due to this fear about the honor and dignity of women that they are discouraged to judge criminal cases and work in public offices. Rahman says with reference to so-called female inferiority: "Men have functional, not inherent, superiority over women, for they are charged with earning money and spending it on women"[28] It is a functional responsibility placed on men, not as a burden but as a trust, which puts men in the position of guardian and protector. In the opinion of Nasr[29],

> *"the relative predominance given to the male function, which brings with it not privilege but rather responsibility, has not in any way compromised the view of Islam that both men and women were born for immortality, that the rites of religion are incumbent upon both of them and that its rewards are accessible to men and women alike ....*
>
> *Even in instances where certain rites are reserved for men, such as the prayer for the dead, this does not imply a particular privilege for though God has not made women responsible for such rites, He still asks them to seek to reach those highest spiritual goals that are the* raison d'etre *of such rites".*

The arrangement of men's predominance through maintaining women and in return women's obedience to men promotes gender harmony within marriage. According to Judith Tucker, "what was owed and what could be expected structured much of this discussion as the material aspects of the marriage arrangement were implemented"[30]. Tucker believes that the objective of such an arrangement between the couple is to guard against discord in the institution of marriage which may lead to greater social disarray; and that marriage is "the fundamental and basic unit of social organization and the recipe for social harmony"[31]. In other words, granting moral predominance to men creates a conducive state to cement an acceptable equilibrium between the roles and duties of men and women, both within marriage and in society, thereby contributing to the cohesive and smooth running of society for all its members[32]. This social vision created by the Muslim jurists is falling apart under the pressure of modernity. The explosive and expanded integration and assimilation of women into the economic sector coupled with their prominence in political and public affairs have increasingly blurred the line of distinction in respect of the defined roles for men and women. In the post-colonial world and since, influence of secularism on Muslim thinking has increased women's access to public life by providing them with greater opportunities for higher education and employment. This does not mean Islam did not give women these rights. Islam recognizes these rights of women. As Nasr puts it, neither "has the complementary role of the two sexes in all walks of life prevented Muslim women from participating in nearly all aspects of life, from ruling countries to owning major businesses in bazaars or even running butcher shops", nor "has the Islamic world been without eminent female religious and intellectual figures such as Fatimah...; 'A'ishah....; Zaynab....; Rabi'ah....; or Sayyidah Nafisah...."[33]. It can be seen that although man and woman are different in respect of their functions due to primarily physiological variations, they have emerged, according to the *Qur'an*, from a single primeval Self (4:1). In their basic human nature and status they are united in the bond of humanity, i.e. they are one and the same, and even in their functions they stand out as complementary to each other, and not as negation of one another. Both possess human dignity and despicableness, if one should add, in equal ratio.

If man and woman are considered as one and the same why, then, is there a difference in terms of their shares in inheritance? Is this not discriminatory? According to an-Na'im the explicit Qur'anic allocations of inheritance (vide verses 4:7-11 and 4:176) are discriminatory because "a woman receives less than the share of a Muslim man whereas both have equal degree of relationship to the deceased"[34]. The argument generally put forward by scholars to justify this discrimination is that when a daughter is married off she receives a dowry from the husband, and the apparent inequality in inheritance actually results in a real greater equality[35]. Another interesting suggestion is that since man is legally obligated to financially maintain not only his wife, but his children, including widowed or divorced daughters and infirm children, and divorced wives during their *'iddah* period, he needs the larger portion of the inheritance. This is not the usual case with woman since she is not religiously obligated to be financially responsible and she can spend the money in any way she deems fit and can even spend exclusively on her self. This, the scholars seem to have feared, may create economic upheaval which, in turn, would disrupt and create societal imbalances.

The above argument rings hollow with the modern woman. She is no longer exclusively dependent upon men for financial support and stability. She has become an economically independent person and contributes financially to her family as well. The modern nation-state has taken over the traditional role of man by claiming to provid material support to those formerly under his exclusive care. Aminah Wadud questions: "If in a family of a son and two daughters, a widowed mother is cared for and supported by one of her daughters, why should the son receive a larger share?"[36] She feels that even though the *Qur'an* does not elaborate on all possibilities, but by "providing a variety of scenarios, it is clear enough that many combinations can and do exist, which must be considered for the equitable distribution of inheritance"[37]. Anderson observes that the changed nature of the family from the extended or tribal to the nuclear creates complications in the Islamic law of inheritance[38]. In many families today, he maintains, close relations with distant cousins, aunts or uncles have been compromised and may not, in actuality exist. For example, according to *fara'id*, in the property of a parent who is survived only by a daughter and a distant agnatic cousin, the inheritors will get equal portions of share in the deceased's estate. This provision seems quite unsatisfactory. The *Qur'an* says that in the wealth of a rich man an unknown poor may receive a share, regardless of whether he asks for it or is prohibited from asking[39]. Therefore, the beneficiary situation of a distant cousin is not, then, strange. The Prophet (s.a.w.) has repeatedly emphasized on keeping and honoring blood relations [*silat al-rahm*]. He reiterated its significance even in his farewell speech.[40]

The sound arguments of al-Na'im, Wadud and Anderson underscore the need for reform in the Islamic law of inheritance. But unluckily this law of inheritance, it must be remembered, is not from the component of *fiqh* but rather it is from the *shari'ah.* The former is alterable but the latter is immutable. They have, simplistically, forgotten the fact that the *shari'ah* principles are applicable in *that* form of society, which Islam seeks to establish. The modern human society, itself a cumulative product of human weaknesses and excesses such as: greed, selfishness, arrogence and other anti-social vices, is in total disagreement with the ideal Islamic one. In an Islamic society the woman remains protected and guarded, whereas in the modern society she, despite her transient glitters stands, over time, exploited at the cruel and unjust hands of unrestained predating men. Islam seeks to bring justice to all, including woman.

Modern scholars have also overlooked the bigger picture of the society. The relentless effort to bring justice by employing woman, cuviously, often by foreign entrepreneurs at the expense of native men has resulted in many social imbalances. We have increased the number of unemployed men who are becoming a liability and threat to the immediate society. By changing the role play in the gender equation, modern society is destroying itself.

Islamic Law and Modern Banking

The Muslim world differs greatly on the acceptance and use of modern banking methods, especially on the modern practice of charging interest on bank loans. The *Qur'an* strongly condemns the practice of *riba* (2:275). The prohibition of *riba* was necessary to establish socio-economic justice. Its backdrop is a situation where if the debtor could not repay the loan on time, the lender would extend the period of repayment by doubling and tripling the amount to be repaid. Obviously this creates vast economic disparity between the lender and the debtor. This is not the case with the present banking system. Some classical *fuqaha'* consider all interests as *riba.* The usage of the term interest in conventional banking is itself misleading and more so when equating it with the concept of *riba.* The English term "interest" has equivocal application in the meanings of usury, dividends, service charges and even penalty for late payment. The closest term describing the concept of *riba* is, however, usury (which is defined as the practice of lending money to people and making them pay unfairly high rates of interest). And the term interest is defined as a charge made for borrowing money or money paid by a bank or financial institution for keeping money in an account therein. There are simple and compound interests. Simple interest is calculated on the sum of money that is invested, while compound interest is calculated on both the sum of money lent or borrowed and on the unpaid interest already earned or charged. From the above descriptions of interest it is evident that not all types of interest are prohibited in Islam. The prohibited type is that which is levied on a loan. In all other cases the interest charged may not constitute prohibition. Even the amount paid as penalty for late payment of loan cannot be, at least in theory, termed as interest. As for the amount earned through keeping the money in a bank account, it may not be considered as interest for it is not derived from a loan transaction. It may fall under dividends. As such this interest should be treated as a *halal* earning and can be utilized in any and all transactions without any restriction including for *zakat*. Because such an imposition would create doubt as to the legality of the interest earned. The restriction imposed by scholars on the use of interest thus earned is perhaps due to *ihtiyat* (caution), since they viewed interest as the equivalent of *riba*. According to Rahman, interest rates are necessary to establish a viable economic system and the charging of interest does not violate the Qur'anic injunctions condemning the practice of *riba*. He says[41]:

> *The abolition of interest presupposes the highest degree imaginable of cooperative spirit and, therefore, cannot be implemented today unless the country's economy and the production are to be left in the direst jeopardy. At present this type of Islamic spirit of cooperation is wanting in our society and, indeed, we are now at the opposite pole from the social order envisaged by the* Qur'an. *This being the case, it will become particularly impossible for the government to raise interest-free loans for its non-profit-making projects.... We, therefore, conclude that the abolition of interest in the present state of our economic development would be a cardinal error.*

Muhammad Asad strongly believes that the term *riba* as mentioned in the *Qur'an* is still in need of reinterpretation. He thinks that the system of *riba* has not been fully clarified in the *Qur'an* and *Hadith.* He says:

> *Considering the problem in terms of economic conditions prevailing at or before their time, most of the early Muslim jurists identified this "unlawful addition" with profits obtained through any kind of interest-bearing loans irrespective of the rate of interest and the economic motivation involved. With all this—as is evidenced by the voluminous juridical literature on this subject—Islamic scholars have not yet been able to reach an absolute agreement on the definition of riba: a definition, that is, which would cover all conceivable legal situations and positively respond to all the exigencies of a variable economic environment. In the words of Ibn Kathir (in his commentary on 2:275), "the subject of riba is one of the most difficult subjects for many of the scholars (*ahl al-'ilm*)". It should be born in mind that the passage condemning and prohibiting riba in legal terms (2:275-281) was the last revelation received by the Prophet, who died a few days*

> *later; hence the Companions had no opportunity to ask him about the* shar'i *implications of the relevant injunction.*[42]

The above quotation makes it very clear that the Prophet (s.a.w.) has, perhaps divinely, left the matter related to *riba* flexible so as to adjust to all economic situations.

The reintroduction of Islamic gold dinar may be considered a step towards the reconciliation of the Islamic law on economic system and the modern macro and micro economies. As can be seen in Malaysia and Saudi Arabia, several banks have adopted and are successfully operating within the banking system based on *shari'ah* principles. Prof. Nejatullah Siddiqi, an internationally recognized expert on Islamic economics and banking, has outlined a system of banking and financing which is in agreement with the fundamental Islamic principles, on the one hand and with the modern needs, on the other. What he has done represents his *fiqh* on Islamic banking through *ijtihad*. The Islamic banking system of today is essentially based on Prof. Siddiqi's *ijtihad*.[43]

Conclusion

Islamic law comprises of two elements: *shari'ah* and *fiqh*. The *shari'ah* represents the divine commands as available in the Qur'an and Sunnah. The *fiqh* symbolizes the contribution of Muslim jurists who derive one or the other ruling on a given issue, on the basis of well-defined principles of *usul al-din* and *usul al-fiqh*, all based on the Qur'an and Sunnah. To all believers, therefore, *shari'ah* does not need to be modernized, as it is immutable. Rather it should be rather understood on its own terms. True Muslims would not take the temporal world as it exists today as the sole reality and judge the relevance or otherwise of various aspects of the eternal *shari'ah* by its degree of conformity with this transition bound modern world. Nevertheless, change, undoubtedly, a constant factor, is enshrined within the structure of *shari'ah*. This is visualized as below:

The principle of gradual change, thus, is fundamental to *shari'ah*. The other component of Islamic law is *fiqh*. It certainly can help modern man apply the immutable Islamic law to the modern settings. It should not be forgotten that Islam seeks to establish a human society on its own. Islamic law is actually for that eventuality. Whatever changes a Muslim country may introduce

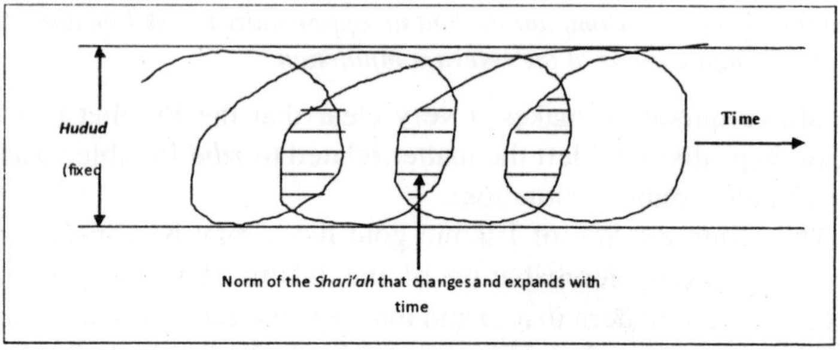

from time to time will not, however, affect the boundaries set by God. It is only in the details of its implementation that a Muslim country differs from another due to its local socio-political realities. The graduated introduction of *shari'ah* in the International Muslim society provides it the opportunity to adjust to changes introduced by it and also enables it to get the various priorities in *shari'ah* correct. Changes brought about by scientific discoveries and innovations in respect of man's multifarious activities will naturally continue to challenge the traditional positions of the earlier scholars. Muslims, however, should not feel threatened by such discoveries and begin mindlessly rejecting them outright. Instead they should actively engage in redefining their space within the divine boundaries. In other words, they can progress by reconciling with the belief that whatever is "modern" would always remain fleeting before the Eternal!

NOTES

1. *Longman Dictionary of Contemporary English*, 3rd Edition, (Essex: Addison Wesley Longman Limited, 1995), p. 913.
2. Wilson, John F., "Modernity" in *Encyclopedia of Religion*, vol. 9, edited by Mircea Eliade (New York: MacMillan Publishing Company, 1987), p. 18
3. *Ibid.*
4. Berger, Peter, *et al.*, *The Homeless Mind: Modernization and Consciousness*, (New York: Vintage Books, 1974), p. 9.
5. *Ibid.*
6. Bellah, Robert Neelly, *Beyond Belief: Essays on Religion in a Post-Traditional World*, (New York: Harper & Row Publishers, 1970), p. 64.

7. *Ibid.*, pp. 72-3.
8. Lloyd I. Rudolph and Susanne Hoeber Rudolph, *The Modernity of Tradition: Political Development in India*, (Chicago: University of Chicago Press, 1967), p. 3.
9. For detailed discussion on this see Lushaba, Lwazi Siyabonga, *Development as modernity, modernity as development*, ASC working paper 69, (Leiden: African Study Centre, 2006).
10. *Encyclopaedia Britannica*, 15th edition, Vol. 24, p. 287a.
11. Eagleton, Terry, *The Illusions of Postmodernism*, (Oxford: Blackwell Publishers Ltd., 1996), pp. 99-100.
12. *Al-Qur'an*, (34:28).
13. Ahmad, Qadeeruddin, "Ijtihad or a Built-in Mechanism for Change in Islam", in *The Changing World of Islam*, edited by Jameel Jalibi and Kazi A. Kadir, (Karachi: University of Karachi, 1986), p. 224.
14. *Ibid.*, p. 225.
15. *Ibid.*
16. Islahi, Amin Ahsan, *Islamic Law: Concept and Codification* (Islamic Publications Ltd., Lahore, 1979), pp. 19-22.
17. *Ibid.* p. 22.
18. An-Na'im, Abdullahi, *Towards an Islamic Reformation: Civil Liberties, Human Rights and International Law*, (Syracuse: Syracuse University Press, 1990), p. 55.
19. Asad, Muhammad, The Message of the Qur'an: Translated and Explained, (Lahore: Maktabat Jawhar ul uloom Publishers and Distributors, n.d.), p. 109.
20. Rahman, Fazlur, *Major Themes of the Qur'an*, (Minneapolis: Bibliotheca Islamica, 1994), p. 49.
21. An-Na'im, Abdullahi, "Human Rights in the Muslim World: Socio-Political Conditions and Scriptural Imperatives", *Harvard Human Rights Journal* 31 (1990), p. 37.
22. *Ibid.*, pp. 37-8.
23. An-Na'im, *Reformation*, *op. cit.*, p. 88. The Hanafite position is based on the limited competence accorded to women as witness in both civil and commercial transactions. Thus they are equally competent to function as judge in similar cases.
24. An-Na'im, *Human Rights*, *op.cit.*, p. 39.
25. Tabandeh, Sultanhussein, *A Muslim Commentary on the Universal*

Declaration of Human Rights, (London: F. T. Goulding and Co., 1970), p. 51.

26. Mawdudi, Abu'l A'la, *Purdah and the Status of Women in Islam*, (Lahore: Islamic Publications, 1979), p. 120.
27. Obviously the stands of both Tabandeh and Mawdudi are based on some textual sources. Their reliance on those *hadiths* portraying women as deficient in intellect (*naqisat al-'aql*), as the majority inhabitants of hell, the non-prosperity resulting from entrusting worldly affairs to women, the interruption caused by the crossing of dog, ass and women, and similar statements, purportedly from the Prophet, is unmistakably prejudicial. The truth or otherwise of these *hadiths* needs to be sieved, in the light of the Prophet's love and respect for women, from the prejudicial historical debris. The possibility of willful suppression of truth, out of ignorance or the sheer hatred for women might have had influenced the narrators of such hadiths. Mernissi's bold, candid and critical appraisal of these *hadiths* shed sufficient evidence to question the continued reliance on them as valid sources. See, Mernissi, Fatima, *Women and Islam: An Historical and Theological Enquiry*, (Oxford: Basil Blackwell, 1991).
28. Rahman, *Themes*, *op.cit.*, p. 49.
29. Nasr, Seyyed Hossein, *Traditional Islam in the Modern World*, (London/New York: Kegan Paul International, 1990), pp. 54-5.
30. Tucker, Judith, *In the House of Law*, (Berkeley: University of California Press, 1998), p. 52.
31. *Ibid.*, p. 40.
32. *Ibid.*, p. 66.
33. *Nasr*, *op.cit.*, p. 54.
34. An-Na'im, *Reformation*, op.cit., p. 176.
35. Rahman, *Major Themes*, *op.cit.*, p. 51.
36. Wadud, Amina, *Qur'an and Woman: Rereading the Sacred Text from a Woman's Perspective*, (Oxford: Oxford University Press, 1999), p. 87.
37. *Ibid.*
38. Anderson, James Norman D., *Law Reform in the Muslim World*, (London: The Athlone Press, 1976), p. 70.
39. *Al-Qur'an*, (51:19) and (70: 25).
40. Sarwar, Hafiz Ghulam, *Muhammad: The Holy Prophet*, (Lahore: Sh. Muhammad Ashraf, 1980), p. 359.

41. Rahman, Fazlur, "Riba and Interest", *Islamic Studies*, March, 1964, pp. 39-40.
42. Asad, Mohammad *The Message of the Qur'an* (Dar al-Andalus, Gibraltar, 1980), p. 622.
43. Siddiqi, Nejatullah, *Some Aspects of Islamic Economy* (Markazi Maktaba Islami, Delhi, 1981), pp. 91-114.

8

Jurists and Legislators in Islam: Origin and Classification of The '*Ulama*'

Sayyid Muhammad Yunus Gilani

'*Alim('aleem)*, '*Alim(aalim)* and '*Ulama*'

'*Ulama*' is the plural of ('*alim* or '*aleem*) but in usage ('*alim* or '*aalim*) is the accepted singular. Both these singulars are Qur'anic terms that are an attribute of Allah (swt)[3] in specific and of man in general, as Allah (swt) has bestowed knowledge to him.[4] An '*alim* ('*aleem*) is one who posses '*ilm*, knowledge, learning or science in the widest sense and in a high degree (*mubalaghah*)[5] or (2) one who possesses the inseparable attribute of '*ilm*. '*Alim*, the active participle of '*ilm* acquired the meaning of a scholar, learned in religious matters and '*ilm* came to be applied to the learning in general at a much earlier date.[6] However, this singular ('*alim*) is used in the Qur'an for Allah (s.w.t) alone[7] and nowhere does the Holy Book use it for man. Its plural '*ulama*' occurs only twice in the Qur'an and there for human beings only.[8] The Qur'anic use of this term '*ulama*' is similar to that of the scientist in our contemporary times and applies to persons who think over various problems of the universe:

> *Seest thou not that Allah sends down rain from the sky? With it We then bring out produce of various colours. And in the mountains are tracts white and red of various shades of colour and black intense in hue.*
>
> *And so amongst men and crawling creatures and cattle are they of various colours. Those truly fear Allah among His Servants (who) are*

> 'ulama' *[scholars or scientists], for Allah is Exalted in Might Oft-Forgiving.*
>
> *(Qur'an, 35:27-28)*

The (sound) plural *'alimun* occurs only at one place and for human beings who ponder (over the divine parables).

> *The parable of those who take protectors other than Allah is that of the Spider who builds (to itself) a house; but truly the flimsiest of houses is the Spider's house if they but knew.*
>
> *Verily Allah doth know of (everything) whatever that they call upon besides Him: and He is Exalted (in power) Wise.*
>
> *And such are the Parables We set for mankind but only the* 'alimun ('ulama' *those have knowledge) understand them (reason it out). (Qur'an, 29: 41-43).*

The plural *'alimin* occurs four times, twice as a "royal majestic" plural (21:52 and 81) for Allah (s.w.t) the One and the only One and twice for human beings (12: 44;30;22):

> *"... and we are not* 'alimin *(knowleageable) in the interpretation of dreams"(Qur'an, 12:44)*

And among His signs is the creation of the heavens, and the earth, and the variations in your languages and your colours; verily in that are signs for *'alimin* (knowledgeable). (Qur'an, 30:22)

'Ilm in the first instance, was knowledge of Traditions *(hadith)*, the *fiqh* and theology, and *'ulama'*, being the custodians of that tradition, were canonists and theologians. The agreement or consensus, *ijma'*, of the Islamic society was represented by *'ulama'*. It is they who ultimately decided the qestions of law, constitution and theology. They were a check over the de-facto rulers, who tried to tame them or purchase their favour. If a ruler succeeded in buying the loyalty of an *'alim*, the *'alim* would lose public respect provided that his loyalty to the ruler was at the cost of the spirit of Islamic law and society. In such cases the public devotion would shift towards private ulama who refused to be thus governed by the rulers. Thus two types of *'ulama*,those governed by the government and those keeping it in an awe , were found throughout the Islamic history. However ,the organization of *'ulama* was the solid unifying force behind the changing ruling dynasties.*10*

The Quran on the *'Ulama*

He it is Who has sent down to thee the Book: in it or verses *Muhkamat* (basic or fundamental of established meaning); they are the foundation (substance) of the Book; others are *Mutashabihat* (allegorical, not of well-established meaning). But those in whose hearts is *zayg* (perversity) follow (pursue) the *mutashabihat* seeking *fitnah* (discord) and searching for its *ta'wil* (explanation, interpretation, true and hidden meaning). But none knows its *ta'wil* except Allah. And the *rasikhun* (firmly grounded) in *'ilm* (knowledge) [*'ulama*] say: "We believe in it (the Book); the whole of it is from our *Rabb* (Lord)"; and none will grasp the Message (receive the admonition) except those endued with sharp mind (understanding). (Qur'an, 3:7).

And so amongst men and beasts and cattle are they of various colours. Those truly (achieve the virtues of) fearing (heeding) Allah among His *'ibad* (serving creation) are the *'ulama* (the knowledgeable scholars): for Allah is Exalted in Might Oft-Forgiving. (35:28).

Is one who worships devoutly during the hours of the night prostrating himself or standing (in adoration) who takes heed of the Hereafter and who places his hope in the Mercy of his Lord (like one who does not)? Say: " will they ever be equal those who have *'ilm* (*'ulama'*) and those who don't have? It is (only) those who (endured) with sharp mind (understanding) that grasp (receive admonition)." (39:9).

Allah will raise up (exalt) to [suitable or high] ranks [and degrees] those of you who believe and have (been granted) *al-'ilm* (knowledge) [:*'ulama*]. And Allah is well-acquited with all you do. (58:11).

The *Hadith* on the *'Ulama'*

Hadrat Abu Ummah (R.A.) reports that the Holy Prophet said: An "*'Alim* (learned person or theologian) is as much superior to an *'Abid* (worshipper) as I am superior to an ordinary (Muslim) among you; the Holy Prophet () further said: Allah, His angels and all those who live in the heavens and the earth,even the ants in their holes and the fish supplicate for those who instruct people in virtuous knowledge. (Tirmidhi).

Hadrat Abu Darda (R.A.) relates that he heard the Holy Prophet say: A person who starts his journey to acquire *'ilm* (kowledge) Allah eases his passage to paradise, and angels to express their appreciation on his acts, spread their wings and all the creatures that are in the heavens and on the earth, including the fish in the water, ask for forgiveness for an *'alim* (learned person). An *'alim* (learned person) is superior to a worshipper as the full moon is superior to all the stars. The *'ulama'* (learned) are the heirs of the prophets and, the prophets do not bequeath any inheritance (in the shape of) dirhams and dinars (wealth), but they do leave *al-'ilm* (the knowledge) as their legacy. As such a person who acquires *'ilm* (knowledge) acquires his full share. (Abu Dawud and Tirmidhi).

Hadrat Abu Hurairah (R.A) narrates that he heard the (Holy) Prophet say: This world is cursed and so are all things in it except the *dhikr* (rememberance) of Allah and that which He likes, and the *'alim* (scholar) and the *muta'allim* (student). (Tirmidhi).

Hadrat Mu'awiah (R.A) relates that the Holy Prophet said: Upon a person whom Allah desires good, He bestows understanding (the knowledge) of *din* (religion). (Bukhari *and* Muslim).

Hadrat Abu 'Abbas Sahl ibn Sa'ad (R.A) relates that the Holy Prophet said to Hadrat 'Ali (R.A.) : "By Allah even if Allah guides a single person through you that would be much better for you than a whole lot of red camels (a costly species of the camels). (Bukhari and Muslim).

Hadrat 'Abdullah bin 'Amr bin al-'As (R.A) says that the Holy Prophet said: Convey from me to the people though it may be only one verse; and you may narrate events from the accounts of Bani Isra'il, there is no harm in doing so. But a person who deliberately attributes to me something which is not true, should find out his abode in Hell. (Bukhari).

Hadrat Ibn Mas'ud (R.A.) relates that he heard the Holy Prophet say: May Allah, keep the person happy who hears something from us and conveys to others what he has heard, for sometimes the people who hear from others remember it better than the (first) hearer himself. (Tirmidhi).

Hadrat Abu Hurairah (R.A.) reports that the Holy Prophet said: One (an *'Alim*) who is asked something (about the *'ilm*) and he conceals it, (such a person) will be bridled on the Day of Judgement with a bridle of fire. (Abu Dawud).

Hadrat Abu Hurairah (R.A) relates that the Holy Prophet said: A Person who acquires *'ilm* (knowledge) which is being sought for the pleasure of Allah, with the intention to attain some worldly gains such, a person will not get even the fragrance of paradise on the Day of Judgement.

(Abu Dawud)

Hadrat Abdullah ibn 'Amr bin al-'As (R.A) relates that he heard the (Holy) Prophet say: Allah will not withdraw *'ilm* (knowledge) by snatching it from people, but it will be withdrawn as a result of the death of *'ulama'* (learned 'divines' or knowledgeable persons) as such when there will be no *'alim* (learned person), people will appoint *juhhal* (ignorant persons) as their leaders and will ask them (for guidance) and they (leaders) will issue *fatwas* (edicts) without *'ilm* (knowledge). Thus they will go astray themselves and will mislead others.

(Bukhari and Muslim)

Hadrat Ibn 'Abbas (R.A.) relates that the Holy Prophet said: A single *Faqih* (discerning *'alim*) is extremely (heavier) on the Satan than a thousand '*abid*s (ritual worshippers). (Tirmidhi)

'Ulama' Mufassirun

A *mufassir* (pl. *mufassirun*) is an *'alim* who provides *tafsir* of (commentaries on) the Qur'an, the primary and eternal source of divine guidance and way of life (*din*), first of the principles or *usul* of *fiqh*. Scanning summarily the origin and development of *tafsir* (pl. *tafasir*) and *mufassirun* Glasse in his *Concise Encyclopaedia of Islam* (p. 87) observes:

> "**Commentaries on the Qur'an:** *Commentaries which are straightforward explanations by way of background information with some degree of interpretation are called* tafsir; *allegorical and mystical exegesis is more strictly called* ta'wil. *The latter as allegory (but not necessarily as mysticism) has often, rightly, been considered extremely suspect. A standard commentary is that of 'Abd Allah ibn 'Umar al-Baydawi (d. 685/1282),* Anwar al-tanzil wa Asrar al-Ta'wil *("The light of Revelation and the Secrets of Interpretation"). It was frequently used in traditional courses of study and includes some of the more dependable opinions taken from earlier commentaries.*

> *Another famous commentary, quoted by virtually all later commentators, is the* tafsir *of Abu Ja'far Muhammad al-Tabari (d. 320/923), entitled* Jami al-Bayan fi tafsir al Qur'an *("The Comprehensive Explanation of Koranic [Qur'anic] Exegesis"). This is a vast compendium of the first three centuries of Koranic [Qur'anic] exegesis. The* Tafsir al-Jalalayn, *the commentaries of the " two Jalals", Jalal ad-Din as-Suyuti, the historian (d. 299/911) and his teacher Jalal ad-Din al-Mahalli (d. 250/864) is also highly regrded. Also important is the commentary of az-Zamakhshari (d. 538/1144),* al-Kashshaf 'an Haqa'iq at-Tanzil *("The Unveiler of the Truths of Revelation"). This commentary is Mu'tazilite and regards the Koran [Qur'an] as created.*

"All of these are based upon oral traditions of the Prophet [] and the Companions, and in particular upon the interpretations of the nephew of the Prophet, 'Abd Allah ibn al-'Abbas, called the *Bahr al-'Ilm* ("Occean of knowledge") [and *Habr al-Ummah* (The Scholar of the Community)].

"Many later Muslim scholars wrote commentaries on the Koran [Qur'an], most, if not all of them, incomplete. Some commentaries are specifically Shi'ite and others again,such as those of Ibn 'Arabi and al-Qashani, are mystical. Fakhr ad-Din ar-Razi (d. 606/1209) wrote a commentary called *al-Tafsir al-Kabir* ("The Great Commentary") which, on the one hand, is an Ash'arite answer to Mu'tazilite ideas, but which also introduced philosophical thinking into Koranic [Qur'anic] commentary. The science of Koranic [Qur'anic] study is part of the *'Ilm al-usul,* or "science of the 'roots', or principles, of law".

"Much of Islamic Koranic [Qur'anic] commentary resembles the *midrash* of Judaism in two ways: in content, because many commentaries to Biblical stories were supplied by converted Jews and are therefore, called *isra'iliyyat;* but above all in form, because the method, which is common to all traditional civlizations, is similar. A parable or story is constructed to bring out one or another intention or possibility of the text. Such commentary by parable is usually not to be taken literally, but rather as the expression of an abstract idea."

'Ulama': Muhaddithun

A *muhaddith* (pl. *muhadithun*) is an *'alim* of (the *'ilm* of) *hadith.* Together with the Qur'an, *hadith* constitutes the main principal, root or source of the divine guidance or *din*. The *fuqaha'* (*'ulama* of *fiqh*), the *qudat* (qadis) and the *'ulama'* of the theoretical as well as the applied (Islamic) *'ulum*, the religious *'ulum* as well as the social sciences, do have *hadith* along with the Qur'an as the reference, source of inspiration, instruction and direction. Historically speaking *'ilm* of *hadith* has been the earliest science developed by Muslims. Referring to *hadith*, its origin and early development Cyril Glasse in his *Concise Encyclopaedia of Islam* (pp. 141-142) states:

> *"**Hadith**: (lit. "speech", "report", "account") Specifically, traditions relating to the deeds and utterances of the Prophet as recounted by his Companions. Hadith are divided into two groups:* hadith qudsi *("sacred Hadith)", in which God Himself is speaking in, as it were, a complementary revelation through the Prophet , and* hadith sharif *("noble Hadith)", the Prophet's own acts and utterances. Hadith may enunciate doctrine or provide a commentary upon it. They deal with the contents of the Koran [Qur'an], social and religious life, and everyday conduct, down to the tying of sandlas. They are the basis, second only to the Koran [Qur'an], for Islamic law* (shari'ah).

"The most famous collections of Hadith are the *Sahih* ("the Authentic") of Muhammad Ibn Isma'il al-Bukhari (d. 256/870) and the *Sahih* of Abu-l- Husayn Muslim ibn al-Hajjaj (d. 261/875) usally called 'Muslim'. These two *sahihs,* or *as-Sahihan* (the Arabic dual of *Sahih*), are the most authoritative of the six well-established collections. The others are those of Abu Dawud (d. 261/875), al-Tirmidhi (d. 279/892), an-Nasa'i (d. 303/915), and Ibn Maja (d. 273/886). These make up the "six books" (*al-kutub as-sittah);* however, equally famous are the *Muwatta* of Malik ibn Anas, the first collection ever written down, and the *Musnad* of Ibn Hanbal. Many other Hadith are found in such books as the *Hilyat al-Awliya'* ("Adornment of the Saints") of Abu Nu'aym. There are also a number of small collections, the most notable being the *Forty Hadith* of Nawawi, which contain those sayings generally considered to be of the greatest importance and the essential minimum for a Muslim's education.

"The collection of Bukhari and Muslim were scrupulously compiled in the first century and a half of Islam, their authenticity being proved by the criterion which the people of the time found most valid, namely an authoritative *isnad,* or chain of transmission. The method was based on the assumption that it was unthinkable for God-fearing men to lie about matters which they held sacred; each human link in the chain vouchsafed the others. If there were pesons in the *isnad* whose integrity could be doubted for any reason, however small, the authenticity of the Hadith was to that extent weakened; conversely if there existed several distinct accounts and varied chains of transmission for a single *Hadith,* its authenticity was to that extent strengthened.

"The Shi'ite call Hadith by another word, *khabar* (''news'', pl. *akhbar).* For Shi'ites, the authenticity of Hadith is guaranteed not by an *isnad* which begins with the Companions, but by its transmission through. 'Ali and the Imams of Shi'ism.The Shi'ite collection of Hadith, which were made during the Buyid period from 320-454/ 932-1060, are considerably larger than the Sunni ones, and contain references to the Imams not found in Sunni collections.

"Western scholars have often affirmed that Hadith have been invented in order to justify some legal opinion or school of thought; this is undoubtedly true and even the early compilers rejected large numbers of Hadith as fabricated. However, the sceptical tendency among Western scholars at one time went so far as to reject *ipso facto* any Hadith which appeared to support a particular school or tendency. One orientalist was thus led to maintain that the Sufis had invented the saying: ''Remember Me [God] I will remember you'', since it so evidently fitted their teachings. In fact, this is not a Hadith at all, but a quotation from the Koran [Qur'an] (2:152). Even if, from a historical point of view, a particular Hadith is false, it does not necessarily follow that the opinions, practices, or doctrines linked with it are suspect. A Hadith may be false in the sense tht the Prophet never spoke the words, but nevertheless true in that it is wholly consistent with his message.

" Islam views the actions of a Divine Messenger as providential and unlimited in their inner nature. Therefore, it is with the authority of the Koran [Qur'an], which states: ''You have a noble example in God's messenger'' (33:21) that Islam bases its Sunnah upon the *Hadith* in addition to the Koran [Qur'an]. If the Hadith were to play such an important role in the developmnt of an entire civilization, their scope must be vast. Throughout the centuries, as Islam evolved, it searched out the traditions of the Prophet's life to guide the faithful in [all] situations [especially] not touched by the Koran [Qur'an]. "

'Ulama': Mujtahidun

Ijtihad literally means effort or exerting one's self. It is a technical term in Islamic law and comes from a Hadith in which the *Shaari'* (Lawgiver) i.e, the Holy prophet asked one of his delegates, Mu'adh ibn Jabal (r.a) by what criteria he would administer the regions (in Yemen) assigned to him. "The Qur'an", Mu'adh replied "And then what?" The Prophet asked. "The *Sunnah*" (or example of the Prophet), "And then what?" "Then I will make a personal effort [*ijtihad*] and act accordingly." And this the Prophet approved. *Ijtihad* is applied to those questions which are not coverd by the Qur'an or Sunnah, that is, by established precedent *(taqlid)*.[11]

However, more accurately, it is a technique and method to arrive at injunctions of the Qur'an and *Sunnah* in new and unique cases. Firstly it was used in general for individual reasoning, later it came to be applied in a restricted sense for the use of the method of reasoning by analogy (*qiyas*),[12] or legal extrapolation from the principles (*'usul*) to the specific cases. It implies the stage of the religious learning of an *'alim* to the degree of having the privilege of forming an opinion on the basis of the Qur'an and *Sunnah* and passing independent judgement in religious matters. A *mujtahid*, one who performs *ijtihad*, thus is a lawyer (qualified to have this privilege) or a Muslim 'divine' of the highest degree of learning.[13]

Every *mujtahid* can have his *ijtihad* or judgement on the religious questions. However, as he is free to use his own opinion *(zann)*, he is not considered as infallible.[14] According to a Tradition of the Prophet , a *mujtahid* receives a reward for his *ijtihad* even though his decision be wrong and receives double reward if it is right. *Ijtihad* of the whole Muslim people leads to *ijma'*, consensus or agreement and is considered unerring.[15] As a whole the Muslim people are not *miujtahid,* therefore, it is practically the *ijma'* of *mujtahid'ulama'* that is taken into account.

A few prominent *'ulama'* followed by *muqallids* (imitators or followers who did not exercise independent reasoning powers) came to be considered as *mujtahids* with the passage of time in Islamic history.[16] Next to the four Rashidun Caliphs and mujtahidun among *Sahabah* (e.g Mu'adh, Ibn Mas'ud, Ibn 'Abbas, r.a. etc.) and *Tabi'un,* the founders of the four (Sunni) legal schools *(madhahib)* are assigned an *ijtihad* of first rank[17] and some people restrict the title of *mujtahid* for these four *mujtahids* only.[18] They possessed a "right" to work out all questions from the very foundations, *usul,* using the Qur'an , the *Sunnah, qiyas, istihsan, istislah, istishab* etc. and they were *mujtahids* absolutely *(mutlaq).* The other *mujtahids* who could pass judgement on minor matters were assinged a secondary rank. They included *mujtahids fi al-madhhab,* who exercised *ijtihad* within their schools *(madhahib),* and all the *muftis* known as *mujtahidun bi 'l-fatwa* for giving legal opinions. Literally speaking all the *mujtahids* are also *muftis* in a wider sense for they are the 'givers of *fatwas (muftis).*[19] The right of *ijtihad* was held by some *'ulama'* to be the sole privilege of the four *mutlaq mujtahids* only. However, some leaders like Ibn-Taymiyyah (1263-1328) and al-Suyuti (1445-1505) claimed for themselves this right.[20] It is said that around 900 A.D it was held that the gate of *ijtihad* had been closed. There are, however, evidences suggesting a date for this closure at least two centuries later[21] when *mujtahids* like Mawardi (d. 1058), Al-Juwayni (d.1085) and his student Al-Ghazzali (d.1111) flourished. "Nevertheless, it is also clear that *ijtihad* is always necessary and unevitable because of the need to act in situations which are new or unique, or because information is lacking or competent authorities not present. As long as an individual is responsible for himself until the Day of Judgement, every believer finds himself, at one time or another,in the position of Mu'adh [Ibn Jabal, r.a] and has to fall back upon the *ijtihad* of personal decision."[22] The emergence of *mujadids* (renovators), *muslihs* (reformers) etc. in every age speaks of continuity of the dynamic tradition of *ijtihad* in this Ummah. Thus the doors of *ijtihad* actually were never and can never be closed.

'Ulama' and *Ijma'*

The Prophet said, "My people will never agree on an error". The saying "disagreement is a mercy from Allah", is also attributed to him. This seems to mean that the diversity of interpretations among the *'ulama'* "should set the consicience of the Faithful at rest by leaving them the choicee of a decision".[23] *Ijma'*, the third and practically the most important principle of the Islamic law, is based on these Traditions. Theoretically *ijma'* is the unanimous agreement of the *ummah* on the regulation *(hukum)* imposed by Allah.[24] Some *'ulama'* hold the *ijma'* to be the privilege of the Companions *(Sahaba)* and their immediate successors *(tabi'un)*.[25] However, during the historical process of Islam the consensus of *mujtahids* in various times formed the *ijma'* for they are the heirs of the prophets (A.S) according to a Tradition of the Prophet . To them falls the mission of 'binding and loosing' *(al-hal wa'l-'uqd)*. Thus *ijma'* is defined as the agreement between the *'ulama'* of a certain period. The tradition of *al-salf al-salih,* pious ancestors, is supposed to be transmitted from one generation to the other through its *ijma'*.[26]

There are three foundations of *ijma'*[27] (i) *ittifaq Qawli,* unamimous consent expressed in declaration of opinion; (ii) *ittifaq fi'li,* expressed in unanimity of practice; (iii) *ittifaq Sakuti,* tacit assent of the majority expressed by silence or non-interference, to the opinins of the minority.

"A perfect *ijma'* is possible, but is difficult to achieve because of the divergence of religious views and the lack of authority recognized by all parties. Thus *ijma'* does not mean that there are no dissenting views, but that agreement exists among a greater or lesser majority."[28] Hence unanimous opinion of *jamhur* (general public majority of the *'ulama'*) is also referred to as established *ijma'* (of the competent authorities). The tacit approval of the *'ulama'* (especially *fuqaha'*) to the opinions or practices, *vox populi* (the voce of the people) also passes on as (de facto) *ijma'* of the *ummah* (community) and *vox dei* (the voice of God). Hence voices of dissent become very important and form the trends and movements of *islah* (reform), *tajdid* (renewal) and *ihya'* (revival). A silent spectator (with knowledge) of a public error is reported to have been dubbed by the Prophet as a "dumb satan". There is also a popular *hadith*:

> *"Any one of you who sights a* munkar *(evil) should change it with his hand, if he cannot then by his tongue, if he cannot [do even that] then by his heart and that is the weakest [level of]* iman." *(Muslim)*

The doctrine of *ijma'* is of great importance. Alongwith the Qur'an, Hadith and *Sunnah* it is a basis which legitimises law. In the early formative period of the *Shari'ah* it marked the limit between the permitted and the forbidden. The silent majority, mainstream of Islam or the orthodox Muslims called themselves *ahl al-Sunnah wa'l-Jama'ah,* the poepole of the *Sunnah* and the people of *Jama'ah* (society) for they subscribed to the decisions of *ijma',* the unanimous agreement and consensus of the Islamic society.[29]

'Ulama': Muftis

The *'ulama* are regarded as the authorized interpreters of *ijma'*. It is on the basis of their *fatwa* that a judge may decide a case or an individual may regulate his personal life. A *fatwa* (pl. *fatawa)* is a formal legal opinion given by a *mufti* in answer to a problem submitted to him by a *qadi* (judge) or the simple Faithful. The *fatwas* are based on the Qur'an, the *Sunnah,* the doctrine of the (four) schools, and lastly on *ijma'*[30] and *ijtihad* generally based on *qiyas* (analogy). Two parties can go to a judge whose decision is binding or they can go by an agreement to a *mufti,* the giver of *fatwas,* and abide by his ruling.In the ideal Islamic state where *shari'ah* would rule eompletely all the precedent *fatwas* would be backed by state authority.[31]

By the 1000 A.D some *muftis* had become officials. The *mufti* was below the judge in rank, yet the judge would state a case to the *mufti* and accept his decision.[32] Some Muslim states tend to favour one or the other of the (four) legal schools. The Ottomans throughout upheld the Hanafi school, appointed Hanafi judge and admitted the *fatwas* of Hanafi *muftis* only. The other *muftis* wherever appointed were meant for the private convenience of the followers of the other schools.[33] The *fatwa,* condemning the pilgrimage to tombs of saints and even the tomb of the Prophet as a form of idolatry, issued by Ibn Taymiyyah in the fourteenth century, was perhaps the most famous in the Islamic history.[34]

'Ulama': Shaykh al-Islam

Shaykh al-Islam is one of the titles of respect and it first appeared in the second half of the fourth century. A.H.[35] This title has always been reserved for *'ulama'* and *sufis* (mystics).

This title gained most glory when it was applied to the *Mufti* of Istanbul (Constantinople) who was the chief *mufti* of the Ottoman

Sultanate/ Caliphate. There this dignity was first created by the Ottoman Sultan Muhammad II in 1453 after the *fath* (liberation) of Constantiniople.[36] The *shaykh al-Islam* was the supreme head of *'ulama'* and *muftis.* He headed the judges. His office in the Ottoman Sultanate gradually had acquired a religious and political importance and prominence unparalleled in other Muslim countries.[37] He was the most important person and European travellers have compared him to a cardinal or even to the Pope for the high authority he held in the Sultanate.[38] Stavrianos compares his position to the Supreme Court of the United States.[39]

The *Shaykh al-Islam* was formerly entrusted with the job of issuing *fatwas.* He was soon replaced by *'fetwa Emini'* to satisfy the demand for *fatwas* by private individuals. The *fatwas* relating to the questions of policy and pulic discipline had great importantce.[40] It was the duty of the *Shaykh al-Islam* to see that the laws made by the Sultan did not contradict with the law of Islam. Though appointed by the Sultan but the latter could be deprived of his office at his will.[41] However, in 1620 the Sultan deprived the holder of this office of all his powers for he did not sanction the murder of the Sultan's brother. In 1632 the Sultan had the *Shaykh al-Islam* murdered but the importance of the office was not affected.[42]

In the 19th and the 20th centuries the *Shaykh al-Islam* did not play that important political role. However, when policy required it, the appeal was made to the traditional authority of this office. Such instances are: the deposition of Sultan 'Abd al-Hamid in 1909, the proclamation of *jihad* in 1914 and the *fatwa* against the Nationalists of Angora (Ankara) in 1920. The *fatwas* of 1914 are addressed to the whole of the Muslim world. The *fatwa* of the *Shqykh al-Islam* of Turkey had a great impact in Afghanistan and India during World War I and led to tribal revolts against the British. This is a factual revelation of the pan-Islamic conception of the function of the office of the Ottoman *Shyakh al-Islam.*[43]

'Ulama': Fuqaha (Faqihs)

Islam being the complete code of conduct and a perfect religion, *al-Din,* ruling all the affairs and spheres of Muslim community, necessitated the development, formation and the codification of law and jurisprudence in the very beginning of its history. The spread of

Islam outside Arabia and the institutionalisation of the Caliphate helped and promoted the need for the formulation of *fiqh,* (literally wisdom or discernment), the jurisprudence. The *fiqh* includes all the obligations imposed by *Shari'ah* or *Shar'*, the Qur'anic law, on the Muslim as a believer, a citizen and a subject of the Caliphate.[44] From the very beginning the circumstances led to the emergence of *fuqaha* (sing *faqih*), the jurists trained in *fiqh.* They were the special scientists of law and jurisprudence.

Fiqh, jurisprudence, is the first term whose meaning has changed by limitation. It has been limited to the knowledge of ordinary legal cases including the mastery of the minute details of the origin of these cases, the disputations on them and the various related opinions.

In the early period of Islam, *fiqh* was applied to the science of 'the path of the hereafter'. It was held to bring a warning against the 'defects of the soul[92] making a person more pious and righteous. The Prophet said, "... the *faqih* [a profoundly discerning man] is he who has not induced people to the depair of the mercy of Allah;not made them feel safe [rather than urge them to repent] during the period of respite which Allah, out of patience [has] given unto man; nor made them lose hope in the spirit of Allah, nor discarded in favour of something else".[46]

An *'alim* was distinguished from a *faqih* in the early period of Islamic history. Ibn 'Umar (r.a) was considered to be *jayyid al-hadith* but not *jayyid al-fiqh.* Ibn 'Abbas (r.a) was termed and known as *'alim* in connection with the decisions handed down by Tradition. He was *afqah* in new cases which involved one's own judgement foı there was no precedent. Zayd ibn Thabit (r.a.) was *faqih fi'l-Din 'alim fi'l-Sunnah.* Sa'id al-Musayyib (r.a.) is referred to as the *faqih al-fuqaha'* and *'alim al-'ulama'.* Among the *Tabi'un* there were *fuqaha' wa-'ulama',* i.e., those who had authoritative *'ilm* of the transmission of *hadith* (Traditions of the Prophet) and *athar* (Traditions of his *sahabah*,Companions) and were competent to give *fatwa* and were authorities on *fiqh.* With regard to *'ilm* and *fiqh* both, Abu Thawr was *ahad a'immat al-dunya.*[47]

Originally *fiqh* (discernment), used for jurisprudence later on, was synonymous with *fahm* (understanding).[48] With the passage of time it came to be applied to the science including and co-ordinating all the branches of knowledge derived from the Qur'an, the *Sunnah, ijma'* and *qiyas*, the four roots. The masters of this sceince came to be known as *fuqaha'* or jurists. *Fiqh* consisted of the result of deductions derived from the sources of *Shari'ah* and the sum total of these deductions.[49] The *Faqih*, the *'alim* or scholar engaged in this field, is so much a professional jurisconsult. He is more a theologian and a moralist.[50] Since every *'alim* studied at least the principles of *fiqh* and every *faqih* had some knowledge of the other subjects of Muslim education, there could be no watertight compartmentalisation.[51] Qadis (givers of the decisions, judges) were among the *fuqaha'* who were *'ulama'* themselves.

'Ulama' and the *Madhahib* (Madhhabs/Schools) of *fiqh*

In the early period of Islamic civilization every *'alim* could be a *faqih*. In the absence of a *nass* or clear text in the Qur'an or the *Sunnah,* one could perform *ijtihad,* employ *qiyas* and *ijma'*. However, with the passage of time some definite schools of *fiqh* emerged. The 4th A.H./10th A.D. century is supposed to mark the closure of the gate of *ijtihad mutlaq* (independent and absolute *ijtihad*) and the end of the formative priod of Islamic *fiqh.* The old masters were recognised and followed as if infallible.

The Hanbali, the Awza'i and the Thawari were the most important schools of *fiqh* in the beginning. However, the Hanbalis were held to be more Traditionists (*muhaddithun*) than *faqihs.* The school founded early by the Syrian *faqih* Awza'i (d. 774 A.D.) soon disappeared and was overshadowed by the Malikis in Spain.The Qadi of Damascus who died in 347 A.H./958 A.D. is said to have been an Awza'i. The last great jurist of the Thawri school who delivered lectrues in the Mansurah *Masjid* at Baghdad died in 405 A.H./ 1014 A.D. At or about the beginning of the 3rd A.H./ 9th A.D. century some five hundred schools of *fiqh* are said to have disappeared.[52]

The Zahiri school, founded by Da'ud of Isfahan (d. 270 A.H./ 883 A.D.), was prominent in the 4th A.H./ 10th A.D. century. Like all the extremists it aimed at purification. They were known as Zahiris for they interpreted the Qur'an and the *sunnah* according to the *zahir* or apparent meaning. The school had following in Spain and al-Maghrib.[53] In Iran [and Sindh] too it had distinguished followers: *qadis* and other judicial officers.[54]

The famous historian Tabari (d. 310 A.H./ 923 A.D.) also founded a *fiqh* school. Tabari's friend ibn Shajarah (d. 350 A.H./ 951 A.D.) likewise had his own line of thought. The *qadi* of old Cairo, Ibn Harbawayhi (d. 319 A.H./ 913 A.D.), a Shafi'i, decided according to his own light.[55]

Some of the prominent jurists whose schools survive even today and stood the test of the times are Imam Ja'far al-Sadiq (d. 148 A.H./ 765 A.D.) Imam Abu Hanifah (d.150 A.H./ 767 A.D.) Imam Malik Ibn-Anas (d.179 A.H./795 A.D.), Imam al-Shafi'i (d. 204 A.H./ 819 A.D.), Imam Ahmad Ibn-Hanbal (d. 241 A.H. /855 A.D.). Imam Abu Hanifah (al-Nu'man ibn-Thabit) is popularly held to be *al-imam al-a'zam*. However, these *fuqaha* never intended to found legal schools. They never meant to make their opinions valid for ever. The names were given to these schools posthumously. "Most of the important differences between the legal schools did not outlive them. The students of one jurist often migrated to other provinces of the Islamic world- state, studied under jurists of another schools, and a cross-fertilization of ideas took place.[56] Al-Shafi'i was a pupil of Imam Malik in Madinah and a student of the Hanafi school in Iraq where he studied with Imam Muhammad al-Shaybani. His experiences led him to give opinions recognized as his Iraqi or "earlier school" and the opinions given by him in Egypt, when he settled there and changed some ideas, were known to be his Egyptian or "new schools" interpretation.[57]

'Ulama': Qudat (Qadis)

In the Islamic state of Madinah all the disputies were referred to the Prophet who solved them. Later his office was held by the Caliphs who in person looked into the disputes or appointed arbiters (*hakams*). It was the *'ilm* of the scholar in the Islamic society that replaced the wisdom of the *hakam* of the *Jahiliyya* times.[58] To W.M. Watt, it was during the Umayyad (Umawi) period that the office of judge (*qadi*) developed.[59] However, there are evidences of the establishment of the institution of judgeship (*qada'*) during the period of Rashidun Caliphs.[60] The famous *Qadi* Shurayh was appointed as *Qadi* of Kufa by Caliph 'Umar (R.A.) and flourished as such for 75 years.[61] The administrators could perform the duties of a *qadi* and decided the cases according to the Qur'an and the *Sunnah*.

It was gradually that a full-time office of *qadi* developed. He was chosen from among the *'ulama'*.[62] He was a delegate of the powers of the Caliph. For this very reason he was expected to conform to the doctrines of the Caliph. Through the passage in history even his dress points towards this delegation.[63] In the 'Abbasi Caliphate the *qadis* were tested as to their views, *mihnah* (inquisition) was set up (A.D. 833) for the purpose when[64] the Mu'tazilah held power under Ma'mun, Mu'tasim and Wathiq (827-847).[65]

Even in the beginning of the 'Abbasi period there was no full compartmentalization between the offices of the governor and that of the *qadi*. As it became too heavy for the governor to discharge all his duties, a separation between the two offices occurred. The Caliph appointed the *qadi* himself or at least confirmed the appointment.[66]

Theoretically, a *qadi* decides all the cases but in practice his jurisdiction has been limited with the passage of time to the questions closely connected with religion.[67] These include personal statute, succession, inheritance and (pious) endowments *(awqaf)*. He applied the *hudud-Allah* (Divine limits) in the criminal matters referred to him by the civil authorities. He is at once judge and notary. He is the guardian of orphans. He administers and supervises the *waqf* properly.[68]

The *qadi* has to be a Muslim *'alim* of blameless character *('adl)*. He should be well-versed in the *Shari'ah* and some *madhahib* demand him to be a *mujtahid*. However, the later times saw the *muqallid qadis* adhering only to the *fiqh* rules laid down in the books.[69]

The independence of the *qadis* was ensured by forbidding them to take presents etc. and even by avoiding engagement in trade. However, all these regulations seem to have been of little avail. The "bad *qadis*" are found side by side the upright *qadis* in the Islamic history.[70]

"Qadi (pl. *qudah*): A judge , appointed by a ruler or a government on the basis of his superior knowledge of Islamic law. This Arabic word is sometimes rendered as "cadi" in English, and produced the Spanish *alcalde*, for "mayor". The *Qadi's* decisions are binding and final. In the Sunni world, the "door of *ijtihad*", or decisions made on one's personal assessment, has been "closed", and judges are thus expected to apply only the precedents of the past in making their decisions. In practice, howerver, judges have applied new solutions (*ijtihad nisbi,* "relative *ijtihad*") to legal problems, at least by small increments, finally producing a new corpus of legal decisions; this could be called *ijtihad* by degrees. In the Shi'ite world, on the contrary, a decision is made only by a *mujtahid*, a high religious authority, and is a new "unique" decision, even if an identical precedent exists.

"The *qadi* must be free of business interests which could compromise his impartiality. Because *qadis* are subject to great pressure from political authorities, the office has sometimes been turned down by men of repute to avoid the stigma of complicity with the political power.

"Although a *qadi* is a necessary functionary for a community, many disputes are decided by civil authorities such as Shaykhs and Governors, since legal power and political authority are inseparable in traditional Islam. In West Africa the term *qadi* has a broader meaning, being sometimes used to designate any man who is well-informed on religious matters but has no official position; such a one would be called a *fiqh* in North Africa."[71]

'Ulama'- Imams

The word *imam* is synonymous with the president or leader.

> *I will make you an* Imam *to the people (Qur'an 2:124)*
>
> *...and make us* imams *to [lead] the righteous. (Qur'an 25:74)*
>
> *One day We shall call together all human beings with their (respective)* imams. *(Qur'an 17:71)*

The earlier Caliphs were used to be called *imams.* The four *Rashidun* Caliphs and the doctors of the four orthodox schools of Sunni *fiqh* are also called *imams.* The Shi'ahs use this epithet for their twelve great leaders. In common parlance it is used for the person who leads the dailyprayer and receives the revenues of the mosque.[72] In modern period as well as in the earlier periods some famous leaders were also called the *imams,* e.g. Imam al-Haramayn ("the *imam* of two Sancturies"), a title for the theologian al-Juwayni, (d. 478/1085), the teacher of Imam al-Ghazzali, (d. 505/1111), Imam Hasan al-Banna (the founder of Ikhwan al-Muslimun in Egypt) and Imam Khumaini . Since the *imams* are learned in the religious sciences or at least possess the knowledge sufficient to lead the prayers, they form a part of the *'ulama'*.

'Ulama': Mulla, Mawlawi and Mawlana

The word "*mulla*", literally means "full" and as a title it has been applied to an *'alim* whose bosom is full of *'ilm.*[73] Some scholars hold "*mulla*" to be corruption of the word *mawla,*[74] which in Arabic means the lord, the (great) friend or protector or the master. The Qur'an states that *Wa Allahu Mawlakum* (3:150; 8:30; 22:78; 66:2). The same word (*mawla*) used for Allah (s.wt.) is used for man in the Qur'an (44:41). S.R. Shafaq is of the view that this title, *mulla,* came into usage mainly in the Safavid Iran in the sixteenth century and spread to the rest of the Islamic world, especially to India.[75] However, Mawlana Muhammad ibn Mawlana Sharaf al-Din Muhammad 'Uthman (d. 901 A.H./ 1495 A.D), generally known as *Mullazadah* (i.e., son of a *mulla*), who belonged actually to Mawara al-Nahr (Transoxiana)[76] lived in the fifteenth century at Herat before Iran came under the Safavid rule. His appelation *Mullazadah* suggests that the term *mulla* had been in use even before him.

Mawlawi, is any one (*'alim*) related to the Eternal and Ultimate *Mawla*[77] (Lord or Master) i.e., Allah, hence it is somewhat synonymous with the term "divine". The great Muslim divine and *Sufi* poet Mawlana Jalal al-Din al-Rumi (d. 1273 A.D.) proudly referes to his own self as Mawlawi.[78]

Mawlana i.e., "our *mawla*" (lord or master) was used first by Anas ibn Malik (r.a.) a Companion of the Prophet , refering to Hasan al-Basri (d.728 A.D.) as Mawlana al-Hasan for "... he preserved 'ilm while as we forgot it".[79] The Qur'an has used this term referring to Allah Himself: (2:286; 9:51).

Mawlawi and *mulla* are used for any person educated in religious sciences, especially those assuming the office of a teacher.[80] *Mulla* is a title of varied usage given to officials of different ranks but generally applied to men who have received some degree of education in a *madrasah,* or higher mosque-schools. They hold generally certificates testifyng thereto. It is also a generic term applied to such officials as a class.[81]

It seems that the appelation *mawlana* has been used for *'ulama'* of greater scholarshp and capability and not for ordinary *mulla* or *mawlawi.* All the three titles have been more common in non-Arab Islamic societies where they have substituted the appelations *Shaykh, imam* and *mujtahid* generally. The term *mulla* has specially been used in Persia (Iran) and South Asia and it seems to be unknown to the Arabs. The Arabs, especially the Egyptians, used the term *mawlawi* (or even *mawlana),* for anyone related to a royal dynastiy or ruling class.[82] In South Asia, the term became an honorific appelation and was also used for leaders e.g. Mawlana Muhammad Ali, Mawlana Showkat Ali, Mawlana Hasrat Mohani, Mawlana Zafar Ali Khan, who were not religious *'alims* in the limited sense of the word but Islamic leaders in various fields of socio-political life of the Ummah. The Quranic *ayat* (quoted above) and the *'amal* (act) of an *'alim sahabi* (cited above) prove beyond doubt that using this divine attribute *(mawla, Mawlana)* of Allah (s.w.t.) as epithet for an *'alim* or Islamic leader is very much acceptable. The connotation and the context differ with the change of referent. The Quran refers both to Allah (2:143;9:117) and to the holy Prophet (9:128) as *ra'uf* (compassionate) and *rahim* (merciful).

References

1. S. R. Shafaq (1955), "The Clergy in Islam" in S. N. Fisher, *Social Forces in the Middle East,* Ithacca, p. 185.
2. H. A. R. Gibb and H. Bowen (1957), *Islamic Society and the West,* vol. I, Pt. 2, London, p. 70.
3. The Qur'an, e.g. 15: 25; 41:36; 23:51.
4. *Ibid,* e.g. 51:28; 7:112; 10:79.
5. D. B. Macdonald, "Ulama" in *The Encyclopaedia of Islam,* Leiden, Ist ed., vol. IV.
6. *Encyclopaedia of Islam,* New (2nd) Edition, vol. 3, Leiden, 1971, article "Ilm" by the editors, p. 1133.
7. The Qur'an e.g. 59:22; 23:92; 35:38.
8. The Qur'an 26: 197; 35:28.
9. The Qur'an 21:51; 21:81.
10. D.B. Macdonald, "Ulama", *loc. cit.*
11. Cyril Glasse (1989), *The Concise Encyclopaedia of Islam,* London, p. 182.

12. J. Schacht "idjtihad" in *The Enclopaedia of Islam,* vol. 3 (new edition), p. 1026.
13. T. P. Hughes (1975), *Notes on Muhammadanism,* Delhi, p. 61.
14. S. R. Shafaq, *op. cit,* p. 187.
15. D. B. Macdonald, "idjtihad" in *Encyclopaedia of Islam,* vol. 3 (New Ed.), p. 1026.
16. S. R. Shafaq, *loc. cit.*
17. D. B. Macdonald, *loc. cit.*
18. S.R. Shafaq, *loc. cit.*
19. D.B. Macdonald, *loc. cit.*
20. S.R. Shafaq, *loc. cit.*
21. W.M. Watt, *Islamic Political Thought,* Edinburgh, 1968, p. 73.
22. Cyril Glasse, *loc. cit.*
23. H. Lammens, *Islam: Beliefs and Institution,* Delhi, 1979, p. 93.
24. I. Goldziher, "idjma", *Encyclopaedia of Islam* (New ed.), vol. 3, p. 1023.
25. T.P. Hughes, *op. cit.* p. 62.
26. H. Lammens, *op. cit.,* p. 94.
27. T.P. Hughes, *op. cit.,* p. 61.
28. Cyril Glasse, *loc. cit.*
29. H. Lammens, *loc. cit.*
30. *Ibid.,* p. 101.
31. H. A. R. Gibb, and J. H. Kramers, *Shorter Encyclopaedia of Islam,* Leiden, 1953, p. 102.
32. A. S. Tritton, *Islam: Belief and Practice,* London, 1954, p. 112.
33. Gibb and Kramers, *loc. cit.*
34. A. Guillaume, *Islam,* Penguin Books. 1956., p. 103.
35. "Shaykh al-Islam" *Encyclopaedia of Islam,* vol. 4, p. 275.
36. D. B. Macdonald, *Development of Muslim Theology, Jurisprudence and Constitutional Theory.* Lahore, 1960, p. 113.
37. "Shaykh al-Islam" *Enclopaedia of Islam, loc. cit.*
38. A. S. Tritton: *loc. cit.*
39. J. J. Saunders, *Muslim World on the Eve of Europe's Expansion,* N. J., Prentice-Hall, 1966, p. 116.
40. "Shaykh al-Islam", *Encyclopaedia of Islam, loc. cit.*

41. Lammens, *loc. cit.* B. Lewis, *Emergence of Modern Turkey,* O.U.P., 1961. p. 70.
42. Tritton, *loc. cit.*
43. "Shaykh al-Islam", *Encyclopaedia of Islam, loc. cit.*
44. H. Lammens, *op. cit.*, p. 82.
45. Al Ghazzali, *The Book of Knowledge,* Trans. N.A. Faris, Lahore, 1962, p. 80.
46. Al-Ghazzali, *Ibid.*, pp. 81-82.
47. I. Goldziher 'Fikh', *The Encyclopaedia of Islam,* New ed. 1960-64, vol. 2, p. 886.
48. Al-Ghazzali. *loc. cit.*
49. I. Goldzher, *Encyclopaedia of Islam, op. cit.*, p. 887.
50. H. Lammens, *op. cit.*, pp. 82-83.
51. H. A. R. Gibb and H. Bowen, *op. cit.*, p. 81.
52. Adam Mez, *The Renaissance of Islam,* Delhi, 1979, pp. 211-212.
53. H. Lammens, *op. cit.*, p. 84.
54. A. Mez, *op. cit.*, p. 212.
55. *Ibid.*, p. 213.
56. S. W. A. Husaini, *Principles of Environmental Engineering Systems Planning in Islamic Culture...(.unpublished dissertation), California.*, p. 31.
57. *Idem.*
58. W.M. Watt, *Islamic Political Thought,* p. 41.
59. *Idem,* and Gaudefroy-Demonbynes, *Muslim Institutions,* London, 1950, p. 148.
60. P. K. Hitti, *History of the Arabs,* London, 1970, pp. 173-225.
61. Ibn Khallikan, *Wafayat al-A'yan,* Trans. M. de Slane, Delhi, 1996, Vol. 2, pp. 430-432.
62. H. Lammens, *op. cit.*, p. 102.
63. Gaudefroy-Demombynes, *Muslim Institutions, London, 1950,* pp. 152-53.
64. D. B. Macdonald, *Development,* p. 156.
65. See Prof. S. K. Hamarneh, 'Al-Mutawakkil Imam Shafi'i and the Mu'tazilites (Revivial of the Sunnah), *Hamdard Islamicus,* XXIII: 1, 2000, pp. 7-13.
66. A. Mez, *op. cit.*, pp. 216.

67. Gibb and Kramers, *Shorter Encyclopaedia of Islam.* p. 201.
68. H. Lammens, *loc. cit.*
69. Gibb and Kramers, *loc. cit.*
70. *Idem.*
71. Cyril Glasse. *op. cit,* pp. 320-21.
72. T. P. Hughes, *op. cit.,* p. 156.
73. K. Niyazi, *Islam Hamara Rahnuma Hay,* Delhi, Taj Co., 1984. p. 103.
74. S. R. Shafaq, *op. cit.,* p. 188.
75. S. R. Shafaq, *loc. cit.*
76. For biography of Mullazadah 'Uthman see Faqir Muhammad Jhilmi, *Hada'iq al-Hanafiyyah,* Lucknow, Nawal Kishore, 1906, p. 354.
77. K. Niyazi, *op. cit.,* p. 104.
78. "*Mawlawi hargiz na shud mawlai Rum Ta ghulam-i Shams-i Tabrizi na shud*".
79. K. Niyazi, *op. cit.,* pp. 103-104.
80. T. P. Hughes, *op. cit.,* p. 157; Hamid Algar, *Religion and Society in Iran,* Berkeley, 1969, p. 18.
81. W. Popper, "Mulla" in *The Encyclopaedia of Religion and Ethics,* Edinburgh, 1915, vol. III. p. 909.
82. K. Niyazi, *op. cit.,* pp. 104-105.

9

Contemporary Issues in Terrorism and their Islamic Perspectives: A Comparative Assessment

Abdul Haseeb Ansari

Introduction

Terrorism has blighted human civilizations for as long as we can remember.[1] It is hard to believe that a word like 'terrorism', which is used so frequently these days in different context in causal, colloquial, political, and legal discourses, does not have a universally accepted definition.[2] Black's Law Dictionary defines it as: "the use of threat of violence to intimidate or cause panic…" In common parlance, it is an act by which people in general feel terrified. Technically speaking, it is an act or a series of acts generally committed by an organization, or a state, which terrorize people discriminately or indiscriminately with or without an ulterior motive or gain. The word 'terrorism' is of recent origin, but terrorist acts are as old as the history of man. Initially, terrorist acts were sporadic and limited to only certain parts of the world. Now, the menace of terrorist activities knows no boundaries and the scourge of such activities is engulfing the whole world. It has become endemic. It is a nightmare to a vast majority of the world's population, especially to those living in such states that are terrorizing some parts of the world in the name of eradicating terrorism. Terrorism is a maniacal regime built on cruelty and violence that invariably violates human rights. Because of this, it has always been condemned, considered as outrageous, abominable and abhorrent, and declared illegal. The United Nations Security Council in its Resolution 1373, which was passed after the 11 September 2001 horrendous act, rightly considered terrorism a threat to international peace and security. Islam also holds the same view on terrorism. However, to consider those, who are fighting for liberation of their territories occupied by others, as terrorist has been a debatable issue.[3] But this causes difficulty, as one person's freedom fighter can be a terrorist for another person. 'Terrorism', thus, is a polymorphous term, its meaning changes with the change of situations under which acts are committed. In 1988, one international scholar noted 109 different definitions, but none among them, is considered to cover all aspects of terrorism. Laws have always been there for abatement and control of terrorism. The scope of laws is being widened with the emergence of new dimensions of terrorism, like cyber-terrorism, bio-terrorism, and economic terrorism.[4] But the irony is that the world is fighting a war against terrorism, without having a widely acceptable definition for it. This is because none of the definitions suits all. It does not mean that further attempts should not be made.[5] In fact, efforts, at all levels, are still being made to have a viable definition.[6] We need an all-encompassing definition because it is more than a mere synonym to dismay as it seeks to impose a degree of order to a subject and establishes a common frame of reference, and because due to a series of legal, political, social, and economic consequences of describing someone as a terrorist, or an action as terrorism.[7] We need to have it as it is a growing concept and relates to diverse groups.[8] In this respect, Thomas H. Mitchell writes that the word 'terrorism' suffers from the following obstacles: 1. It suffers from an implicit condemnation. 2. It is a heterogeneous phenomenon. 3. It does not take into account constantly changing nature of tactics, targets, and strategies, as well as impacts of the technological innovations such as new techniques of media coverage and advanced weapons.[9] This paper examines some of the definitions, including the one given by the Organization of Islamic Conference (OIC), for that reflects the collective will of Muslim states.[10]

All religions are for fostering peace, amity among the human kind and their ultimate salvation and reward. So is Islam. It is highly unfortunate that Muslims are associated with many of terrorist organizations around the glob, for whatever reasons. Some lopsided western thinkers and media are identifying them with Islam, which has virtually proven to be counter productive and resulted in the state of conflict between two popular religions of the world, which is differently put as clash of civilization. This perception exists even though truly speaking a vast majority of Muslims of the world is against terrorism and is fighting by all means against extremists. The paper sheds some light on this aspect of terrorism.

We know that prisoners of war (POWs) have to be treated in accordance with the III Geneva Convention Relative to Treatment of Prisoners of War 1949 (Hereinafter Geneva Convention).[11] But there are grave violations of the treaty norms of the Convention. This is because of the envy feelings of some states and their soldiers against POWs besieged their minds. Islam's teaching on POWs is against this kind of feelings, as it is based on clemency. The paper will make a humble attempt to delineate comparison and contrast of the two laws.

Inhuman treatment of POWs, humiliating them and their religions and inflicting all kinds of torture on them is also exceedingly common at the detention places, including the Abu Graib prison of Iraq and the Guantanamo Bay detention camp. This is a grave violation of the Geneva Conventions and the Anti Torture Convention, but powerful countries do not care about such laws. Islam's teaching is entirely different than this. This aspect of Islamic law will be discussed.

We have noticed that most of the detainees at various detention camps, including the detainees of the Guantanamo Bay, have so far spent more than 2-6 years, which is a sheer denial of their right to access to court, e.g. 'due process'. Islam's teaching, on the contrary, is to release them unconditional, or to try and punish them if they have committed any crime, for which they can be subjected to penalties, or to free them on payment of ransom, or to exchange them with the prisoners in their countries. It opposes to detain any of the POWs for a longer period. This Islamic law will be discussed.

In view of the predominant feeling of national integrity and protection of human rights that are invariably being threatened by subversive terrorist acts, many states have made anti-terrorism laws. Legislations generally provide, along with prescribing certain activities as terrorist acts, subjecting terrorists to stringent penalties, and for detention of suspected terrorists. But most of these legislations, especially that of the United States and the United Kingdom, are considered to have severely violated universally acclaimed human rights.[12] The worst aspect of these legislations is that they, in effect, discriminate foreign nationals from their own citizens and provide for illegal deportation. In fact, these legislations serve the interests of the state only.[13] Laws against terrorism that also provide for detention and interrogation of suspected terrorist on the basis of administrative orders are warranted. But in view of grave misuse of such laws, it is necessary to suggest for striking a meaningful balance between the state interests and the protection of human rights. The paper will critically examine provisions of some of the legislations from this point of view. This kind of preventive detention is against the Islamic teaching. Islam subscribe to the idea either try and punish or free. It opposes even normal interrogation in captivity. This aspect of Islamic law will also be examined.

To Have A Viable Definition

In spite of the fact that there exists a myriad of definitions of the polymorphous word 'terrorism', various dimensions of the word is well understood–which is the result of intellectual exercises made individually by certain experts,[14] by states through terrorism legislations,[15] and by collective efforts of states[16] through various global conventions made mainly under the auspices of the United Nations.[17] But none of the definitions is widely accepted because most of them generally cover the functional aspects of 'terrorism', or because some of them, along with this, cover only limited dimensions of terrorism. For example, most of the definitions do no encompass state terrorism; some of them are limited only to the political reasons of terrorism; some others do not consider those who are fighting for liberation of their territories as an exception to 'terrorists'; most of the conventions on terrorism merely define certain terrorist crimes and prescribe punishments for them; and some definitions, contained in state legislations, go beyond their territories.[18] Presidents and Prime Ministers of 160 countries met at the 60th United Nations General Assembly on 14-16 September 2005 and deliberated on various aspects of terrorism, including its definition, but in spite of the EU arguments in favour of adopting the Draft UN Comprehensive Convention on International Terrorism, including a legal definition of terrorist acts, consensus in favour of a viable definition could not be reached.[19] This kind of effort has also been made by the Convention of the Organization of the Islamic Conference on Combating International Terrorism 1999. The definition given in the Convention runs as: "Terrorism means any act of violence or threat thereof notwithstanding its motives or intentions perpetrated to carry out an individual or collective criminal plan with the aim of terrorizing people or threatening to harm them or imperiling their lives, honour, freedom, security or rights or exposing the environment or any facility or public or private property to hazards or occupying or seizing them, or endangering a national resource, or political unity or sovereignty of independent states." According to the Convention, 'terrorist crime' means any crime executed, started or participated in to realize a terrorist objective in any of the contracting states or against its nationals, assets or interests or foreign facilities and nationals residing its territory punishable by its internal law. It also includes terrorist crimes prescribed in the 12 international conventions already existing before it was made.[20] This definition is too wide to cover an extensive spectrum of terrorist activities. However, it does not mention about sate terrorism or sate-sponsored terrorism. We can note that the OIC Convention, for penalizing terrorist acts, depends on the state law. This will always lead to the variegated approach of penalizing such acts. Dr. Rao has rightly pointed out that reliance on the internal law of the state could create different standards for punishing a particular conduct. Further, no action against a terrorist offence would be possible when the conduct involved is not prohibited by the internal law of the interested state, even if the law of the requesting state and the provisions of the relevant international convention treated such conduct as a terrorist crime.[21] It will be appropriate to say that the definition given by the OIC Convention is of immense value it is in conformity with the Islamic teachings on terrorism and all Muslim States endorse it. It does not mean the definition contained in the OIC convention on terrorism is all encompassing and will be acceptable to all states. This definition has also been subjected to criticism.

So as to make it acceptable to a maximum number of states, it can be revised or a new definition, which does not violate the rules of divine wisdom contained in Qur'an and *sunnah* (Prophetic traditions) can be devised. Towards this end, the 1999 Convention on Suppression of the Financing of Terrorism is notable. Efforts are being made to have a Global Convention on terrorism. The UN General assembly is already discussing a Draft Global Convention on International Terrorism. It has a comprehensive definition of 'terrorism'. Although it is not acceptable to all states, it can be an alternative to the definition contained in the OIC Convention, and as it does not violate divine injunctions it will be acceptable to Islamic states as well. The author is of the opinion that further discussions should be augmented soon so that a workable and widely acceptable definition is finally reached.

Although it has been stressed time and again that there should be a universally accepted definition,[22] it is an arduous task, which suffers from numerous difficulties because 'terrorism' is a polymorphous term. Some of the difficulties that need to be hammered out amicably are:

General or Specific Definition

Definitions are either general and applicable to all kinds of terrorist acts or specific, or limited to certain acts to be considered as terrorist acts. In the first case, states or courts have more right to interpret and widen the scope of the definition as they wish. On the contrary, with respect to a specific definition, only literal interpretation is possible. The first one can be preferred, but the fear in this kind of definition is that there is possibility to determine certain acts to be terrorist acts even though the acts were committed without any such motive, or were committed by a group of people who were fighting for freeing their territory from foreign occupation, or were committed by those who are being persecuted and are left with no option but to resort to it.

However, the modern approach is the combination of both. Usually, the first part of the definition is general and the later part specifies certain acts committed within or outside the state to be terrorist acts. They include all possible kinds of terrorist acts. This part is inclusive so that any newer kind of terrorist activities could also be included. The definitions of the United States, the United Kingdom, Canada, Australia and New Zealand are of this kind. The author is of the opinion that this kind of definition should be negotiated at international level and states should be asked to bring definitions contained in their local legislations in line with this. Towards this end, the definition of terrorism supported by Muslim countries and contained in the OIC Convention can appropriately be amended, without violating the injunctions of the Qur'an and *Sunnah*, to include certain acts–in the *maslahah mursalah* (public interest)- to be terrorist acts. Muslim countries might not have any objection on it. A question arises here: will it be acceptable to non-member countries? The answer to this question is that it will be, if it is based on objective criteria suited to all states.

Judicial Solicitude

Although courts could have contributed through their decisions towards reaching a comprehensive definition suited to all countries, but they, as interpreters of law limited their activities only to interpreting and applying terrorism laws on given facts.[23] It is submitted that this attitude of courts failed to provide guidance to the legislature in various states. Justifying this attitude of the courts, Ben Golder and Jeorge Williams write that capacity for judicial flexibility does not outweigh the argument for a greater legislative role. Definition containing key features of terrorism has several advantages. These operate with particular strength given several consequences that can flow from the use of the word 'terrorism' when attached to a person, act or organization. The most important role for the legislature is that as peoples' representative and a sovereign democratic forum it can be the best place because to define terrorism is a mixed political and legal matter.[24] It can further be argued that in absence of a statutory definition, for comprehend it one will have to look into a gamut of cases; and the effort may be futile in case of lack of uniformity of approach.

In view of this, it will be appropriate to say that for an intricate matter like terrorism, legislature should take initiative to define. Judiciary's role is to evaluate the definition and interpret it properly while applying it. It is notable that the legislature always has the superiority over the judiciary, as it can abrogate any of the judicial interpretations, which restricts or widens the scope of the definition and that is not in conformity of the policy of the government.[25] On the contrary, if a judicial endeavour goes co-extensive with government's policy, the law is better understood.[26] The author is of the opinion that judiciary can guide the legislature in manifest ways. The Islamic history reveals that on many occasions, *Qazis* (judges) have guided *Ameers* through their decisions. Thus, if *Qazis* fulfill the qualifications to be a *Mujtahid* (person who does *ijtehad*), they can do *ijtehad* (developing rules on the basis of analogy), or can refer the matter to the *Fatawa Committee,* if it exists in a state, and can base their decisions on the *fatawa* (religious ruling) given by the committee. So, in an Islamic legal system also, there is ampoule opportunity to a *Qazi* to guide the state on defining terrorism. For Muslim states the OIC definition is acceptable; they will accept it even if it is suitably amended. And if it is based on objective criteria, as stated above, it would be accepted to other states also.

Objects

Terrorism as political violence possibly stems out from its root as a political term applied to the French Revolutionary Tribunals during that country's 'Reign of Terror', with terrorism's political connotations continuing to feature throughout much of its historical development.[27] It is also said that terrorism is inherently and fundamentally political in nature.[28] However, in spite of the fact that most of the terrorist activities are being perpetrated for political motives, this view is not so widely accepted. Some reject the element of motive altogether. For them, motive is not an important factor. They concentrate on the cause and effect of terrorist activities that takes lives or destroys properties or both. Thus, Eqbal Ahmad holds the view that motivations make no difference. Likewise, Jessica Stein is of the opinion that the definition of terrorism is not limited to perpetrator or purpose. To Stern, it is the 'the deliberate evocation of dread is what sets terrorism apart from simple murder or assault'.[29] Although it is said that individuals are not to be considered as terrorists, there are terrorist organizations, and individuals can be terrorists if they are perpetrating terrorism on the behest of any such organization or prompted by a state. It is argued that if individuals are perpetrating terrorism, they can be charged under terrorist legislations. The author is of the opinion that political motivation is a reason of perpetrating terrorism in most of the cases, but it does not apply in all cases. Therefore, motive is an important factor for defining terrorism.

There is another opinion that terrorism has a motive. It can be political, ideological, or economic, and the activity can be traditional or non traditional like environmental terrorism, consumer terrorism, cyber terrorism or state terrorism. Although it is argued that such a wide connotation will dilute the purpose of war against terrorism, and risks making the term so elastic as to deprive it form its functional meaning.[30]Psychological object of terrorism is also material in a large number of cases. People or state is terrorized so that they concede to the demand of the terrorists. In some cases, the sole purpose is to kill or destroy. In some other cases, the purpose is to retaliate. In the last case the motivating factor is revenge. The author is of the opinion that all these factors should be taken into consideration while attempting to have a widely acceptable definition.[31]

In Islam, terrorist acts have to be judged on the basis of motives of its perpetrators, as all human acts are to be categorized as *marufat* (virtues) or *munkarat* (vices) on the basis of the motive of doing them. However, all forms of terrorism, as it is understood, is certainly a non-virtuous act and, thus, prohibited in Islam.[32]This is because Islam not at all subscribe to kill and terrorized innocent people.

Individual Terrorist

It is widely accepted that terrorism is related to organizations that are perpetrating terrorism for a particular purpose. Individuals can be considered as terrorists when they work for terrorist organizations. To consider a single person to be a terrorist is a debatable issue. For many, he should not be considered as a terrorist and should be dealt with the criminal law of the state. However, some others subscribe to the view that if an individual perpetrates terrorism, using the method that are generally used by terrorists, for any of his own personal reason, including personal pleasure or egoistical ends, should also be considered as a terrorist.[33]

The second view is close to the Islamic *Shari'ah* on terrorism, as on the Day of Judgment, every one will have to give *hesab* individually. So, any despicable act one has committed individually or collectively will be subjected to punishment.

Means

Means that terrorists adopt for achieving their object(s) are not constant. The commonly used means now is suicide bombing, which was largely practiced by the Japanese Army during the Second World War and at times practiced by LTTE, including the ones that took lives of two heads of states. Generally, tactics adopted by terrorists do not involve heavy weapons. Those who adopt guerilla warfare tactics generally use heavy weapons. This happens in case of war. But the difficulty arises when terrorist groups also adopt this technique. Another difficulty is the use of biological weapons, and possibility of using dirty bomb or any other such weapons of mass destruction. In view of these, it is difficult to distinguish terrorist means from non-terrorist means.

The position will be the same in Islam also. In Islam terrorism, practiced by application of whatever means, is prohibited.

State Terrorism

For many, there is nothing like state terrorism. For them, terrorism is generally perpetrated by groups of individuals through their members. This is true that around the glob there are hardcore organizations, generally constituted for accomplishing political, ideological, economic objectives or to counter the intimidations and persecutions inflicted to them, and they have adopted the path of terrorism and are engaged in various means of terrorist activities. Nevertheless, a section of intellectuals believe that states are also responsible for escalating terrorism, or are directly or indirectly engaged in terrorist activities. This view can be substantiated when we turn the pages of the history or look at the causes and effects of present international terrorism. Although state terrorism had existed in some or the other from throughout in the past, during the second world war the world experienced two significant acts of state terrorism, large number of Japanese suicide bombers and the horrendous act of dropping of atom bombs on Nagasaki and Hiroshima. Creation of Israel on the Palestinian lands after the Balfore Declaration became the turning point. Ever since the creation of Israel, struggle to liberate the occupied land is continued. The action and retaliation are continual. It is notable in the whole episode that retaliations have hardly been proportionate. This trend became more serious after destruction of nuclear facilities of Iraq by Israel, the Gulf War and the horror of Sabra and Shatila.[34] It is submitted that had there been negotiations with concerted efforts made by the world community for bringing about peace in the region rather than reiterating that what Israel has been doing is its right of self-defence, there would have been entirely different scenario. In fact, the West took a lackadaisical attitude and supported wrong principle that 'offence is the best defence'. What Israel had been doing was nothing but acts of terrorism: poor and armless people were very often persecuted, arrested, killed and their properties were destroyed. This kind of attitude escalates terrorism rather than alleviating it. The author is sorry to see no change in the attitude of the West.

In the Vietnam War, thousands of hectares of mangrove forests were destroyed by the American Army presuming that forests were hideouts of Vietnamese Army. This was the clear violation of the principle of 'discrimination' of the law of war, and because of this, a large number of forest inhabitants were terrified and killed by the American bombardments. This can be classified as an act of state terrorism. This mistake was repeated subsequent wars. It is notable that so as to deter warring countries from committing such acts again, in 1977, Environment Modification Treaty (ENMOD) and 1977 Protocol to Geneva Conventions of 1949 were made. In spite of these legal instruments and the principle of 'discrimination' and 'proportionality' of the international law of war, the allied forces destroyed civilian facilities, and the Iraqi Army in first Iraq war used oil as a weapon. Both are some kind of environmental terrorism perpetrated by states. So is the case of using biological and chemical weapons used by Iraq for suppressing Qurds.

After the Afghanistan war, terrorism was dying its own death, because terrorists and states that were supporting them were demoralized and defeated. But the attack on Iraq on the false pretext and without support of the UN Security Council, which killed seemingly a large number of civilians and extensively destroyed civilian properties and crippled infrastructure, provided a justification to rejuvenate their struggle. It is more than obvious that the present state of terrorist activities in and around Iraq, including the horrendous acts of terrorism experienced in Madrid and London may have links with the Iraq war. The terrorist activities in Pakistan, including the deadly attack on the Marriot hotel of Islamabad, may have link with the *de facto* occupation of Afghanistan. Who is responsible for the present conditions in Iraq and Afghanistan? If it is true that Iran is helping one of the two religious groups in Iraq, what is it? If it is true that terrorist groups are being funded by some states, what is it? All these can be classified as state terrorism. War against terrorism has always been counterproductive. Here a question arises: Are the US, the UK and their allies are not responsible for terrorism? For many, the answer will be positive. Some others consider the attack on Iraq and killings of innocent people, when most of the Saddam's guards had melted away and the attacking forces were not facing any effective resistance, tantamount to terrorism.[35] Nevertheless, there were grave violations of the law of war and Geneva Conventions. In the continuous chain deaths occurring in Iraq, deaths caused by the US Forces and their allies are not insignificant. Moreover, the responsibility of the present state of affairs in the country is on them because the countries that attacked Iraq did not make proper calculations of the law and order situations in the aftermath of the war and did not pour in enough forces and support personnel. Excessive use of force for suppressing any movement, ideological or economic, within a state or supporting or conniving communal riots can also be labeled as state terrorism. Excessive use of force against Maoists in Nepal and in some other states are opt quoted examples by some of the western countries and Human Rights Watch. The problem is that many countries do not believe in state terrorism. They oppose the definition that attempts to consider such state activities tainted with terrorism.

In Islam, sovereignty of the state is with the Allah (*s.w.t.*). There is, thus, a representative government run on the basis of divine injunctions contained in the Qur'an and *Sunnah*. There can be man-made laws, but these laws for their validity have to be in conformity with the primary source of law. The primary purpose of the state is good to its people and cordial relations with its neighbors. It can be inferred from the divine scheme that no state can, directly or indirectly, be involved in terrorist activities. If a state is involved in such activities, the ruler will be accountable for it.[36]No state is allowed, in Islam, for establishing its might on another state, or occupying it for some ulterior objective. State is duty bound to protect the Islamic character of the state and to protect it from any foreign aggression. If an Islamic state has been attacked, holy war *(jihad)* is the option. However, at any point of time, for establishing peace, compromise (*sulh*) is a solution. Thus, those, who fight for protecting their country from a foreign aggression or foı taking it back, are, in fact, keeping up the Islamic precept. They cannot be called as terrorists.

Pre-emptive Strikes

According to international law, states have an inherent right to defend themselves against armed attacks. This is justified on the ground of self-defence.[37] The right is based on necessity and limited by proportionality.[38] It presupposes the absence of any alternative means for protection of fundamental rights of the state. Article 51 of the UN Charter, grants the right of self-defence. But this has wrongly been imagined to provide the basis for pre-emptive strikes in view of serious and eminent danger of attack. States' right to resort to force under the Charter is only until the Security Council has taken the measures necessary to maintain international peace and security, thus, restricting the extent of availability of the right. There are two prominent interpretations of the applications of the Article: First, Goodhart says that the right is available as a matter of right, the Charter only limits the right. Second, Kelsen is of the opinion that the right becomes available only when there is an armed attack. The International Court of Justice (ICJ) in the Nicaragua Case held that self-defence was a pre-existing right of customary nature. The supporters of the first view are of the opinion that the right arises in case of attack or *serious and imminent danger of attack*, which may arise by posting large number of force along the border or by sending bands of force into the territory of another country, because this can be a case of indirect armed attack. But in all cases, the serious and eminent danger of attack must be proved before exercising military activities for self-defence.[39] The author is of the opinion that the right is available only in case of armed attack with the requirement for invoking Article 51 that the response of the defending state must be 'close in time' or 'immediate response to attacks'.[40] Article 2(4) of the UN Charter has clear prohibition on threat or use of force. Michael Bothe and A. M. Frankfurt have written: "Lawful self-defence requires the actual existence of an armed attack, or a situation to be considered as equivalent to an armed attack. A threat may be so direct and overwhelming that one cannot require the victim to wait to act in self-defence until the attack has actually started. This principle of necessity and immediacy is still part of customary international law."[41] If right of self-defence is liberally interpreted as the United States is doing for justifying pre-emptive strikes, which will be sheer misinterpretation of Article 51 of the UN Charter; and if it is accepted, no state will be safe.[42] Pre-emptive strike can never be self-defence. It will itself be no less than an armed attack.[43] The doctrine of pre-emptive strike practiced by the United States and Israel for their national security, thus, is illegal and an unacceptable expansion of the right of self-defence.[44] It cannot be justified as a customary international law also.[45] It will be even worst if the scope of pre-emptive strike is widened in the name of 'long war' on global terrorism. It will result into a sense of insecurity among many countries of the world. The situation of Iraq was different than Afghanistan.[46] There was no attack nor an eminent danger of attack by Saddam Hussain, as he did not have weapons of mass destruction. The UN inspectors before the attack said this. Colin Powell has admitted this in his recent interview given to ABC.[47]

It can very well be concluded that there is nothing like pre-emptive strike, which is justified under the 'Caroline Principle', in international law, as it can neither be justified under the UN Charter nor under the customary international law. If it is practiced, it will be an illegal act, and will itself amount to a kind of state terrorism. This should be included in a comprehensive definition. But the problem is that this might have opposition of the United States and its close allies.

According to the traditional *Sunni* view, for a war, there has to be a just cause viz, the imperative to extend the boundaries of the territory of Islam. For this, invitation has to be sent by a Muslim ruler to a non-Muslim ruler either to accept Islam or to pay tribute. There can be a war on refusal and that has to be fought according to the Islamic values.[48] But according to *Shi'ite* view, use of force is allowed only for *defa'* (defence), when war is imposed by hostile and aggressive political forces.[49] This view is fairly common among the contemporary *Sunni Ulama* (religious experts), especially of Egypt. To support this, Mahmood Sultan in *Qur'an and Fighting* (originally published in 1948) for example, presents the thought of a formidable Sunni scholar, eventually the *Shaykh al- Azhar*, and argues fighting cannot be an essential part of the Islamic mission…it can be justified only in cases of defence…to stop aggression, to protect the mission of Islam, and to defend religious freedom. The author agrees with this reformist approach.[50] However, from the practices of the Prophet, it can be inferred that a Muslim country can attack another country in case of an eminent danger of attack by that country, which can be established on facts. This is in conformity with the Qur'anic authority to fight given to those who were driven out of their place.[51] Had it not been there, some men would have suppressed others.[52]

In view of this it can be said that an Islamic state has to have cordial relations with other states and to fight against any state or group of people to defend its territory and its people only when there is an attack by the other state. Otherwise, it will be considered as an act of aggression, which is not allowed. It can, thus, be said that Islam does not subscribe to pre-emptive attack. More appropriately, almost all Muslim states are bound by the customary international law. They also have to follow treaty norms of the treaties to which they members, because in Islam, there is a Qur'anic injunction to all keep their promises.

Self-Determination

In many countries, secessionist activists have adopted the path of terrorism and justify their movements on the basis of the international principle of self-determination. They will be considered as terrorists and will be governed by specific legislations made for abatement and control of terrorism. We know that the principle has limited scope of decolonizing a colonized state. After the Second World War, based on this principle, a large number of countries were decolonized. A secessionist movement, especially armed rebellion, cannot be justified on the principles of external as well as internal self-determination. If the principle is applied today, insurgency will get encouragement and sovereign states might break. However, for a justifiable cause and for a peaceful co-existence, based on peace agreements between activists and the government, within the constitution, some kind of autonomy can be allowable. There are many examples of this. In exceptional cases, where activists perpetrate terrorism and continue perpetrating it and don't negotiate peace, only they can be considered as terrorists and their activities will be covered by a comprehensive definition of terrorism.[53] This is because there are some genuine insurgency movements and they have not resorted to terrorist acts.[54] But the problem here is that countries that support armed rebellion tainted with terrorism will oppose the attempt of including such acts within the definition of terrorism.

In Islam, there cannot be a state within a state. Thus, all kinds of secessionist movements are illegal. They are considered to be rebellious activities and have to be suppressed by application of force. However, if a territory is illegally occupied by another country, the people will have right to fight for the freedom of their territory from illegal occupation. This will be allowed and their activities will not be tainted as terrorist activities, as long as they do not kill innocent people. This is notable that even in case of rebellion, revolution or people's war (civil war), which are known as 'irregular war', the rules of war have to be observed, but rebellions have to be dealt with severely. In a civil war, Ali the Caliph took a soft approach against those Muslims who fought against him. Al-Shaybani reports that Ali the Caliph said in the Battle of Camel:[55] "Whoever flees (from us) shall not be chased, no prisoners of war will be killed, no wounded in the battle shall be dispatched, no enslavement of women and children shall be allowed, and no property of a Muslim shall be confiscated".[56]

International Terrorism

We have noted above that terrorism has now engulfed the whole world. Whatever may be reasons, it is evident that many terrorist organizations are operating now borderless. Their bases are not known and their targets are unpredictable. The American definition of 'terrorism' has attempted to bring such international terrorist activities within the scope its. The Australian definition also prescribes for taking action under the Australian law against those who cause harm to Australian nationals or their properties. Cross-border terrorism is also a kind of international terrorism, which is blighting relations of many countries, including the India-Pakistan. This category of international terrorism can be most dangerous if because of that war between two countries takes place.[57] The country that supports such activities, opposes any definition that includes this.

We have already stated above that international terrorism or cross border terrorism are prohibited in Islam. This is also accentuated from the below discussion.

Terrorism and Islam

Islam is Against Terrorism

Objectively speaking, all religions are for peace, amity and peaceful co-existence of followers of all religions. They all disapprove hatred, enmity and violence.[58] In Islam, Qur'an and *ahadith* (traditions of Prophet Muhammad, *hadith* is singular of *ahadith*), which are based on divine wisdom, clearly establish them. Islam is a religion of peace co-existence, harmony and tolerance. It disapproves all kinds of terrorism and upholds equality, human dignity, non-aggression, tolerance, non-violence, and assistance to those who are in distress. The Qur'an says, "...if any one slew a person...it would be as if he slew the whole people. And if any one saves a life, it would be as if he saved the life of the whole people..."[59] Although plants and animals are subservient to man, Islam permits to take benefits from them and prohibits their wasteful use. Islam ordains to be nice to them and maintain congenial relations with them.[60] In spite of this fact, it is unfortunate that Islam is identified with terrorism. It is sheer misrepresentation when Muslims inflict strikes, and BBC and CNN call them as Islamic terrorist attacks and identify perpetrators with jihadists. This attitude can be counterproductive; innocent Muslims might be misguided by it and might tend to Muslim terrorist groups.

Considering terrorism as *Jihad* is nothing but, ignorantly or deliberately, projecting a diversely opposite picture of the religion. *Jihad* (holy war)[61] has generally been misinterpreted. The word has wide connotation. It means intense efforts, total endeavour, and strive hard towards spiritual and moral struggle, not to be guided by ego, to be God conscious *(taqwah)*, setting forth good conducts (*marufat*, virtues) and abstain from prohibited and disliked conducts (*munkarat*, vices), excelling in all areas of knowledge that are for public interest. It also includes conflict with enemies in circumstances where believers are persecuted and their existence is endangered.[62] A Yusuf Ali, while commenting on *Sureh Taubah, ayah* 20, aptly writes, "Here is a good description of *jihad.* It may require fighting in God's cause as a form of self-sacrifice. But its essence consists in: 1. true and sincere faith; and 2. earnest and ceaseless activity, involving the sacrifice of life and property in the service of God. Mere brutal fighting is opposed to the whole spirit of *Jihad*..."[63] It is clear that quoting *ayah* (verses) to justify terrorism is entirely a wrong notion.

The most pertinent *hadith*, which clearly demonstrates that Islam is against terrorism, is: "And I dislike using any kind of intimidation against anybody."[64] On the contrary, he (saw) visited Jews when they were sick, protected their personal law in the Constitution of Medina, and preached to be nice to neighbors, irrespective of their religion.[65]

Islam teaches restraint in the face of provocation, and supports for forgiveness. Qur'an says, "The recompense for an injury is an injury equal thereto: but if a person forgives and makes reconciliation, his reward is due from God ..."[66] Likewise, *Tirmizi* records a *hadith,* "Once a person from Quraysh broke a tooth of another person from Ansar camp. The victim then made a petition before Mua'viyah the khaliph for seeking justice. The accused requested the *khaliph* to be soft towards him. But Mua'viyah was not agreeable to that. A senior companion of the Prophet by the name of Abu al-Darda', who was sitting beside the *khaliph* said that on one occasion the Prophet said that if a person forgave another person for a crime commit to him, he would be rewarded greatly. Upon this, the victim forgave the accused. The *khaliph* showed his happiness on this and ordered the victim to be recompensed."[67] It is also worth noting that Islam encourages for justice and compassion and forbids oppression. Justice is considered as a sacred trust and the best among all virtuous deeds. Oppression is opposite of justice. This can be inferred on reading various *ayahs* in the Qur'an pertaining to justice.

Those who identify Islam with terrorism generally misinterpret and misquote *ayah* 191 of chapter II of the Qur'an which reads, "And slay them wherever you catch them, and turn them out from where they have turned you out; for tumult and oppression is are worse than slaughter..." This *ahyah* has to be read and interpreted only in the context in which it was sent. Even after the migration of Muslims from Makkah (*hijrah*) to Medina, the oppression and persecution by Makkans continued. They also looted the business caravan of Muslims. Muslims were hesitating because Makkans were close relatives of those who had migrated to Medina (*muhajerun*). This *ayah* encouraged Muslims to fight giants them. This interpretation gets support from *ayah* 190 of the same chapter that reads, "Fight in the Cause of God those who fight you, but do not transgress limits..." The irony is that in spite of the clear indication of the context by the commentators of the Qur'an to which the *ayah* 191 refers to, orientalists, whose mission is to prove that Islam encourages terrorism, have misinterpreted it. The irony is applying Qur'anic verses, which have been descended to meet war situations, during peacetime. *Ayah* 191 of chapter II is to be applied only during war situations; it cannot be given generated application. Muslims, who are perpetrating terrorism in preparing self-styled jihadists, also misinterpret for motivating innocent Muslims for militancy.

It is, therefore, suggested that all Qur'anic *ayah* and *ahadith* must be read and interpreted in their relevant contexts. On the contrary, they are going to be misinterpreted, resulting in undesired results. It is the responsibility of *ulama* and jurists to put forth correct Islam. It is *sine qua non* for fighting Muslim militancy.

In fact, a vast majority of Muslims are against all kinds of terrorism. Those who are perpetrating it constitute small minority. There is a kind of civil war among them. Terrorism will end only when the right-minded majority wins this war. In view of this, it is suggested that all states that are waging war on terrorism must provide all kinds of strength, individually and collectively, to the majority group.[68] If it is not done, the recently renamed 'long war' on global terrorism can turn into an undifferentiated campaign against Muslim in general and Muslim insurgencies, wherever they emerge, in specific. This will be a great mistake. We cannot target any insurgency movement just because al-Qaeda helps it. Some Muslim causes may be just and deserve international support. In view of this it is suggested that the United States should pick its fight very carefully.[69] The best example is Muslim insurgency of Moro Islamic Liberation Front in Mindanao, Philippines. This has nothing to do with the West. There has been peace talk between insurgents and the Government of Philippines. A conventional military approach might engulf whole southern Philippines. This problem can be solved through negotiations. In the peace process West can help. Kit Collier and Malcon Cook have rightly written that US, Australia and other countries must pick up political slack and build the government's capacity to deliver a sustainable peace agreement for Mindanao.[70]A long-lasting peace can be achieved within the within the constitutional framework by granting an agreeable autonomy to the region.

Madarasah are for Religious Teachings

Madarasah is a school where religious teachings are given to Muslims. However, in Pakistan, some of them bordering with Afghanistan have been allegedly blamed for teaching militancy rather than teaching Islam. This is a misuse of *Madarsahs* for sinister purposes, which is tarnishing the image these religious institutions. Those who are involved in it find it easy to distract and motivate those young people who have seriously suffered by the war on terrorism. As a part of clean up activities, General Musharraf ordered for registering all *Madarasahs* and for scrutinizing their syllabi.[71] This kind of activity has not been reported in India. In India, *Madararahs*, notably Deoband, are actively participated in the independence movement, and ever since then they are busy in imparting religious teachings only.

Terrorists Are Not Martyrs

We may conclude that it is wrong to say that Islam supports terrorism. Extremism is clearly prohibited by it. So-called jihadists are not actually jihadists. Islamic Scholars condemn terrorism.[72] Those who die or kill themselves while perpetrating terrorism are not martyrs.[73] Some have made distinction between the suicide bombings of those who are trying to defend themselves from occupiers, from those who kill civilians for the sake of perpetrating terrorism. For them, it is something different.[74] The author is of the opinion that it is the duty of Muslim Scholars to tell the world about the true Islamic view on terrorism, *jihad* and martyrs. If necessary, inter-faith dialogues should be organized so that the theory of conflict of civilizations is falsified.

It is clear from above paragraphs that the Islamic approach of terrorism is the same as the western perception about it. It has to be stopped by all means. Identifying Islam with terrorism and considering terrorists as jehadists will be a great mistake. Western countries should provide all kinds of help to the vast majority of right-minded Muslim so that they become empowered enough to counter the fallacious propaganda of those who are perpetrating terrorism.

Prisoners of War

Taking Prisoners of War

It is a general rule that enemy soldiers can be captured during a war and made POWs. Non-combatants, while helping the enemy army in any ways can also be captured and made POWs. According to the Geneva Conventions,[75] the following, who have fallen into the hands of enemy, can be taken as prisoners of war: members of the armed forces of a party to the conflict; militia or volunteers forming part of that military group operating with or outside their territory; members of armed forces who profess allegiance to a government or an authority not recognized by the detaining power; civilian associates of the armed forces; crew members of a merchant ship or civil aircraft; and inhabitants of non-occupied territory, who on the approach of enemy spontaneously take up arms to resist the invading forces.[76]

After the war is over, there has to be no captures in the name of enemy combatants, and thereafter making captives as POWs. In case of doubt or so long their status of captives is not determined, they have to be considered as POWs. This rule of customary international law and explicitly incorporated in the Geneva Conventions is being gravely violated. Many individuals, against whom there exists no proof of being enemy soldiers or helping enemies during war in any way, have been apprehended and put in detention camps without giving them POW status.

In Islam, the law on becoming a prisoner is clear and the same as set out in the IV Geneva Convention. Enemy soldiers, and those who are helping them, including women and children, can be taken as POWs. Allah (*s.w.t.*) ordains in the Qur'an, "It is not for a prophet to have prisoners of war until he has thoroughly subdued the land (enemy).[77] It means before making POWs the enemy must be subdued. It has been re-iterated as: "If you meet in battle those who disbelieve, smite their necks. Then, if you have thoroughly subdued them, bind a bond firmly, so there will be a time for either generosity or ransom for them until cessation of the war."[78] It is rightly said that the second *ahyah* does not abrogate the ruling of the first one, as both convey essentially the same thing.[79] This view is supported by Sheikh Rashid Rida in his commentary of the Qur'an entitled *Tafsir al-manar* in these words: "The gist of these verses is that it is not the tradition of the prophets nor of those who follow them to have prisoners of war whom he ransoms or releases except after gaining some ascendancy over the enemies of Allah."[80]

It is clear that Muslim commanders have to fight until the enemies are subdued. If an enemy fighter embraces Islam during the war without any compulsion, he will neither be killed nor taken as a POW. This is because there is no compulsion in religion. Once a person embraces Islam, he will no more remain an enemy pertaining to that war. Once enemy combatants are captured as POWs, they will not be pressurized to embrace Islam.

It is notable that Islamic law of war and POWs is based on divine wisdom. Most of the Islamic rules are in conformity with Geneva Convention and Anti Torture Convention (see *infra*). Some rules are not in conformity with them. These rules are not applicable now because as a member of these treaties they will be bound with the norms enshrined in them. According to the *siyar* (International law) of treaties, as derived form Islamic law of contract, Muslim states as a member of treaties will be bound with them.

Illegal Detentions

We know that most of 558[81] detainees of the Guantanamo Bay were not captured from the war zone. They were captured elsewhere. Some of them were brought to the Guantanamo Bay on certain incentives given to the states which captured them. They are being detained there as enemy combatants for years without granting them the POW status and without producing them before a competent court.[82] Their fundamental human right to meet with their family members and the access of human rights bodies like Amnesty International is denied. We have already stated above that in case of doubts, Geneva Convention applies and they get all rights, including those, guaranteed by the Convention. The law clearly demonstrates that detainees can either have the POWs status or they can be considered as an ordinary criminal. In the second situation, they should be presented before courts of competent jurisdiction within the shortest possible time and should be treated according to the decision of the courts; or they should be freed.[83] The United Nations and Britain, Germany, Denmark and several human rights groups have urged the US to close the detention camp.[84] President Bush forestalled the Europeans during June 21-22, 2006 EU-US Summit by raising the issue of Guantanamo Bay saying that he understood their concerns and expressed his deep desire to end the programme. He said, "He would like to end the Guantanamo. I would like it to be over with."[85] In spite of this, detainees are being considered as enemy combatant and are being kept in detention. Even if they are so, their rights to access to justice cannot be denied.[86] The Supreme Court of the United States has categorically accepted this right of the detainees of the Guantanamo Bay.[87] In the light of these decisions, we can say that detainees at other places, secretly or openly, will also have the same right. These cases have provided impetus to detainees to go to the High Court. Over 200 cases have already been filed. Recently Chinese detainees are planning to go to the High Court.[88]

In the light of the US Supreme Court's *Rasul* v. *Bush* case,[89] where the Supreme Court decided that the US court system has the authority to decide whether foreign nationals held in the Guantanamo Bay were rightfully detained. The Court further held that District Courts had the jurisdiction to hear habeas corpus writs of the detainees of the Guantanamo Bay. In view of this, the US Government on 7th July 2004, created the Combatant Status Review Tribunal (CSRT), a body composed of three noncommissioned officers, to examine the legality of detainees. Thereafter, the United States District Court dealing with the habeas corpus petitions of the Guantanamo Bay rules that the CSRT proceedings "deny fair opportunity to challenge these incarcerations" and thus fail to comply with the terms of the Supreme Court ruling given in *Rasul* case.[90] The legitimacy of the CSRT was challenged in *Hamdan* v. *Ramsfield*[91] in the US Supreme Court and it was expected that the court would give its judgment on it within the year 2006.[92] The decision has come now and the Court has decided that the Bush administration had no authority to order for establishing such tribunals, as it contravened the Geneva Conventions. In a 5-3 decision the court warned the Bush administration saying that it had no 'blank cheque' to decide how to try terror suspects. More appropriately, under the Geneva Conventions, Hamdan, as a prisoner of war, was entitled to a court hearing that followed the same procedures. The Bush administration is now looking for means to avoid the effect of the Court's verdict. Professor George Fletcher writes that the Bush administration is now left with an embarrassing position. It does not want to prosecute the Guantanamo detainees in American courts, but it is unlikely that it can prosecute them under the law of war as interpreted in the Hamdan case.[93] The Bush administration is now looking for means to avoid the effect of the Court's verdict by any suitable means.[94] The Government has already established the Administrative review Board for annual review of detentions. It is submitted that this also will not be in conformity with the Supreme Court's decisions.

On 17 October 2006 President Bush signed Military Commissions Act 2006, which authorizes tough interrogation of terror suspects and smoothing the way for their trials before military commissions. The Act was passed just six weeks after he acknowledged that the Central Intelligence Agency had been secretly interrogating suspected terrorists overseas. It is notable that the Act reaffirms the US plan to try terrorist suspects before military tribunal rather than regular courts. The American Civil Liberties Union has registered the following comments on it: 1. It does not protect due process; 2. It fails to meet international treaty obligations.[95]

On 12 June 2008 the Supreme Court of the United States took even a tougher stand in *Boumedine* v. *Bush.*[96]By 5:4 majority, the Supreme Court reiterated its view that the Federal Courts have the jurisdiction to hear the cases of detainees. Justice Anthony Kennedy rejected the Bush administration's argument that prisoners could be held for years without a fair process for assessing evidence against them. It means that the Federal Courts–which are equipped with the procedures necessary to protect sensitive national security information - will now be able to examine the basis for detainees' claims that that they are wrongly held. In reading its decision the Court rejected the administration's assertion that the procedure established in the Detainee Treatment Act 2005 and the Military Commissions Act 2006 were adequate substitute for habeas. The Boumedine ruling is based on the U.S. Constitution, unlike the decision in *Rasul* u. *Bush*, which could make it more difficult to overrule by legislation. Although Attorney General Michael Mukasey said that the ruling would not affect the on-going trails at the Military Tribunal, in view of this decision the credibility of the trials at the Military Tribunal has become doubtful. The United States has now started ether freeing and sending detained to their home country to face trial there. It is better if the detainees are tried in their home country provided the United States provided evidence against them. This case has given a sigh of relief to those human rights groups which have been lamenting for long about illegal detentions that gravely violated the Geneva Conventions and the Due Process rule. It will certainly give rise to a number of cases filed by them to see the detainees free.

In spite of these cases, the brutal interrogations and torture of detainees is continued. This has been stated by Sami al-Hajj, an *Al Jazeerah* cameraman.[97]

The Islamic law about POWs is clear. In Islam, there can be two categories of detainees pertaining to a war: one, who had committed a crime for which they could be penalized; and the second, who are simply POWs. So far the first category is concerned, they have to be indicted and penalized accordingly, including death penalty. If the heinous crimes committed by them are already known and for that they deserve death penalty, they can be executed without subjecting to any trials. In such an exceptional situation of war crimes, Prophet Muhammad (*s.a.w.*) gave such ruling against some POWs. In the Battle of Badr 70 enemy soldiers were captured. Three of them, namely Uqba ibn Abi Ma't, An-Nadr ibn al-Harith and Tu'aymah bin Udday, were executed.[98]He also approved the execution of all of Banu Qurayzhas for breaking the peace treaty and pledge to fight against any outside enemy and instead joined the enemy forces. It is notable that although as the head of the state it was prophet's job to conduct the trial, he made Sa'd bin Mu'adh to be the arbitrator. Sa'd gave the award that their men be executed and the Prophet (*s.a.w.*) enforced the verdict.[99] From this, we cannot draw a conclusion that POWs can be killed without following the 'due process' rule. There are a good number of scholars who are of the opinion that prisoners of war should not be killed.[100] One can draw a conclusion that the rule is that POWs will not be killed. The exception to this rule is that if a POW has been involved with crime for which death is the penalty, he can be killed if so decided by the *Qazi.* According to Mohammad Hamidullah,[101] a big number of Muslim jurists are of the opinion that prisoners cannot be held liable for damage they inflicted on Muslims lives or property while combatants. In view of above, this does not seem to be a correct approach.

Other POWs, according to the Qur'an,[102] can have any of the four fates: Freed gratuitously conditional or unconditional, or exchanged with ransom, exchanged with Muslim POWs in enemy's hands.

Preventive detention is allowed in Islam only to prevent a detainee from absconding, because freedom of movement is one of the fundamental rights of the man guaranteed by Qur'an.[103] Jurists (*fuqaha*) have forbidden detention except when necessary to facilitate a criminal trial. *Habs* (imprisonment) for them is wide enough to include arrest and preventive detention. In effect, it is deprivation of the right of personal liberty.[104] Jurists are of the opinion that *Qazis* have to inspect jails and make order to release those who are kept there unjustly.[105] Thus, in this limited sense, Islamic jurists recognize preventive detention as a legitimate state function for some specific purposes. Some call it *habs ihteyat* (precautionary detention), some others call it *kashf wa istebarh* (discovery and acquittal arrest), or *ikhtibar* (trail or examination arrest). In all cases, arrests have to be for a temporary period,[106] more appropriately during the trial. To this effect, Al-Mawardi is of the opinion that, 'there are different opinions on it. Some say one month, others say it is undetermined and should be left to the *Imam's* independent reasoning–the last is more likely'.[107] Even though it is left to the discretion of *Imam*, it cannot be beyond the trial and conviction. It is not appropriate to detain a person for a longer period in the name of investigation. In *al-Mabsut,* Sarakhsi has rightly expressed his view that if someone is accused of adultery or rape, has to be kept in custody until the guilt is proved or disproved. This is to prevent the accused from escaping. This is applicable to other crimes also.[108]

It can, therefore, be said that detaining any person for an unlimited period in the name of preventive detention or in the name of investigation is against the Islamic law. It is clear from the above paragraphs that a preventive detention is to detain the person until the disposal of the criminal case so that he does not abscond and thus escape the punishment. Some scholars hold the opinion that Islam provides for compensation to the accused who is placed under detention as a precaution but whose innocence is later established. As a proof they cite the ruling of Ali for compensation (*ghurrah*) to be paid to the mother when miscarriage resulted from an official's mishandling of her detention.[109] The author is of the opinion that the right of the detainees has to be judged *vis a vis* the states security. For this a meaningful balance has to be created. We can strike a balance only when judicial authorities frequently review detentions. This will be an exceptional situation.

Torture to Prisoners

Detainees, wherever they are, have been given frightful treatment. It is known to the world now from photographs and stories narrated by prisoners released from the Guatanamo Bay detention camp and the Abu Ghraib prison.[110] The vivid photographs of heinous abuse of prisoners of the Abu Ghraib prison accentuate that detainees were undermined, humiliated and tortured in manifest ways by the US Army, with or without the consent of the Army Commanders of the US Army.[111] It is said that they are happening because the Bush

Administration has abandoned the Geneva Conventions for the war against the Taliban and al-Qaeda on the grounds that they are not legitimate warriors as defined in the Geneva Convention.[112] The British army has also caused atrocities to Iraqi prisoners. All kinds of maltreatments of prisoners are grave violation of the Geneva Convention, the Convention against Torture and Other Cruel, Inhuman or Degrading Treatment or Punishment 1948 (Anti-Torture Convention), which has come into force on 26th June 1998. The heinous act of sexual torment by prostitutes in the course interrogation is serious and despicable. This has been revealed in a draft manuscript obtained by the Associated Press. The author writes that he witnessed about 20 such interrogations, where interrogators, who were female hired civilians, wore miniskirts and bathing costumes and while asking questions they rubbed their bodies against detainee's bodies and commented on their erections.[113] This kind of interrogation is against the law of every civilized country; it is violation of prisoner's rights and freedom of religion also.[114] Referring to an independent report the BBC News on February 5, 2005 said that some of the detainees due to abuse and staying away for so long time might develop some kind of irreversible psychological symptoms.

Donald Rumsfeld, the Defence Secretary of the United States, has tried to justify these heinous acts by saying that the inmates of the Guantanamo Bay were not 'common prisoners'. They are enemy combatants.[115] So, they should not be considered as ordinary criminals or POWs. He said so to deny them a fair trial to them. Jan Clabbers has rightly written, "Indeed, the very proclamation by a state that it is engaged in a war against terrorism, or against certain specified terrorist network, invoking the right of self-defence and relying on the seeming acquiescence of the world community in this conceptualization, would seem to imply the applicability of humanitarian law. One cannot after all claim to be engaged in warfare, yet also claim to be entitled to ignore the applicable rules; one cannot, as the saying goes, blow hot and cold."[116]

Similarly, when cruel, humiliating and degrading treatment of Abu Ghraib prisoners became a blatant cause of worldwide criticism of the U. S. Army, Donald Rumsfeld stated that Geneva Conventions would apply to all detainees in Iraq. But now U. S. is mulling to deny this protection. Pentagon opened the door to denying this protection to foreign fighters captured in Iraq, saying legal analysis by government lawyers suggests that individuals could be exempted on a case-by-case basis.[117] They are, thus, trying to create an exception to the applicability of the Geneva Convention, and the Anti-Torture Convention, which, according to the author, is based on surmises.[118]

All kinds of torture inflicted to prison inmates at the Abu Graib prison or secret prisons and at the Guantanamo Bay detention camp are violation of the Anti Torture Convention. On 19 May 2006, the UN Committee against Torture directed the US to close any secret prison abroad and the Guantanamo Bay facility saying they violate the Anti Torture Convention. The Committee said, "The Us should ensure that no one is detained in any secret detention facility under its de facto effective control" and to "investigate and disclose the existence of any such facilities." It further said, "Detaining persons in such conditions constitutes, per se, a violation of the Convention." This has also been said by 10 independent experts, who examined the US record at home and abroad, also urged President Bush's administration to 'rescind any interrogation technique, that constituted torture or cruel treatment.[119] In view of the UN Committee's request, the US has no moral right to maintain prisons and the detention camp. They should be closed. Prisoners should either be tried or freed.

The Detainee Treatment Act 2005 and the Military Commissions Act 2006, the United States have authorized tough interrogations and has provided protection to interrogators. The stories of atrocities caused to detainees are being accentuated by those who have been released recently, including citizens of Pakistan, Britain, Australia and Sudan. This is nothing but ignoring the UN Committee's request and negations of the willingness expressed earlier to respect the feelings of the EU, UN and the rest of the world.

By virtue of the 1945 International Military Charter of the Nuremberg, Articles 3, 5 and 147 of the Geneva Convention and Article 1 of the Anti-Torture Convention, all kinds of torture inflicted on detainees can be said to be war crimes and those who are responsible should be tried war commit it. The best court for their prosecution is the International Criminal Court as Article 27(1) says of the Rome Statute says that no one is above the law; and according to Article 27(2) immunity will not apply to them. But the problem is that the Unites States is not a party to the Rome Statute.

The United States is trying some Army men that have been highlighted worldwide by the media, under the criminal justice system of the US Army. We know the prosecution case of a lady officer, who was found guilty of making pyramid of naked Iraqi detainees and putting them chained in the Abu Graib prison. Recently, Lewis Welshofer, a high-ranking officer was found guilty of negligent homicide of an Iraqi General during brutally designed interrogation.. This is notable here that this lesser degree crime carries the maximum penalty of three years imprisonment. This case has been has been criticized by David Danzing, the manager of a campaign to end torture for Human Rights First, a New York Based group. He said that the trail showed there was of great confusion about what soldiers had been doing in Iraq.[120] These kinds of comments are also there with respect to other trials. The Hague Convention (IV) Respecting the Laws and Customs of War on Land 1907 and Hague Convention (X) Adapting to Maritime War of the principle of the Geneva Conventions 1907 provide for 'command Responsibility'[121] It provides that there is a relationship of junior and superior officials; and the superior one will be liable if the superior one had the knowledge, and he negligently failed to control.[122] Under this law there should have been many prosecutions, but the irony is only one high-ranking officer has been punished and that too with lower degree of punishment. This shows insincerity of the United States.

In Islam, POWs are dealt with a predominate sense of compassions and clemency. POWs have right not to be abused or tortured. To abuse POWs because they fought against those who captured them is totally prohibited. This is because it will amount to revenge, which is strictly prohibited. Also, it is notable that belligerency during the war as such is not a punishable crime. During Prophet's time and even after that during *Khulpah Rashedun's* time, there is no case of abuse or torture. Punishment is allowed to know information about the enemy. However, it should never reach the level of outright torture and must not affect the health of the prisoner. Sheikh Salman al Oadah in "Who is there for our prisoners of War" notes a *hadith*: The prophet (*s.a.w.*) fought against the people of Khayber until they were forced to retreat to their castle... There was an agreement between them and the Prophet (*s.a.w.*) that they will leave the place and handover all gold and silver they had. They concealed a purse. On interrogation the responsible person replied that all the money of the purse was utilized in the war.[123] With mild punishment, he told the truth. One can infer from this *hadith* that mild punishment can also be given in order to know the truth. When Imam Malik was asked whether it was permissible to torture a POW to extract from him information about the enemy's weaknesses, he said that he had never heard of such a thing. It is clear form the *hadith* discussed above and the view of the jurist Imam Malik that abuse and torture to POWs is totally prohibited. However, mild punishment, without inflicting any serious injury or mental agony, is allowed so long it is for knowing the truth or secret of the enemy if war is continued. According to a *hadith*, a slave belonging to the enemy was captured. He was being beaten by the companion's of the Prophet (*s.a.w.*) to reveal the hideouts of Abu Sufyan and his companions. He told about others except Abu Sufyan as he did not know about him. He was further being beaten. The Messenger of Allah (*s.a.w.*) had been praying. When he saw that excessive beating, he stopped praying and said, "I swear by Allah in whose hand is my soul, you beat him when he tells you the truth and let him go when he lies to you."

We can infer from the above paragraphs that all acts of torture and abuse of prisoners of war that is commonly being practiced in Abu Graib prison, Guantanamo Bay or elsewhere are prohibited by Islam. On the contrary, the Islamic teaching to treat POWs is based on compassion and clemency. In *Surah Al- Insan*, *ayah* 8, Allah (*s.w.t.*) told us one of the characteristics of a pious Muslim as: "And they give food...to the *miskin* (poor), the orphans, and the captive." Qatadah, while commenting on this ayah said that Allah (*s.w.t.*) had ordained us to nice to captives.[124] It has been stated in *Tafsir Ibne Kasir* that Muslim and non-Muslim captives will be treated alike.[125] It is accentuated by a *hadith* "*Istausu Bil-Usari khairan*", meaning be nice to captives.[126] The following are some notable rights that are based on *ahadith* and opinions of jurists:

1. Right to nourishment–We have seen above that this right has the basis of ayah 8 of *surah Al-Insan.* It is accentuated by a *hadith* also. There is a famous *hadith* that a woman brought food for Prophet Muhammad (*s.a.w.*). He asked the lady to give that food to captives.[127]
2. Right to remain on his religion–It is loud and clear in Islam that there is no compulsion in religion. Thus, captives have right to change their religion on their free will. If any one wants to do that, he will be converted to Islam. POWs were never forced to accept Islam. There is a famous *hadith* to prove it: Thamamah was arrested by the Muslim Army. He was brought to a mosque and was tied with a pillar. Prophet (*s.a.w.*) asked from him, 'What have you, O Thamamh?" Thamah replied, "Actually I have a lot going for me. If you kill me, you kill a man whose blood will surely be avenged. If you are generous, then you are generous to a man who knows how to be grateful…"He was left in that condition. Next day same thing happened, Third day when he gave the same reply, Prophet Muhammad (*s.a.w.*) freed hem. Afterwards, he embraced Islam.[128]We can draw one more conclusion form this *hadith* that in case a captive repents, he can be freed without ransom.
3. Right to remain silent–POWs have right to remain silent. Any confession taken under duress will not be considered as an acceptable confession.[129]
4. Right of clothing–There is a *hadith* narrated by Jabir, that, "After the Battler of Badr, POWs were brought. Among them was Al-Abbas. He did not wear a shirt, so the Prophet (*s.a.w.*) provided his a shirt of his size.[130] It is clear form this *hadith* that POWs should be given nice cloth to wear.
5. Right of lodging–As during Prophet's time there was no proper jail system, POWs were kept in mosque, houses. Once brought one prisoner to his house also. But in all cases, they were treated nicely. Jurists are of the opinion that POWs should not be kept at a dark or damp place.[131] Prophet (*s.a.w.*) saw that some captives were kept in scorching sun. He asked their wardens to keep then under at a shaded place, to provide them water to drink and to give them chance to sleep.[132]

6. Right to treatment–Prisoners have right to get treatment. Prophet (*s.a.w.*) asked his companions not to do any hardship to injured POWs.[133] It is clear from this *hadith* that injured POWs should properly be treated.
7. Right to be with family members–It is said that a mother should not be separated from her child, nor should that child be separated from its father. Brothers also have to be kept together. Prophet (*s.a.w.*) on one occasions said, "Whoever separates a mother from her child will be separated from his own loved ones on the day of judgment."[134]
8. Right to write a will–According to Islam detainees have right to write will. Their wills have to be executed by the state or the other state.

The above discussed Qur'anic *ayah* and *ahadith* command to be compassionate towards POWs and treat them nicely. Perhaps in view of these, the Universal Islamic Declaration of Human Rights writes in its Article VII: "No person should be subjected to torture, in mind or body, or degraded, or threatened with injury either to him or to any one related to…"[135]

Denial of Procedural Justice

The 'due process' rule is a widely accepted rule of procedural justice. It serves to restrain governments from arbitrarily depriving a person's life, liberty or property. It stresses the need to protect individuals' liberty, which is an important constitutional right. Examples of due processes rights are: right to remain silent, right to counsel, right to bail and right to a speedy and public trial.[136] According to this rule, thus, all detainees, foreign or local, have to be presented before the court within the shortest possible time, which is generally determined as 24 hours. This rule was first developed by the House of Lords, but very soon became a universally accepted rule. In the United States the Fifth Amendment to the Constitution has a due process clause. Denial of the due process rule is considered as denial of justice and thus violation of a well established human right (emphasis added). In *Baker* v. *Wingo*[137], which is considered as an epoch-making judgment, Justice Powell, in his judgment discussed four strong arguments-length of delay, reason of delay, the defendants assertion of the right of failure to assert it, and prejudice caused by the delay - that could possibly be leveled against the 'due process' rule and rejected all of them. According to him, the rule is imperatively demanded to ensuring justice.[138]

The detainees of the Guantanamo Bay, as discussed above, cannot be considered to be POWs. Therefore, they have to be treated as alleged criminals and should be brought before the court of the US or be sent to the country of which they are the subjects. The United States is not presenting them before the regular court of the country or the military court of the country. President George W. Bush unveiled a plan of establishing a system of military commissions to try the detainees that proved to be tainted with arbitrariness. The Attorney General of Britain has also expressed this kind of feeling on it. Recently, High Court ruled that President Bush had no authority to order such tribunals, which it said, contravened the Geneva Conventions.[139]

In Epoch-making judgments of the US Supreme Court given in 2004 and 2008, noted above, the U. S. Supreme Court ruled that the war on terrorism did not give the American Government a 'blank cheque' to hold a U S citizen and foreign-born terror suspects in legal limbo. The Court refused to endorse a central claim of the Bush Administration that the government has authority to seize and detain terrorism suspects and indefinitely deny access to courts and lawyers while interrogating them. This case, according to authors, has provided opportunity to the detainees to go the Federal Court against their detentions and seek justice. The American Post has rightly commented that the ruling is the most significant test so far of executive power in the fight to root out and contain global terrorism.[140]Based on this ruling, some cases have started coming in the District Courts, but the results there are not so encouraging.[141]Same kind of feelings has also been expressed by the UN General Assembly. The General Assembly also wants them to be tried or freed.

This is far from clear that detaining them without a fair trial of international standards will be sheer violation of the 'due process' rule. Any other kind of trial or presenting them before any administrative committee or board will also be its violation. In most of the cases, these will generally result in extension of the detention.[142] This gets support from the recent judgment given by the House of Lords in *A (FC) and Others* v. *Secretary of State for House Department* and *X (FC) and Another* v. *Secretary of State of House Department*[143], where appeal by 9 detainees of the Belmash prison, who are being held there indefinitely, said: "detaining foreign terrorist suspects without trial breaches human rights law." and "Measures are incompatible with European Human Right laws. Lord Nicholls has remarkably said in his judgment that "Indefinite imprisonment without charge or trial is anathema in any country which observes the rule of law." To the surprise of the authors and many others, instead of honoring the verdict of the court, the Home Secretary said that the prisoners would remain in the prison until the law was reviewed. And in the mean time, the Government would review the law and if possible would make necessary changes to address the concern raised by the House of Lords.[144] Author is of the opinion that the verdict of the Court is clear and the detainees should either be charged or released; detaining them is violation of the European human rights laws. To say to review the law is nothing but a delaying tactic. The detainees should go to the European Court.

The situation of detention before deportation hearing is also the same. It has been clarified in the *Harvard Law Review* notes on cases entitled "The Supreme Court, 2002 Term: Leading Cases: 1. Constitutional Law: D. Due Process."[145] In the United States, under the Supreme Court's century-old plenary power doctrine, immigration matters 'are so exclusively entrusted to the political branches of the government as to be largely immune from judicial enquiry or interference.[146] At the same time, however, the Court has required the government to choose 'a constitutionally permissible means of implementing' its immigration policy. In balancing these two principles, the Court has generally followed two trends. First, it has typically limited the plenary power doctrine to 'substantive criteria for admission and exclusion, while applying mainstream constitutional principles to 'procedural' matters such as deportation hearings. Second, the Court has traditionally afforded robust constitutional protection to permanent resident aliens, even while withholding such protection from other categories of non-citizens.[147] In *Demore* v. *Kim*[148] the Supreme Court contravened both of these trends by invoking the plenary power doctrine to hold that the mandatory detention of criminal resident aliens pending their deportation hearings does not violate the Due Process Clause of the Fifth Amendment. The author is of the opinion that *Demore* is not a correct approach, as the plenary power doctrine has not received wide support, because of violation of human rights in arbitrary detentions.[149] The due process law should be applied without any discrimination.

Notwithstanding the existence of a double standard across constitutional cultures in the United States, the line between citizen and non-citizen has not been particularly firm one. The PATRIOT Act does not specifically mention about discrimination. But in practice, foreign citizens in the name of investigation are being detained for a longer period, violating the due process rules.[150] This kind of practice has been criticized by Non-Governmental Organizations (NGOs) working for protecting human rights, the media and the public.[151]

The United Kingdom is not different than the United States. The Anti-Terrorism, Crime and Security Act 2001, in effect, is not different than the U. S. law discussed above. The Act gave the police sweeping new powers, including the right to detain foreigners indefinitely only on suspicion of their involvement with terrorism. There are many foreign nationals detained in the United Kingdom without charge or trial. There is discrimination between foreigners and citizens of the country; and to the surprise of the authors, the British Courts are supportive to this practice. In *A and Others* v. *Secretary of State for the Home Department*[152] the respondent detainees were non-nationals resident in the United Kingdom. They were detained under Anti-Terrorism, Crime and Security Act 2001, which gave the Secretary of State extended powers to detain resident aliens who could not be expelled in the ordinary way if he suspected that they were terrorists. The power to detain involved derogation from the right to liberty guaranteed by the European Convention for the Protection of Human Rights and Fundamental Freedom 1950 (as set out in Schedule 1 to the Human Rights Act 1998). The detainees appealed to the Special Immigration Appeals Commission on the basis, *inter alia*, that the 2001 Order made under the Act and the 2001 Act violated the prohibition on discrimination under Article 14 of the convention as they allowed only suspected terrorists who were non-nationals to be detained when there were equally dangerous British nationals who were exactly in the same position and who could not be detained. This contention was accepted by the Commission which found section 23 of the 2001 Act incompatible with Articles 5 and 14 of the convention, in so far as it permitted detention of suspected international terrorists in a way that discriminated against them on the ground of nationality.

The Court of Appeal reversed the decision. The court held that section 23 of the 2001 Act and the 2001 Order were not incompatible with the Convention. Although the Convention required an actual or imminent emergency before a contracting state might lawfully derogate from the protections afforded by Article 5, there was ample material on which the Secretary of State could conclude that *an emergency of requisite quality* existed. The Terrorism Act of 2006 presents a refined version of the 2001 Act. It has some preventive measures that will if given effect remove the element of arbitrariness to some extent. British Courts can play a positive role in preventing unnecessary and excessive violations of human rights.[153]

The author is of the opinion that creation of an exception on the given basis will have ample scope of arbitrary use of the exception. This will result in undermining the human rights guaranteed by various international and national legal instruments. Preventive detention can be justified for protecting the security and integrity of a country.[154]Such detentions are made either on the basis of specific constitutional provisions or specific legislations. These legislations have no provision for bail and judicial review from time to time, which is warranted for protecting human rights and broadly speaking for ensuring a laudable justice system. In *Aksoy* v. *Turkey*[155] the European Court of Human Rights expounded that "The Court would stress the importance of Article 5 in the convention system: it enshrines a fundamental human right, namely the protection of the individual against arbitrary interference by the state with his right of liberty." Unjustified detentions amount to arbitrary interference of states with internationally acclaimed right to liberty and due process rights. The author has written above and would like to reiterate that for protecting human rights, especially personal liberty, a meaningful balance has to be created between preventive detention and the national security. This is only possible when detentions are reviewed every three-months by the regular courts of the country.[156] The court in *Aksoy* has emphasized this, also. The Court says in that case that judicial control of interferences by the executive with the individual's right of liberty is an essential feature of the guarantee embodied in Article 5 which is intended to minimize the risk of arbitrariness and to ensure the rule of law.[157] The preventive detention law should apply uniformly to aliens and nationals.[158]

There has been a general practice in many countries that for convictions the level of proof required should be 'beyond reasonable doubt'. This threshold is applicable in trials of terrorists also. The Home Secretary of the United Kingdom wants to apply a lower evidence threshold for terror cases. He suggests the following three important changes in the existing law, which is already considered as too harsh and violative to human rights: 1. Terror cases should have a lower evidence threshold, perhaps requiring the prosecution to prove the case on the 'balance of probabilities'. 2. Terrorism trials should partly be held in secret, with certain elements not being communicated to the defence, so as to protect British intelligence sources.[159] 3. Setting up a group of anti-terrorism judges who alone would be entitled to examine information judged sensitive for national defence and which would not be made public. This attempt to toughen the anti-terror law has been criticized by human rights activists. Liberty Campaigns Director Mark Littlewood told the Press Association: "Britain already has the most draconian anti-terror laws in the Western Europe... Further undermining trials by jury and radically reducing the burden of proof is wholly unacceptable. The plan for such highly secretive trials, involving security-vetted judges sitting without a jury will simply undermine civil rights. The threat of terrorism needs to be dealt with in increasingly sophisticated ways." Neil Durkin form Amnesty International U. K. commented: "We would be extremely concerned at any further erosion of the right to receive a fair trial in the U. K. in the name of combating terrorism. What is particularly worrying about these comments from the Home Secretary is the suggestion that there might be some wider introduction of internment–like measures that have already created a small-scale Guantanamo bay in our own backyard by imprisoning more than14 foreign nationals without charge or trial."[160]

The author is of the opinion that the move to further tighten the law will promote further erosion of human rights of personal liberty and fair trial. Undermining the trials by reducing the threshold from 'beyond reasonable doubt' to 'on the balance of probability' will not be in the interest of justice. There can be a special court comprising specialist judges. But to have a secret trial is not acceptable because it will undermine the due process rights.

We have noted above that according to *Shari'ah*, if any POW is found guilty of any crime, he has to face a trial; and if he is found guilty, he is accordingly punished. We have also noted that detaining any person for a short period to prevent him from absconding or during the trial is permitted. In Islam, there is no concept of keeping anybody as captive for years in the name preventive detention is dilation of human right as Allah (*s.w.t.*) has clearly said that "He it is who hath made the earth subservient unto you, so walk in the paths thereof and eat His providence."[161]It is clear from this ayah that except when necessary, arrest and detention will be violation of this *ayah*. It is required that detainees must be informed of the crime they have committed, and he should be provided right to defend himself. Although *Shari'ah* is not explicit about right to attorney, it has not explicitly been denied. This is because in absence of this right there will be chances that a smart and vocal person will win the case.[162] It is, therefore, suggested that for ensuring justice to the person who really deserves it, right to attorney should be available to litigants or accused persons.

It is clear that in the *Shari'ah* the modern concept of preventive detention has no place. It is rather prohibited. If someone is unnecessarily detained for a longer period will be entitled to claim compensation (*ghurrah*). But this claim can be entertained when he is presented before a court and the court determines him not guilty. However, in the changed circumstances and for protecting the interest of a state, preventive detentions, other than that the detentions at the Guantanamo By, is a debatable issue.

Conclusion

All efforts, including the Convention on Nuclear Terrorism 2005, have failed to have a viable definition of 'terrorism', which can widely be acceptable. The fight against terrorism, thus, has become directionless. It is necessary, therefore that all states should show willingness to forge a viable definition, and should make efforts to have consensus on it. It will be better if the United Nations formulates a definition taking into account all aspects of terrorism and its acceptability by almost all states.

Detaining people of different nationalities as enemy combatants in the name of war against terrorism, and torturing them in brutal form of interrogations and not presenting them before civil courts is illegitimate as it is denial of the 'due process' rule and violation of Geneva Conventions. Presenting some of them before a military tribunal and releasing some others on political pressure is just eyewash.[163] Their illegal detention and abuse is a blatant violation of human rights. What The United States and some other countries are presently doing is no less than an act of state terrorism.[164]The Amnesty International has rightly concluded that war on terrorism has led to widespread human rights abuse in Iraq, Afghanistan and at the Guantanamo Bay detention camp.[165] It is for this reason that in its 2008 decision, the US Supreme Court has ruled that detainees of the Guantanamo Bay have right to file habeas corpus writs before the US courts. It has rightly been desired by the United Nations that without any further delay, all detainees-where ever they are - should either be presented before courts of competent jurisdiction or be released. Islam wants prisoners of war be tried without any delay, or exchanged or released.

All kinds of physical or mental torture, humiliation or insult are inhuman and grave violation of the Geneva Conventions and the Anti-Torture Convention. They should be stopped immediately. In order to ensure the compliance of the treaty norms of the Conventions, the International Committee of the Red Cross (ICRC) should be allowed to have frequent visits to all jails and other placed where prisoners of war are kept.[166] Those who are abusing helpless prisoners and committing the act of torture and the high-ranking officers under whom these criminal acts are being committed are culprits of war crimes, thus be tried at the International Criminal Court. Francis Amar, the Head of the ICRC Regional Delegation, based in Kuala Lumpur, is also of this opinion.[167] It is also necessary to strictly enforce the principle of 'command responsibility', because the higher authorities, who have either connived or permitted torture, are also equally liable.

It is better if war against terrorism is fought in more collective way and organized manner. It will be better if we have regional co-operations about sharing information and making joint efforts to fight terrorism. It is appropriate to have a regional task force. Developed countries should support these forces. Islam is against all kinds of physical and mental torture inflicted on detainees/prisoners of war. States have to be nice with them. All kinds of interrogations in captivity is prohibited.

Prevention and control of terrorism requires immediate preventive measures to be taken by beefing up security around nuclear power generation plants. Likewise, adequate measures should be taken to storage and movement of nuclear materials, which can be used in making dirty bombs. The Director General of the IMO has expressed his concern, with the escalating trend of terrorism, the danger of using a ship as a bomb and hitting it with another ship or with a busy port cannot be ruled out. If it happens, it will certainly leave disastrous results. In view of this, possibility, he rightly emphasized on effective security to ships, ports and international straits, where a large number of ships pass through narrow watercourses. The author shares his concern and solicits for prudent efforts for avoiding any such possibility.[168]

Islam is a religion of peace and amity. It prohibits all kinds of terrorism. The religious concepts of '*jihad*' and 'Islamic brotherhood' have bean misinterpreted and exploited by Muslim terrorists for their sinister and menacing objectives. They are not at all jihadists. To call terrorists as jihadists will be counterproductive. Terrorists should never be considered as martyrs also. Today's terrorism, in fact, is a civil war within Islam between a majority of normal people and a small minority. War on terrorism cannot be won unless the right-minded majority wins this war, and for that all states must help them. It is also warranted that 'long war' on global terror has to be sensibly enforced, as there are some Muslim insurgencies that require international support. They should not be fought with because al-Qaeda is providing extending some helps to them. On the contrary, it might turn into an undifferentiated campaign against Muslim insurgencies, which is not at all desirable.

James Dobbins has rightly written that in the long war on al-Qaeda and terrorism, America should guard against being bogged down in a campaign of indiscriminate reactions against all Muslim insurgencies, regardless of their provenance. The best example is the insurgency of Mindanao. This has nothing to do with the West. The solution of this problem is negotiation within the constitutional framework of the Philippines, and negotiating some kind of amicable autonomy to the region. The west can play a meaningful role in it. Resorting to military action is not at all a solution.

Illegal detentions and torture of POWs and other detainees are totally against *Shari'ah* on POWs. Islam commands for compassion and clemency towards them. *Shari'ah* on POWs is well developed and generally humane. It is in total conformity with the Geneva Convention[169] and the Anti -Torture Convention, except that POWs can be taken as slaves. The author is of the opinion that in the contemporary world, no POW can now be enslaved because all Muslim countries are members of the Geneva Conventions, and it is also not provided in the Universal Islamic Declaration of Human Rights. As members, they have to follow the treaty norms arising out of the Geneva Convention, because *Shari'ah* ordains them to keep their promises.

Notes

1. Shad S. Farooqi, "Agony and Ambivalence about the War on Terrorism", Paper presented at *Civilization and Terrorism: A Round Table Dialogue*, one-day seminar, UiTM, Malaysia, 26 February 2002.
2. The word 'terror" was first used to describe the Jacobin 'Reign of Terror' that followed the French Revolution in 1789. The legal response to terrorism seen in various events convened in various capitals of European countries throughout 1920s and 1930s. See Johhn F. Murphy, "Defining International Terrorism: A Way Out of Quagmire" 19 *Israel Yearbook on Human Rights*, 1989, p. 14; Geoffrey Levitt, "Is 'Terrorism' Worth Defining, 13 *Ohio Northern University law Review*, 1986, p. 97; Susan Tiefenburn, "A Semiotic Approach to A Legal Definition of Terrorism", 9 *ILSA Journal of International and Comparative Law* (ILSA J. Int. & Com. L.), 2003, p. 357, at p. 358.
3. This comes within the fold of self-liberation. Everyone knows that Palestinian lands have illegally been occupied by Israel. Brutal,

merciless, bloody and destructive incursions into Palestinian camps, which can never be justified on the principles of law of war, are also open facts. Palestinians, on the other hand, are fighting with limited means they have, for liberation of their land. But the irony is that Israel, which has no respect to UN Security Council Resolutions and has invariably violated international law, is justified by so called depositories of the peace of the world; and they consider the freedom struggle of Palestinians as terrorist acts.

4. Tun Dr. Mahathir Mohamad, the former Prime Minister of Malaysia, in his speech delivered at the Lankawi International Dialogue 2002 in Lankawi, Malaysia, on August 1, 2002, specifically discussed "Economic Terrorism". He said, "They [newly independent countries] are terrified or being colonized once again through economic pressure coupled with the propaganda of the media. They are being terrorized; terrorized in the same way that the terrorists are threatening the world. See Mahathir Mohamad, *Terrorism and the Real Issues*, Hashim Makaruddin (ed.) (Subag Jaya: Pelanduk Publications, 2003), p. 97.
5. At the Special ASEAN Ministerial Meeting on Terrorism, Kuala Lumpur, May 19-21, Abdullah Ahmad Badawi, the Prime Minister of Malaysia, made a remark that the meeting stopped short of adopting a common definition of terrorism. It would pose political difficulties. See *New Straits Times*, 22 May 2002.
6. See G. Levitt, "Is Terrorism Worth Defining?", *Ohio Northern University Law Review* (Oh. NULR.), 1986, Vol. 13, p. 97; D.C. Rapoport and Y. Alexander, *The Morality of Terrorism: Religious and Ethical Implications* (New York: Pergamon, 1982), p. 30; W. Laqeur, *The Age of Terrorism* (Boston: Little Brown, 1987), p. 11; T. H. Michell, "Defining Terrorism", in D. A. Charter (ed.), *Democratic Responses to International Terrorism* (New York: Ardsley-on-Hudson, 1990), p. 9; N. W. Provizer, "Defining Terrorism", in M. Slann and B. Schechterman (eds.), *Multidimensional Terrorism* (Boulder: Lynne Reiner, 1987), p. 3; Ashraf Abdullah, "Defining clearly what is terrorism", *New Straits Times*, 19 September 2001; Munir Majid, "Terror: still searching for answers", *New Sunday Times*, June 9, 2002. Abdul Haseeb Ansari, "Terrorism, National Integrity and Human Rights", 3 *Malayan Law Journal* (MLJ), 2002, pp. ccv-ccxI.
7. See Richard R. Baxter, "A Skeptical Look at the Concept of terrorism", 7 *Akron Law Review* (ALR), 1974, p. 380.
8. See B. Jenks, "The Study of Terrorism: Definitional Problems", in Yonah Alexander and John Gleason (eds.) *Behavioral and*

Quantitative on Terrorism (New York: Pergamon, 1981), pp. 3-10; Abdul Haseeb Ansari, "Terrorism, National Integrity and Human Rights", *The Malayan Law Journal*, ccv, at p. ccviii; Susan Tiefenburn finds two difficulties in defining terrorism: First, it is necessary to distinguish between three different conceptions of terrorism: terrorism as a crime in itself, terrorism as a method to operate other crimes, and terrorism as an act of war. Second, there is no universally accepted definition. According to her, it is necessary to resolve the underlying paradoxes. Authors feel that terrorism exists *sui generis* as a crime. See Susan Tiefenburn, footnote 2, at p. 359-359.

9. Thomas H. Michell, "Defining Terrorism", in D. A. Charter (ed.) *Democratic Responses to International Terrorism* (New York: Ardsley-o-Hudson, 1990), p. 9, at p. 11. Similar points have also been given by Jean-Mark Sorel, in "Some Questions about the Definition of Terrorism and the Fight Against its Financing", 14 *European Journal of International Law* (EJIL), 2003, p. 365.
10. This may be noted here that United Nations is proposing to have a comprehensive legal regime on terrorism. This will also have a definition.
11. See infra.
12. The United States and the United Kingdom, who were critical of preventive detention laws of other countries, now have even worst quality of laws that do not have any regard for human rights at all.
13. It is because an excessive use of power by the state might results in injustice, and that might itself perpetrate violence or threat of violence.
14. Notable among them are: Thompson P. Thornton, "Terror as Weapon of Political Agitation", in H. Eckstein (ed.) *International War: Problems and Approaches* (New York: Free Press, 1964), pp. 73-74, 77-78; Micheal Stohl, " Demystifying Terrorism: The Myths and Realities of Contemporary Political Terrorism", in Micheal Stohl, *The Politics of Terrorism,* 3rd Edition (New York: Dekker, 1988), at P. 3; Arend and Beck, "Do Not Tread on US: International Law and Forcible State Response to Terrorism", 12 *Wisconsin International Law Journal,* 1994, p. 148 at p. 153; Yonah Alexander and Edger H. Brener, *Terrorism and Law* (Inc.: Transnational Publishers, 2001) at p. 7; Cherif Bassiouni, *International Terrorism: Multilateral Conventions* (1937-2001) (New York: Transnational Publishers, 2001), p. 4; Jean-Mark Sorel, "Some Questions About the Definition of Terrorism and the Fight Against its Financing", *European Journal of International law*, 2003, at p. 365. Among Muslim leaders who have contributed in reaching at a viable definition, Dr Mahathir

Mohammad's contribution is remarkable. See *New Straits Times*, 2 April 2002.

15. For a critical appraisal of various definitions, see Abdul Haseeb Ansari, "Terrorism, National Integrity and Human Rights", [2002] *Malayan Law Journal* (MLJ), p. ccv; Abdul Haseeb Ansari and Nik Ahmad Kamal, "Terrorism, Law and Human Rights", *IKIM Law Journal*, vol. 9, 2005. p. 13; (US) Anti-Terrorism Act, 1996; (US) Anti Terrorism Crime and security Act 2001; United States Patriotic Act 2001; United States Financial Anti-Terrorism Act 2001; (UK) Prevention of Terrorism (Temporary provision) Act 1984; Prevention of Terrorism (temporary provision) Act 1989; United Kingdom Terrorism Act 2000; and Security Legislation Amendment (Terrorism) Act 2002.

16. See Abdul Haseeb Ansari, and Abdul Haseeb Ansari and Nik Ahmad Kamal, *ibid.*

17. The following 14 treaties specifically deal with terrorism: Convention for the Prevention and Punishment of International Crimes, 1937, and Convention for the Creation of International Criminal Court, 1937 (These conventions did not come into force due to want of ratification); Convention on the Prevention of and Punishment of Crimes Against Internationally Protected Persons, Including Diplomatic Agents, 1973; International Convention Against the Taking of Hostage, 1979; International Convention for the Suppression of Terrorist Bombing, 1997; International Convention for the Suppression of the Financing of Terrorism 1999; Convention on Offences and Certain Other Acts Committed on Board Aircraft 1963; Convention for the Unlawful Seizure of Aircraft 1970; Convention for the Suppression of Unlawful Acts Against the Safety of Civil Aviation 1971; Convention on the Physical Protection of Nuclear Material 1980; Protocol on the Suppression of Unlawful Acts of Violence at Airports Serving International Civil Aviation, Supplementary to the Convention for the Suppression of Unlawful Acts Against the Safety of Civil Aviation, 1988; Convention for the Suppression of Unlawful Acts Against the Safety of Maritime Navigation, 1988; Convention on the Making of Plastic Explosives for the Purpose of Detection 1991; and Convention for the Suppression of Acts of Nuclear Terrorism, 2005, which has been adopted by the General Assembly on 13 September 2005. This Convention calls for states to make nuclear terrorism activities criminal offences and for sharing information and extradition of suspects in such cases. It also calls for outlawing and condemning terrorist activities, along with:

- demonstrating global unity in opposition to terrorism; and
- treating terrorism as a matter subject to domestic and international law; and challenging states to use, and if necessary adapt, their domestic legal systems to combat terrorism.

18. See Abdul Haseeb Ansari and Nik Ahmad Kamal, footnote 15 at p. 32.
19. See *New Straits Times*, 16 September 2005. For the EU arguments, visit <*www.parliament.org.uk/docs/0507/doc06.htm*>
20. For the full text of the OIC Convention, see *International Instruments Related to the Prevention and Suppression of International Terror* (UN, New York, 2001), at pp. 187-209.
21. See Dr. S. P. Rao, "International Terrorism, Self-Determination and National Liberation", in R. K. Dixit and C. Jayaraj (eds.) *Dynamics of International Law in the New Millennium* (New Delhi: ISIL, 2004), p. 115.
22. While opening the session of ASEAN Ministerial Meeting on Terrorism in Kuala Lumpur, Abdullah Ahmad Badawi said that the global effort to combat terrorism would remain arduous if the international community does not commit to a definition of terrorism. See *New Straits Times*, 21 May 2001.
23. The following cases may be referred: *T.* v. *Secretary of state for Home Department*, [1996] AC 742 (HL); *R.* v. *Secretary of State for Home Department and Another*, [2002] All ER 327; *R.* V. *Secretary of State for Home Department*, [2002] EWHC Admn. 644; *Secretary of State for Home Department* v. *Rehman*, [2003] AC 153 (HL); *Suresh* v. Canada *(Minister of Citizenship and Immigration)*, [2002] 1 SCR 3; *Fuents* v. *Canada (Minister of Citizenship and Immigration)*, [2003] 4 FC 249.
24. See Ben Golder and George Williams, "What is 'Terrorism': Problems of Legal Definitions", 27 *University of New South Wales Law Journal* (UNSW Law Journal) 2004, p. 170, at pp. 192-293.
25. Row of legislature and the judiciary in India on Land reform legislations is the best example.
26. In India, the definition of industry was widened enough by the judiciary to include municipal corporations, hospitals and universities within the fold of the definition of the term 'industry'. None of the cases were abrogated by the Parliament.
27. See Mark Burgess, "Terrorism: The problem of Definition", <http://studies.edentura.ru/centers.cdi/definition>; Mark Burgess, *A Brief History of terrorism* (USA: Harvard University Press, 1999), p. 11.

28. Bruce Hoffman, *Inside Terrorism* (New York: Columbia University Press, 1988), p. 14.
29. Eqbal Ahmad, "Terrorism: Theirs' and Ours", in Russell D. Howard, and Reid L. Sawyer, *Terrorism and Counter Terrorism: Understanding the New Security Environment* (Guilford: McGraw-Hill, 2003), pp. 46-53. Jessica Stern, *The UltimateTterrorists* (Cambridge: Harvard University Press, 1999), p. 11.
30. Adrian Guelki, *The Ultimate Terrorists* (New York: I.B. Tauris, 1998), p. 1.
31. Paul R. Pillar, *Terrorism and US Foreign Policy* (USA: Brookings Institution Press, 2001), pp. 13-14.
32. See *infra.*
33. See Mark Burgess, infra.
34. For the atrocities of Sabra and Shatila, see Shad S. Farooqi, "The forgotten horror of Sabra and Shatia", *New Straits times*, 14 September 2005.
35. See *New Straits Times*, 10 -11 September 2005.
36. See S.A. A' la Maududi, Editor Khurshid Ashmad, *The Islamic Law and Constitution* (Lahore, Islamic Publications, 1983); S. A. A 'la Maududi, *Islamic State and Constitution* (Lahore, Islamic Publications, 1990) 10th Edition.
37. Collective self-defence is allowed only when there is a request from the attacked state and supported by the United Nations. 1999 Gulf War is the example. This may be noted that for the Gulf War the UN Security Council invoked Article 51 of the UN Charter and passed the Resolution 671 for collective self-defence. It takes place when one or more than one states joint to provide defence to an ally under armed attack.
38. This is based on Caroline Case, 29 BFSP 1137-8. For a detailed analysis of the case, see R. Y. Jennings, "The Caroline and Acleod Cases", 32 *American Journal of International Law* (AJIL), pp. 82-89.
39. For the contrary view, see J. L. Hargrove, "The Nicaragua Judgment and the Future of the Law of Force and Self-defence", 81 *American Journal of International Law* (AJIL), 1987, p. 135; Justin N. B. Frank and Javaid Rehman, "Assessing the Liability of the Attacks by the International Coalition Against Terrorism: An Enquiry into the Self-Defence Argumant Under Article 51 of the Charter", 67 *Journal of Criminal Law* (Jo. C. L.), 2003, p. 415, at p. 418.
40. This may be noted here that in the *Nicaragua case* ICJ held that, "It may be considered to be agreed that an armed attack must be understood as including not merely action by regular armed forces

across international borders, but also the dispatch of armed bands of terrorists into the territory of another state." The necessary condition that can be noted here is 'the dispatch of armed bands of terrorists', which is not against the authors' view.

41. "Terrorism and the Legality of Pre-emptive Force", 14 *European Journal of International Law* (EJIL), 2003, p. 227.
42. According to Article 31 of the Vienna Convention on Law of Treaties, provisions should be given simple meaning in the light of its object and purpose. It has been rightly said by Micheal J. Glennan that the United States had wrongly made the case for pre-emting threats that were not immediate, but merely prospective, as in the case of Iraq. See Micheal Glennan, *New York Times*, 21 Nov. 2002. This has been agreed by Rahmatullah Khan. See Rahmatullah Khan, "The War on Terrorism", 45 *Indian Journal of International Law* (IJIL), 2005, p. 1.
43. See Y. Dinstein, *War, Aggression and Self-Defence*, (London: Cambridge University Press, 1988), p. 184; Randelzhofer, "Article 51", in B. Simma (ed.), *The Charter of the United Nations: A Commentary*, 2nd Edition, 2002, p. 803; Kirgis, "Per-emptive Action to Forestall Terrorism", *ASIL Newsletter*, July/Sep. 2002 at p. 5.
44. See Joan Fitzpatrick, "Speaking Law to Power: The War against Terrorism and Human Rights", 14 *European Journal of International Law* (EJIL), 2003, p. 241; P. Glennon, "The Fog of War: Self-Defence, Inherence, and Incoherence in Article 51 of the United Nations Charter", 25 *Harvard Journal of Law and Public Policy* (Harv. J. L. & Pub. Pol.), 1002 539; Emanuel Gross, "Thwarting Terrorist Acts by Attacking the Perpetrators or Their Commanders as an Act of Self-Defence: Human Rights Versus the State's Duty to Protect its Citizens", 15 *Temple International and Comparative Law Journal* (Temple Int'l & Comp. L. J.), 2001, p. 195. This may be noted here that Tony Blair, in one of his speeches delivered in March 2004, demanded for amendment of the international law for legalizing pre-emptive strikes. It means he accepts that under the present law, it is illegal.
45. The rules about pre-emptive strike were spelt out as long ago as 1837 in a dispute between Great Britain and the United states involving a vessel, The Caroline. This right was made available if it could be shown that "necessity of self defence is instant, overwhelming and leaving no choice of means and no moment of deliberation." This is known as 'Caroline Principle'. Since then, Israel and the United states have resorted to it several times. This principles has not been accepted a principle of customary international law.

46. The United States and the United Kingdom to surprise of the world did not even wait for the decision of the Security Council. This shows that the attack was pre-determined.
47. Mr. Powell said that his speech in February 2003 to the UN making a case for war was a "painful blot on his record". See *New Straits Times*, 14 September 2005.
48. See John Kelsey, *Islam and War- A Study in Comparative Ethics* (Kentucky: John Knox Press, 1993), pp. 35-36.
49. See Abdulaziz Sachedina, "The Development of Jihad in Islamic Revelation and History", in James Turner Johnson and John Kelsey, *Cross, Crescent, and Sword* (New York: Greenwood Press, 1990).
50. Mahmud Shaltut, The Qur'an and Fighting, in *Jihad in Mediaeval and Modern Islam* (translated by Rudolph Peters) (Leiden: E.J. Brill, 1977) at p. 51.
51. See Abdullah Yusuf Ali, *The Meaning of the Holy Qur'an* (Brentwood: Amanah Corporation, 1992), pp. 832-833.
52. See the Qur'an , *Al-Haj* (20):39-40.
53. See P. S. Rao, "International Terrorism, Self-Determination and national Liberation", in R. K. Dixit and C. Jayaraj (eds.) *Dynamics of International Law in the New Millennium* (New Delhi: ISIL, 2004), p. 115.
54. The difference between simple terrorists and insurgents is that the former use violence and kill innocent people to register their grievance, often in the hope that it can lead to some type of change in the policies of their enemies, while the later simply seeks to over through and replace the government or to get back their illegally occupied territory.
55. It was a civil war between two Muslim groups.
56. Al-Shaybani, *Kitab al-Siyar al-Kabir*, translated by Majid Khadduri, *the Islamic Law of Nations* (Baltimore: John Hopkins University Press, 1966), sec. 1372.
57. India and Pakistan had that kind of situation in 2002.
58. C. G. Weeramantry, "Religion, Law and Human Rights", 6th Professor Emeritus Ahmad Ibrahim Memorial Lecture, Organized by Ahmad Ibrahim Kulliyyah of Laws, International Islamic University, Malaysia, and delivered at the Crown princess Hotel, Kuala Lumpur, 23 July, 2005.
59. Qur'an, *al-Maeda* (5): 32.
60. See Abdul Haseeb Ansari and Parveen Jamal, "Towards an Environmental Jurisprudence", *Religion and Law Review,* Vol. X-XI, 2001-2002, p. 79.

61. According to Islamic traditions, the 'great jihad' is the struggle with one's own heart, the attempt to bring oneself into accord with the will of God. This is because whatever a man does are for the pleasure of Allah.
62. Henry S. Williams, "Terrorism and Religions",< *www.religion_online.org/showarticle.asp?title=2457*>
63. See The Holy Qur'an , Translation and Commentary, note 1270.
64. Bukhari, *Sahih* (Beirut: Dar Ihya' al-Turath al-Arabi, 2000) Vol. 5, p. 644, *hadith* no. 5432, ; Muslim, *Sahih* (Dar al-Ma' rifah, Beirut, 1997), Vol. 4, p. 578, *hadith* no. 2189.
65. There are numerous of Qur'anic *ayah* and *ahadith* on these.
66. The Qur'an, *Shura* (42): 40.
67. Tirmidhi, *Sunan* (Beirut: *Dar Ihya' al-Turath al-Arabi*, 1995), vol. 4, p. 14, *hadith* 1397.
68. For similar view, see Joseph S. Nye, "The soft-power secret of defeating terror", *New straits Times*, 2 May 2006.
69. James Dobbins, "Picking the right fight against the global terror", *New Straits Times*, 4 May 2006.
70. "Closing Mindanao's Sanctuaries of Terror", *New Straits Times*, 6 May 2006.
71. See *New Straits Times*, 13 September 2005.
72. See *New Straits Times*, 14 August 2005.
73. See *New Straits Times*, 17 July 2005.
74. *Ibid.*
75. There are four Geneva Conventions. The I Geneva Convention was re-affirmed by the II Geneva Convention for the Amelioration of the Condition of Wounded and Sick in Armed Forces. The III Geneva Convention Relative to Treatment of Prisoners of War followed the second one. The fourth Geneva Convention is Relative to the Protection of Civilian Persons in the Time of War. It also re-affirms the three previous Conventions. The user of 'Geneva Conventions' refers to the IV one, which re-affirms the previous three also.
76. See Article 4 of the Convention.
77. The Qura'n, *al-Anfal (8)*: 67.
78. The Qura'n, *Muhammad* (470): 4.
79. See Sheikh Salman al-Oadah, "Who is there for Our Prisoners of War?" (Part 2 of 3), at <*www.islamtoday.com*>
80. *Ibid*, p. 2. Also see Syed R. Hassan, *The Reconstruction of Legal Thought in Islam* (Lahore: Law Publishing Company, 1974), p. 171.

81. This figure has recently been released by the Pentagon. Originally, the figure was more than six hundred. Of them, some have been released. See *The Star*, 21 April 2006.
82. In the detention camps of the Bay, foreign citizens are kept. They are terrorist suspects arrested and brought from different parts of the world. American citizens are in the US jails.
83. This has been said by the UN- Economic and Social Council, Commission on Human Rights, Sixty-second Session, E /CN.4/2006/ 120. After the suicide committed by three detainees at the Guantanamo Detention camp, has ignited new calls to shut down the detention camp. Saudi Arabia said it was stepping up efforts to free all Saudi detainees. Waleed al-Tabtaie, a former Member of Parliament, said that the US should release the prisoners or give them fair trials. See *New Straits Times*, 13 June 2006.
84. See *New Straits Times*, 13 June 2006.
85. New Straits Times, 23 June 2006.
86. Joan Fitzpatrick, footnote 44, at p. 241.
87. In *Hamdi* v. *Rumsfeld: US*, 542 US 570 (2004), the Supreme Court of the United States held: "...We hold that ..., due process demands that a citizen held in the US as an enemy combatant be given a meaningfull opportunity to contest the factual basis for that detention before a neutral decision maker." At pp. 14-15. In *Rasul* v. *Bush*, and *Al Oadah* v. *US* (consolidated), 542 US 466 (2004), the Supreme Court said that the right to *habeas corpus* is not dependent of citizen status. The detainees, therefore, were free to bring suit challenging detention as unconstitutional. At pp. 4-16.
88. See 17 January 2006, *the Washington Post* at: *<www.Washigtonpost .com>*
89. 542 US 466 (2004).
90. See the US District Court for the District of Columbia, decision 16 January 2005 in *re Guantanamo Detainees*, 355 F. Supp. 2nd 443, at pp. 468-478.
91. 548 US 557 (2006)
92. See *New Straits Times*, 13 June 2006.
93. "Beginning of the end for Guantanamo Bay", *New StraitsTimes*, 20 July, 2006.
94. See *New Straits Times*, 1 July 2006.
95. *See New Straits Times*, 18 October 2006.
96. 553 US 655 (2008).

97. *Al Jazeerah*, 6 May 2008. Also see, *The Muslim World*, 2nd Issue of May 2008.

98. See Sheikh Fysal Mawlawi, "Islam and Kidnapping Innocents", at *<http://islamonline.net/english/Contemporary/2004/09/Article01.shtml>*

99. *Ibid.*

100. Ibne Rushd expresses his view in *Bidayat Al-Mujtahid* (Beirut: *Dar al-Fikr*, n.d.), p. 98. It is also mentioned in Ibne Kathir, *Tafseer Ibne Kathir* (Beirut: *Dar Ihya' al-Turath al-Arabi*, 2000), Vol. 4, p. 173.

101. See Mohammad Hamidullah, *Muslim Conduct of State* (Lahore: Mohammad Ashraf, 1996) p. 214.

102. See the Qura'n, *Muhammad* (47): 4.

103. The Qur'an, *al-Mulk* (42): 15.

104. Awad M. Awad, "The Rights of the Accused Under Islamic Criminal Procedure", in Cherif Bassioni (ed.) *The Islamic Criminal Justice System* (London: Oceans Publications, 1982), p. 91.

105. See *Al-Fatawa Al-Hindiyya* (This is a collection of *fatawa* compiled during the reign of the Mughal King Aurangzeb) See at : *<www. al-Islam>*.

106. There is no consensus about the time, but it has to be the shortest possible time. See Al-Mawardi, *Al-Ahkam Al-Sultaniyya* (Beirut: Dar al-Kitab al-Arabi, 1994), p. 386.

107. See *Al-Ahkam Al-Sultaniyyah*, *ibid*, pp. 386-387.

108. Awad and Awad, "The Right...", footnote 104, at p. 103.

109. Taha J. al 'Alwani, "Rights of the Accused in Islam", 11 *American Journal of Islamic Social Sciences*, 1994, p. 504.

110. The United States has asserted that at the Guantanmo Bay detention camp, detainees are not abused, psychological and physical. This has been falsified by the stories of abuse told by some of the detainees who were released from the camp, including the story of abuse narrated by Mr. Mubanga, one of the four British citizens, released from the camp on the request of the United Kingdom. See *New Straits Times*, 5 December 2005. The International Committee of the Red Cross (ICRC) also prepared 24 pages confidential report on which disclosed the abuse and ill treatment of prisoners in Iraq between March and October 2003. This report could not remain confidential. See *New Straits Times*, 31 May 2004, and 27 July 2004.

111. See *New Straits Times*, 28 September 2005 and 3 October 2005.

112. See Andrew Sullivan, "How torture became a matter of routine", *The Times*, 2 October 2005.

113. See *American Post* 28 January 2005. This has been re-printed in *New Straits Times*, 29 January 2005.
114. It is an act of deliberately eroding the religious values of Islam. It is needled to say that most of the detainees profess Islam as their religion.
115. See *New Sunday Times*, 15 February 2004. This may e noted here that those terrorists cannot be considered under the international law as enemy combatants.
116. "Rebel with A Cause? Terrorists and Humanitarian Law", 14 *European Journal of International Law* (EJIL), 2003, p. 299.
117. See *New Straits Times*, 28 May 2004.
118. We may note here that President Bush, after the September 11, 2001 attacks on the United States, declared that al-Qaeda and Taleban fighters captured in Afghanistan or elsewhere were unlawful combatants not covered by the Geneva Conventions. However, they will be treated humanly nonetheless "in the manner consistent with the Geneva Conventions".
119. *New Straits Times*, 20 May 2006.
120. See *New Straits Times*, 23 January 2006.
121. It is "Responsibility commanders and other high officials for war crimes committed by sub-ordinate members of the armed forces or other persons subject to their control."
122. See Timothy Wu and Yong-Sung King, "Criminal Liability for Actions of Subordinates–the Doctrine of Command Responsibility and its Analogues in the United States Law", 38 *Harvard International Law Journal* (Harv. ILJ), 1997, p. 290; M. Feria Tinta, "Commander on Trial: the Balakis Case and the Doctrine of Command Responsibility under International Law, 47 *Netherlands International Law Review* (NILR), 2000, p. 293; Leslie Greene, "Command Responsibility in International Humanitarian Law", 5 *Transnational Law and Contemporary Problems* (TLCP), 1995, p. 319.
123. Ibne Hibban, *Sahih* (Beirut: *Moassah al-Risalah*, 1993), vol. 11, p. 607, *hadith* no. 5199.
124. See Al-Tabari, *Tafseer Al-Tabri* (Beirut: *Dar al-Fiqr*), vol. 29 p. 209.
125. See vol. 42, p. 456.
126. See Tabrani, *Muajjam Kabir* (Kairo: *Maktb al-Ulum Wa al-Hukm*, 1983), Vol. 22, p. 393.
127. Abu Daud, *Sunan* (Beirut: *Dar al-Fikr*, 1863), vol. 3, p. 244, *hadith* no. 3332.
128. Bukhari, see supra, Vol. 67, p. 644, *hadith* no. 4372.

129. See S. A. Farar, "Islamic jurisprudence and the role of the accused: a re-examination", 23 Legal Studies, p. 587; Taha j. al Alwani, "The Rights of the Accused in Islam", 11 *The American Journal of Islamic Social Sciences*, p. 506; Ibn Hazm, *al-Muhalla* (Beirut: *Dr al-Aa al-Jadid*), Vol. 11, p. 141.

It is notable here that starving, beating, consignment are considered as duress. See Abd al Razzaq, *al- Musannaf* (Beiru: *al- Maktab al-Islami*, 1403 Hijri), Vol. 10, p. 193.

130. *Al-Bukhari,* supra note , vol. 3, p. 1095, *hadith* no. 2846.

131. Zakaria Al-Ansari, *Asnal Matalib*, vol. 9, p. 366. See at: *<www. Al-Islam>.*

132. Al-Waqedi, *Maghazi*, p. 515. See at: *<www. al-Islam>.*

133. Al Hakim, *Mustadrik* (Beirut: *Dar al-Kutub al-Ilmiyyah*, 1990), Vol. 2, p. 168, *hadith* no. 2662.

134. Al-Tirmidh, *Sunan* (Beirut: *Dar Ihya' al-Turath al-Arabi*, 1995), Vol. 3, p. 580, *hadith* no. 1283.

135. See at: *<www.kavkazcenter.com/eng/islam/hrislam>*

136. See Howard Abadinsky, *An Introduction to American Legal System* (New Jersey: Prentice Hall, 2002), 5th Ed. p. 62-65; Daniel E. Hall (ed.), *Criminal Law and Procedure* (New York: West Legal Studies Pub., 2002), 3rd Ed. p. 48-51.

137. 404 US 514 (1972).

138. He expounded in this case that determination whether a particular defendant has been denied seedy trial is to be made on case-by-case basis. Judges must look at the length of the delay, reasons for the delay, timely assertion for the right to a speedy trial and prejudice to the defendant as a result of the delay.

139. See *New Straits Times*, 1 July 2006.

140. See *New Straits Times*, 30 June 2004.

141. See *New Straits Times,* 26 June 2004.

142. Recently, in view of the Supreme Court's decision, the Bush regime has decided that military will review the individual cases of the detainees of the Guantanamo Bay. For this purpose a panel of three military officers is reviewing the detention cases. Perhaps, the United States is doing this so that it could plead before the Federal Courts in cases filed by the detainees that they were provided protection of the 'due process' rule.

143. [2004] UK HL 56.

144. *BBC News*, 8:1, 16 December 2004.

145. 117 *Harvard Law Review* (Harv. L. Rev.), 2003, p. 287.

146. See *Harisiades* v. *Shaughnessy*, 342 U. S. 580 (1952); *Kleindienst* v. *Mandel*, 408 U. S. 753 (1972). Also see David Cole, "In Aid of Removal: Due Process Limits on Immigration Detention", 51 *Emory Law Journal* (Emory L. J.), 2002, p. 103.

147. See *Zadvydas* v. *Davis*, 533 U. S. 678 (2001); *Landon* v. *Plasencia*, 459 U. S. 21 (1982).

148. 123 S. CT. 1708 (1982).

149. See David Cole, footnote 150 (infra), at p. 108. .

150. See David Cole, "Terrorism and the Rule of Law", A Review of Ronald Daniels, Patrick Macklem, Kent Roach (eds.) *The Security of Freedom: Essays on Canada's Anti-Terrorism Bill* (Toronto: University of Toronto Press, 2001), p. 499.

151. See Lisa Finnegan Abdolian and Takooshian, "The USA PATRIOT Act: Civil Liberties, the Media, and Public Opinion", 30 *Fordham Urban Law Journal* (Fordham Urb. L. J.), 2003, p. 1429; N. Chang, "The USA PATRIOT Act: What Is So Patriotic About Trampling on The Bill of Rights?", < http://www. sevenstories.com >; N. Chang, *Silencing Political Dissent: How Post-September 11 Anti-Terrorism Measures Threaten Our Civil Liberties* (New York: Seven Stories Press, 2002); A. Clymer, "Anti-Terrorism Bill Passes: US Gets Expanded Powers", *New York Times*, 26 October, 2001; A. Goldstein, "A Deliberate Strategy of Disruption", *Washington Post*, 4 October, 2001; Abdul Haseeb Ansari, footnote 6 at p. ccxxxv.

152. [2003] 1 ALL ER 816.

153. See Razman Bin Abdul Rahim, "The United Kingdom Terrorism Act 2006: From the Bill to the Act", [2008] 4 MLJ cxlii.

154. This may be noted here that preventive detentions are made either on the basis of a specific constitutional provision or a specific legislation like the Internal Security Act of Malaysia. Preventive detentions are different than detentions of suspected terrorists. Those who are detained under the preventive detention law can remain under detention for a longer period without producing before the court, but their detentions have to be reviewed by the competent administrative authority or the court, as the case may be, from time to time.

155. (1996) 1 BHRC 625.

156. This should be noted that most of the countries have given the power to review to the High Court. Some other countries have made tribunal for this purpose.

157. At p. 643. Also see *Chahal* v. *UK*, (1996) 1 BHRC 405. In this case, pertaining to Article 5 the Court said, "Everyone has the right to liberty and security of person. No one shall be deprived of his liberty save in the following cases and *in accordance with a procedure prescribed by law*...(f) the lawful arrest or detention of a person...against whom action is being taken with a view to deportation." This odes not mean that the detentions will be arbitrary and for unlimited periods.

158. The Court of Appeal in *R.* v. *Secretary of State for Home Department*, [2002] All ER 373, has also expressed the same view. The Court says that a person cannot be detained because he lacks British nationality. In order to detain him there must be some other justification, such as that he is suspected of having committed a criminal act. If there is to be an effective derogation from the right to liberty enshrined in Article 5 in respect of suspected international terrorists, -and we can see powerful arguments in favour of such a derogation-the derogation ought rationally to extend to all ...suspected terrorists. This is a cautious approach of the Court. The popular view of the courts is that derogation is allowed only by the grave emergency threatening terrorist attacks.

159. The idea is that close door trials will be conducted by "security-cleared" judges. It will be a part of a two-tier trial system-first hearing in close door in a special court and the second hearing before the conventional court-enabling the use of intelligence material in terrorism cases. The second hearing will be based on the summary prepared by the court of first hearing.

160. See *New Straits Times*, 3 February 2004. This may be noted that in the United Kingdom, about 561 detainees of different nationalities are there in different jails. See *New Straits Times*, 1 June 2004. This number is increasing.

161. *Sureh al-Muluk* (67): 15.

162. See Awad M. awad, "The Rights of the Accused under Islamic Criminal Procedure", footnote 104, pp. 97-99.

163. The United States has done it in wake of the forthcoming presidential election in the country.

164. Some of the examples of state terrorism are as follows: 1. Attacking a country for falsely alleged reasons; 2. Threatening a country to attack for no reasons; 3. Illegally occupying territory of another country; 4. During war, not following the principles of proportionality, discrimination and necessity; 5. Committing or supporting the act of genocide; 6. Use of weapons of mass destruction, e.g., chemical,

biological, or nuclear weapons; 7. Supporting a despotic regime; 8. Supporting an illegal insurgency. 9. Performing illegal incursions in another country and killing innocent people and destroying properties; 10. Supporting terrorists by any means, or harboring them; 11. Weakening or dominating the economy of a country; 12. Giving subsidy on those agricultural items that substantially contribute the economy of developing or underdeveloped country or countries; 13. Supporting one or some of the groups involved in rioting in a country; and 14. Detaining people for indefinite period for no substantial reason (s).

165. This may be noted here that the United States is of the view that by this war 50 million people have been liberated and their civil and political rights have been protected. See *New Straits Times*, 28 May 2004.

166 Abdul Haseeb Ansari and Nik Ahmad Kamal "Terrorism, Law and Human Rights", Paper presented at the International Conference on Muslims and Islam in the 21st Century: Image and Reality, 4-6 August 2004, PWTC, Malaysia, Organized by the IIUM, Malaysia. The paper was later published in the *IKIM Law Journal,* Vol. 9, No. 1, p. 12. Also see Abdul Haseeb Ansari and Nik Ahmad Kamal, "Contemporary Issues in Terrorism", in Abdul Rashid Moten and Noraini M. Noor, *Terrorism –Democracy–The West and the Muslim World* (Kuala Lumpur: Thompson, 2007) p. 119.

167. See Ruslina Yusuf, "An eye on political prisoners", *New Straits Times*, 31 May 2004.

168. See Abdul Haseeb Ansari and Nik Ahmad Kamal, "Prevention, Abatement and Control of Pollution of Straits: An Appraisal with Special Reference to the Straits of Malacca", *Malayan Law Journal*, pp. xxxvii-lxxvi.

169. The following rules are common: POWs will be in custody of the state; The state can exact labour from them; The detaining sate will be responsible for their maintenance, which will be subject to repatriation; They will be subjected to humane treatment; they will obey the laws of the detaining state; they will be permitted to perform their religious rites; their wills will be executed; they will not be exposed to brutality to procure information useful for the conduct of operation; and they should be released and repatriated without delay after the cessation of active hostilities.

10

The Contract of Ja'alah and The Modern Banking Business: Juristic Analysis

Hafiz Ali Ismail

The Meaning and Nature of Ja'alah

In its literal meaning, *ja'alah* (rewarding) is the term for the consideration offered to a person in return for a performance[1]. In the contract of *ja'alah,* the party, who undertakes to pay a reward, is called *ja'ail* or rewarder; whereas, the party, who is required to perform, is called *majaul lahu* or rewardee[2].

According to the Maliki school of thought, *ja'alah* is the undertaking to pay a reward in return for a utility or *Manfa'ah.* However, to Ibn Arafah, who is a Maliki jurist, *ju'al* or reward is a contract of exchange in which the reward is given in return for a certain performance, provided that the reward does not accrue from the subject-matter of the contract of *ja'alah.* Moreover, the reward will only be earned upon complete performance, whereas the partial performance gets nothing[3].

The Maliki definition emphasizes the essence of *Ja'alah* the utility which may or may not occur, as the contract of *ja'alah* involves the element of uncertainty or *Gharar.* Although the definition is consistent with that of Ibn Arafah, he gives great emphasis to separation of reward from the subject-matter. As such, the consideration in *Ja'alah* shall not be given out of the subject-matter of *Ja'alah*, in the sense that it must be a separate consideration. In contrast to the opinion of Ibn Arafah, the majority of jurists maintain that the partial performance in *ja'alah* requires the payment of wage or *Ujr* which is normally the prevailing market rate. The partial performance may not entitle a person to the reward offered, otherwise the contract is considered invalid[4].

Ja'alah according to the majority, is legitimate unilateral contract, its legitimacy rests in a Qur'anic verse in which Allah (*s.w.t.*) says "*They said: "We miss the great beaker of the king; For him who produce it, Is (the reward of) A camel load; I will be bound by it"*[5] . The *hadith* has also been quoted to reinforce it. This occurred when companions passed on Arab village without being hosted. The head of the village had been poisoned and was in urgent need of treatment. The group initially declined to cure him unless a flock of goats to be the consideration. The head of the village was cured when one of the groups started reciting Qur'anic verses. Subsequently the Prophet (*s.a.w.*) asked about the legitimacy of taking a reward (the goats) in return for the deed. The Prophet (*s.a.w.*) approved the taking of the reward in return for the work[6].

In addition, *ja'alah* is permissible so as to satisfy the needs of people wherever the required performance cannot be done without the making of such contract; or the rewarder has not been able to perform the act personally and there is no one to perform the act free of charge. There may be some types of performance which by their very nature are not capable of being the subject-matter under a contract of *Ijarah,* and may be performed on *Ja'alah* basis for the satisfaction of the people's needs[7].

On the other hand, jurists of the Hanafi school of thought do not recognize *Ja'alah* on the ground that the contract involves element of uncertainty or *Gharar* in respect of its eventual objective, as well as the contract duration. However, they recognize that the payment of a reward on *Ja'alah* basis in return for recovery of a slave who escaped from his master. The reward for recovering the slave may be fixed in term of sum of money. The Hanafi school of thought seems to regard *Ja'alah* as synonymous to *Ijarah.* Thus any specified performance must be a valid subject-matter for *Ijarah* contract rather than *Ja'alah* [8].

As for the requirements of formation, *Ja'alah* is a reward offered by a party in means of words, or written means to the public or to specified or unspecified person or persons demonstrates on the express intention of the rewarder to contract on a *Ja'alah* basis for specified or unspecified performance. Where the offer has been made by the rewarder to a specific person, the contract would be concluded upon the acceptance of the other. In case the offer of reward has been made to unspecified persons the contract is considered entered into upon the commencement of the actual performance. As a general rule, formal acceptance of the rewardee is not an essential requirement for formation. It may be interesting to note that an offer may not always be made by the rewarder himself in the sense that the reward can be suggested by the other party. Thus, and to that effect, al-Zarkashi has pointed out that where the rewardee himself has taken the initiative to suggest a performance of specified act in return for a fixed reward, the contract is created and would take its legal implications if, the rewarder consented[9].

The clearness of the words expressed by the rewarder in making the offer is highly significant in determining whether a permission is given to commence the performance or not. Where the act has been performed without the consent of the recipient of benefit, the party, who undertakes the performance, will not be entitled to the reward, and the performance in question will only be regarded as made voluntarily of charitable basis. The rule is also applicable where the rewarder requests in his own right the rewardee to perform the act but was performed by another without a valid right.

It is established that the party who undertakes the performance must have sound knowledge of the requirement. Mere performance of the act without prior knowledge may not entitle the other party who performed the act to get a reward in return, though the permission is given.[10]

The essence of *Ja'alah* is the performance of the act. Therefore, the unspecific acts that are not capable of being good subject-matters under the contract of *Ijarah* can be performances subject to the contract of *Ja'alah* so as to satisfy the people's needs. The jurists, however, have difference of opinion regarding the performances which are specific and accordingly capable of being subject-matters for *Ijarah*. The first view seems to have supported the specific performance to be a good subject-matter for *Ja'alah* contract as well, in the sense that the party is given the option either to enter into the contract of *Ijarah or Ja'alah*. The second view, however, maintains that the specific performance is only restricted to *Ijarah* contract. It would seem that the first view which supports the specific performance to be a subject-matter for *Ja'alah* contract is more flexible and may also be convenient to the parties as *Ja'alah's* main principles are in some ways different from *Ijarah,* therefore the parties may find it more beneficial to them to enter into *Ja'alah* rather than any other contract.

Ja'alah, in civil law terms, would be the promise to the public to undertake the payment of a reward in return for specific performance. The person who undertakes the performance will be entitled to the reward where he has performed the required act without a prior knowledge of the reward. As such, where a promise has been made unknown to the performer the reward would be earned upon the actual performance[11]. The promisor would be permitted to withdraw his promise by a subsequent offer made to the public to that effect, provided this does not affect the right of any person who has completed the required performance before the withdrawal. The contract of *Ja'alah* is also relevant to other types of performances in the commercial and marketing sectors and the sport games as well. In addition rewards are also offered in return for performances which are consistent with state and government policies in different fields of knowledge made for the purpose of encouragement.

It is generally understood by many that the contract of *Ja'alah* applies only to the traditional performances which were earlier elaborated by the jurists. However, a careful examination to the writings of the jurists from various schools of law reveals that the list of performances on the basis of *Ja'alah* is comprehensive and includes all the traditional performances, in addition to some other performances which are much similar and more relevant to our modern banking business, thus, it is appropriate to attempt identifying all these performances as discussed by the jurist even before the emergence of the modern banking system. Our discussion may also slightly toughs on the view of a contemporary scholar who has tried to relate the contract of *Ja'alah* to some banking business.

Attraction of Savings

Reference to the main principles of *Ja'alah* reveals that the safe keeping of property or *Wadi'ah* is capable of being a subject-matter for *Ja'alah* contract provided that the property must be specified as well as the safe keeping has to be for a certain period of time[12]. This assumption is where the safe keeping of property is made essentially as the safeguard of any sort of transgression or destruction, to illustrate this if a person says to another safe keep my property in return for a reward, then it is permissible *Ja'alah* as noted by al-Ansari, the most important requirement is the specification of the property and the time limit for safe-keeping. However, the question which may arise here is whether the concept of banking deposits, which is normally made by the depositors for the safe-keeping of their money, can be a valid performance on the basis of which a reward is deserved. Taking into consideration the legal maxim that maintains that the rule in contracts is the permissibility *Ibaha,* unless there is a presumption to indicate the contrary. In addition to the flexibility of *Ja'alah* as the contract, the bank may offer a reward for the purpose of attracting deposits on the legal basis of *Wadiah.*

The justification may be that banking has become a huge industry necessary for any community in the world. Banks have to depend heavily on the customers' deposits in the first place in order to mobilizes the funds and make such funds available to the money users or the investors. One of the most important money users for the customer funds is the government represented by the central bank. The government may normally receive the customer's funds in terms of borrowings. Therefore, in order to finance vital projects through indirect borrowings the banks and the government, as a matter of policy, may encourage the habit of saving at the individual level for the well being of the whole community. It is submitted, therefore, that encouraging the habit of savings among the customers by rewarding may be acceptable performance under the contract of *Ja'alah.*

In the view of a contemporary scholar, one of the main functions of banking is to act as an intermediary between the customers and the investors. The commercial bank, for instance, mobilizes funds and makes them available to investors who may be interested in receiving funds for their investments. The bank on its capacity as a financial intermediary may offer such service to its customers. The service rendered in term of arranging capitals from the depositors fund will be made on the basis of dormant partnership or *mudaraba*, accordingly the bank may be entitled to get a reward for the service rendered[13]. Thus the service rendered by the bank has been considered valid performance whereby the bank deserves a reward in return. The reward which the bank is entitled to take in return for the service may be justified on the light of the following two factors:

1. As the consideration for the work or the performance done in which the bank will be entitled to take a wage or *Ujr*.
2. In addition to the wage, the bank will be entitled to a reward as it shares the profit generated which belong to the capital supplier (the depositors), and for that purpose the depositors will be required to donate part of their shares in the profit in favor of the bank which undertakes the performance[14].

Scholars continue to maintain that there are occasions in which the bank may be in need to attract more deposits from the public so as to make such deposits or funds available for investments. The attraction of deposits from the public may be made by means of making use of the contract of *Ja'alah*, in the sense that the depositor, who originally involves in dormant partnership *Mudaraba* as the capital supplier, will be entitled to a reward in addition to the ratio of sharing the profit generated which must be fixed in advance with certainty. As such, the concept of taking reward may be justified based on the authorization given to the bank as an intermediary in investing the capitals with the respective investors and that is deemed to be a valid performance under *Ja'alah*[15].

It seems that the above idea is focused mainly on the deposits that had and received on the investment account which normally operates on the basis of *mudaraba*. However, banks also accept deposits from the customers who seek safe custody of their funds and absolute convenience in their use in form of current or saving accounts. The attraction of deposits in saving or current accounts in return for a reward may also be made on the basis of *Ja'alah* contract.

Arrangement of Loans

In Islamic banking, most money lending can be done by making use of debt financing instruments which are basically sale contracts.

Lending on loan basis is still allowed in Islamic law, but it has to be without interest or *Fa'aidah.* This type of lending is known as the benevolent loan or *Qard Hasan.* This contract is therefore more relevant in the social welfare sector of the economy, or where there is a social implication such as in dealing with government rather than in the private or commercial sector of the economy[16]. However, arrangement of loans in return for a fixed reward is proven to be valid performance under the contract of *Ja'alah.* The legal basis for such practice has been found in scattered statements made by prominent jurists. Ibn Qu'damah while elaborating the rules which govern the contract of loan, has pointed out that where a person has requested or instructed another to arrange specified amount of money, such as one hundred in return for ten, for him on loan basis from certain person in return for a reward to be given to the requested person, it is permissible *ja'alah*[17].

To the same effect, al-Mawardi has maintained that where a person has requested another to arrange a loan for him from either specific or unspecific person it is a permissible *Ja'alah.* The view of al-Mawardi gives the requested person an absolute option regarding the loan arrangement whether from specific or unspecific person. al-Mawardi has also illustrated such practice in a manner similar to that maintained by Ibn Qu'damah[18]. Moreover, al-Mawardi has also confirmed that such practice is approved by al-Imam Ahmed.

Further views have been attributed to al-Rawyani, where a loan has been arranged in return for a consideration such as one hundred in return for ten it is a contract of *ja'alah*[19]. It would be interesting to note that the illustration given by the jurists is the same, as to the amount of the loan and the rate of the reward. As such the reward would amount to 10% out of the principal amount of the loan made. However, subject to the contract of *Ja'alah* and its terms and conditions, the reward rate could be more than that as long as its rate is dependent on how beneficial the performance is to the rewarder. Therefore, in *ja'alah* it is not necessary for the reward given to commensurate with the actual efforts undertaken in the performance. However, this requirement may be necessary for the contract of *Ijarah.* It may also be interesting to note that al-Bahwati, while discussing the various aspects of *Ja'alah,* has mentioned that the arrangement of loan in return for a reward is valid as the reward has nothing to do with the loan or *Qard* contract[20]. Rather the reward is deserved by the rewardee for being good in contact and able enough in convincing the lender to pass the loan to another person.

Moreover, according to al-Ansari, the statements made by the jurists in relation to loan arrangement may be categorized under the contract of *ja'alah*. The person who moves the request may be regarded as borrower, in the sense that the loan would pass to his ownership. Hence he would be required to repay the equivalent of it to the lender at the time of settlement. In reviewing the practice, al-Ansari maintained that such practice has a relation with agency *Wakalah*[21]. Indeed, the element of agency is involved in arrangement of loan. However the reward given was not only in return for playing the role of an agent on behalf of the borrower, but essentially for the efforts made out in looking for fund and this is the essence of the loan arrangement. Assume the borrower was able to contact the lender directly and borrow the money there would be no need for an intermediary to arrange the loan. The rewardee in arranging the loan would be required to act as an agent in adding the loan to the name of the lender inasmuch as the contract of loan would not be valid unless the agent has added the principal amount borrowed to the ownership of the loan grantor. To sum up, it would be erroneous to consider the reward given in return for acting as an agent only, the reward is given originally in return for all the efforts undertaken to locating the fund as well as passing the loan to the rewarder.

It is submitted that the statements made by jurists in respect of arrangement of loans predicates that the money is to be owned by a third party in the first place. Their statements will not in any way amount to *Riba* which is strictly prohibited, where the loan has been made from any fund belonging to a third party. To my mind, bringing such practice in commercial banking needs complete separation between shareholders fund and the depositors fund, in addition to some amendments relating to the underlying legal basis for the money had and received in the depositors fund and this will be highlighted in a separate paper.

Debt Collection

Banking commercial instruments may mainly include bills of exchange and cheques. The bill can be defined as unconditional order in writing addressed by one person to another, signed by the person giving it requiring the person to whom it is addressed to pay on demand or at a fixed or determinable future time a sum certain in money to, or to the order of a specified person, or to the bearer. The cheque is a bill of exchange drawn on a banker payable on demand[22]. A commercial bank normally extends the service of debt collection to its customers in its capacity as an agent. Accordingly the bank may charge the customer a certain sum of money on the legal basis of *Ujr*. Imam Malik is reported to have said where a person requested another for collection of debt or *Qabd al-Dayn* from a third party in return for a part of it, is permissible *Ja'alah*. The view of Imam Malik was further supported by Ibn Rushd provided the reward is a portion of the debt itself. The time for deserving the reward, however, may either be at the time of contracting or after the commencement of actual collection of the debt[23].

Further views have also been expressed as to the collection of bills of exchange. It is reported that the bank will be entitled to a reward upon the actual collection of the bill of exchange. The collection of bills of exchange has been given the same legal basis of recovering the missing objects. And no doubt the recovery of missing objects is considered permissible performance under the contract of *Ja'alah* whereby a reward is earned[24].

Thus, wherever the bank has collected the amount of the bill of exchange on behalf of its customer, the bank would deserve a reward for the work done or the service rendered. The bank, however, would not be entitled to take any reward if it has not collected the amount. Although some others, have said that the bank would deserve a reward once the bank has made a claim on behalf of the customer and not necessarily the collection of the bill of exchange in itself[25].

Letter of Guarantee

One of the banking practices is to issuance of letters of guarantee or *Khitab al-Daman* in favor of a customer. Where a letter of guarantee has been legalized on the basis of guarantee or *Kafalah* injunctions, no wage or commission should be paid in return. This argument seems to be based on a norm laid down by the jurists whereby charging hire or commission in return for the issuance of a letter may be classified under the granting of loan which accrues benefit to the issuer, because the guarantor will be required to effect the payment where a claim to that effect has been made. However, another view has based the issuance of a letter of guarantee on the agency injunctions; hence, a bank will be allowed to ask for hire in return for the service rendered.

In line with charging a wage or *Ujr* in return for the issuance, the Association of Islamic Jurisprudence holds the view that the hire is legitimate where it has been taken as a consideration for the actual expense incurred and not as the consideration for the effect of payment regarding the claim made. Subject to *Ja'alah* contract, it has been claimed that taking a consideration in connection with a personal guarantee is a permissible reward on the basis of *Ja'alah*[26]. However, one of the principles, which has been elaborated by the jurists in conjunction with the subject-matter of the contract is that whatever, is held capable to be a subject-matter for *Ijarah* can also be a subject-matter for *Ja'alah.* Accordingly the issuance of a letter of guarantee can also be a valid performance whereby the reward may be deserved.

Leasing Services

Leasing or *Ijarah* is defined as simply as transfer of property in usufruct for specified payment. It may also indicate the sale of usufruct which includes rendering of service. The modern banking finances businesses in terms of *Ijarah* after purchasing the assets with the view of subsequently leasing such assets to the customers at an agreed rental for fixed period of time[27]. The specified subject-matter of *Ijarah,* in theory, is held to be a valid subject-matter for the contract of *Ja'alah* as well, in the sense that the parties have been given the option to elect which contract they intend to conclude.

The traditional performances, which were given by jurists, are those of construction, examples building of a wall, or a house etc. in addition to preparation of a thing such as sewing of clothes[28]. The construction and preparatory performances may be extended to include industrial and manufacturing works. However, it must be taken into consideration that where work has been performed partly the rewardee deserves only the equivalent payment subject to the market price, provided the partial performance has achieved some benefit to the rewarder who undertakes to pay the reward for a complete performance.

Brokering businesses

According to a contemporary scholar, the *Ja'alah* contract includes also the works which are of brokering nature[29]. The brokering business has been held to be permissible performance capable of being valid subject-matter of the contract. It is attributed to Imam Malik that whoever plays an intermediary role in respect of purchase and selling of goods in return for specified amount of money is entitled to a reward on *ja'alah* basis. For Imam Malik such practice cannot be categorized as *Ijarah.*

However, Ibn Sirrin and others are of the view that the broker who is acting as an intermediary in trade is entitled to get a payment in return for his efforts. Hence, the effort undertaken by the broker is held to fall under the permissibility in general. Moreover the effort undertaken is considered similar to hiring a person to do specific work[30]. And as mentioned earlier, the contract of *ja'alah* is capable of including all types of performances whether specific or unspecific. As such the effort undertaken by the broker may fall under the contract of *Ja'alah* rather than that of *Ijarah* by its very nature necessitate the performance to be specific and certain. Conversely, where the performance is not specific and certain, it can be valid subject-matter for the contract of *Ja'alah* which is flexible enough to cover all types of uncertain performances.

Requirement of Hardship

In connection to performance under the contract of *Ja'alah,* jurists have laid down a requirement stipulates that the performance must include hardship *Mashaqah* incurred by the rewardee[31]. Hardship, however, has been a subject of differences among the jurists, inasmuch as the hardship is always connected to the nature of the required performance. Some jurists, however, have demonstrated unlimited numbers of performances capable of being permissible subject-matter under contract of *Ja'alah.* The hardship may readily be conceivable in some of those performances, whereas in others it may hardly be established.

As a general rule, however, in establishing the degree of the hardship incurred, it is not necessary that the reward offered be in accordance with the degree of hardship incurred. As such, the reward can be surprising compared with the exact hardship incurred by the rewardee so long as it determined only by the rewarder on his absolute discretion. Conversely, where a complete performance is required in return for a reward, the rewardee would not be entitled to get the reward in case of failure at the last moment to complete the performance irrespective of the degree of the hardship incurred[32]. Thus, it is evident that the rewarder may lose his efforts, in addition to any expense incurred in connection with the performance. It would seem that the above mentioned requirements have been laid down by the jurists in order to justify the reward in return for performance.

On the other hand, jurists have established a rule whereby even an appointed rewardee will not be required to perform the act personally. Accordingly, the rewardee is permitted to authorize another to perform[33]. Thus, where the rewardee has been given the right to transfer the performance to a third party based on the concept of agency *Wakalah*, the hardship would be transferred by the rewardee to another despite the fact that the reward would only be deserved by the rewardee, The transfer of the performance whether, wholly or partly would be valid provided that the rewarder has accepted such transfer. However, any transfer of performance must be based on reasonable grounds. Upon completion of the required performance, the rewardee would be entitled to the reward as a principal because the performance has been done by another in the capacity of agent only.

The Reward

The jurists have laid down a requirement in which the reward *ja'al* should be known and fixed in advance whether in the form of specified amount of money or otherwise. As mentioned before, the contract of *Ja'alah* has some of the main features of *Ijarah* contract. Therefore, it is a requirement that the reward must always take the form of money[34]. The absence of the reward, however, may render the contract void. The contract is also held void where the reward involves any element which is strictly prohibited by Islamic law such as lack of ability to deliver the reward or the reward has been given out of *ja'alah*' subject-matter.

In case where the rewarder has provided the necessary expense for the performance of the work, the reward has to be paid as a consideration for the work done. However, where the rewardee has undertaken to provide the materials, tools and any other essential expense in connection with the performance the rewardee is expected initially to make an estimation of all the operational costs with reference to the prices of the materials and tools, wages to be paid and the amount and arrangements that the rewardee has envisaged for receipt of his own fees and then declare a definite and fixed amount as a reward acceptable to him[35].

It may be appropriate to distinguish between wage or *Ujr, reward* or *Ja'al*, and Commission or *umulah.* As pointed out before, there is a distinction between the three. The wage which is the consideration of *Ijarah* should always commensurate with the level of the required performance. Hence, and most probably the amount of the wage may be estimated according to the market price. Normally, the reward *Ja'al* in the contract of *Ja'alah* can be more than the amount of the wage. The main characteristic regarding the *Ja'al* is that it is not subjected to the market price in any way. As such *Ja'al* can go much higher, and it cannot be controlled in amount unless by the rewarder himself, because the contract of *Ja'alah* in Islamic law was made lawful in order to satisfy the people's need. Therefore, its amount depends mainly on how and to what extent the performance is beneficial to the rewarder, and of course the rewarder is in a better position to decide on his own benefit and interest after making the necessary calculations according to the ordinary surrounding circumstances.

On the other hand, the commission or commitment fee *umulah* has been used as synonymous to wage or *Ujr*, Hence the commission would be legitimate where it has been given as the consideration for real service rendered. The criterion in deciding whether such commission is legitimate or not under Islamic law is whether the commission which normally takes the form of specified amount of money, is a consideration given in return for a work done, service rendered or effort made. If the answer positive then the commission will be legitimate, otherwise it is not. It should be noted, however, the term " service charge" in the context of banking practice may indicate the actual expense incurred in providing the service to its customer.

Expense of Reward

Reward or *ja'al* is originally given in return for performance of the act. The necessary expense needed for the performance is dependent on the nature of the performance required. Therefore, where a complete performance is required the rewardee may lose any expense incurred by him in order to facilitate such performance upon failure to complete the performance within specified period. Moreover, any failure in making the performance available is going to have the same legal effect.

The loss of the expense may normally occur in cases where there has been no direct link between the parties such as the reward offered to the public which by its very nature necessitates the rewardee to incur the normal expense needed for the required performance. As mentioned earlier, *Ja'alah* is flexible contract, in the sense that the finance of a certain work or project can be made by the rewardee himself. For instance the promise to reward any one of the public for translation of a book may require the expense to be borne entirely by the rewardee.

Therefore, the rewardee will be required to provide all the materials such as paper, dictionaries, a computer and other equipment in order to translate the book. As such the reward offered is expected to cover all the expenses incurred, in addition to some specified amount over and above the expense incurred. Hence, in response to the offered reward the rewardee may calculate all the expenses to make sure that the reward is eventually profitable.

However, once the complete performance has been successfully done within the specified period of time, the reward will be due. In line with this type of performance where there is a condition whereby the reward will be given to the first one who completes the performance, the rest of rewardees may take the risk of losing any expense incurred. Furthermore, where the utilization is not satisfied unless upon the complete performance the rewardee may lose his efforts made, in addition to any other expense.

Reward as the rule necessitates the necessary expense to be incurred by the rewarder, for instance where the subject matter of

Ja'alah is the construction or building of a house, the rewarder may provide all the necessary materials, equipments or tools to facilitate the performance. However, and as far as the contract of *ja'alah* is flexible in nature the necessary expense may also be borne by the rewardee based on the permissibility which is the general rule in contracts. Accordingly, the rule of creditor debtor relationship will be crucial in governing contractual obligations of the parties and as such the rewardee will be allowed to secure such debt.

Negotiability of Reward

The general rule is that the reward is binding upon completed performance, whereas the Maliki school of thought maintains that once an agreement is put into commencement, the reward is binding on the respective parties[36]. The reward is negotiable in nature before the commencement of the performance, however, it becomes binding after the commencement of the performance, in the sense that the reward is no more negotiable between the parties. Another view, however, has extended the negotiability of the reward until before the completion of the performance[37].

In negotiating the reward it is immaterial whether the rewardee who undertakes the performance of the act accepts less than the reward offered, for instance where the rewarder offers $1000.00 (reward) in return for specific performance, he will be bound to pay the specified amount even if the rewardee accepts the sum of $ 500.00 in return for the performance. Thus, the reward always remains as pointed out by the rewarder mainly because the acceptance of rewardee is not a requirement for the contract formation.

The general rule in the contract of *Ja'alah* is that the reward should not be delivered to the rewardee who undertakes the performance unless upon the completion. There may be occasion, however, in which the reward may pass to the rewardee before the commencement of the performance or after the commencement but before the completion of the performance. The delivery of the reward although it is contrary to the practice, however, is held acceptable so long as it has done by the consent of the rewarder. Accordingly, the reward can pass to the rewardee on the basis of al-*Wadiah*. The rewardee, however, may also be permitted to utilize and make use of the *Wadiah* as the reward, but he will not be permitted to acquire any title to it. In case the reward has been destroyed on his hand, then he would be required to guarantee the refund of the same.

According to Maliki school of thought, it is a requirement that the period of the contract must be made open, in the sense that no time limit is fixed for the contract[38]. The above requirement seems to be a preventive measure against the occurrence of unfair dealing and also disputes between the contracting parties, as the fixing of a certain period as the contract limit may cause damage to the rewardee resulting in losing his efforts and expense. Others, however, are of the view that the determination of the contract limit must be in accordance with the very nature of the performance itself.

Legal Implications

According to the majority reward is classified as non-binding contract, in the sense that the parties have the right to rescind the contract before the completion of the performance. However, after completion, the parties would not be allowed to rescind the contract. On the other hand and according to the Maliki school of thought, reward has been considered a binding contract to the rewardee upon the commencement of the performance. The reward is due once the performance has been completed[39].

There has been considerable debate as to the effect of invalid reward. Most of the jurists are unanimous that the invalid form of reward necessitates the payment of an equivalent hire to the rewardee who undertakes the performance. The hire should be given according to the prevailing market price[40]. Thus it is evident that since the contract of *Ja'alah* is held lawful for satisfaction of the people's need the reward will always be much higher than the amount of hire. The reward in arranging loans for instance, as has been illustrated by a number of jurists is10% of the loan amount. However, as mentioned before the amount of reward can be much higher than the hire amount, and in fact it is difficult to draw a limit for the reward.

It is submitted, however, that the only factor, that we may depend on in order to draw certain limit to the reward, is the consent of the rewarder himself. The rewarder can make careful assessment of his needs and determine how beneficial the performance to him is. Thus, it would be erroneous after all to consider the wage or *Ujr* as synonymous to reward. The hire is always determined in accordance with the level of performance and subject to the prevailing market price. Therefore, offering a reward on the basis of contract of *Ja'alah* is always much higher than *Ujr*.

One of the issues not discussed by most of the jurists in connection with *Ja'alah* contract is the liability of the rewardee over any properties provided by the rewarder in order to facilitate the performance. However, al-Nawawi has maintained that the hand of the rewardee over the property provided to facilitate the performance is the hand of a trustee. Hence, the rewardee is not required to guarantee the property unless upon fault, negligence or transgression attributed to him. Moreover, al-Nawawi has continued to maintain that the rewardee can also claim any expense needed in connection with the performance where there has been a custom to that effect. This view, however, is made with respect of the normal expense necessary for the performance.

Ja'alah is a permissible contract for the parties to enter into. Therefore, any of the contracting parties enjoys the right to rescind the contract before the completion of the required performance. In all cases however, *Ja'alah* is a binding contract after the completion of the required performance, accordingly the rewarder will not be allowed to rescind the contract any more[41]. It is submitted that since the subject matter of *Ja'alah* is the performance of an act in return for a reward, the Maliki view seems to be the reasonable because it prevent the occurrence of any damages to the parties and in particular to the party who undertakes the performance. The view is also helpful in stabilizing commercial dealings. Hence when the performance commences the contract become binding in nature and no party is allowed to rescind it unless upon the mutual consent of the parties.

Conclusion

The contract of *Ja'alah* is legitimate based on the Qur'an and the tradition of the Prophet (*s.a.w.*). The people may resort to such contract for satisfaction of their needs. *Ja'alah* signifies the consideration offered to a person in return for a performance which may be specified or unspecified. It is generally understood by many that the contract's subject-matter is only restricted to the traditional performances. However, the elaboration of the principles of *Ja'alah* by jurists reveals that there are other performances which are similar and much relevant to the modern banking business. The performances that related to banking business, as identified, include attraction of savings, arrangement of loans, debt collection, letter of guarantee, leasing services, and brokering businesses. In connection to performance under *Ja'alah* contract jurists have laid down a stipulation that the performance must include hardship incurred by the rewardee. It is also requirement that the reward must be fixed in advance with certainty, and only it can be earned upon the complete performance. Any expense needed to facilitate the performance can be incurred by the rewardee and the amount of the reward may remain negotiable until before the completion of performance. *Ja'alah* is classified as non-binding contract. Therefore, any party is permitted to revoke the contract at any time before the completion of performance.

Notes

1. Shams al-Din Mohamad al-Ansari, *Nihayat al Muhtaj ila Sharh al-Minhaj,* (Cairo: Maktabat al-Halabi, 1967), pp. 465.
2. Throughout the paper the writer is using the terms rewarder and rewardee to indicate the Ja'ail and Majaul lahu respectively.
3. Abd Allah Mohamad Ibn al-Maghrabi al-Hatab, *Mawahib al-Jalil* (Cairo: Dar al-Fikr, 1978),Vol. 5. p. 452.
4. *Ibid*
5. Surah Yusuf, v. 72.
6. See *Sahih Muslim* at 10/169.
7. See al-Ansari at p. 465.
8. Wahbah al-Zuhili, *Al-Fiqh al-Islami wa Adilatuhu* (Beirut: Dar al-Fikr, Beirut, 1989), Vol. 4, p. 784.
9. Yahyah ibn Sharaf al-Nawawi, *Rawdat al-Talibin* (Beirut: al-Maktab al-Islami, 1405 H) Vol. 4, p. 335.
10. See al-Ansari at p. 466.
11. Civil Transactions Act of Sudan, Section, 137.
12. See al-Ansari at p. 467.
13. Mohamad Baqir al-Sadr, *al-bank al-larabwi fi al-Islam* (Beirut: Dar al-Ta'aruf, 1983), p. 41.

14. *Ibid*
15. *Ibid*
16. Islamic Banking Practice, *Bank Islam Malaysia Berhad, Kuala Lumpur*, 1994, p. 21.
17. Muwaffaq al-Din Abdallah ibni Qudamah, *al-Mughni* (Cairo: Maktabat al-Kahirah, 1969), Vol, 4, p. 244.
18. Abi al-Hassan Ali ibni Mohamad al-Mawardi, *al-Hawi al-Kabir* (Beirut: Dar al-Fikr,1994), Vol, 5, p. 212.
19. See al-Ansari at p. 481.
20. al-Shikh Mansor ibni Yunus al-Bahwati, *Sharh Muntaha al-Iradat* (Cairo: Alam al-Kutub, 1996), Vol. 2, p 373.
21. See al-Ansari at p. 481.
22. D. P. Whiting, *Elements of Banking* (London: Macdonald & Evans Ltd. 1985), p. 78.
23. Mohamad al-Atabi al-Qurtubi, *Al-Bayan wa al_Tahsil* (Beirut: Dar al-gharb al-Islami, 1988), Vol. 8, p. 414.
24. See Baqir al-Sadr at p. 223.
25. *Ibid*
26. *Ibid*
27. See Islamic Banking Practice at p. 38.
28. Mansor ibni Yunus al-Bahwati, *Kashf al-Qina* (Beirut: Dar al-Fikr, 1982), Vol. 4, p. 578.
29. Mohamad Kamal Atiah, *Muhasabat al-Sharikat wa al-Massrif fi al-Nizam al-Islami* (Beirut: Dar al-Fikr1984), p. 100.
30. Mustafa Abdallah al-Hamshari, *al-Amal al-Masrafiah wa al-Islam* (Beirut: al-Maktab al-Islami, 1983), p. 125.
31. See al-Nawawi at p. 337.
32. For more details see al-Ansari at p. 465.
33. *Ibid*
34. See al-Bahwati at p. 578.
35. Habib Shirazi, *Islamic Banking*, 1990, p. 73.
36. See al-Hatab at p. 455.
37. See al-Nawawi at p. 340.
38. See al-zuhili at p. 788.
39. See al-Hatab at p. 455.
40. See al-Nawawi at p. 338
41. See al-Hatab at p. 455.

11

Judicial Control In The Islamic System

Nayel Musa Shaker Al-Omran

Introduction

Question is if the Islamic legal system had known the principles of judicial control over the constitutionality of laws, especially the constitutional suit, in their present form. If the answer was in the negative, then, would the adoption of this suit contradict the Islamic system? If the latter is true, then how should the control over the constitutionality of Islamic law be?

But if the Islamic system and civilisation had generally known what may be named as the constitutional suit, the inevitable questions here would be: what is the particularity of the constitutional suit in the Islamic legal system? And what are the aspects of concurrence and difference about the constitutional suit in both the American and Egyptian systems? Finally, what are the possibilities of each system benefiting from the advantages of other systems in developing the performance and capacity of the constitutional suit?

If the objective of the judicial control is to prevent the legislative authority which represents the constitutional faith of a country, from putting forward unconstitutional laws, the wisdom of such a principle is to deny the rules in the Islamic law from wording legislations that contradict the legitimacy and higher divine rule demanded by Allah (*s.w.t.*) for mankind.

Before studying the control over the constitutionality of laws in the Islamic System, the elements that helped to establish the judicial control in the Islamic System must be discussed, and then discussion must be made regarding the historical and political background of that control.

Elements of the Emergence of Judicial Control in the Islamic System

Jurists link the emergence of judicial control in the Islamic System to various factors, noted among which are:

1. Separation of Powers in the Islamic System
2. The principle of the rule of law
3. The principle of Judicial Independence in the Islamic System

Separation of Powers in the Islamic System

Many jurists of Islamic and modern law said that Islamic *Shari'ah* knows the principle of separation of powers, and the predominant opinion of Islamic jurists also hold that the Islamic legal system knew the principle of separation of powers in the country's legislative, executive and judicial branches, but all their powers were governed by the Prophet (saw) and his four orthodox caliphs.[1]

The principle of separation of powers was applied in the early days of Islam, where the Prophet (saw) used to invest judicial powers into a provincial government, but later on, he used to appoint a judge independently of any political or administrative consideration.[2] After the conversion of Arabia, when a large number of people came under the sway of Islam, the Prophet (saw) appointed various functionaries for the different parts of the peninsula. Whenever the Prophet (saw) appointed a governor and a military commander, the caliph usually took good care to appoint a judge as well over whom these officials had no jurisdiction.[3]

There are many examples of this practice in the *Sunnah* of the Prophet (saw) and the caliphs, among which are: It is reported that the Prophet (saw) asked Mu'adh ibn Jabal questions upon the latter's appointment as judge to Yemen, in answer to which Mu'adh told the Prophet that he would resort to his own *ijtihad* in the event that he failed to find guidance in the *Qur'an* and *Sunnah*, and the Prophet was pleased with this reply, and patted him on the chest and said: "Praised be God, who has caused the messenger of God's Messenger to please the latter!"[4]

"أنَّ رَسُولَ اللَّهِ صَلَّى اللَّهُ عَلَيْهِ وَسَلَّمَ لَمَّا أَرَادَ أَنْ يَبْعَثَ مُعَاذًا إِلَى الْيَمَنِ قَالَ كَيْفَ تَقْضِي إِذَا عَرَضَ لَكَ قَضَاءٌ قَالَ أَقْضِي بِكِتَابِ اللَّهِ قَالَ فَإِنْ لَمْ تَجِدْ فِي كِتَابِ اللَّهِ قَالَ فَبِسُنَّةِ رَسُولِ اللَّهِ صَلَّى اللَّهُ عَلَيْهِ وَسَلَّمَ قَالَ فَإِنْ لَمْ تَجِدْ فِي سُنَّةِ رَسُولِ اللَّهِ صَلَّى اللَّهُ عَلَيْهِ وَسَلَّمَ وَلَا فِي كِتَابِ اللَّهِ قَالَ أَجْتَهِدُ رَأْيِي وَلَا آلُو فَضَرَبَ رَسُولُ اللَّهِ صَلَّى اللَّهُ عَلَيْهِ وَسَلَّمَ صَدْرَهُ وَقَالَ الْحَمْدُ لِلَّهِ الَّذِي وَفَّقَ رَسُولَ رَسُولِ اللَّهِ لِمَا يُرْضِي رَسُولَ اللَّه"

Through the abovementioned example, it is obvious that two basic rules are confirmed:

> *First: written law, as the Muslim judge neither gives his judgment according to custom and usage nor on the basis of an order given to him by the caliph or the ruler, he rather gives his judgment according to the* Qur'an *and* Sunnah, *and if he does not find any rule in them, he gives his opinion on the basis of his own* ijtihad.

Second: that judiciary in Islam is an independent authority that is not subordinate to any particular person. The judge rather follows the texts before him that comprise of firs the *Qur'an* and then the *Sunnah* and by the inspiration of his conscience, understanding and discernment in order to arrive at justice.

Therefore, there is a relationship between the judicial and executive authorities with respect to appointment and dismissal, without any interference with the judiciary's primary function and that is hearing and deciding cases and disputes.

Also, the first caliph, Abu Bakr, after being chosen as caliph, invested 'Umar with judicial powers. During the 'Umar ibn al Khattab's period, he was the first caliph who directly charged other persons for the exercise of the judge's functions. He appointed Abu Darda'as a judge with him in Medina, *Shari'ah* as a judge in Basrah and Abu Musa al-Ash'ari as a judge in Kufah.[5]

There are many events which happened in Islamic history in which the principle of separation of powers was applied. But the researcher will mention some of them as examples: in the story of Mu'awiyah, the governor of Sham, with Ubadah ibn al-Samit, the judge of Palestine and Jordan, as narrated by al-Awza'i, who said "the first to take the position of judge in Palestine was Ubadah ibn al-Samit, and Mu'awiyah had then refused to execute a ruling by Ubadah, but Ubadah stood by his decision, so Mu'awiyah spoke aggressively to him, thus Ubadah said, "I would never again live with you in one area," and he left for Medina. So the caliph 'Umar said to him: "what brought you here?" 'Ubadah told him what had happened, and 'Umar replied: "go back to your position, repugnant is a land in which you and your likes are not." Then 'Umar wrote to Mu'awiyah: "you have no authority over 'Ubadah."[6]

If we look at this story we will find that 'Umar ibn al-Khattab emphasised on the separation between the judicial authority and the executive authority, and made a direct relationship between the caliph and the judge. As a result, there appeared the features of independence of the judiciary in the Islamic country. Thus it can said that Islam had known the principle of separation of powers, and especially the independence of the judiciary and its separation from the other authorities, since the seventh century C.E., while contemporary nations had known it only in the late eighteenth century.

Perhaps the story of the conquest of Samarqand is a unique one in human history and it is a story that points out the clear understanding of the early Muslims of the principle of separation of powers and its implementation.

The people of Samarqand said to Sulayman ibn Abi al-Sirri, the governor appointed by 'Umar ibn 'Abd al-'Aziz, that "Qutaba ibn Muslim, the Military leader, had deceived and oppressed us and took our country, and that Allah (*s.w.t.*) has shown justice and equity, so allow us to send a delegation to the Commander of the Faithful (*Amir al-Mu'minin*) to complain about the injustice towards us, that if we had a right we shall have it for we need it." So he allowed them. Thus they sent a delegation that met with the caliph, who then wrote for them to Sulayman ibn Abi Sirri, asking him to appoint a judge to look into their grievance, and the judge Jumai' ibn Hadir was appointed, and he ordered that the Arabs of Samarqand leave and return to their camp."

The researcher observes that 'Umar ibn 'Abd al-'Aziz fully recognises the principle of separation of powers. That is because when he knew the grievance of the people of Samarqand he did not decide the case himself, although he could have as he is the caliph of Muslims, and although the interest of Muslims lay in that. In addition he did not entrust the governor of Samarqand, Sulayman ibn Abi Sirri with that, fearing that he might be bias. Further, because he was the governor appointed by the caliph, he refused to let him decide the case, and did not authorise the military leader who committed the offence against the rules of the *Shari'ah*. Rather, he ordered that a judge for them who was not affected by military or political interests be appointed and did not give any consideration except for the rule of Allah (*s.w.t.*), enforcing the rules of *Shari'ah* as they are stated.

The examples mentioned above represent sample cases of the separation of powers during different periods of Islamic history, especially during the Umayyad and Abbasids periods where this principle was practically implemented.

The Rule of Law

It was seen that the principle of the rule of law means, in the positive system, that the ruler and ruled submit to the rule of law. This principle became stable after the struggle of people against tyranny, injustice and absolutist authority that was not restricted or limited by any bounds. An example is the struggle of the people in the French revolution, which took place in 1789.

While the principle of the rule of law in the Islamic system was considered as the basis or cornerstone which Islam was founded on as Creed and *Shari'ah*, because Islam came to remove injustice and fighting tyranny and to demolish the pillars of absolutist authority. Therefore, that principle found its basis in the *Qur'an, Sunnah* and the consensus (*ijma'*) even during the centuries that people grappled with despotism.[7]

(مَن لَمْ يَحْكُم بِمَا أَنزَلَ اللهُ فَأُولَـئِكَ هُمُ الْكَافِرُونَ)

Allah says: "*And if any fail to judge by (the light of) what Allah hath revealed, they are (no better than) wrongdoers*".[8]

(وَمَن لَمْ يَحْكُم بِمَا أَنزَلَ اللهُ فَأُولَـئِكَ هُمُ الظَّالِمُونَ)

Also, He (*s.w.t.*) says: "*let the people of the Gospel judge by what Allah hath revealed therein. If any do fail to judge by (the light of) what Allah hath revealed, they are (no better than) those who rebel.*"[9]

(وَمَن لَمْ يَحْكُم بِمَا أَنزَلَ اللهُ فَأُولَـئِكَ هُمُ الْفَاسِقُونَ)

And in another Verse He (S.W.T.) says: "*if any do fail to judge by (the light of) what Allah hath revealed, they are (no better than) Unbelievers.*"[10]

يَا أَيُّهَا الَّذِينَ آمَنُوا أَطِيعُوا اللَّهَ وَأَطِيعُوا الرَّسُولَ وَأُولِي الأَمْرِ مِنكُمْ فَإِن تَنَازَعْتُمْ فِي شَيْءٍ فَرُدُّوهُ إِلَى اللَّهِ وَالرَّسُولِ إِن كُنتُمْ تُؤْمِنُونَ بِاللَّهِ وَالْيَوْمِ الآخِرِ ذَلِكَ خَيْرٌ وَأَحْسَنُ تَأْوِيلًا

Allah (*s.w.t.*) in other *Surah* says: "*O ye who believe! Obey Allah, and obey the Messenger, and those charged with authority among you. If ye differ in anything among yourselves, refer to Allah and His Messenger, if ye do believe in Allah and the last Day: that is best, and most suitable for final determination.*"[11]

According to Mohammad Asad:

> *Obey God and obey the Apostle and those in authority from among you," leads us inescapably to the conclusion that those who are to wield supreme authority in the Islamic state and are to be responsible for the shaping of its policies should always be Muslims: and this not merely* de facto, *by virtue of their majority in the country, but also* de jure, *by virtue of a constitutional enactment. If we are resolved to make Islam the dominant factor in our lives, we must have the moral courage to declare openly that we are not prepared to endanger our future by falling into line with the demands of that spurious "liberalism" which refuses to attribute any importance to us than the mere accident of his having been born or naturalised in our country.*[12]

Also, the judge must implement *Qur'an* and *Sunnah* in every dispute brought before him, but if he does not implement that, his conduct and deeds will be annulled, this matter is derived from the following Verse where Allah (*s.w.t.*) says: "*O ye who believe! Obey Allah. And obey the Messenger, and make not vain your deeds*!"[13]

The *Sunnah* came to support, emphasise and clarify these *Quranic* Verses. Therefore, Prophet Muhammad (S.A.W) said: "Obedience of a human being is disallowed, if it is considered disobedience to the creator (Allah)." (S.A.W) also said:

"السَّمْعُ وَالطَّاعَةُ عَلَى الْمَرْءِ الْمُسْلِمِ فِيمَا أَحَبَّ وَكَرِهَ مَا لَمْ يُؤْمَرْ بِمَعْصِيَةٍ فَإِنْ أُمِرَ بِمَعْصِيَةٍ فَلَا سَمْعَ عَلَيْهِ وَلَا طَاعَةَ"

"Hearing and obeying is binding on a Muslim, whether he likes or dislikes the order-so long as he is not ordered to commit a sin; but if he is ordered to commit a sin, there is no hearing and no obeying."[14]

"لَا طَاعَةَ فِي مَعْصِيَةٍ إِنَّمَا الطَّاعَةُ فِي الْمَعْرُوفِ"

"No obedience is in sinful matters: behold, obedience is due only in the way of righteousness "*fi al-ma'ruf.*"[15]

" لَا طَاعَةَ لِمَخْلُوقٍ فِي مَعْصِيَةِ اللَّهِ عَزَّ وَجَلَّ "

"No obedience is due to him who does not obey God"[16] and he said

" لا طاعة لمخلوق في معصية الخالق

"No obedience is due to him who rebels against God."[17]

" مَنْ أَحْدَثَ فِي أَمْرِنَا هَذَا مَا لَيْسَ فِيهِ فَهُوَ رَدٌّ

He (S.A.W) also said "every act that does not conform to our order is rejected."[18]

In the Islamic system, everyone, head of state, government and masses, is subject to the law. The Prophet (S.A.W) himself was subject to it, and was the most obedient person to the *Qur'an*. He was "*'Abd Allah wa rasuluh*," the servant of God and his messenger. In the Islamic system, the head of state cannot invoke any immunity from impeachment. The principle, "Be you ever so high, the law is above you" has always been there in Islamic law, to include the Prophet (*s.a.w.*) himself. Just before he died, the Prophet (*s.a.w.*) made the following short speech:

> *I swear by God that I have made lawful only those things that the Qur'an made lawful and I have made unlawful only those things that the Qur'an made unlawful. If I have taken the money of any of you, here is my money, let him come and take it, and if I have lashed the body of any, here is my body, let him take back his right.*[19]

Therefore, the past Verses supported with these *ahadith* indicate that every dispute that happens in Islamic society between individuals, between groups of people, or between people and the government, or among parts of the government and its people, must be judged by the fundamental law which we received from Allah (*s.w.t.*) and His Messenger. According to this principle, the country must have an institution that judge among people by the *Qur'an* and *Sunnah*, and that institution is the judicial authorities."[20]

Another example with regards to the rule of law according to the *Shari'ah* is in the report of 'A'ishah that:

عَنْ عَائِشَةَ رَضِيَ اللَّهُ عَنْهَا

"أَنَّ قُرَيْشًا أَهَمَّهُمْ شَأْنُ الْمَرْأَةِ الْمَخْزُومِيَّةِ الَّتِي سَرَقَتْ فَقَالُوا وَمَنْ يُكَلِّمُ فِيهَا رَسُولَ اللَّهِ صَلَّى اللَّهُ عَلَيْهِ وَسَلَّمَ فَقَالُوا وَمَنْ يَجْتَرِئُ عَلَيْهِ إِلَّا أُسَامَةُ بْنُ زَيْدٍ حِبُّ رَسُولِ اللَّهِ صَلَّى اللَّهُ عَلَيْهِ وَسَلَّمَ فَكَلَّمَهُ أُسَامَةُ فَقَالَ رَسُولُ اللَّهِ صَلَّى اللَّهُ عَلَيْهِ وَسَلَّمَ أَتَشْفَعُ فِي حَدٍّ مِنْ حُدُودِ اللَّهِ ثُمَّ قَامَ فَاخْتَطَبَ ثُمَّ قَالَ إِنَّمَا أَهْلَكَ الَّذِينَ قَبْلَكُمْ أَنَّهُمْ كَانُوا إِذَا سَرَقَ فِيهِمْ الشَّرِيفُ تَرَكُوهُ وَإِذَا سَرَقَ فِيهِمْ الضَّعِيفُ أَقَامُوا عَلَيْهِ الْحَدَّ وَايْمُ اللَّهِ لَوْ أَنَّ فَاطِمَةَ بِنْتَ مُحَمَّدٍ سَرَقَتْ لَقَطَعْتُ يَدَهَا"

> *Verily as for the Quraish the affair of a woman of Makhzumiyyah tribe who had committed theft gave them much anxiety. They said: who will plead for her before the Messenger of Allah? They said: who will dare*

it than Usamah son of Zaid, who is a favourite of the Messenger of Allah? Then Usamah pleaded before him. The Messenger of Allah said: you plead for a crime out of the crimes ordained against by Allah! Then he got up and delivered a sermon. Afterwards he said: Verily those who were before you were destroyed because when a noble man from among them committed theft, they passed no sentence on him. By Allah, had Fatimah, the daughter of Muhammad, committed theft. I would have cut off her hand.[21]

In the same way, Abu Bakr, the first successor and caliph of the Muslim state, in his acceptance speech said:

أمّا بَعْدُ أيّها النّاسُ فإنّي قدْ وُلّيت عَليْكمْ ولَسْت بِخَيْركُمْ فإنْ أحْسَنْت فأعِينُوني ؛ وَإنْ أسأت فقوّمُوني ؛ الصّدْقُ أمَانَة وَالكَذِبُ خِيَانَة وَالضّعِيفُ فِيكُمْ قويّ عِنْدِي حَتّى أُريحَ عَليْهِ حقّهُ إنْ شَاءَ اللهُ وَالقويّ فِيكُمْ ضَعِيفٌ عِنْدِي حَتّى آخُذَ الحَقّ مِنْهُ إنْ شَاءَ اللهُ لا يَدَعُ قوْمٌ الجِهَادَ فِي سَبِيلِ اللهِ إلا ضَرَبَهُمْ اللهُ بِالذّلّ وَلا تَشِيعُ الفَاحِشَةُ فِي قوْمٍ قط إلا عَمّهُمْ اللهُ بِالبَلاء أطِيعُونِي مَا أطعْت اللهَ وَرَسُولهُ فإذا عَصَيْتُ اللهَ وَرَسُولهُ فلا طاعَةَ لِي عَليْكمْ .

O people! I have been appointed over you, but I am not the best of you. Support me if I did good and remove me if I did badly... a weak person of you is strong before me as long as I maintain his right for him. And a strong one of you is weak before me until I take back a right from him... Obey me as long as I obeyed Allah and his Messenger. If I disobeyed them there is no obedience of me upon you.[22]

Under the issue of respect for justice, an example can be found in one of the transactions that 'Umar ibn al-Khattab had entered into, where the caliph purchased a horse and on approval, allowed a rider to try it. The horse was injured in the course of the ride, and the caliph wanted to return the horse, but the owner refused to take it back. The dispute was referred to the judge who observed: "if the horse was used for the purpose of riding with the permission of the owner, it could be returned, otherwise not!" the caliph was pleased with the judgment and promoted the judge as the *qadi* of *al-Kufah*.[23]

On another occasion in which 'Ali ibn Abi Talib was a party, the same issue of respect for justice and submission to the law arose, where: Once the caliph lost a coat-of-mail belonging to him in his way to Siffin. After the termination of the war he returned to *al-Kufah*, and told him: "This armor is mine; I neither sold it nor gave it away." The Jew replied, "it is my armour and in my possession." Later, both the caliph and the Jew went to the court of Shurahİ. Shuraih said: "Proceed, O prince of the faithful!" He said: Yes, this armour which is in the hands of this Jew is my armour- I neither sold it nor gave it away." Shuraih exclaimed," what does thou say, O

Jew?" He replied: " It is my armour and in my possession." Then Shuraih said:" Hast thou any proof, O prince of the faithful?" He said: "Yes, Kambar and al-xasan are witnesses to the fact that the armour is mine." Shuraih replied, "The evidence of a son is not admissible in favour of the father."

The result was that the judgment was given in favour of the Jew. At this, the Jew exclaimed," I testify that there is no god but God, that Muhammad is His Apostle, and that this armour is thy armour."[24] It can be deduced from the above and other scenarios that rulers in the Islamic system submit to the rule of law and the judiciary, without allowing any bias treatment to them, on the account of the citizens.

Below a relevant portion from the reported speech of Mu'adh ibn Jabal was reported, which he made before the ruler of Syria. In his speech, Mu'adh clearly states that the rule of law is binding to the ruler and the ruled alike; he further warns the ruler against violating the law and reminds him of power of the people. Mu'adh says:

> *Our leader in one of us; if he implement among us the teaching of our Religious Book (i.e., The Qur'an), and Sunnah of our prophet, we shall have him over us. But if he goes against it we shall depose him. If he commits theft, we shall amputate his hand; if he commits adultery, we shall flog him. If he abuses anyone of us, we will abuse him as he (the leader) did. If he injures us, we will take retaliation from him. He will not hide himself from us, nor will he be self-conceited. He will not reserve for himself the booty which God bestowed on us. He is a person as good as we are.*[25]

In the application of the principle of legality, which is one of the basis that the Islamic system of rule is based on, it is seen that Muslim rulers, after the first Islamic century, were confined to implement the same principles of *Shari'ah* that were applied by their predecessors. So, the ruler submitted to the rules of the judiciary as ordinary individuals. Also, they always, in their conduct and in deeds, try to implement the Islamic system. This matter states that the principle of legality was not a mere personal method but it is a principle that stabilised in the conscience of people, and it existed since the establishment of the Islamic government.[26]

In addition to that, some rulers rejected the execution of the caliph's orders because they violated the principle of legality, such as when al-Hakam ibn Amir al- Ghafari, deputy of Ziyad ibn Abi Sufyan, and Wali of *Khurasan*, invaded al-Asall Mount and got a lot of money. Then Ziyad wrote to him that the commander of the faithful, Mu'awiyah, requested from him to collect gold and silver from the booty and send it to the treasury, but al-Hakam refused and answered that the book of Allah (*Qur'an*) has priority over the book of the commander of the faithful.[27]

After that it becomes clear that the principle of legality or the rule of law in the Islamic system was the cornerstone which the independence of the judicial authority was based on. So if this principle had started politically in the secular system, as a result of the struggle of the people against absolutism, then it became after that a legal principle in its essence. While in the Islamic system, the aforementioned principle of validity started as a legal principle and main center for the *'aqidah* and *Shari'ah*, since the early days of the Islamic government's missionary work, because law is divine. So, Muslim judges rejected the application of any law, order or decision that is passed by the caliph or his officers, if that law, decision or order contradicted the general principles of the *Qur'an* and *Sunnah*. The Islamic system has known the principle of the rule of law, and thus the independence of the judicial authority, as a natural result from that, before that came to be known in the positive system by several centuries, because it is the legislation of Allah, Who created humans.

Muhammad Salim al-'Awwa went on the *Medinan* polity as the world's first State: The Islamic state in *Madinah* was the oldest example of a political society organised in the form of "state." This claim rests on the fact that it was an organised society based on "rule of law." The Supremacy of rule of law is a distinguishing factor between a "state," and other forms of organised political societies. It presupposes that all organs and agencies of the government are subject to and will abide by the rule of the same legal system which governs the individual citizen.[28]

Diya' al-Din al-Rayyis says that none of the Muslim rulers and Jurists dispute that obedience is not allowed except in conformity with the *Shari'ah, Qur'an* and *Sunnah*, and no one ever said that obedience is allowed in transgression.

Judicial Independence in the Islamic System

The independence of judiciary must be a principle of the constitution. No person in an Islamic State, not even the elected Head, can be above the law, and he is as such subject to the *hudud* "punishments for major crimes" as anyone else. The *Qur'an* repeatedly enjoins the administration of justice in an impartial manner, even though the decision may go against a judge's own kinsmen or his own community.[29]

Emile Tyan in his article mentioned that, Muslim judge does not have an independent or even autonomous position, especially during the early stages of the establishment of the Islamic state. He added that the head of state (caliph), at that time, derived his judicial power from no one but subordinates by virtue of his position. Tyan also asserted in his article that the concept of delegation in Islam was the complete lack of separation between the judicial authority and the executive authority.[30]

In summary, it appears that during the period of the pious caliphs, the judicial system was independent and integral. The judge had no register in which his judgments were recorded, because those judgments were carried out by the judge himself.

During the *Umayyad* period the Muslim law was characterised by two main features:

First, the judge exercised his discretion (*ijtihad*), because the four schools of Muslim law, by which judges had to abide, were not established until the early *'Abbasi* period. At that time, the judge drew his own judgment from the *Qur'an* and *Sunnah*, or the *ijma'* (consensus), or to use his own discretion (*qiyas*).[31]

Second, the judge was not influenced by politics; he was independent in his judgment, far from being affected by the tendencies of the ruling dynasty. His authority was unlimited and the governors of the provinces, the collectors, and even the caliph had to submit to his judgment.[32]

During the *'Abbasi* period, there were several important characteristics of the judiciary system:[33]

The appointments of judges representing the four orthodox schools in each province were made. Every one of these judges was entrusted with the task of dealing with cases related to the persons who adhered to the teaching of their particular school.

Another feature was the introduction of the system of permanent, trustworthy witness after verifying their good character from the outward, without regard to their hidden character.

A remarkable improvement was the registers, in which matters related to legacies and debts, were recorded.[34]

N. J. Coulson, in his article, mentioned that, the *qadi* Abi Khuzaymah refused to annul the marriage of a woman on the application of members of her tribe, Bani 'Abd Kulal. The plaintiffs approached the ruler, Yazid ibn Hatam, who, not wishing to offend this strong and loyal tribe, ordered the *qadi* to annul the marriage on grounds of non-equality. The tribe of the husband, he declared, was inferior to the Bani 'Abd Kulal. Abi Khuzayma refused. "I do not allow, he said, what Allah (S.W.T.) has forbidden, and I do not forbid what Allah (S.W.T.) has allowed. The woman was given in marriage by her *wali*: therefore the marriage must stand." The governor then separated the couple himself.[35] Coulson considered this interference by the executive power in the judicial power.

The researcher believes that this case does not indicate the lack of independence of the judiciary in the Islamic system, because the *Shari'ah* gave the caliph or ruler the right to interfere in certain matters to solve them, if the *qadi* passed his judgment in that dispute, without acceptance from the adversary parties. In addition to that, the equality between the two spouses in certain matters is a condition for the validity of marriage contracts to be binding in many Arab countries until now. Furthermore, equality between the two spouses is considered a necessary requirement for the validity of marriage contracts by some Muslim schools. Therefore, the caliph has the right to annul some contracts or judgments if these contracts would result in great harm.

The researcher agrees that several cases, that had taken place in Islamic judiciary, illustrated that the executive power interfered with the independence of the judicial power. For example, there is a case that took place when Ma'mun (813-833 C.E.) proclaimed the doctrine of the createdness of the *Qur'an* as the true creed; he ordered his governor to test the fidelity of the *qadi*'s of their provinces to this proclaimed doctrine. Al-Ma'mun had punished several scholars of *Shari'ah* for their acceptance of this doctrine especially Ahmad ibn Hanbal.[36]

In one of his articles, N. J. Coulson asserted that the *qadi* appeared in early *Umayyad* times as the legal secretary of the governor. And these were delegated, through appropriate measures, to the subordinate state officials. N. J. Coulson also asserted that the political authority, which defined the scope and nature of the *qadi*'s jurisdiction, and naturally the decisions given and actions taken by the *qadi,* were subject to the approval or otherwise of the governor.[37]

The Islamic history has shown many eminent judges, who were distinguished by their faith, strong belief, manners, morals, dignity, knowledge, deep wariness of rules, courage and independence.

Many of them stood fast against the interference of the executive, rejecting, in firm determination, such interferences. They refused all kinds of direct and indirect influence or orientation. Marvelous were their courage, dignity and readiness to resign as soon as exposed to pressure from the rulers, their relatives' friends, or assistants.

During the life of Prophet Muhammad (*s.a.w.)* he was the leader and Chief of judicial authority in the Islamic State. However, he also appointed several close companions to assist him in the administration of the law.[38]

During the reign of the *Rashidin* caliphs, the judicial authority took a form similar to that in the period of the prophet (*s.a.w.*). There was no demarcation of judicial authority with that of other powers. The *Rashidin* caliphs upheld and respected the independence of the judiciary, especially both caliphs 'Umar and 'Ali who had had occasion to appear and plead their cases before the *qadi* like any other parties to litigation and both have exhibited sensitivity and concern not to be given preferential treatment in court. So that, the *qadi* would accept a suit against the person of the head of state and would try him in an open court; this feature of the Islamic judiciary is an indication of its independent status.[39]

However, there was a significant change in the period of the *Umayyad* and the *'Abbassi* caliphate. The judges enjoyed freedom especially in the exercise of independent *ijtihad.* Moreover, Caliph Mu'awiyah was the first to abdicate all his judicial powers to appointed judges. The judiciary was completely independent from the executive authority without any exceptions.

In the period of the *'Abbassi* caliphate, all the judicial powers were transferred to a specially appointed person. Consequently, the caliph no longer played an active role in the administration of the Islamic legal system and the operation of the judicial authority. During this period, there was a special appointed person who was called *qadi al-qudah*. Harun al-Rashid was the first caliph to be instituted in the office of *qadi al-qudah,* Abu Yusuf was the first chief judge (*qadi al-qudah*) appointed by the caliph Harun al-Rashid. In addition, Harun al-Rashid did not appoint any judge without consulting Abu Yusuf (the delegated head of judiciary), also the *qadi* exercised judicial authority in the capacity of a *hakim* (ruler), not a *muwazzaff* (task of *al-qudah* officer).[40] In several cases they deserved the explicit respect "judicial independence" and appreciation of the caliph and rulers.

Shurayk ibn 'Abd Allah is very distinguished and famous for his courage and strong judicial personlaity. After many refusals to be a judge, Caliph al-Mahdi, obliged him to accept, but under his condition approved by the caliph al-Mahdi. An essential condition is that there should be no interference in justice, from any, from any person or any side what so ever.

> *A woman once came to Shurayk complaining from the 'Abbasi prince Musa ibn 'Isa, the governor of the caliph, saying that the prince wanted to force her to sell him her garden, and when she refused, he destroyed her fence. The judge ordered the prince governor to come to court. When the latter sent instead, the chief commander of police, Shurayk ordered him to be put in jail. The same happened as the prince sent his chamberlain, and after wards group of the noble men of Kufah who were friends of Shurayk. Because intermediation is strictly forbidden in judicial matters, the firm and independent judge Shurayk sent all to prison, as a disciplinary measure, so that they refrain from mediation to the judge and from carrying the message of an unjust. At night, the prince governor ordered the door of prison to be opened and the said prisoners to be released.[41] The judge made up his mind to go from Kufah to Baghdad to resign before the caliph, saying "we did not ask to be judge; they obliged us to do. We accepted only provided that our dignity and independence should be guaranteed". The prince begged him not to go, and accept that all the prisoners be returned to jail! This done, the judge ordered the prince governor to come and stand the same as his adversary, the complaining woman, before the court. The case was seen and the judgment was issued to the favour of the woman against the oppressor. That is a slide of Islamic justice!![42]*

Indeed, the independence of the judiciary is considered a healthy development to ascertain contemporary demands and needs. It made the role of the judicial authority more prominent and effective in the state. Although the judicial authority had changed hands, the caliph was still highly responsible in regard to the judiciary institution.

Therefore, if we made a comparative study about the independence of the judiciary in the Islamic legal system and Western countries, we will find in these Western countries that the executive is the strongest authority, stronger than both the legislative and the judiciary. So, the people in these countries until now feel that there is no true progress or development in the independence of the judiciary.

Therefore, several conferences were held during 1985 to 1989, which established a number of basic principles for the independence of the judiciary. The essential points mentioned in the events are:[43]

The principle of independence of the judiciary should be respected and guaranteed without any encroachment by the head of the state or by any other influence.

Impartiality should be considered by the judiciary, without restrictions, improper influence, inducements, pressures, threats or interference, direct or indirect, from any party or for any reason.

To protect judges and lawyers, who are harassed or persecuted, as a result of carrying on their professional duties.

The judiciary should ensure that judicial proceedings are conducted fairly, and that the rights of the parties are respected.

Judges should be free to form associations of judges- or other organisations, to represent their interests, to promote their professional training and protect their judicial independence.

Summary

The judicial role is not merely a career or profession." It is so vital, important and noble, that it is considered to be a sacred message, a kind of worship. And that is not a matter of theory or hope. Islamic basic principles of justice and judicial independence were actually and practically implemented in many countries of the world, through different ages of history. The real outcome was security, freedom, fairness and legality, through the sovereignty of the *Shari'ah*."[44]

The Background of Judicial Control in the Islamic System

Judicial Control over the Constitutionality of Laws in Shari'ah

All principal sources of the Islamic political system, the *Qur'an* and *Sunnah*, stipulate the obedience by the individuals or groups to the Head of State, but this obedience is not absolute but is restricted to conformity with the conduct of the Head of State, irrespective of whether it were legislative or administrative, with the *Qur'an, Sunnah* and consensus of *Shari'ah* scholars on legal rulings.[45] Therefore, if any government orders contradict the authority of these sources, they are void and should not be obeyed. Therefore, the Islamic judiciary, in centuries where injustice was at its most, rejected any order, law or decision that was not in conformity with the *Shari'ah*.[46]

The researcher will study this subject through two fields of research, which are: First, Judicial control over the acts of legislative authorities; second, the control over acts and deeds of caliph and his workers and delegates.

Judicial Control over the Acts of Legislative Authorities

We cannot study judicial control over the acts of legislative authorities, whether individual or in groups, without first studying the nature of the Islamic constitution and Islamic legislation. This is followed by a discussion on the manner of judicial control.

The researcher will divide this subject into two branches: Firstly, the nature of Islamic constitution and legislation, and secondly, the manner of judicial control.

Nature of the Islamic Constitution and Legislation

If judicial control was established on the principles of legality and separation of judicial authority from other public powers in the country, then the nature of the constitution and legislation in Islam has two meanings the influence of which is reflected on that control.

They are explained in the following paragraphs.

(a) Nature of constitution: The constitution in positive legal systems is a collection of legal rules that show the ruling system, its type in the country, and the organisation of public powers, limitation of individuals' rights, and their obligations or duties. This definition does not conflict with the ruling system in Islam. However, the researcher finds that the constitution in the Islamic legal system has a deeper and more comprehensive meaning than that of the constitution in the positive legal system. The Islamic constitution is concerned with expressing faith in Allah (*s.w.t*) and solidarity in implementing Allah's orders and abstinence from his prohibitions.[47] Also, that the *Qur'an* and *Sunnah* are the convention of people and that the realisation of interests and the repelling of harm in order to realise the aims of *Shari'ah* is an obligation, and that *ijtihad* must conform to the rules of the *Shari'ah*.[48] Therefore, the constitutional rule in the Islamic legal system differs from the constitutional rule in the positive system.

There is controversy about the sources of *Shari'ah* among jurists, but they are said to be of three main sources: *Qur'an*, *Sunnah* and *al-ra'y* (opinion),[49] and this is what the former Imam of al-Azhar, Mahmud Shaltut, had deduced. However, there is a group that said that the sources are divided into two levels: the first is *Qur'an* and *Sunnah*, and the second is *al-ra'y* (opinion) and *qiyas*. They also considered that the *Qur'an* and *Sunnah* are both constitutional legislations.[50] While the principles that derived from other sources and fell under the heading *al-ra'y* are similar to normal legislations.

The analogy between the Islamic *Shari'ah* and constitutionalism was first made in the nineteenth century and became more common in the late twentieth century. Despite the analogy, there are some differences between Western and Islamic forms of constitutionalism.

First, Western constitutionalism has expressed itself most frequently in human-authored constitutional texts that generally reflect the idea of popular sovereignty; the Islamic *Shari'ah* is based on the will of God. This difference is not as great as might initially appear, because many constitutional scholars acknowledge that the root of Western constitutionalism lies in religious sources.[51]

Second, Western constitutionalism has generally focused on procedural ways of limiting government authority and rendering it accountable. Western constitutions and other constitutions based on Western models devote most of their attention to creating structures of government and clear lines of authority and accountability.[52]

Western constitutions do contain substantive as well as procedural limitations on government (such as guarantees of free speech), but even some of those substantive limitations are presented in procedural form (the famous first amendment to the U.S. Constitution states that Congress shall make no law abridging freedom of the press). The Islamic *Shari'ah,* on the other hand, provides much guidance on what the substantive law should be but far less on the procedures of government.[53]

(b) Nature of legislation and domain of *Shari'ah*: There is a big difference between the nature of legislation in an Islamic system and nature of legislation of the secular system. The lawmaker in manmade systems can legislate on any matter except matters that are explicitly excluded by the constitution. Whilst the legislation in the Islamic legal system must conform to the *Qur'an* and *Sunnah*, the interest that it aims to achieve must not contradict the text of the *Qur'an* and *Sunnah*. So there are several points that limit the domain of *shura* as legislative authority, which include the following:[54]

There is agreement among scholars of *Shari'ah* that *shura* is a kind of *ijtihad* in public opinion on various affairs: legislative, economic, political and social. Also, *ijtihad* is not allowed where there is a conclusive text in the *Qur'an* or *Sunnah.*[55]

Concerning the implication of non-conclusive texts, there is room for individual *ijtihad,* so public *ijtihad* would be *in priori* for the prevention of chaos. Such public *ijtihad* would take place by giving preference to some interpretations of one text over other interpretations.[56]

If there is no text of *Qur'an* or *Sunnah* or its counterpart of *qiyas or ijma'* (consensus of opinion) then the scope is open for *shura.* In this case, most of the political or governing issues derive their rules through the *shura* council on the basis of interest, and *sadd al-dhari'ah* In other words, legislating *ijtihad* systems for the realisation of legislation in the country and organisation of its administration and institutions in every subject that has no text, and that is based on the interests of *fiqh.*[57]

'Abd al-Wahhab Khallaf expressed and conveyed this point where he said that legislation has two meanings: finding a new legislation and this in Islam could not be except by Allah (*s.w.t.*) only; and secondly, illustrating a judgment required by existing legislations and this is the meaning in Islam, and judicial control extends to three domains of *shura*. Its controi extends in the first kind, decreases in the second, and dwindles in the third, and in all these kinds the judiciary checks the conformity of legislations to the public principles of *Qur'an* and *Sunnah* and *ijma'*, and what the *salaf* agreed upon as to that in which interest does not change.[58]

What is the jurisdictions and scope of the legislative authority in the Islamic State? The researcher believes that the legislative power in Islamic system has several jurisdictions to perform.

First, explanation of the directives of God and his Messenger are available, in spite of the fact that the legislative authority cannot replace or change or amend them; the legislative authority alone will be competent to legislate them in the shape of sections, devise relevant definitions and details, and make rules and regulations for the purpose of enforcing them.

Second, provisions and injunctions in the Holy *Qur'an* and *Sunnah* construed and interoperated, in the same instance, in various manners. So, it is to the legislature to choose which interpretation to be brought into operation.

Third, if there was no explicit provision in the Holy *Qur'an* and *Sunnah* pertaining to a subject, it would be incumbent on the legislature to enact laws pertaining to that subject in line with the spirit of Islamic and public interest.

> *Sayyid Qutb has said: If sovereignty lies with God, so does legislative authority, leading Islamic constitutionalists to affirm the absolutely binding nature of the Shar'ah. Any action by any human government has to be measured against the requirements of the Shar'ah, and any man-made rule, policy, or regulation that contradicts any provision of the Sha 'ah is invalid.*[59]

> *Rashid al-Ghannushi has said that Islam makes the binding nature of provisions a basis for legitimacy of the state and makes the ruler bound in the decisions he takes, the procedures and the commands he issues-by the provisions of the Islamic Shar'ah.*[60]

> *Tawfiq al-Shawi, member of the Muslim brotherhood, says that, the application of the Islamic Shari'ah is not confined to applying the Islamic fiqh to relations among individuals in the society, whether in civil, commercial or other aspects. But it is the state itself be bound by compliance with the sovereignty of the Shari'ah. All the organisations, institutions, and individuals who represent (the state) must be bound to comply with its principles and rules and apply them on themselves*

and on their own exercise of authority before they apply them on the general population and the individuals within society.[61]

Muhammad Salim al-'Awwa mentioned in his book, that the messenger of Allah left the matter of choosing the ruler and the determination of the system of government "also left without specifying details" to Muslims to decide according to their interests and the requirements of time, place and changing circumstances; and nothing decreed was binding on them except the general rules of Islamic law in regard to consultation, justice and equality, and the ordinances and moral values which the Prophet had promulgated during the Madinan *period, that is, from the inception of first Islamic state until he passed away.* [62]

'Awdah simliarly accepted the idea that the Shari'ah was the defending feature of Islamic politics. He wrote "The basic constitution for the Muslim is the Islamic Shari'ah and "Islam forbids each Muslim from obeying a law or command that violates the Shari'ah of Islam and exceeds limits established by God and his prophet". Positive legislation thus has a sharply limited role. Not only must it be contained within the bounds of the Shari'ah, it is only legitimate for one of two purposes:

The first: implementing legislation that aims at guaranteeing the implementation of the Shari'ah of Islam. The second: organising legislation, to organise the group, defend it, and meet its needs on the basis of the principles of the Islamic Shari'ah. This legislation can only exist where the Shari'ah is silent and there are no particular texts. Such legislation must agree with the general principles of Shari'ah and its legislative spirit.[63]

The Control of Islamic Judiciary over the Constitutionality of Laws

Originally, the judge should, when making his decisions, depend on the *Qur'an*, *Sunnah* of the Prophet (*s.a.w.*) and consensus, and if he does not find any (ruling) he should exercise judicial interpretation (*ijtihad*) to derive at the *Shari'ah* ruling from other evidence in order to apply it to the facts before him.

What can be conceived in the field of judicial control over the constitutionality of laws, as far as Islamic *Shari'ah* is concerned, is that it is implemented on legislation passed by the parliament which is known as (*Ahl al-Hall wa al-'Aqd*). Legislation here is based on judicial interpretation (*ijtihad*) solely, because the definitive rulings that are found in the *Qur'an* and *Sunnah* are considered constitutional texts over which the judge has no control, and what has been passed by way of consensus is infallible and there is no control over that as well, yet control can be had over rulings of the source which is judicial interpretation (*ijtihad*).[64]

What is known is that one of the functions of "parliament" is juridical interpretation (*ijtihad*) and legislation, and that is where it uses juridical interpretation in cases where there exists no text from the *Qur'an* or the *Sunnah* or consensus in order to derive the *Shari'ah* ruling. If these derived rulings were drafted as laws for the judiciary to implement, then the judicial control over the constitutionality of law and their legitimacy would appear, because the judge in the Islamic system is not allowed to implement a law which he sees as conflicting with the *Qur'an* and *Sunnah*, as there is no obedience to a human in disobedience to the Creator.

There are two kinds of Verses in the *Qur'an*, namely, absolute and presumptive, the latter being those which are capable of different interpretations. The decisive Verses are the basis of the book and contain the fundamental principles of religion. So, whatever may be the differences of interpretation over allegorical Verses, the fundamentals of religion are not affected by them.[65]

The Court has articulated this principle on numerous occasions. In 1996, for instance, a father brought a case to the Court involving an administrative decree issued by the Minister of Education barring female students from wearing *niqab* "a veil covering the full face in contradistinction to the permitted *hijab*, a veil covering only the hair" in state schools. The proponents of a *Shari'ah* -based constitutional jurisprudence finally seemed to have a strong case. The challengers could cite not only Article 2, but also personal rights provisions of the constitution. The father claimed that the minister's decree violated both the Islamic *Shari'ah* and rights of a liberal provenance. The court rejected the claim, however, laying out once again a view that grants executive and legislative authorities tremendous latitude:

It is not permitted for a legislative text to contradict those *shura* provisions definitive in their certainty and meaning *"qat'i al-thubut wa-al-dalalah."* These rules alone are those for which *ijtihad* is forbidden because they signify the comprehensive principle and fixed roots of the *Shari'ah*, accepting neither interpretation nor substitution...The judgment of reason, where there is no text, develop on a practical basis and are more compassionate to humankind and more dedicated to their affairs in their content. [The judgments based on reason] are more protective of humanity's true interests, which the [*shura*] provisions are prescribed to realise in terms of what is appropriate for these interests. The underlying factor is that the essence of God's *Shari'ah* is truth and justice. Being limited by the *Shari'ah* is better than widespread depravity.[66]

For [the *Shari'ah*] to be closed upon itself is neither acceptable nor necessary. The statements of an expert of *fiqh* on a matter related to the *shura*, are not granted any sanctity, or placed beyond review reexamination. Rather they can be replaced by other [such statements]. Opinions based on *ijtihad* in debated questions do not in themselves have any force applying to those who do not hold them. It is not permitted to hold [such opinions] to be firm, settled *Shari'ah* law that cannot be contravened. To do so would be to end contemplation of and reflection over Almighty God's religion; it would deny the truth that error possible in all *ijtihad* .....The challenged decree does not contradict...the text of article 2 of the constitution. The rule has-in debatable questions-the right of *ijtihad* to facilitate the affairs of the people and reflect what is authentic in their customs and traditions, so long as overarching purposes of their *shura* is not abrogated ....

An attempt to use Article 2 as the basis for the application of a *Shari'ah* - based law must now overcome one of two hurdles. First, one might resort directly to the Court. Yet, by rejecting any claim that is not a clear and permanent injunction of the *shura,* the Court has made this barrier formidable. Others have distinguished between unalterable sources of law "the *Qur'an* and *Sunnah,"* on the one hand, and those based on human judgment, on the other.

The jurists have the right to make sure that *ijtihad* in the non-peremptory provisions is achieving the interest of the people.

Ijtihad is a brainstorming process to deduct practical rules to regulate the life of people and achieve their interest. Hence *ijtihad* should cope with the context of events prevailing at the time. It does not have a binding power but on those who believe in it. This sign of God's mercy that permitted different *ijtihad* to encourage people to think and avoid the possibility of human error. Thus, the Islamic *Shari'ah* is always developing and flexible to accept *ijtihad* of the responsible people to achieve the utmost interest of the people.

A number of Muslim jurists have shown that Islamic *Shari'ah* has known, in theory, the control system over the constitutionality of law, but did not practice it. Among them is the Muslim scholar Abu al-A'la al-Mawdudi who says:

> *Does Islam permit the judiciary to reject some legislation that are passed by the legislative council as being contradictory to the Qur'an and Sunnah? I did not look into a text under this topic and there is no doubt that what the work of the orthodox caliphs (al-Khulafa' al-Rashidin) indicate that the judiciary had no such powers, at least we have not found until now an example of this matter, but the reason for this as I see it is that all the members of parliament (Ahl al-Hall wa al-'Aqd) were at that time very knowledgeable in the Qur'an and Sunnah, and on top of them were the orthodox caliphs who did not pronounce in any way an issue that is in contradiction to the Qur'an and Sunnah.*[67]

Although the researcher agrees with many aspects of this opinions, but the researcher is of the view that the legislative council consists of normal people who are human beings and are affected by matters that all people are affected by. So, some might have made mistakes according to the circumstances, thus the promulgation of a legislation that is not in conformity with the *Qur'an* and *Sunnah* is not an impossible proposition. On the contrary, it is a conceivable proposition and the objective behind the promulgation of such legislation is not the contradiction of the *Qur'an* and *Sunnah per se*, it might rather be caused by the absence of discernment or the actual purpose behind its promulgation.

The Islamic system, during the period of the four pious caliphs, did not know the principle of judicial control over the constitutionality of laws or acts. There was no room in Islam for the judiciary to reject or to restrict the powers of the legislature in respect of enacting laws in contravention of the *Qur'an* and *Sunnah*. During this period, the caliphs proved that the judiciary did not enjoy or exercise such powers at the time. There was no instances of any *qadi* taking such an action. This is because the members of the legislative authority at that time had very deep and true insight in the

Qur'an and *Sunnah* and almost all the caliphs too were the most reliable persons in all respects. In addition to that, under their authorities, there was no real danger of any such legislation taking place which was contrary to the spirit of the *Qur'an* and *Sunnah*. While the principle of judicial control over the constitutionality of laws appeared after the end of this period, the judicial authority gave the right to declare void, and *ultra vires* of the constitution, all laws and legislation enacted in contravention of the *Qur'an* and *Sunnah*.

Perhaps, the best example to be given here is where Caliph Umar ibn al-Khattab (may Allah be pleased with him) refused to divide the conquered lands of Iraq among the conquerors while most of the Prophet's companions, who formed the legislative council (*Ahl al-Hall wa al-'Aqd*), were asking for that division and the most eager amongst them was Billal ibn Rabah. But 'Umar was able to convince them using evidence from the *Qur'an* and *Sunnah* and by showing the wisdom behind the refusal of such a division among the conquerors which was the fear of stoppage of the Islamic conquests and the defense of the wide Islamic borders. He also explained to them that the decision not to divide was not based on his own desire but was rather in agreement with the *Qur'an* and *Sunnah*.[68] Thus we can say that the Islamic judiciary has the power to reject any law that is not in conformity with the *Qur'an* and *Sunnah*, and not give a judgment based on it for its illegality. Moreover, the judge is bound, in exercising his function of giving a judgment, by what Allah (*s.a.w.*) has revealed. The Prophet (*s.a.w.*) said: "there is no obedience to a human in disobedience to the Creator,"[69] and Allah (*s.a.w.*) revealed: "*... If any do fail to judge by (the light of) what Allah hath revealed, they are Unbelievers*."[70] Thus, it is obvious that the Islamic *Shari'ah* has control over the constitutionality of law before the positive law systems have.

Furthermore, the right of control that the judiciary has over the constitutionality of law, the source of which is juridical interpretation (*ijtihad*), is not absolute, as a judge may not merely claim that a law contradicts the *Shari'ah*. This is because the juridical interpretation that emanates from people who have the correct mechanism of juridical interpretation, and the law that is promulgated on its basis and is met by the approval of the leader after its promulgation must be implemented by the judge even if it contradicts the judge's own interpretation. This is because it is a well established legal maxim in the science of jurisprudence that one judicial interpretation (*ijtihad*) does not become overruled by its like.[71]

"لَا يُنْقَضُ الِاجْتِهَادُ بِالِاجْتِهَادِ"

Among the most important jurists who talked about the control over the constitutionality of law is Ibn Hazm al-Andalusi where he said: "no ruling is permitted unless it is based on what Allah (S.W.T.) has revealed to His Prophet (*s.a.w.*) and it is the truth, and all that is not, is considered injustice and tyranny, and any ruling based on it is not permitted and must be annulled if the judge ruled by it."[72] Ibn Hazm supported his view by some Verses of the Holy *Qur'an,* such as the revelation of Allah (*s.w.t.*): "... *and any who transgresses the limits of Allah, does verily wrong his (own) soul*..."[73] and added: "the approval of injustice may not be permitted and the wrong may not be let to pass."[74]

It is to be noted that even though rules based on *ijma'* and *ijtihad* are not directly based on the *Qur'an* and *Sunnah*, these rules are to be in conformity with the principles of *shura* and its spirit which is directly derived from the *Qur'an* and *Sunnah.*

Abu Hanifah said, "If I said a statement in non-conformity with the *Qur'an* and *Sunnah* of the Prophet, do not take my saying."[75]

He also said, "It is not permissible to anyone to adopt our opinion or saying unless he knows where we took it from."[76]

Imam Malik said, "I am a human being and I can be right or wrong. So look at my opinion, if it is in conformity with the *Qur'an* and *Sunnah* take it, but if it is not in conformity with the *Qur'an* and *Sunnah*, leave it."[77]

Al-Shafi'i said, "If you find in my book things that do not conform to the *Qur'an* and *Sunnah*, do not take my opinion and abide by the *Qur'an* and *Sunnah.*"[78]

Ibn Hanbal said, "Do not imitate me and do not imitate Malik, Abu Hanifah, al-Shafi'i, and al-Thawri, and you take from where they have taken."[79]

Conclusion

It is clear then that the Islamic legal system has known judicial control over constitutionality or legitimacy of laws. As well as, it has applied the judicial control in practice in several occasions that had taken place in the Islamic history and civilisation especially during the Ummayyad, 'Abbasi and the Ottoman periods. However, there is no scope to mention these occasions or cases in this study as we feel there is no need to go into details, because that could be explained in future studies which could elaborate more.

While during the orthodox caliphs period there was no room in the Islamic system for the judiciary to reject or to restrict the powers of legislature in respect of enacting laws in non-conformity with *Qur'an* and the *Sunnah.* We believe that during the period of the pious caliphs the judicial power did not enjoy or exercise such powers at that time. At least there is no instance of any *Qadi* taking such an action. Because, the members of the legislature at that time had very deep and true insight in the *Qur'an* and the *Sunnah* and almost all the Caliphs too were the most reliable person in all respects. Under them, therefore, there was no real danger of any such legislation taking place which was contrary to the principles and spirit of the *Shari'ah* or the *Qur'an* and *Sunnah* provisions.

Notes

1. Zafir al-Qasimi (1974), *Nizam al-Hukum fi al- Shari'ah wa al-Tarikh al-Islami: Al-Sultah al-Qada'iyyah* (Bayrut: Dar al-Nafa'is), at p. 403.
2. ManÎur Muhammad al-Hafnawi (1989), *Sultat al-Dawlah fi al-Manzur al-Shar'i.* (1st ed.), (Al-Qahirah: Matba'at al-Amanah), at p. 349.
3. Anwar Ahmad Qadri, *Justice in Historical Islam,* Lahore, SH Muhammad Ashraf, 1968, at p. 8. See also Úafir al-Qasimi (1974), *Nizam al-Hukum fi al- Shari'ah wa al-Tarikh al-Islami:,* at p. 404. See also Hasan al-'Alkim (1991), *Al-Nizam al-Siyasi al-Islami: Hiwar Ma'a al-'Almaniyyah.* Mu'assasat al-'Ayn li al-Tawzi' wa al-Nashr, at p. 178.
4. *Hadith* no. 3592, in *Sunan Abi Dawud.* (2001). (Beirut: Dar al-Kutub al-'Ilmiyyah). See also, Mohammad Hashim Kamali, *Principles of Islamic Jurisprudence,* Second Edition, (Kuala Lampur, Ilmiah Publishers 1998), at pp. 45, 217 and 218.
5. *Ibid,* at 18.
6. Al-Qurtubi, Abu 'Abd al-Barr (2002), *Al-Istishab fi Ma'rifat al-Ashab* (Beirut: Dar al-Kutub al-'Ilmiyyah), at p. 356. See also Ahmad Fathi Bahnasi (1984), *Mawqif al- Shari'ah Min Nazariyyat al-Difa' al-Ijtima'i.* (Beirut. Dar al-Shuruq), at, p. 3.

7. Yasin Umar Yusuf (1995) *Istiqlal al-Sultah al-Qada'iyyah*, at p. 298. See also Al-Ma'had al-'Alami li al-Fikr al-Islami (1981), *Al-Dawlah: Al-Fikrah wa al-Arkan wa al-Mu'assasat*, (USA: Grove Street, Herndon), at pp. 66-67. See also Diya'al-Din Muhammad al-Rayyis (1976), *Al-Nazariyyat al-Siyasiyyah al-Islamiyyah*. (Al-Qahirah: Maktabat Dar al-Turath), at pp. 365-375.
8. Abdullah Yusuf 'Ali (trans.) (1984), *The Qur'an, Text, Translation and Commentary*, (Jedda: Islamic Education Center. Reprinted by the Muslim Converts Association of Singapore), *Sura*, 5, 44. See also Hasan al-'Alkim. *Al- Nizam al-Siyasi al-Islami*, at 65.
9. Abdullah Yusuf 'Ali (trans.) (1984)..., *al-Qur'an* 5: 45.
10. Hasan 'Alkim, at p. 65. See also Muhammad Yusuf Musa (1964), *Nizam al-Hukm fi al-Islam*. (2nd ed.). Al-Qahirah: Dar al-Kitab al-'Arabi, at 74.
11. *Ibid*, at 4,59. See also al-Sabuni, Abd al-Rahman, *Mukhtasar Ibn Kathir li al-Sabuni*, Vol. 1, at 520.
12. Mohammad Asad, *The Principles of State and Government in Islam*, Cibraltar: Dar Al-Andalus 1980, at 34, 38.
13. Tirmidhi, *al-Jami' al-Sahih*, Vol 1, at 319. See also Diya' al-Din Muhammad al-Rayyis. (1967), *Al-Nazariyyat al-Siyasiyyah al-Islamiyyah*, at p. 340.
14. Bukhari, Abu 'Abd Allah Muhammad ibn Ismail, *Kitab al-Jami' al-Sahih*, Vol. 9, at 52. See also Muslim, Abu al-Husayn ibn al-Hajjaj al-Nisaburi. (n.d.). *Sahih Muslim*. n.p. Ed.m., at 111. *Sunan al-Tirmidhi*. See also Mohammad Asad, *The Principles of State and Government in Islam*, (Cibraltar: Dar al-Andalus 1980), at pp 34-6. See also Diya' al-Din Muhammad al-Rayyis (1976), *Al-NaĐariyyat al-Siyasiyyah al-Islamiyyah*. Al-Qahirah: Maktabat Dar al-Turath, at p. 362. See also Al-Ma'had al-'Alami li al-Fikr al-Islami (1981), *Al-Dawlah:* at pp. 84,85.
15. Muhammad Muhsin Khan. (trans.) (1970), *Sahih al-Bukhari*, Vol. 9 (Al-Medina al-Munauwara: Islamic University), at p. 271.
16. Ibn Hanbal, Ahmad (1998), *Al-Musnad: Musnad al-Ansar*, Vol. 7 (Beirut: Dar 'Alam al-Kutub), at p. 540.
17. *Musannaf Ibn Abi Shaybah* (1989), Vol. 7 (Bayrut: Dar al-Fikr), at p. 736.
18. Muhammad Muhsin Khan. (trans.) (1970), *Sahih al-Bukhari*. Vol. 3, at pp. 535-536.
19. *Hadith* no. 15119, in Al-Tibrani, Abi al-Qasim Sulayman ibn Ahmad, *Al-Mu'jam al-Kabir*, Vol. 13, (Al-'Iraq: Ihya' al-Turath al-Islami, 1984).

20. Waki', Muhammad ibn Khalaf ibn Hayyan (2001), *Akhbar al-Qudat.* (1st ed.), (Bayrut: 'Alam al-Kutub), at p. 357. See also, Yasin Umar Yusuf (1995), *Istiqlal al-Sultah al-Qada'iyyah fi al-Nizamayn al-Wad'i wa al-Islami,* at p. 300.
21. Muhammad Muhsin Khan (trans.) (1970), *Sahih al-Bukhari.* Vol. 8, at pp.512-513. See also Anwar Ahmad Qadri, *Justice in Historical Islam,* at pp.11-12.
22. Ibn Hisham, Abu Muhammad Abd al-Malik (1980), *Sirat al-Nabi Muhammad.* Vol. 3. (Al-Qahirah: Maktabat Dar al-Turath), at pp. 340-341.
23. Anwar Ahmad Qadri, *Justice in Historical Islam,* at p. 23.
24. *Ibid,* at 27.
25. Ahmad Hasan (1969), "The Political Role of *Ijma'*", *Islamic Studies.* Vol. 2, at 138. See also Manoucherhr Paydar, *Aspects of the Islamic State Religious Norms and Political Realities,* at 2972.
26. Ahmad Fathi Bahnasi (1984), *Mawqif al- Shari'ah Min Nazariyyat al-Difa' al-Ijtima'i.,* at p. 111.
27. Ibid. See also, Muhammad Abu Zahrah (1997), *Usul al-Fiqh* (Al-Qahirah: Dar al-Fikr al-'Arabi), at p. 92.
28. Muhammad Salim al-'Awwa (1983), *Fi al- Nizam al-Siyasi li al-Dawlah al-Islamiyyah* (Al-Qahirah: al-Maktab al-Misri al-Hadith), at p. 1.
29. Farooq Hassan, *The Concept of State and Law in Islam,* University Press of America, at p. 65. See also Ahmad Hasan, "The Political Role of *Ijma',*" *Islamic Studies, Journal of the Islamic Research Institute,* Pakistan, Vol. VIII, No.1, 1969, at p. 188.
30. Emile Tyan (1955), "Judicial Organization." Majid Khadduri. (ed.). *Law in Middle East,* at p. 236.
31. Mahmud A. Faksh, "A Review of Islamic Culture," *The Islamic Quarterly,* Vol. xxviii (Number 1), England: The Islamic Culture Centre, 1984, at p. 110.
32. Hassan Ibrahim Hassan, "Judiciary System from the Rise of Islam," at p. 567. (C.E. 1171).
33. Ibid. See also Ahmad Ibrahim, "The *Shari'ah* Court and Its Place in the Judicial System,", paper presented at the International Islamic Conference on The role of Judiciary in The Development of Islamic Law, November 21 St- 23RD 1986, Malaysia, at 70.
34. Hassan Ibrahim Hassan, "Judiciary System from the Rise of Islam," at p. 567. (C.E.1171). Ali Abd Al-Kader, *"A Review of Islamic Culture",*

The Islamic Quarterly VI Numbers 1, 2, England: the Islamic Culture Centre, 1961, at p. 24.

35. N. J. Coulson, "Doctrine and Practice in Islamic Law," *Bulletin of the School of Oriental and African Studies,* Vol. xviii, University of London: Published by The School of Oriental and African Studies, 1956, at p. 215. See also Manouchechr Paydar, *Aspects of the Islamic State: Religius Norms and Political Realities*, 1973, at pp. 95-97.
36. Sami Zubaida, *Law and Power in the Islamic World,* London: I. B. Tauris- 2003, at p. 42.
37. N. J. Coulson, "Doctrine and Practice in Islamic Law," *Bulletin of the School of Oriental and African Studies*, at p. 214.
38. Masudul Hasan, *Reconstruction of Political Thought in Islam* (Pakistan: Islamic Publications (PVT) Limited, 1988), at p. 207.
39. Mohammad Hashim Kamali, "Appellate Review and Judicial Independence in Islamic Law", *Islamic and Public Law,* 1993, at 53-54.
40. *Ibid*, at 55.
41. Husayn Abd Allah 'Uthman (1993), *Al-Qada' fi al-Islam: 'Ilm wa Qiyam* (Al-Qahirah: Dar al-I'tisam), at pp. 32-33.
42. *Ibid*, pp. 36-37.
43. Muhammad al-Ghazali, "Introduction to a Draft Islamic Constitution," *Islamic Studies, Journal of the Islamic Research Institute*, Vol. 20, 1981, pp. 155-160.
44. Husayn Abd Allah 'Uthman (1993), *Al-Qada' fi al-Islam*, at p. 40.
45. Muhammad Salim al-'Awwa (1983), *Fi al- Nizam al-Siyasi li al-Dawlah*, at 397.
46. Sulayman Muhammad al-Tamawi (1976), *Al-Sultat al-Thalath fi al-Dasatir*, at 329-330.
47. Yasin Umar Yusuf (1995), *Istiqlal al-Sultah al-Qada'iyyah,* at 328. See also, Sulayman Muhammad al-Tamawi (1976), *Al-Sultat al-Thalath,* at p. 330.
48. Mahmud Shaltut (1959), *Al-Islam: 'Aqidah wa Shari'ah*. Kuwait, at p. 398.
49. *Ibid*. See also, Sulayman Muhammad al-Tamawi (1976), *Al-Sultat al-Thalath*, at p. 328.
50. *Ibid.*
51. Sulayman Muhammad al-Tamawi (1976), *Al-Sultat al-Thalath*, at p. 330.

52. Fathi al-Dirini (1987), *Khasa'is al-Tashri' al-Islami fi al-Siyasah wa al-Hukm*, (2nd ed.) (Beirut: Mu'assasat al-Risalah), at p. 444.
53. *Ibid.*
54. *Ibid.*
55. Abd al-Wahhab Khallaf (1937), *Al-Sultst al-Thalath fi al-Islam: Bahth fi Majallat al-Qanun wa al-Iqtisad*, at pp. 565-570.
56. *Ibid*, at p. 577.
57. Fathi al-Dirini (1987), *Khasa'is al-Tashri' al-Islami fi al-Siyasah wa al-Hukm*, at p. 447.
58. Abd al-Wahhab Khallaf (1988), *Al-Siyasah al-Shar'iyyah*, (Kuwait: Dar al-Qalam), at p. 9.
59. Sayyid Qutb (1983), *Ma'alim fi al-Tariq*, at pp. 20-12.
60. Rashid al-Ghannushi (1993), *Al-Hurriyyat al-Ammah fi al-Dawlah al-Islamiyyah* (Beirut: Markaz Dirasat al-Wihdah al-Arabiyyah), at p.105.
61. Tawfiq al-Shawi, (1992), *Fiqh al-Shura wa al-Istisharah* (Al-Mansurah: Dar al-Wafa´), pp. 168-170.
62. Nathan J. Brown, *Constitutional in a Non Constitutional World (Arab Basic Laws and the Prospects for Accountable Government* (New York: State University of New York Press, 2002), at p. 168.
63. 'Awdah, 'Abd al-Qadir (1951), *Al-Islam wa al-Wad'iyyah al-Qanuniyyah* (Beirut: Mu'assasat al-Risalah), at p. 61.
64. Munir Hamid al-Bayyati (1994), *Al- Nizam al-Siyasi fi al-Islam: Muqaran bi al-Duwal al-Qanuniyyah.* (2nd Print). (Amman: Dar al-Bashir), at p. 281.
65. Farooq Hassan , *The Concept of State and Law In Islam*, at 36.
66. Case 8, judical Year 17, issued by the Supreme Constitutional Court 18 May, 1996.
67. Abu al-A'la al-Mawdudi (1985), *Tadwin al-Dustur al-Islami* (Al-Sa'udiyyah: Dar al-Sa'udiyyah), at p. 61.
68. Abu Yusuf Ya'qub Ibrahum (1970), *Kitab al-Kharaj* (Beirut: Dar al-Ma'ifah), pp. 28-38.
69. Al-Bayhaqi, *al-Sunan al-Kubra*, Vol. 3, 122. See also *Sunnan al-Nasa'i: Kitab al-Qada´*. (n.d., n.p.).
70. Abdullah Yusuf 'Ali (trans.) (1984), *The Qur'an, Text, Translation and Commentary, al-Qur'an* 5: 44.
71. Munir Hamid al-Bayyati (1994), *Al- Nizam al-Siyasi fial-Islam*, at p. 283.
72. Ibn Hazm al-Andalusi (1956), *Al-Muhalla*, Vol. 6. (Beirut: Dar al-Fikr), at pp. 362- 363.

73. *Al-Qur'an* 65: 1.
74. Ibn Hazm al-Andalusi (1956), *Al-Muhalla*, Vol. 6 (Beirut: Dar al-Fik), at p. 362.
75. Al-Imam al-Hafiz, Abu Umayr Yusuf ibn Abd al-Bar al-Nimri al-Qurtubi. (n.d.), *Al-Intiqa' fi Fala'il al-Thalathah al-A'immah al-Fuqaha'* (Al-Qahirah: Maktabat al-Quds), at p. 20.
76. Ibn al-Qayyim, Shams al-Din Abu Abd Allah Muhammad al-Dimashqi. (1969). *A'lam al-Muwaqqi'in 'An Rabb al-'Alamin*. Vol. 1. (Beirut: Dar Ihya' al-Turath al-'Arabi), at p. 302.
77. Al-Imam al-Hafiz, Abu Umayr Yusuf ibn Abd al-Bar al-Nimri al-Qurtubi. (n.d.). *Al-Intiqa' fi Fala'il al-Thalathah al-A'immah al-Fuqaha'*, at p. 20.
78. *Ibid*, at 72.
79. Al-Nawawi, Yahya ibn Sharaf al-Din. (n.d.). *Takmilat al-Majmu' Sharh al-Muhadhdhab* (Al-Madinah al-Munawwarah: al-Maktabah al-Salafiyyah), at p. 63. See also Ibn al-Qayyim, Shams al-Din Abu Abd Allah Muhammad al-Dimashqi (1969), *A'lam al-Muwaqqi'in 'An Rabb al-Alamin*, at p. 361.

12

Regulation of Islamic Banks and Allegations of Lax Control of Money-Laundering

Norhashimah Mohd. Yasin

Introduction

In recent years, particularly since the terrorist attacks in New York on 11 September 2001, the spotlight has been cast on the role of Islamic Banks in money laundering and terrorism financing. The main allegation, particularly from American law enforcement agencies and the US State Department,[1] is that regulations of Islamic banks is lax compared to that of conventional banks. The allegations are often of a blanket nature and do not distinguish between countries. It is notable that the Financial Action Task Force (FATF), which is the leading body for the combating of money laundering and terrorism financing, has not passed such type of comment in any of their reports.

The State Department said:

> *"Some terrorist groups may also use Islamic banks to move funds. Islamic banks operate within Islamic law, which prohibit the payment of interest and certain other activities. They have proliferated throughout Africa, Asia and the Middle East since the mid-1970s. Some of the largest Islamic financial institutions now operate investment houses in Europe and elsewhere. Many of these banks are not subject to a wide range of anti-money laundering regulations and controls normally imposed on secular commercial banks nor do they*

undergo the regulatory or supervisory scrutiny by bank regulators via periodic bank examinations or inspections. While these banks may voluntarily comply with banking regulations, and in particular, anti-money laundering guidelines, there is often no control mechanism to assure such compliance or the implementation of updated anti-money laundering policies."[2]

While it may be true that some countries may be lax in their regulation of Islamic banks,[3] this is certainly not the case in countries that intend to be global leaders in Islamic banking. As it is not possible to examine the regulation of Islamic banks in every Muslim country, this article will focus on the two leading countries in global Islamic banking– Malaysia and Bahrain.

The related issues of Islamic charities which are alleged to be engaged in terrorism financing having accounts at Islamic banks, and that of so-called 'underground' banking will also be touched on.

This Article intends to show that the allegations levelled at Islamic banks, vis-à-vis money laundering and terrorism financing, do not apply to Islamic banks operating in these two countries.

Malaysia[4]

Islamic banking is still a relatively small part of the overall banking sector.[5] 11 Islamic banks hold about 12.2% of total banking assets.[6]

Conventional banks (including those that also engage in Islamic banking)[7] are governed under the Banking and Financial Institutions Act 1989 (BAFIA). Islamic banks are governed by the Islamic Banking Act 1983 (IBA). Both types of bank come under the supervision of the Central Bank of Malaysia (CBM).[8]

With regards to money laundering, both types of banks are treated equally; Islamic banks are subject to the same legislation and regulations as conventional banks.[9]

All Malaysian banks have to adhere to the Anti Money Laundering and Anti Terrorism Financing Act 2001 (AMLATFA),[10] especially Part 4 that deals with compliance. The Central Bank has also issued guidelines, i.e. UPW/GP1[1]: Anti-Money Laundering and Counter Financing of Terrorism (AML/CFT) Sectoral Guidelines 1 for Banking and Financial Institutions.[11] In addition, all banks are also subject to the general guidelines for all reporting institutions' namely UPW/GP1: Standard Guidelines on Anti-Money Laundering and Counter Financing of Terrorism (AML/CFT) with effect for banks on 15 November 2006.

Islamic banks are listed in the First Schedule of AMLATFA as 'Reporting Institutions' and have been subject to the Act since it came into force on 15 January 2002. As such, under Part 4 of the Act, the compliance requirements for Islamic banks operating in Malaysia, whether local or foreign, are exactly the same as for conventional banks. Islamic banks must file 'Cash Transaction Reports'[12] (CTRs) and 'Suspicious Transaction Reports' (STRs) to the Central Bank's Financial Intelligence Unit in exactly the same way as conventional banks do.

UPW/GP1[1] does make slight reference to Islamic banking. In section 4 (Customer Due Diligence), it says:

> *"...Whether the transaction involves a new type of service or product or engages new technology, which alters the delivery mode and transaction process, whereby, care must be taken to ensure that customer identification and verification requirements are adequately complied. To ensure that new conventional or Islamic products or services as well as delivery mode does not create an avenue for money laundering and terrorism financing activities, the reporting institution must ensure that prior to the launch of any new conventional or Islamic products/services or engagement of a new technology, controls to combat money laundering and terrorism financing practices are in place to address any risks these new products/services or technology may pose; and..."*[13]

Unlike conventional banks that simply take the customer's deposit, use it for lending or investment, and pay interest on the principal amount, Islamic banking products work on the principles of partnership or involve buying and selling property, or even commodities. Although the act of buying and selling commodities could give scope for money laundering, this activity is done by the bank or the bank appointed customer as its purchasing agent. The customer must still deposit money with the bank in the normal way, and 'Customer Due Diligence', and any CTR or STR, will likewise be carried out in the normal way. This section of the Guidelines creates an obligation on the Islamic bank to ensure that new products, for example Commodity *Murabaha*,[14] cannot be used as a vehicle for money laundering.

Appendix 2 of UPW/GP1[1] lists the various general types of product offered by Islamic banks in Malaysia, i.e.:

Deposit	*Wadiah* (safekeeping) Mudharabah (profit sharing)
Investment	*Mudharabah* (profit sharing) *Bai' Bithaman Ajil* (deferred payment sale)
Retail Financing	*Bai' Bithaman Ajil* (deferred payment sale) *Mudharabah* (profit sharing) *Musharakah* (joint venture)
Hire Purchase	*Al-Ijarah Thumma al-Bai'* (hire purchase)
Credit Card-i	*Bai' al-Inah* (sell and buyback arrangement)

Appendix 2 briefly explains how each type of product works, but does not state what would constitute a 'red flag' so as to trigger suspicion. The reason appears to be that the various concepts involved already fall into the various categories listed in Appendix 3 (Examples of transactions that may trigger suspicion).[15]

A recent report by the Asia/Pacific Group (APG) on Money Laundering regarding Malaysia's compliance with the FATF Recommendations found no particular problems with the supervision of banks vis-à-vis money laundering.[16] The APG report does not make any observations regarding Islamic banks, so it can be assumed that Malaysian Islamic banks are regarded as being no different to conventional banks.

Malaysia has allowed offshore banking to take place on the island of Labuan, near Sabah, since 1990. This is known as the International Offshore Financial Centre (IOFC).

Banks are governed by the Offshore Banking Act 1990 (OBA). As there is no specific piece of legislation for offshore Islamic banks in Malaysia, the OBA is deemed to apply.

With regards to money laundering, Offshore Islamic and conventional banks are treated in exactly the same way by the Labuan Offshore Financial Services Authority (LOFSA).

As Labuan is part of Malaysia, AMLATFA applies to all institutions listed in Part 2 of Section 1 of the Act. LOFSA has also issued guidelines which are similar to those issued by the Central Bank (Bank Negara).

These are the 'Standard Guidelines on Anti-Money Laundering and Counter Financing of Terrorism (AML/CFL)' for all institutions and the 'Sectoral Guidelines 1 for Offshore Financial Institutions Licensed and Registered under Offshore Banking Act 1990.' Reporting institutions on Labuan, including Islamic ones, must report STRs to both the LOFSA Anti-Money Laundering Unit (AMLU) and the FIU of the Central Bank.

A 2004 report by the International Monetary Fund (IMF)[17] found no serious problems regarding supervision of offshore banks with regard to compliance with money laundering legislation and guidelines. As no attention was drawn to Islamic banks, this implies that the IMF does not regard offshore Islamic banking in Labuan as having a higher risk than offshore conventional banking.

Bahrain[18]

28 of Bahrain's licensed banks are classified as Islamic banks. Their assets make up about 4% of the banking system.

With respect to money laundering, all banks in Bahrain are governed by the 'Anti Money Laundering Law 2001.'[19] It is a very short Act compared to the Malaysian AMLAFTA, with only 13 Articles. As such, there is great dependence on rules and regulations.[20]

Two sets of money laundering rules[21] have been issued by the Central Bank of Bahrain,[22] one for conventional banks, the other for Islamic banks. Both sets of rules are, however, essentially the same.[23]

The money laundering rules relating to Islamic banks are in Part A of Volume 2. They are in the section called Business Standards under the Financial Crimes heading.

Despite conventional and Islamic banks coming under different Volumes of the Rulebook, the Central Bank treats all issues of compliance with those rules by Islamic banks, as well as money laundering legislation, regulations and orders, exactly the same as for conventional banks.

All banks, Islamic and conventional, must report CTRs and STRs to the Anti Money Laundering Unit of the Interior Ministry, as well as to the Central Bank's Compliance Unit.

A recent report by MENAFATF[24] has not found any particular problems with the supervision of banks. As no attention is drawn to

Islamic banks, it can be presumed that in terms of there regulation, vis-à-vis money laundering, there is nothing to make them out as a greater risk than conventional banks.

Charities

Islamic charities, particularly in the United States as evidenced by the fact that several have been closed-down,[25] are frequently accused of fund-raising for terrorist purposes. Connected to this, Islamic banks are accused of not conducting sufficient CDD in regard to Islamic charities.

Malaysian charities, Islamic or otherwise, are not reporting institutions. Therefore banks, including Islamic banks must, under UPW/GP1,[26] carry out CDD on charities by requiring the relevant documents and to establish the identity of the office bearers and who is authorised to represent it. In addition, under UPW/GP1[1],[27] banks must verify the identity of at least two of the signatories, and must "closely scrutinise" the accounts "in order to detect discrepancies in the transactions and account activities."

Malaysian charities must either be registered under the Registrar of Societies or as companies under the Companies Commission of Malaysia as the case may be.[28] If registered as a company, the bank will apply the CDD procedure for corporate customers as per section 5.3 of UPW/GP1.

The Bank Negara Standard Guidelines, UPW/GP1 (for all reporting institutions), state the following:

5.4. Clubs, Societies and Charities[29]

> *5.4.1. In conducting customer due diligence on a club, society or charity, the reporting institution should require the club, society or charity to furnish the relevant constituent documents (or other similar documents) including certificate of registration and the identification of the office bearer and authorisation for any person to represent the club, society or charity.*

The Central Bank of Malaysia 'Sectoral Guidelines' for banks and other financial institutions, UPW/GP1[1] requires charities to be placed under extra scrutiny:

4.7. Clubs, Societies and Charities[30]

4.7.1. In addition to the customer due diligence measures on clubs, societies or charities, as provided in the Standard Guidelines on AML/CFT, the reporting institution should verify the identity of at least two signatories through the customer due diligence process. In the event that there is a change of signatories, care should be taken to ensure that the identities of at least two current signatories have been verified.

4.7.2. The reporting institution should also closely scrutinise the accounts of clubs, societies or charities in order to detect discrepancies in the transactions and account activities.

In Bahrain, a bank must not provide any services to a charity unless it has authorization from the relevant Ministry. Banks must also monitor transactions by charities more strictly. The banks must report to the Bahrain Central Bank any transaction by a charity exceeding 3,000 Dinar, and give an increased level of monitoring to the account as required by the relevant section of Volume 2 for Islamic banks:

FC-1.6 Enhanced Due Diligence: Charities, Clubs and Other Societies

FC-1.6.1 Financial services must not be provided to charitable funds and religious, sporting, social, cooperative and professional societies, before an original certificate authenticated by the relevant Ministry confirming the identities of those purporting to act on their behalf (and authorising them to obtain the said service) has been obtained. For Clubs and Societies registered with the General Organisation for Youth and Sports (GOYS), Islamic bank licensees must contact GOYS to clarify whether the account may be opened in accordance with the rules of GOYS.

FC-1.6.2 Islamic bank licensees are reminded that clubs and societies registered with GOYS may only have one account with banks in Bahrain.

FC-1.6.3 Charities should be subject to enhanced transaction monitoring by banks. Islamic bank licensees should develop a profile of anticipated account activity (in terms of payee countries and recipient organisations in particular).

FC-1.6.4 Islamic bank licensees must report all payments and transfers of BD3,000 (or equivalent in foreign currencies) and above,

> *from accounts held by charities registered in Bahrain. The report must be submitted to the BMA's Compliance Unit (see FC-5.3 for contact address), giving details of the amount transferred, account name, number and beneficiary name account and bank details. Islamic bank licensees must ensure that such transfers are in accordance with the spending plans of the charity (in terms of amount, recipient and country).*[31]

Charities come under the supervision of the Directorate of Development and Local Societies, which is part of the Ministry of Social Affairs (MSA). Ministerial Order 3/2004 makes it a requirement that any payment by a charity of more than BD 1,000 must pass through a financial institution, and so will be subject to reporting requirements.[32] Furthermore, any payment of greater than BD 3,000 to a foreign jurisdiction needs MSD permission,[33] which ties in with FC-1.6.4 for Islamic banks.

Hawala and Money Transfer

It has to be noted that '*hawala*' or '*hundi*,' a traditional informal means of money transfer or remittance system in South Asia and the Middle East, is not an official part of Islamic banking, even though the authorities in several non-Muslim countries tend to link them together.

Hawala is an alternative parallel remittance system. It exists and operates outside or parallel the traditional banking system. It was developed in India before the introduction of Western banking system. This system is also referred to as "underground banking". The components of *hawala* that distinguish it from other remittance system are trust and the extension use of connections such as family relationships or regional affiliations. Unlike traditional banking, *hawala* makes minimal use of any kind of negotiable instruments like cheques, bank drafts etc.

There appear to be no references as to whether *hawala* exists or not in Malaysia,[34] but anyone who did engage in this activity would be committing a number of offences which are all predicate offences under Schedule 2 of AMLATFA. This would include illegal deposit taking under s25 of BAFIA and carrying out banking or money-broking business without a license under s4 of BAFIA or subsection 3(1) of the IBA.

For legal funds remittance by 'wire transfer' a Malaysian Islamic bank, like a conventional bank, must carry out customer due diligence for any transaction exceeding RM3,000.[35]

In Bahrain, according to a recent MENAFATF[36] report, *hawala* does not exist to any great extent:

> *In reality, alternative or "underground" transfer systems do not appear to be a significant element of the financial landscape. The Authorized Money Transferors provide extremely cheap and efficient service, including "door to door" service. However, it is worth noting that the BMA is currently following up on two reported* hawala *situations, both very small operations.*

SAC Resolution on Source of Funds

It should be noted that there seems to be an unusual conflict between Malaysian money laundering legislation and regulations and a Resolution issued by the *Shari'ah* Advisory Council (SAC)[37] of the Central Bank of Malaysia. In response to the question:

> *"In relation to Islamic banking deposit, is it permissible in* Shari'ah *for the Islamic banking institution to accept every deposit without the need to screen its source?"*

The SAC issued the following Resolution:

> *"The Council in its 58th meeting held on 27th April 2006/28th* Rabiul Awal *1427 resolved that Islamic banking institutions may, generally, accept any application for placement of deposit or investment fund from individual or corporate customers* without the need to investigate the status of the sources of fund; *either* Shari'ah *compliant, non-*Shari'ah *compliant or a mixture between the two."*[38]

If this was followed literally there is a risk that it could be contrary to the money laundering regulations, as there is an obligation to know something about from where a customer derives the deposited funds.[39] However, money laundering legislation and regulations do apply to all banks, including Islamic banks and other Islamic financial institutions. It could be agued that this Resolution is mainly referring to funds which are from an unlawful source (*haram*) which may not be illegal under Malaysian laws such as AMLATFA.

The Shari'ah Review Bureau (SRB)[40] in Bahrain does not appear to have such a resolution.

This issue demonstrates that *Shari'ah* advisors do need to be aware that Islamic banks are subject to the same anti-money laundering requirements as conventional banks.

Conclusion

As can be seen, the statements by sections of the American Government, which seem to imply that Islamic banking is poorly regulated, cannot be taken to apply to all Islamic banks in all countries. This situation may well be true in some counties but does not apply to either Malaysia or Bahrain. In these two countries, Islamic banks are subject to the same strict supervision as conventional banks with regard to money laundering and terrorism financing.

The United States Bureau for International Narcotics and Law Enforcement Affairs, in its 2007 report, can find no problems with Islamic banking in Malaysia, vis-à-vis conventional banking:

> *Malaysia's Islamic finance sector is subject to the same strict supervision to combat financial crime as the commercial banks. A combination of legacy exchange controls imposed after the 1997-98 Asian financial crisis in addition to robust regulation and supervision by BNM makes the Islamic financial sector as unattractive to financial criminals as is the conventional financial sector.*

In the same report the Bureau finds the same situation for Bahrain:

> *Given the large share of such institutions in Bahrain's banking community, the BMA has developed a framework for regulating and supervising the Islamic banking sector, applying regulations and supervision as it does with respect to conventional banks.*

Due to the strict adherence to the FATF Recommendations, Malaysia and Bahrain are well-placed to continue as leaders in Islamic banking, as any doubts about the integrity of their Islamic banks with regard to money laundering and terrorism financing do not stand up to scrutiny.

Notes

1. The USA's Home Ministry.
2. International Narcotics Control Strategy Report, Bureau for International Narcotics and Law Enforcement Affairs, State Department, March 2004.

3. If this is the case, the regulation of conventional banks is likely to be equally lax.
4. Malaysia is not a member of FATF, but is a member of the Sydney, Australia-based Asia-Pacific Group on Money Laundering (APG), which exists to implement the FATF Recommendations in the region.
5. Institutions licensed under BAFIA and the IBA.
6. This compares with 22 conventional commercial banks. There are also 14 merchant/investment banks.
7. Specifically, Section 124 of the Banking and Financial Institutions Act 1989 (BAFIA). These 'Islamic Windows" have been encouraged to convert to stand-alone Islamic banks taht are subsidiaries of the parent conventional bank.
8. Bank Negara Malaysia (BNM).
9. Part 1 of the First Schedule of AMLATFA puts institutions carrying-out Islamic banking business under the Islamic Banking Act 1983 as reporting institutions. Among the main functions of reporting institutions is to report any transactions which are above the threshold amount (cash transaction report) and anything suspicious (suspicious transaction report). It is beyond the scope of this Article to discuss about the details of AMLATFA as it has already been examined by the same author extensively elsewhere. See Norhashimah Mohd Yasin, *Legal Aspects of Money Laundering from the Common Law Perspective* (Kuala Lumpur: LexisNexis, 2007), see also Norhashimah Mohd Yasin, "An Examination of the Malaysian Anti-Money Laundering Act 2001 (AMLA)", *Current Law Journal*, [2002] 6 CLJ, pp. i-xxiii.
10. An Amendment Act passed in 2003, has among other things, renamed it as the Anti Money Laundering Act (AMLA). The Amendment came into force in March 2007. This amendment, along with amendments to the Penal Code, criminalizes various aspects of terrorism financing.
11. This came into force on 15 November 2006, replacing BNM/GP9 issued in December 1993, and applies to any institution under the Banking and Financial Institutions Act 1989, the Development Financial Institutions Act 2002 and the Islamic Banking Act 1983. There are 7 other sectoral guidelines which have been issued by the CBM which are related to insurance & takaful industries, licensed money changers and/or non-bank remittance operators, non-bank affiliated charge & credit card issuers, licensed casinos, designated non-financial businesses and professions and licensed gaming outlets.
12. The threshold amount is RM50, 000 per day.
13. In 4.1.1 General.

14. As this product involves the buying and selling of commodities involving several parties, often in different countries, banks have to ensure the integrity of its staff and of the other parties such as commodity brokers.
15. Such as, cash transactions, International banking/Trade finance, Employees and agents, private banking and trust services, secured and unsecured lending, and Credit cards.
16. In the APG Mutual Evaluation Report on Malaysia against the FATF, there are 40 Recommendations (2003) and 9 Special Recommendations, July 2007.
17. International Monetary Fund (IMF), Labuan, Malaysia: Assessment of the Supervision and Regulation of the Financial Sector-Review of Financial Sector Regulation and Supervision, December 2004.
18. Bahrain is not a member of FATF, but is a member of the Manama, Bahrain-based Middle East & North Africa Financial Action Task Force (MENAFATF), which exists to implement FATF Recommendations.
19. Also known as the Decree Law No. (4) of 2001 With Respect to the Prevention and Prohibition of the Laundering of Money. The law was amended to cover terrorism financing by Law No. 54 of 2006 with Respect to amending Certain Provisions of Legislative Decree No. (4) of 2001 With Respect to Prohibition of and Combating Money Laundering.
20. 'Ministerial order no. 7 of 2001 with respect to the obligations governing institutions concerning the prohibition and combating of money laundering' with effect December 2001, and 'BMA Regulation 6/2001 -Money Laundering Regulation' with effect October 2001 are still in force. The former Finance Ministry Order deals with issues such as record keeping, customer identification and reporting. The latter Central Bank Regulation deals with compliance by banks.
21. The money laundering rules were issued in April 2005.
22. It has recently renamed itself from the Bahrain Monetary Agency.
23. This is because conventional and Islamic banks follow different rulebooks, Volume 1 and Volume 2 respectively, and this is done simply to fit into this format.
24. Mutual Evaluation Report of the Kingdom of Bahrain on Anti-Money Laundering and Combating Financing of Terrorism, November 2006.
25. Such as, the Benevolence International Foundation, Global Relief Foundation, Holy Land Foundation and International Islamic Relief Organisation.

26. S5.4.
27. S4.7.
28. Malaysian Islamic charities are also supervised by the Islamic Religious Councils of each state that they operate in.
29. UPW/GP1.
30. UPW/GP1[1].
31. From Central Bank of Bahrain, Volume 2 (Islamic Banking), Part A, Business Standards, Financial Crimes, Customer Due Diligence.
32. Article 7.
33. Article 85.
34. As various international anti-money laundering bodies do not mention *hawala* in respect of money laundering in Malaysia, it can be assumed that it does not exist to any great extent. This activity would, in any case, be illegal.
35. UPW/GP1[1] 4.1.4 and 4.4.1-9. The CDD requirements are given in s5 of GPW/GP1.
36. The MENAFATF Mutual Evaluation Report of the Kingdom of Bahrain on Anti-Money Laundering and Combating Financing of Terrorism, 2006.
37. Section 16B of the Central Bank of Malaysia Act 1958, in its 2003 Amendment Act, has provided that SAC is the authority for the ascertainment of Islamic law for the purposes of Islamic banking business, *takaful* business, Islamic financial business, Islamic development financial business, or any other business which is based on *Shari'ah* principles and is supervised and regulated by the Central Bank.
38. Central Bank of Malaysia Kuala Lumpur, *Shari'ah* Resolutions in Islamic Finance, 2007 at p. 46.
39. There is actually a *hadith* (Prophetic tradition) that states the following: Narrated by Nasa'i "There will be a time when one will not be concerned about the source of the property, whether legal or illegal." It is not the intention of this article to dispute the above SAC resolution and to explore the Islamic aspects of money laundering as this requires a separate article. Suffice to state here that the Islamic concept of *Shari'ah*-compliant funds is actually wider than that illegally obtained as per AMLA under its various predicate offences in Schedule 2. In other words, lawfully or legally obtained funds/ proceeds under AMLA might not necessary be *Shari'ah*-compliant as they might be derived from interest-based proceeds or from licensed gaming outlets. Briefly, under Islamic principles, the funds or the

proceeds of the transaction or activity must be free from the elements of interest (*riba*), gambling (*maysir*), uncertainty (*gharar*) and un-Islamic elements such as those which are alcohol and pork related.

40. The SRB is part of the Accounting and Auditing Organisation for Islamic Financial Institutions (AAOIFI), based in Bahrain.

13

Woman in the *Shari'Ah* Courts: A Study of Malaysia and Indonesia

Ramizah Wan Muhammad

Introduction

The function of the judiciary is to dispense justice to the parties involved in cases. To ensure justice, the courts must be independent of executive and legislature so that the decisions are made by them without fear or favour. The most important element in judicial institution is to give rights to whom it is due without looking at whether the parties involved are rich or poor, adult or child, man or woman.

In Islamic literature, there are quite a number of discussions pertaining to woman as dispenser of justice; and most of them are pessimistic. In other words, for them, woman is not qualified to hold the post of a judge and to sentence the accused accordingly. There are various reasons given by the classical Muslim jurists. However, their *dalil* or authority from the *sunnah* of the Prophet (*s.a.w.*) is ambiguous, as such open to varying interpretation. The Holy Qur'an is silent on that issue.

This paper attempts to understand the Islamic stand on this issue and to empirically verify the status of women vis-à-vis the court in two Southeast Asian countries, Malaysia and Indonesia. The first part of the paper analyses the status of women pertaining to dispensation of justice based upon the Qur'an, *Sunnah* and the precedent of the companions of the Prophet (*s.a.w.*). Next two sections are devoted to the situation in Malaysia and Indonesia. The concluding section summarizes the findings and offers suggestions for future directions.

Status of Women in Islamic Society

In Islam, man and woman are equal in terms of human dignity, reward, accountability of personal conduct and matters pertaining to property rights, morality and religion. However, there is disagreement among scholars pertaining to the woman's participation in public affairs and government.[1] Likewise, there is disagreement among Muslim jurists on the case of woman to be appointed as a judge.[2]

However, one has to take note that the companions of the Prophet (s.a.w.) were actually the mediators towards the development of Islamic law. The companions of the Prophet (s.a.w.) were close to him and helped him in making the message of Islam and Islamic law understandable to Muslims and non-Muslims. These people formed the vanguard of Islam whose lives were illuminated directly by that "lamp of that spread light".[3] The companions were not confined to man but to woman as well. However, women companions can be categorized into two: woman companions and wives of the Prophet (*s.a.w.*).

The wives of the Prophet (*s.a.w.*) were the source of narrating the *ahadith* of the Prophet. Hence, the Muslims and non-Muslims could benefit from them in understanding the Islamic ruling and apply in their daily lives. Prominent among the woman narrators of *ahadith* are Aishah Binti Abu Bakar, Ummu Salamah, Fatimah Binti Muhammad, Fatimah Binti Qais, Asma'Binti Abu Bakr.

Before the advent of Islam, the status of woman in the period of ignorance (*jahiliyyah*) was very dismal. Women were treated similar to chattel to the extent that they can be inherited by the heirs of the deceased. The news of birth of a daughter was considered as a great disgrace and shame to her family.[4] However, after the Prophet Muhammad (*s.a.w.*) was sent to the Arabs, Islam upgraded their status equal to the men.

In the Holy Qur'an, there is one chapter *al-Nisa'*.[5] It is interesting to note that in the Holy Qur'an also Allah (*s.w.t.*) mentioned 57 times the word "*al-Nisa*"[6] and 57 times the word

"*Rijal*".[7] These signify the fact of equal importance of man and woman in Islam and their contribution in development of Islamic law. At the same, it shows that man and woman are equal.

Islam does not lay any restrictions on spiritual, social, economic and political activities of a woman. Both are equal in terms of right and responsibilities by looking into the nature and circumstances of a person. Generally, men by nature is physically strong than a women. By virtue of this, men are not considered superior to women. Both have been granted by Islam more or less equal status. And where ever women have been discriminated, it is for their good. Islam granted women those rights which were not available to them in the rest of the world; they could get it only after a long struggle.

Judge's Qualification

The Prophet Muhammad (*s.a.w.*) was the Chief of Justice during his lifetime as the leader to the Muslim nation and the Messenger of Allah for 23 years. In article 23 of the Constitution of Medina, it was proclaimed that 'the Prophet is the Chief of Justice and an avenue to settle dispute'. Thus, the qualification of the Prophet (s.a.w.) as the judge was exclusive and cannot be made a benchmark for any man in this world.

In the Prophet's lifetime, many among Muslims of Medina and Mecca had helped him in spreading the teachings of Islam. Muslims, who had lived and met with the Prophet (*s.a.w.*) were knowas the prophet's companions. They were those who were closest to the Prophet (*s.a.w.*). They were actually the quintessence of the Prophet's success in spreading the faith of Islam. They were also those who helped the Prophet (*s.a.w.*) in shaping an innovative and positive thinking to the *Ummah*. These companions of the Prophet (*s.a.w.*) were also the early judges appointed to carry out the responsibility as an upholder of justice after the Prophet (*s.a.w.*).

Many among the companions were appointed as judges outside the city of Medina. The appointment of the companions as the representatives of the Prophet (*s.a.w.*) was to safeguard the interest of the *Ummah* which was ever expanding and was also in line with the development of Islam in that era. The criteria of their selection were based on revelation from Allah[8]. Among the companions, who were appointed as judges, were Muadz Bin Jabal in Yemen, Utrnan

Bin al-Ass in Ta'if, Muhajir Bin Abi Umayyah in San'a and Ataab Bin Asid in Mecca[9].

It should be noted that the position of a judge is not a ticket to an easy life, nor is it to obtain any privileges. Verily it is a very heavy task which has to be carried by anybody who is entrusted to hold such a position.

During the period of the Prophet (*s.a.w.*), Khulafa' al-Rashidun, 'Umayyah, and 'Abbasiyyah, the selections were made based on two conditions, which are:

1. Through the utilization of specific knowledge of the caliph himself, for instance, any man who is widely known for his ability and experience in settling cases previously, Such as the appointment of 'Ali Bin 'Abu Talib and Abdullah Ibn Mas'ud.
2. By way of examination and interview in order to assess the capability of the person whom are intended to be appointed[10].

The above methods are being used in the contemporary period. The first method is seen from the perspective of the experience of the candidate as a judge, a registrar, chief registrar, *sharie* lawyer, *Sulh* officer and others. The second method is widely prevalent and is followed in all the employment sectors.

Fundamentally, a judge, according to the majority of *fiqh* scholars, must be a Muslim, male, major (*baligh*), sound mind, free, committed to impart justice (*'adil)*. He must not be a handicapped in hearing, sight and speech, and must have knowledge of *hukm Sharai*. According to Imam al-Mawardi, man is given priority by reason that man has the advantage from the viewpoint of the mind and physical strength[11].

There are other scholars who have laid down the following conditions of a judge:

1. Muslim,
2. Baligh,
3. Sound mind,
4. Free,
5. Male,
6. 'Adil,
7. Understands the meaning of the verses of the Qur'an and *Sunnah*,

8. Acquainted with *ijma'* of *ulama* and the *ikhtilaf* between them,
9. Familiar with the Arabic language,
10. Knows the basis of *qiyas,* and
11. Possess perfect sight and hearing[12].

Basically, to be a judge, the candidate must be a man with perfect senses in order to ensure the importance of the law of procedure and evidence. There are also who added that the qualifications of a judge are similar to that of a witness. Whilst according to Mazhab Hanafi, male is not an exclusive condition to hold the position of a judge. In other words, Muslim women who are qualified are allowed to hold the top positions in the judicial institution in the Islamic state[13].

Views of Muslim Jurists

The Muslim jurists' view can be divided into two, the proponents and opponents. A brief explanation of these is as follows:

1. The Opponents: The opponents form *jumhur's* view or the unanimous view and consist of jurist from Shafie, Hanbal and Maliki schools of thought. They unanimously agree that woman is not allowed to be appointed as a judge in any case including cases involving the admissibility of woman's testimony. If there is any appointment, that will be categorized as void including the decisions made by them.

The authorities which they relied upon are some verses of the Qur'an which say to the effect:

> *"Men are protectors and Maintainers of Women, because Allah has given the one more strength than the other and because they support them from their means.*[14]

The next authority is from the *hadith* of the Prophet (*s.a.w.*) which says:

> *"A nation which entrusts its affairs to a woman will never be prosper"*[15]

2. The Proponents: The proponents consist of those belonging to Hanafi School, especially Ibn Jarir and Ibn Hazm. According to one view from Hanafi School of law, it is permissible for a woman to be appointed as judge only in cases other than *Hudud* and *Qisas*. There are some of them who oppose and believe they formed part of the jumhur.

According to Ibn Jarir al Tabari, it is permissible for a woman to be appointed as a judge in all cases, but as usual there are some scholars who oppose he said so.

The last Muslim Jurist is Ibn Hazm who holds that the ruling on the appointment of a woman as judge in all cases is permissible.[16]

Analysis of The Juristic Opinions

Having discussed the views of above authorities pertaining to the issue of woman as a judge, it is quite clear that there is no definite *dalil* or authority, which forbids woman to be a leader. There is no Qura'nic verse as well that clearly disallowed woman to be a judge. There are a number of verses where Allah commands us to uphold justice without referring to a Muslim man or a Muslim woman.

> *" Allah doth command you to render back your trust to those to whom they are due, and when you judge between people that you judge with justice"*[17]

In another Qurnaic verse, Allah says to the effect:

> *"O! Dawuud, We did indeed make you a vicegerent on earth, so judge thou between them in truth and justice"*[18]

From the above two verses it is clear that it is a duty of every Muslim, be he a man or a woman, to uphold justice. The verses make no distinction on this issue.

With regards to the *hadith* mentioned, it is clear that the meaning of the *hadith* is speculative and open to interpretation. The Prophet (*s.a.w.*) used a word "no prosperity", which indicates disapproval or absolute prohibition. Or it can be the ruling of disapproval or prohibition only in the context of leadership of a country but not in the judge's tenure ship.

The Holy Qur'an has put a great emphasis on the equality of the sexes, saying that they only differ in the extent of their piety and righteousness.[19] Man and woman are equal in terms of acquiring property, knowledge and rewards. The most important element in the practical side is how much one puts his sincerity in the given task. However, one also can say that quality does not necessarily mean justice.

Malaysian Position

From a perusal of the Malaysian law it can be said that in Malaysia, there is no specific and clear prohibition on the appointment of females as judges. According to the Islamic Administration (Federal Territories) Enactment 1993, the qualifications of a candidate to be a judge are as follows:

1. Must be a Malaysian citizen; and
2. Have experience as a Qadi in a subordinate court or Syari'ah High Court or as a public prosecutor or even a Court Registrar or a person who is knowledgeable in *Hukm Syara'* (*hukum sharai*).

The provisions of the Administration of Islamic Law (Selangor) Enactment 2003, section 56 and 58 also mentioned the same criteria for candidates to be appointed as judges of the High Court and the Subordinate Courts. The above provisions state that those who are qualified to be appointed as a judge are:

(a) A citizen; and

(b) For a period of not less than 10 years before appointment have practiced as a *Syarie* lawyer in any Subordinate Courts or a member of a *Syariah* (in Malay language, *Shar'ah* is written as *Syariah*) Court or possesses expertise in Islamic law.

While provision of section 43(3) of Administration of Islamic Law Enactment 2001 of the state of Pahang mentions the qualifications for the post of Chief *Syarie* Judge and High Court Judge as follows:

(a) He is a man;

(b) He is a citizen; and

(c) For a period of not less than 10 years before appointment he had practiced as a *Syarie* lawyer in any *Syariah* Court or a member of *Syariah* court or possesses expertise in Islamic law.

Only the Pahang state's provisions show that a woman is not qualified to hold the position of a High Court Judge and a Chief *Syarie* Judge. That provision must have been in accordance with the view of the majority of scholars who agree that women should not hold the position of a judge. Definitely there are those who stress that the above provisions do not deprive women from holding the position of a judge of a subordinate court. But at the same time, if the same reasoning is to be used, one aspect which may be raised is that the provision denies the right of a female judge of a subordinate court to be promoted.

In article 8, the Federal Constitution of Malaysia states that there shall be no discrimination on the ground of race, religion, and lineage or also from the aspect of gender[20]. Thus, it can be understood that if a female who is qualified but not appointed as a judge just because she is a woman, that decision is against the Constitution. Similarly, in any provisions of the law which is based on such discrimination as above are void and contrary to the constitutional law. As a result, it can be generally understood that the provision in the state of Pahang is inconsistent with the Malaysian Federal Constitution.

Therefore, it becomes clear that in Malaysia, all the existing laws in Malaysia can be considered as not preventing women from being appointed as judges. Hence, it becomes permissible for qualified Muslim women to hold the position of a *Syariah* Court judge. The issue of woman to be appointed as a judge came into limelight in 2000 when it was highlighted in the media that there was indeed a need to have more *Syariah* court judges including female judges[21]

Nevertheless, according to Y.A.A Datuk Abu Naim and Y.A.A Datuk Sheikh Ghazali Abdul Rahman, priority is to be given to male candidates and at the same time, the appointment of existing male judges is due to necessity[22]. Accordingly, the author is of the opinion that it is not prohibited to appoint females to be judges in Malaysia. Rather, the Malaysian law encourages appointment of female judges if necessary. Those, who are opposing this move are, in fact, acting against the *shari'ah* and the Malaysian civil law.

In the National Usul Fiqh Seminar organized by the International Islamic University College on 15-16 of December 2004, Datuk Sheikh Ghazali[23] was asked about the position of Muslim Women as female judges in the Malaysian *Syariah* Courts. According to him, a *fatwa* had already been made back in 1982 giving permissibility to the appointment of females as judges based on the view of Ibn Jarir al-Tabari. However, as yet, no appointment has been made of females who are truly qualified to sit as a judge in the *Syariah* Court.[24]

However, in September 2001, Madam Noorhadina Binti Mohd Zabidi was appointed as the registrar of *Shariah* court of Federal Territory. One year later in 2002, she was appointed as the chief registrar of the same court. Currently, she is the chief registrar of *Syariah* High Court of Selangor.[25] Actually, she is one-step short of becoming the first female court judge in future.

Datuk Sheikh Ghazali mentioned that so far she is the top choice for becoming the first woman to be a *syariah* court judge in Malaysia by looking into the expernce she has now. However, he said, it depends also upon her whether she is ready or not to hold the post.[26]

According to the opinion of the recipient of Ma'al Hijrah award for the year 1426 Hijrah, Dr. Uthman El Muhammady, women are allowed to be appointed as judges based on two fundamental aspects: 1. from the view of the need for female expertise in such fields; and 2. from the mercy for the Muslim *Ummah* which is in need of qualified judges including female judges. He also added that Islam had never closed its doors in not allowing a woman to be appointed as a judge. It is however reminded by him to all Muslims to be cautious of the elements of feminism which have been brought from the West which is based on human intellect alone without any consideration for the divinity of Allah's revealed laws.

It is mentioned in the laws that a judge must be a person who is knowledgeable in Islamic law. This phrase is too general to include both male and female. Thus, it may be defined as a person who has an academic qualification in the field of *Syariah*, including family law, Islamic criminal law, banking and also law of evidence. One of the conditions is that a candidate to be appointed as judge must be qualified to be a *mujtahid*. *Mujtahid* is a person who is able to do *ijtihad*. According to the opinion of scholars, it is not necessary that a person who merely knows how to exercise *ijtihad* be categorized as a *mujtahid*, along with other qualifications he/she must be an *alim* with *amal*.

The current situation in Malaysia is that in the *Syariah* Judicial Department, there are 26 *Syariah* female officers who could eventually become *shari'ah* court judges. They are comprised of

Sulh Officer[27], Registrar, Chief Registrar, Research Officer, *Syarie* Lawyer and *Syarie* Prosecutor.[28] This is an encouraging sign. These people have to be groomed so that they are ready to hold such an onerous task in future.

Indonesian Position

In Indonesia, the government took a serious view regarding the qualifications of a candidate for the position of a judge. This was necessitated by the fact that the recruitment of religious court judges was done haphazardly. Thus, in the early 1970s, there were 12 Islamic Court Chairmen in the whole of Indonesia. They were graduates of State Islamic Institute but none of them obtained law school degrees.[29] Consequently, the government cited the selection, promotion and supervision of the judges as needing urgent improvement to elevate and integrate Islamic courts into a national judicial system.

The consequence of such a realisation is the formulation of current government policy to recruit only law graduates for the position of a judge of religious court.[30] Additionally, a candidate must:

(a) Be the citizen of Indonesia;
(b) Be a Muslim;
(c) Be a pious person;
(d) Be loyal to *Pancasila*[31] and *Undang-Undang Dasar (UUD) 1945;*[32]
(e) Possess a degree in *Shar'ah;*
(f) Be at least 25 years of age;
(g) Be charismatic, honest, just and of good behaviour; and
(h) Must not be a member of any Communist Party or any other organization declared illegal like *Gerakan Kontra Revolusi* G.30 S/PKI.[33]

The above criteria are the minimum required of all Religious Court judges. However, a candidate aspiring to be promoted to a higher position must fulfil additional requirements. The candidate must be:

(a) At least 40 years of age, and

(b) Must have acquired at least 5 year's experience as a *Ketua* (Chief) or *Wakil Ketua* (Deputy Chief) *Peradilan Agama*[34] or 15 years as a judge in *Peradilan Agama*.

A candidate meeting all the requirements becomes eligible to sit for a written examination prepared by the Supreme Court to test the candidate's knowledge of general civil law and State Ideology as well as Arabic language and Islamic laws.[35]

After passing the written test, the candidates have to undergo a psychological examination conducted by the Department of Psychology of the University of Indonesia and administered by the Supreme Court. Later, they have to take a training course and serve as a clerk for two years before actually assuming responsibility as a judge.[36]

It seems that the policy of Indonesian Government towards the training of judicial members is to familiarise them with the administrative work before they could be appointed as a judge in a *Shari'ah* Court. This kind of approach is not followed in Malaysia with the exception of the final year students in a higher institution. They are required to do practical internship in a company or an institution for graduation. The Indonesian approach is useful for a judicial institution in that it makes the judge fully aware of administrative responsibilities involved and helps him/her understand the nature and the technical matters of the job.

In Indonesia, there were female judges going as far back as 1964[37]. Up until February 2002, there were 429 female judges in the *Peradilan Agama* of Indonesia. Nevertheless, the jurisdiction of females judges are limited to family law which has been the jurisdiction of the *Pengadilan Agama* according to the Marriage Law 1974.

The appointment of females as judges in the *Peradilan Agama* in Indonesia is based on several justifications. Among such is Chapter al-Imran verse 104 of the Qur'an that rules:

> *"Let there arise out of you a band of people inviting to all that is good, enjoining what is right and forbidding of what is wrong, and they are the ones to attain felicity"*

The above verse indicates that it is the common duty of both male and female to enjoin what is good and prevent what is wicked. This is because the above verse did not specify any gender of male or female. Thus, the duty mentioned in the above verse is the duty of all Muslims without any discrimination of man or woman. According to Hamka, the duty to call towards righteousness may be divided into two which are governmental duty and familial duty. For that reason, it is the duty of the leader to call the people towards righteousness, to protect them from any difficulties. Besides, it is also upon the shoulders of the parents as the back bone of the family to ensure that their family lives are articulated according to the tenets of Islam[38].

Conclusion

From the above discussion, it is clear that the Government of Malaysia is at a preliminary stage of appointing woman as a judge in *Syariah* Court. Right now, there is no female judge in the *shari'ah* court system. Hopefully, we will see female *shari'ah* court judges also. The government of Indonesia on the other hand, had started to appoint female *shari'ah* court judges after 19 years of their independence. Malaysia should emulate its neighbour and some Middle East countries, where judiciary is not monopolized by males. This author is of the opinion that if there are female judges in the *shari'h* courts also, the courts will impart justice in a better way. There is no reason to allow women to be judge of civil courts but not of *shari'ah* courts. We have not done it in 50 years of independent Malaysia, does not mean that we should not do it in future.

Notes

1. Mohammad Hashim Kamali, *Freedom, Equality and Justice in Islam*, Ilmiah Publishers, Kuala Lumpur, 2002, p. 61.
2. Najma Moosa, *Women's Eligibility for the Qadiship*, paper presented at II Joseph Schact Confernce, Granada, 16-17th December 1997, Granada, pp. 1-2.
3. Khalid Muhammad Khalid, *Men around the Messenger*, Islamic Book Trust, Kuala Lumpur, 2005, p. xxix.
4. Rafi Ahmad Fidai, *Concise History of Muslim World*, VOl.1, Kitab Bhava, New Delhi, 2001, p. 6.
5. Surah 4 or Surah al Nisa'.
6. See Surah al Baqarah (2):222, Surah Al Imran (3): 14, Surah al Nisa

(4): 4, Surah al Maidah (5): 6 etc. Derivatives such as nisa ukum, nisa ana, nisa ahum etc.

7. See Surah al Baqarah (2: 282, Surah Al A'raf(7):63, Surah al Mu'minun ((23): 25 etc. The word al Rijal and its derivatives such as rajulun, rijalukum, Rajulani etc.
8. Chapter Al-Najm: 3, "Your companion is neither astray nor being misled, nor does he say (aughta) of (his own) desire."
9. Muhammad Hamidullah, "Administration of Justice in Early Islam", *Islamic Culture*, Vol. 11, 1937, pp. 166.
10. Mahmud Saedọn Awan Othman, "Perlantikan Qadi: Tanggungjawab, Syarat dan Cara-caranya", *Jurnal Hukm,* Vol. 3, No. 3, 1983, pp. 172-173.
11. Al-Mawardi, *al-'Ahkam al-Sultaniyyah*, translated by Asadullah Yate, Ta Ha Publishers, London,1996, p. 72.
12. Haji Daud Bin Muhammad, "Tugas Kehakiman Dalam Mahkamah: Pengalaman dalam Mahkamah Syariah", *Sistem Kehakiman Islam*, ed. Abdul Monir Yaacob, IKIM, Kuala Lumpur, 2001, pp. 23-24.
13. Abu al-Hassan al-Mawardi, *Al-Ahkam al-Sultaniyyah*, translated by Asadullah Yate, Taha Publisher, London, 1996, p. 98.
14. Al-Quran Surah Al Nisa' (4): 34.
15. Narrated by Al Bukhari.
16. Ibn Hazm, *al Muhalla*, Vol.1, n.d. Cairo, 426.
17. Al Quran surah Al Nisa' (4): 58.
18. Al Quran Surah Sad (38): 26.
19. Al Quran Surah Al Hujurat (49): 13.
20. (2) Except as expressly authorized by this constitution, there shall be no discrimination against citizens on ground only on religion, race, descent, place of birth or *gender* (emphasis added) in law or in the appointment of any office or employment under a public authority or in the administration of any law relating to the acquisition, holding or disposition of property or the establishing or carrying on of any trade, business, profession, vocation or employment.
21. Bernama News Agency, May 2nd 2000 and May 5th 2000.
22. Andek Masnah Andek Kelewa, "Wanita dan Kehakiman di Mahkamah Syariah", *IKIM Law Journal*, Vol. 1, 1997, pp. 60-61.
23. He was former Director General of Department of Syariah Judiciary of Malaysia and the recipient of Ma'al Hijrah Figure 1428.
24. In a recent development, Datuk Sheikh Ghazali had made an announcement that, to date, there is one female candidate who is

eligible to be appointed as shariah subordinate court in Malaysia. *News Straits Times,* 24th April 2006.

25. A telephone conversation with her on the 24th of January 2007.
26. News Straits Times, 28th July 2006.
27. Sulh officer can also act as a judge in Syariah Subordinate court provided that he has been given " Tauliah Hakim"(Judge's Certificate). To date, in the state of Kelantan, there are 3 Female Sulh officers who have been given tauliah hakim. See "The Theory and Practice of *Sulh* (mediation) in the Malaysian Shariah courts" by the author, *IIUM Law Journal,* Vol. 16, No. 1, 2008.
28. Statistic given by Puan Laila Busyra Hassan from Syariah Judicial Department of Malaysia (JKSM) on the 15th of January 2007.
29. Daniel Lev, *Islamic Courts in Indonesia*, p. 111.
30. *Standarisasi Pengadilan Agama dan Pengadilan Tinggi Agama,* Department of Religion, Indonesia, 1983, p. 94-95. In an interview, the researcher was informed that a person with no less than 10 year experience as a staff in the Ministry of Religious Affair can also be chosen for the post of a judge. The chosen candidate, however, have to undergo training like all other candidates.
31. National ideology.
32. Indonesia's state constitution.
33. Article 13 of Religious Court Act No. 7 of 1989.
34. Chief Justice of Islamic Courts.
35. Mark Cammack, "Islamic Law in Indonesia", *International and Comparative Law Quarterly,* Vol. 38, 1989, p. 70.
36. *Ibid.*
37. Daniel Lev, *Islamic Courts in Indonesia*, Berkley, University of California Press, 1972, p. 110.
38. Hamka, *Tafsir al-Azhar*, Yayasan Nurul Islam, 1965, Jakarta, pp. 40-41.

14

Contract Documentation Under Islamic Law: Redefining Its Role

Suhaib Walid Sharaiyra

Introduction

During the early stages of Islam, written documents were either ignored or discouraged by legal theory that refused to accept them in court, where proof was limited to the oral testimony of witnesses. However, in practice, there was a widespread usage of written documents that consequently gave rise to a separate branch of legal literature devoted to a science of drafting documents that is best known as *'ilm al-shurut*. Such works were conducted with the aim of instructing professional notaries in drawing up sound instruments, and hence contained model documents for the notaries to follow.

Islamic law of contract came to stabilise commercial transactions and settle disputes arising therefrom due to the inability of the parties to remember the terms of the contracts or due to faulty terms included in the contracts by parties who are ignorant of the lawfulness of transactions or parts thereof. Islam as such places emphasis on contract documentation and writing, evidenced by the Verse of the Holy *Qur'an* where Allah (*s.w.t.*) revealed:

> *O ye who believe! When ye deal with each other, in transactions involving future obligations in a fixed period of time, reduce them to writing. Let a scribe write down faithfully as between the parties; let not the scribe refuse to write: as Allah has taught him, so let him write.*

Let him who incurs the liability dictate, but let him fear his Lord Allah, and not diminish aught of what he owes... Disdain not to reduce to writing (your contract) for a future period, whether it be small or big: it is juster in the sight of Allah, more suitable as evidence, and more convenient to prevent doubts among yourselves...[1]

Written documents mainly existed for private transactions. However, many transactions, private or otherwise, were not documented for the simple reason that documents were discouraged as legal proof. "Yet, private contracts of all kinds depended on written instruments, and from the earliest Islamic times they were used extensively."[2] Such usage of contractual documents, hence, had mainly been for the purpose of reminding the parties and the witnesses to the contracts of the terms and contents thereof. For the purposes of this discussion, nevertheless, the writer moves to argue that contractual documents representing Islamic contracts have nowadays become mere mechanisms by which suppliers of goods and services can legalise their exploitation of the public, through using such complicated language and structure in the contractual documents as to be beyond laymen's ability to comprehend or even act upon with full knowledge of the effects and consequences of their execution.

What Is Documentation?

What is meant by documentation, for the purposes of this paper, is not the writing of the contract *per se*, as that falls within the permitted methods of contract formation, where parties are permitted to conduct the contract in writing. To that effect, it is stated in the *Mejelle* that "offer and acceptance may be made by writing as well as by word of mouth."[3] It is also stated in the literature about Islamic law of transactions that "a contract can be concluded in writing if the writing is clear, readable and understandable; and it does not have to be in standard Arabic necessarily, it can be in dialect or slang or in any other language. Contract can be concluded in writing even if the two parties were capable of speaking."[4] However, the documentation referred to here is one of the five methods of authentication of contracts under Islamic law, and these are authentication by way of testimony (*shahadah*), mortgage/security (*rahn*), suretyship (*kafalah*), assignment (transfer of debt-*hawalah*) and documentation (*kitabah*).[5]

A Brief History of Documentation

Documentation is said to have been in existence since the time of Prophet Adam (*a.s.*) as had been narrated by Ahmad on the authority of Ibn 'Abbas as saying:

> *When the Verse of* al-Dayn *was revealed, the Prophet (saw) said: '... Adam asked: O Lord who is that, Allah said: he is your son Dawud, Adam asked: how old is he? Allah said: sixty years, Adam said: O Lord increase in his age, Allah said: No unless I increase for him from your age, and Adam's age was a thousand years, so Allah increased Dawud's age by forty years, ordered that to be documented and took the Angels as witnesses. When Adam was dying and the Angels came to him he said: I have forty years left of my age, then he was told: you have given them to Dawud. Adam said: I did not, so Allah exhibited the document and made the Angels testify.'*[6]

Moreover, documentation existed at the time of the Prophet (*s.a.w.*) where a number of traditions indicate that the Prophet (*s.a.w.*) used to order documents to be drawn up when conducting transactions, among such traditions is where the Prophet (*s.a.w.*) ordered 'Ali to draw up a document in his name at Hudaybiyyah, another is where he (*s.a.w.*) bought a slave from a Companion (al-'Adda' Ibn Hawdah al-Hanafi) and drafted a written contract.[7] Thus, the practice of documenting contracts existed at the early stages of Islamic law and even way before the advent of Islam, as evident by the authorities mentioned above.

The Requirement of Documentation under Islamic Law

Contract documentation under Islamic law is required by virtue of Verse 2: 282 of the Holy *Qur'an*, which is said to apply mainly to two types of transactions, namely the contracts of sale with delayed payment and those payable immediately.[8] Yet the transactions that may be implied by the Verse may include other types of contracts in addition to those of sale, as many of the commentators on and interpreters of the Verse stated and used the term "transaction" in general, and thus any kind of transaction may be implied and not only those of sale.[9] In addition, the word '*dayn*' in the Verse above has been interpreted to mean: any transaction where one of the counter values is present while the other is deferred.[10] It has also been stated that: "The original Arabic word '*dayn*' covers every obligation, for each obligation accepted by one party towards the other is in the nature of debt from the obligee to the obligor. Hence the contract of debt implies all specific transactions including mortgage, purchase of things on credit and the agreement of work."[11] Having said that, the documentation referred to in the above Verse of the Holy *Qur'an* applies to contracts and debts in general, but the question that arises at this juncture is whether documentation of contracts is obligatory or not?

The Recommended Feature of Documentation under Islamic Law

The majority of Muslim scholars state that contract documentation is recommended and not obligatory in nature, especially that the Verse in which the order for writing was revealed contained the statement: "*it is juster in the sight of Allah, more suitable as evidence, and more convenient to prevent doubts among yourselves.*" This statement, the scholars emphasise, show that writing is for the purpose of securing the transaction from future doubts and for being used in evidence, so if the parties feared not from such matters they are not obliged to write down the transaction.[12]

The Verse as stated above indicates three matters that are further supported by the practice of the Companions of the Prophet (saw), and these are:

1. That Allah (*s.w.t.*) permitted the absence of writing when the creditor trusts the debtor and feels secure about the transaction; this implies that writing and even witnessing are not obligatory.
2. The Companions and successors never were too strict about having to document transactions, so had documentation been obligatory they would have not left it.
3. Commercial transactions are largely carried out by people, thus have documentation been obligatory to secure the obligations of both parties that would cause great hardship on people.[13]

Some scholars, however, state that the Verse implied the obligatory nature of documentation, until the rule was later abrogated by the statement in Verse 2:283 which states: "*... and if one of you deposits a thing on trust with another, let the trustee* *(faithfully) discharge his trust, and let him fear his Lord...,*" where the Verse is said to have the effect of recommendation and not obligation for the element of trust comes under consideration.[14]

Only a few jurists held the view that contract documentation is obligatory under Islamic law. These jurists included Ibn Hazm, where he stated that if any transaction had any of its parts based on deferred basis then that transaction must be put into writing. The basis of his view is that the statement in the Verse "*...reduce them to writing...*" has the effect of a direct order, and thus no one can say "I will not write," and similarly the statement in the same Verse "*...and get two witnesses...*" was also revealed as a direct order and thus no one can say "I will not bear witness" otherwise that would be disobedience of a direct order from Allah (*s.w.t.*).[15]

Obligatory or not, documentation of contracts have nowadays become a matter of practice with the increase in the usage of standard form contracts in daily life and for almost every transaction and activity a person has to carry out, this fact brings into attention the purpose which contractual documents have.

The Purpose of Documentation under Islamic Law

A few benefits of documentation can be deduced from the Verse including the preservation of wealth, avoiding disputes as a document may serve as a reference for the parties to the contract, serving as a guide for the parties in knowing the validity of the contractual terms and conditions as the notary documenting the contract would direct their attention to such terms, and to avoid future confusion with regards to the terms of the contract, as if the contract had not been documented the parties as time passes might forget the terms such as the cost price and the time and method of payment.[16] This general statement indicates that documentation is multi-purpose, serving at one point as a reminder for the parties of the terms of the contracts, and at another as a tool of evidence that can be used in the court of justice.

These purposes of documentation are particularly stated in the part of the Verse where Allah (..) revealed: "*... it is juster in the sight of Allah, more suitable as evidence, and more convenient to prevent doubts among yourselves...*" According to Ibn Kathir, this Verse means that:

> *Writing transactions that will be fulfilled at a later date is more just with Allah meaning better and more convenient in order to preserve the terms of the contract. Therefore, recording such agreements helps the witnesses, when they see their handwriting–or signatures–later on and thus remember what they witnessed, for it is possible that the witnesses might forget what they witnessed... This helps repel any doubt. Since if you need to refer to the contract that you wrote and the doubt will end.*[17]

Accordingly, there are three major purposes of documentation, the first of which is achieving justice; the second is the suitability of written documents to be used in evidence, and the third is that written documents serve as a reminder for the parties to the contract of its terms, and thus prevent doubts as to the contents and terms of the contract. Hence, parties to a contract can benefit from its documentation in different ways, namely, seeking the gratification of Allah (*s.w.t.*), achieving a worldly benefit in allowing a form of evidence to be available for the parties, and preventing harm to one's self and to others by reminding them of the actual facts and characteristics of the transaction.[18] These benefits and purposes can be said to be of a more theological perspective; yet, other purposes exist that can be said to be of a more legalistic perspective. It is said that "since the purpose of a document in the case of a debt (as literally understood by the Verse)[19] is to eliminate distrust and forgetfulness, then a document ought to be drawn up for all contracts of sale for the same reason," and the general purpose as such would be "to keep conflicts between the parties at a minimum."[20]

The legal effects of documents are such that they are a written record of the terms of a concluded contract, and thus they are considered to be declarative instruments.[21] Such characterisation is supported by the view that documents are not constitutive instruments as they in themselves do not give rise to any legal obligations, as the transaction has already been completed. This is of course with particular reference to model documents that have been pre-written and where the parties only have to fill in the so-called "blank spaces" and endorse the documents by putting their signatures at the end. Furthermore, documents serve as a record of certain clauses such as guarantee clauses that may bind the parties in the future; something which, even if it would suffice to have witnesses to establish its proof, can only be emphasised and sustained with the presence of a written document.

Having said that it can only be derived that documents serve to establish the validity of any transaction. With the presence of a written document, the validity of the transaction or any of its terms cannot be contested by third parties or the parties themselves in terms of invalidity or irregularity. Moreover, documenting contracts allows for the *Shari'ah* to be followed in its details when conducting the transaction, as more care is taken while documenting any transaction than when the transaction takes place without documentation. Documentation also reduces the possibility of having conflicting testimonies on the part of witnesses if they were called upon in case of conflict.[22]

Another important purpose of documentation lies in the fact that most people do not know how to avoid a defective contract, especially that Islamic law of contracts requires many details to be very closely adhered to, details that ordinary people are usually not aware of, whereas a notary specialised in drafting contracts is capable of avoiding defective contracts and making sure that legal and *Shari'ah* issues are adhered to.[23]

Furthermore, certain details for various contracts differ from one legal or jurisprudential school to another as there is a diversity of views among the legal scholars on details of positive law, and it is necessary that any contract be valid according to all schools in order to avoid conflicting or unsatisfactory judgments should the parties to the contract stand before a judge who is more inclined to the views of one school than another. Drafting contracts can help avoid such diversity of views and their effects on the validity of the transaction especially if great care was taken while drafting the contracts. A notary faced with a contract that is subject to different views on certain details must know the differences of opinion as well as the techniques for making them harmless to the validity of the transaction, and must as well be able to prevent misinterpretation by judges who are ignorant or careless about such diversity of opinion.[24] Hence it is observed, with reference to the early method of contract documentation, that:

> *The notary had to draw up the contract in a way that avoided the inclusion of elements that were subjects of difference between the*

legal schools or that could be interpreted by a qadi *as grounds for judging the contract to be invalid. Many formulae in the contracts were motivated by the need for precaution (*ihtiyat, taaarruz*) against such legal defects.*[25]

The Method of Documentation under Islamic Law

For any document to be accepted as a written proof of any transaction, certain requirements must be present in the document itself as well as in the notary or legal practitioner who has written it, these conditions being inherent by virtue of Verse 2:282 where Allah (*s.w.t.*) revealed: "*...Let a scribe write down faithfully as between the parties; let not the scribe refuse to write: as Allah has taught him, so let him write....*" It can be deduced from the Verse that not any person can write a legal document, as the notary must satisfy certain conditions which are:[26]

(1) That the notary does not reduce or increase the amount of the counter values in the contract, whether it be the subject matter or the price, *i.e.* he must be trustworthy.

(2) That the notary does not prejudice any of the contracting parties by giving the other preferential treatment and reflect that in the document.

(3) Justice: in the sense that what the notary writes be agreed upon by jurists in such a way that no judge can find a way to invalidate the document or misinterpret it.

(4) That the language used in writing the document be bare of generality so that no conflict would arise due to vagueness or haziness of the document or its clauses.

(5) That the notary must have sufficient knowledge of the rules of the *Shari'ah* and those that regulate the transaction that he is documenting, and of the opinions of the different schools on the terms of the transaction so that he can avoid any adverse effects of the diversity of opinions on the validity of that transaction.

Once these conditions are fulfilled in any person, then he can be said to have written the document "faithfully as between the parties" as the Verse orders. Furthermore, the Verse dictates that even if the document was written by a knowledgeable notary it would still be lacking unless the party incurring the liability by virtue of the transaction dictates its terms as a way of recognition of what he is liable for and of its conditions.[27] That is unless that party was incapable of dictation for any reason then his guardian should be burdened with it,[28] while such dictation should be done with fear of Allah (*s.w.t.*) meaning that the dictating party be honest and not diminish what he is liable for, as Allah (*s.w.t.*) revealed: "...*Let him who incurs the liability dictate, but let him fear his Lord Allah, and not diminish aught of what he owes. If the party liable is mentally deficient, or weak, or unable himself to dictate, let his guardian dictate faithfully....*"

In general, there is no fixed rule regarding the method of documenting contracts in Islamic Law, yet there is a specific style of documentation as evident in the writings of early scholars, "for apart from particulars concerning the subject matter, there is not a great deal of difference among marriage contracts, agreements creating partnerships, claims for debts, or deeds of sale."[29] It is noticed that the early scholars have written model contracts that could be followed by notaries for all kinds of transactions, where most if not all of these contracts share a common feature of formalism that has been described by Wakin as "the rigid structure and repetition of stereotyped phrases."[30] However, even though the style of documentation would seem similar in the writings of most scholars, but the divisions within the documents as well as the terminologies used vary considerably among scholars from different schools. Thus to define a specific style of documentation that have been used by early scholars would seem an impossible task.

Nowadays, nevertheless, it is noticed that standard form (pre-written/printed) contracts are being used in almost every transaction, using which the parties enter into the contract according to the terms and conditions stated therein, only having to fill in the blank spaces provided for them, and any additions or changes usually occur only if one of the parties has influence on the other party, either because of his social or economic power. In this regard, it has been stated that:

> *It is now very common for contracts to be made on standard terms prepared by one party and presented by him to the other. Usually such terms are set out in a printed form, which is either the contractual document or one to which reference is made at the time of contracting. Such terms are meant to govern a whole class of contracts, only the individual details being completed in each case. The practice has*

> *obvious advantages. It saves time; and, by creating a standard pattern of dealing, it enables parties to know, in general terms, what sort of risks they will probably have to bear, and to cover by insurance. On the other hand, the practice was also open to abuse, particularly were it was used by commercial suppliers of goods or services when contracting with private consumers. The supplier might put into the printed form a clause limiting or altogether excluding a liability to which he would otherwise be subject, either by virtue of a term implied by law or even irrespective of contract. The customer would often be in a weak position to resist the imposition of such exemption clauses. For one thing, he would generally not read the printed form; indeed, if he did so, its main purpose (of saving time) would be defeated.*[31]

These issues which standard form contracts raise actually defeat the role which contract documentation is meant to play under Islamic Law, defeats its purpose, and lead to a sort of unfair dealings in commercial transactions, or in other words, injustice. It is obvious that the element of "dictation" that was present in the early documents does not exist any longer, or it is that the stronger party does the dictation and not necessarily the party incurring the liability. In addition, it could no longer be said that the scribe writing standard form contracts is doing so "*faithfully as between the parties...*," just as Islam orders, since such contractual documents include as many "legal" mechanisms as to almost completely exclude the stronger party (the party doing the dictation!) from any liability, making any transaction he enters into practically risk-free. In his commentary on this part of the Verse, 'Abdullah Yusuf 'Ali stated that:

> *The scribe in such matters assumes a fiduciary capacity: he should therefore remember to act as in the presence of Allah, with full justice to both parties. The art of writing he should look upon as a gift from Allah, and he should use it in His service. In an illiterate population the scribe's position is still more responsible.*[32]

In the writer's view, illiteracy in the above commentary includes the lack of knowledge of the law or the pillars and conditions of contracts, and not only the ability to read and write. Such illiteracy is a feature of what legal practitioners term as "laymen", and since most people who engage in everyday activities and transactions using standard form contracts are laymen, the scribe should assume more responsibility in reflecting justice in the contractual documents. In fact, such practices of giving preferential treatment to suppliers of goods and services, as reflected in standard form contracts and exemption clauses inserted therein, defeat the principles of justice and fair play that are stressed upon in the Verse of the Holy *Qur'an* where Allah (S.W.T.) revealed: "*O ye who believe! Eat not your property among yourselves in vanities: But let there be amongst you traffic and trade by mutual good-will...*" (Verse 4: 029).

Contract documentation, as such, could not be said to be a mere method for preserving contracts and providing evidence in cases of disputes, it is rather to be looked upon as a mechanism for achieving justice and enforcing honesty in daily transactions; to protect the weak and the poor rather than to allow them to be exploited by the strong and influential parties. "Mutual good-will" does not only mean the mutual consent of both parties to a contract, but also the equal bargaining power which contractual documents can ensure. A scribe is under a religious, moral as well as legal duty to ensure that such equal bargaining power exists, by explaining the contract and its contents to the parties, educating them about its terms and conditions and highlighting their rights and obligations under it. Although scribes writing standard form contracts may not have the opportunity to meet the parties to the contracts and explain their terms to them, but the duties of such scribes still have to be carried out, and that can be achieved by simplifying the wording and structure of contractual documents, thus enabling the parties who are less familiar with the law or the effects of the contracts to understand their rights and obligations. Scribes can, in great many different ways, embody the Islamic rules and conditions governing each transaction in the contractual documents, taking into account the views of the different schools of jurisprudence on each term and condition, thus limiting the possibility of the contracts being disputed due to one of the parties, or the judge hearing the dispute, being more inclined towards the views of one school or another.

Hence, proper documentation of contracts in accordance with the letter and spirit of the *Shari'ah* can in fact lessen the number of commercial disputes; help achieve economic prosperity by reducing exploitation of the public and ensuring a balanced circulation of wealth in the Muslim communities, aside from being a tool for reminding people of their rights and duties under various contracts. Thus documentation of contracts should be given due consideration and approached with diligence like any other professional activity or work, and even more imperatively.

Conclusion

It is clear from the above discussion that documents that were written in the early periods of Islam played more or less the role of a reminder, while nowadays they have more evidential value, and generally speaking, it is difficult to believe that any contract would have a strong effect, if none at all, if it were not documented. Thus the need is more pressing for documents to be worded correctly, embodying every detail of the transaction and avoiding any flaw that is the result of carelessness or unawareness of the diversity of opinions on the validity of the transaction or any of its terms. Hence, any document should not only reflect the terms that the parties wish to stipulate to govern the transaction, but also the rules of the *Shari'ah* that give every single term the stamp of validity in addition to the laws by which both the parties and their transaction are governed. Only once these general guidelines are taken into consideration would the process of contract documentation be up to the expected standards of Islamic law.

Furthermore, what is striking nowadays is that contracts are being formed and documented using such terminology that is difficult, if not impossible, for laymen to understand. The writer believes that the main purpose of documents have been forgotten, that is to remind the parties to a contract of their contractual obligations, and documents have simply become instruments of evidence the language of which is only meant for legal practitioners to understand. It also seems that the assumption, when documenting contracts, have become that the contract would eventually be reviewed or examined by courts, and thus documents are worded in such a way as to enable the parties to use the document for evidence, while forgetting the value of the document as a reminder of the obligations of the parties while executing the contract, and as a reflection of their rights and liabilities thereunder. The writer is not attempting here to deprive the contractual documents of their evidentiary value, but is trying to stress on the fact that documents are, in the first place, for the parties and should thus be written in such a way that is easy for laymen (who are usually the parties to everyday contracts) to understand.

To conclude, contract documentation should reflect the spirit of Islam, as well as the general Islamic principles that govern contracts and transactions, including the principles of justice, trustworthiness, honesty and good faith. To borrow the words of 'Abdullah Yusuf 'Ali:

> *Commercial morality is here taught on the highest plane and yet in the most practical manner, both as regards the bargains to be made, the evidence to be provided, the doubts to be avoided, and the duties and rights of scribes and witnesses. Probity even in worldly matters is to be, not a mere matter of convenience or policy, but a matter of conscience and religious duty. Even our every-day transactions are to be carried out as in the presence of Allah.*[33]

Notes

1. Verse (2:282). See 'Abdullah Yusuf 'Ali (trans.), *The Holy Qur'an: Text, Translation and Commentary*, (Maryland: Amana Corporation, 1989).
2. Jeanette A. Wakin, *The Function of Documents in Islamic Law: The Chapters on Sales from Tahawi's Kitab al-Shurut al-Kabir*, (New York: State University of New York Press, 1972), at p. 5.
3. Article 173; see Hooper, C. A. (Trans.), *The Civil Law of Palestine and Trans-Jordan*, an English translation of the *Mejelle*, (Jerusalem: Azriel Printing Works, 1933).
4. Ala' Eddin Kharofa, *Transactions in Islamic Law*, (Kuala Lumpur: A.S. Noordeen, 1997), at p. 16.
5. Amin 'Abd al-Ma'bud Zaghlul, *Nazariyyat al-Tawthiq fi al-Shari'ah al-Islamiyyah*, (Kuwait: Mu'asasat Dar al-Kutub, 1989), at p. 11.
6. See Hikmat Bashir Yasin (Ed.), *Marwiyyat al-Imam Ahmad Ibn Hanbal fi al-Tafsir*, Vol. 1, (Riyadh: Maktabat al-Mu'ayyad, 1994), at p. 245. See also Ibn Hanbal, *al-Musnad*, Vol. 4, 2270, at 128, and Mohammad Burhan Arbouna, *Islamic Law of Evidence: The Function of Official Documents in Evidence*, (Kuala Lumpur: Syarikat Nurulhas, 1999), at pp. 26-27.
7. See Al-Sarakhsi, *Kitab al-Mabsut*, at 145, and Wakin, *The Function of Documents*, at 6.

8. That is according to Tahawi, as emphasised by Jeanette A. Wakin, *The Function of Documents...*, at p. 29.
9. See for instance *Tafsir Ibn Kathir (abridged)*, Vol. 2, (Riyadh: Maktabat Dar al-Salam, 2003), at p. 85. See also 'Abdullah Yusuf 'Ali (trans.), *The Holy Qur'an*, at 117, and Amin 'Abd al-Ma'bud Zaghlul, *Nazariyyat al-Tawthiq ...*, at 256.
10. 'Abd al-Latif Muhammad 'Amir, "*Al-Duyun wa Tawthiquha fi al-Fiqh al-Islami*", in *Mawsu'at al-Qada' wa al-Fiqh li al-Duwal al-'Arabiyyah*, Vol. 379, (Cairo: Dar Murjan li al-Tiba'ah, 1991), at p. 9.
11. 'Abd al-Qadir 'Udah, *Criminal Law of Islam*, translated by S. Zakir Aijaz, Vol. 1, (New Delhi: Kitab Bhavan, 2005), at p. 60.
12. 'Abd al-Latif Muhammad 'Amir, "Al-Duyun wa Tawthiquha...," at 131.
13. Amin 'Abd al-Ma'bud Zaghlul, *Nazariyyat al-Tawthiq fi al-Shari'ah al-Islamiyyah*, (Kuwait: Mu'assasat Dar al-Kutub, 1989), at p. 258.
14. These were the views of al-Hasan, al-Sha'bi and al-Hakam Ibn 'Utaybah. See ibid, and Abi Hafs al- Hanbali, *Al-Labbab fi 'Ulum al-Kitab*, Vol. 4, (Beirut: Dar al-Kutub al-'Ilmiyyah, 1998), at p. 480. See also *Tafsir Ibn Kathir (Abridged)*, Vol. 2, (Riyadh: Maktabat Dar al-Salam, 2003), at p. 86.
15. 'Abd al-Latif Muhammad 'Amir, "*Al-Duyun wa Tawthiquha...*," at 132, and Amin 'Abd al-Ma'bud, *Nazariyyat al-Tawthiq*, at p. 259.
16. Al-Sarakhsi, *Kitab al-Mabsut*, Vol. 30, Beirut: Dar al-Fikr li al-Tiba'ah wa al-Tawzi' wa al-Nashr, 2000, at 144.
17. Safiur-Rahman al-Mubarakpuri *et al* (trans. & eds.), *Tafsir Ibn Kathir (Abridged)*, Vol. 2, (Lahore: Darussalam Publishers & Distributors, 2000), at p. 90.
18. See Abi Hafs al-Hanbali, *Al-Labbab*, at 501.
19. Brackets are the writer's own.
20. Wakin, *The Function of Documents*, at 30.
21. *Ibid.*
22. *Ibid*, at 31.
23. Al-Sarakhsi, *Kitab al-Mabsut*, at p. 144.
24. Wakin, *The Function of Documents*, at pp. 32-37.
25. Geoffrey Khan, *Arabic Legal and Administrative Documents...*, at p. 7.
26. See Amin 'Abd al-Ma'bud, *Nazariyyat al-Tawthiq*, at p. 263, and Abi Hafs al-Hanbali, *Al-Labbab*, at p. 481. These conditions are not exclusive, other conditions may exist, but these can be directly inferred from the Verse referred to above.

27. Amin 'Abd al-Ma'bud, *Nazariyyat al-Tawthiq*, at 263, and Abi Hafs al-Hanbali, *Al-Labbab*, at p. 481.
28. It is the view of the writer that the incapability of dictation includes the lack of knowledge about the essential elements of contracts and the rules of Islamic law applicable to them, and as such that is where the notary or legal practitioner steps in to take the role of the guardian of the incapable party for the special purpose of dictating the terms of the contract.
29. Wakin, *The Function of Documents*, at p. 38.
30. *Ibid.*
31. Liaquat Ali Khan Niazi, *Islamic Law of Contract*, (Lahore: Research Cell, Dyal Sing Trust Library, 1991), at pp. 74-75.
32. See 'Abdullah Yusuf 'Ali (trans.), *The Holy Qur'an: Text, Translation and Commentary*, at p. 117.
33. 'Abdullah Yusuf 'Ali (trans.), *The Holy Qur'an: Text, Translation and Commentary*, at p. 118.

15

Administrative Ethics of Corporate and Public Administration from the Qur'anic Perspective*

Abdul Razak Abdulahi Hashi

Introduction

At the outset, it is necessary to explain that morals are just and good human relations and human behaviours. Thus, rules that are just and good for the people are considered as morals. A system of morals is known as morality, e.g. Islamic morality. Ethical rules are also moral rules-collectively known as ethics-but they are applicable to only a group of people, e.g. ethics of doctors, lawyers' ethics, and ethics governing administrators and managers of companies and corporations. In civil laws, ethical rules are either codified or exist in the form of traditions. However, in Islam, most of ethical rules applicable to public administrators and executives of companies and corporations are enshrined in the Qur'an and *Sunnah* (Prophetic traditions, known as *ahadith*).

Various Qur'anic verses and numerous *ahadith* remind us the importance of professional and administrative ethics for the overall well being of the community. The Qur'an expresses this in many ways. Sometimes in a form of warning humanity from the grave environmental or social consequences of their misconducts of social administration, or through narrating the stories of the past nations who had engaged with mismanagement and immorality in their individual and collective lives which eventually ended up with complete physical, economic, and spiritual destruction of their civilization. With regard to the warnings, the Qur'anic dictums like "*wala tufsidu fi al-Araḍ ba'd iṣlahiha*",[1] "*wala tulqu bi aydikum ila at-tahlukah*"[2] and "*wala yahiqu al-Makru as-sayi'u ila bi ahlihi*"[3] clearly denote the grave consequences of our social and personal misbehaviours. Furthermore, about the narrations of the previous nations, to mention some, we read the words of prophet *Hud* (*a.s.*) asking his nation (*Ad*) to administer their society with humility and be grateful to Allah for their spiritual, as well as economic strengthen.[4] Furthermore, Prophet *Shu'aib* (*a.s.*) commanded his people that for the sake of enjoying social harmony and economic prosperity, they should maintain commercial and ethical values.[5] He reminded them of social stability and personal happiness which could not be attained without preserving administrative ethical values.[6] In addition, Prophet *Salih* (*a.s.*) addressed his community (*thamud*) in order for them to sustain the economic prosperity and the social security that they had achieved, they should cultivate the administrative ethical values and do not follow the ways of those who put forward extravagant claims for men's powers and material resources and make mischief in the land.[7] Prophet Muhamad (*s.a.w.*) himself repeatedly insisted on various occasions, about the necessity of being administratively just and professional. On one occasion, the Prophet (*s.a.w.*) mentioned that seven groups would be saved on the Day of Judgment, including "the fair public administrator or the leader"[8]; while on another occasion, he announced that fair public administrators would be exempted from any detailed account in the hereafter,[9] while those who had good faith would be those who had better morals including administrative ethics.[10] Thus, these and many countless examples depict how managerial ethics of public and business administrators are important in the Islamic managerial perspective.

Managers, Public Administrators and Administrative Ethics

Scholars of social psychology categorically understood "leader" as "a person influencing another to willingly work toward a predetermined objective,"[11] while manager is "a person who plans, organizes, leads and controls the work of others so that the organization achieves its goals."[12] Administration denotes the act or process of administering, especially the management of a government, or large institution. In addition, "public" in its collective noun[13] means; community or the people as a whole,[14] thus, public administrators are those who administer (this includes planning, organizing, controlling and leading) especially those who work as managers in a business, government agencies, or educational institutions.[15]

On the other hand, in the Islamic administrative perspective, heads of states, directors of incorporated business companies, chancellors and vice-chancellors of educational institutions as well as the persons engaged with welfare organizations are principally classified as *ra'i* and *ajir* in the Qur'anic dictums and Prophetic pronouncements.[16] The Arabic term *ra'a,* which is literally tantamount to 'shivered', is employed to mean 'in charge', 'leader' or 'administrator', while the term *ajara* and its derivatives are applicable to all employees, from domestic servants and factory workers to the caliph or the head of the state.[17] All of them are *ujara* (plural of *ajir*), literally 'hired for a consideration', in both public and private positions.[18] *Imam,*[19] i.e., leader and *ulul-amr*, i.e., the person in charge or administrator are also those who hold public offices. Despite their etymological discrepancies (*ajir, ra'i and ulul amr*), these terms connote anyone who possesses any title of social responsibility.

Finally, regardless of the terminological variety between the terms of modern theories of leadership and that of the Qur'an, all agree that the role of administrators and leader, as the central figurehead of the administration, to be vital, for the success of the organization depends on them. Hence, both interpreters of the Qur'an and modern social psychologists agreed that professional ethics of managers and administrators means: "the normative obligations that cooperate and public administrators owe to the public; of both workmates and clients."[20]

Managerial Ethics in Modern theories of Management and Islam

Many social-psychologists of the past two centuries have shown keen interest in leadership characteristics. Their contentions emphasized on what qualities distinguish between leaders and followers. Nonetheless, many of their writings on management were criticized for their undue emphasis on the organizational structure and work design of the management. They were criticized for having paid less attention to the role of the human elements (satisfaction of workers and employees) in achieving the goals of the organization.[21] This is because though early classical theories of management and leadership like general management theory,[22] bureaucratic theory[23] and scientific management theory[24] presented some contrasting elements, they all gave less attention to the employee's psychological and moral well being, and its impact on work performance. They were criticised for their job oriented conception of management.[25] Perhaps this is what made latter theories of leadership like trait,[26] contingency theory[27] and behavioural theories[28] of leadership to shift their emphasis to the moral and psychological characters of leaders and administrators.[29]

With regard to the leadership characteristics of public administrators, the early Muslim scholars like; Abu Yusuf (731-798 A.D),[30] Ibn al-Muqafa (724-789A.D),[31] Al-Juwayni (1028-1085 A.D)[32] and Al-Mawardi (d.1058 C.E)[33] emphasized on the personal, theological and judicial aspects of the public administrators under the topics: '*al-wali al-adil*', '*as-sultan al-'Adil*' or the '*khalifah*'. They all are equivalent to a 'just leader or administrator'. Besides their enormous effort, which was heavily invested in the descriptions of the "*sultan 'adil*", less intention was given to the professional ethics of public administrators.[34] Many contemporary theologians and ethicists like al-Attas,[35] Shaukat Ali[36] and Qardhawi,[37] offered more precise attention to the subject of managerial ethics than classical theologians.

The Qur'anic Managerial Ethics of Administration

Furthermore, according to the *Qur'anic* perspective of administration, there are three interrelated portions of administrative ethics with regard to the administration and management. *First,* is the ethics towards work structure, *second,* is the ethics towards manpower and human resource, and *third,* is the ethics towards the personality (perception, traits and morality) of the administrators. This encompasses both the *macro* level of managerial behaviour, such as crises management, human resource management and coping with new social changes and development, and *micro* level, such as perception, motivation, personality and career development. Hence, enhancement of administrator's dynamics, his psychological set up and mental satisfaction are fundamental. In the Islamic managerial ethics of management and public administration, administrators were required not to make any decision because they were not psychologically stable; they could easily become angry and sad. On the other hand, one of the essential elements of the principles of social relations in Islam is that social groups should interact through healthy communication which, in turn, will create peace of mind and happiness. The Prophet (*s.a.w.*) teaches to exchange greetings and smiling in front of your colleagues showing them some sort of respect; and that amounts to *sadaqah.* With regards to the work structure, the administrator should be more definite about certain elements of work structure, such as division of work according to specialization and skill, subordination of personal interests, authority and responsibility.

With regard to the division of work, the Qur'an teaches that mutual benefits and group prosperity cannot be realized without such diversification of employment based on variations of talent, profession and need. The group is a constituent element of the humankind, it being understood that group differences are meant for complementary of one another, not for unjust discrimination, as implied in tribalism, provincialism, nationalism and racism. Society's responsibility, as Islam sees it, is that every human may fulfil the function for which he is best fitted.[38] Furthermore, the importance of specialization and division of work are constantly addressed in the Qur'an. In the *Qur'an*, people are advised to refer to *ahl Đikr*, i.e., professional and *ulu al-Ilm*, i.e., knowledgeable or skilful, as an authority to solve their daily social difficulties. The *Qur'an* says: "*fas'alu ahla Đikr in kuntum la ta'lamun*", which means if you do not have enough knowledge about the concerned subject, ask those who specialize in the field. This according to Muslim scholars means to respect the specialization and division of the workload according to the available qualifications.[39]

Similarly, Islamic administrative ethics rejects all kinds of conflict of interest and demands the administrator to subordinate all personal interests to the public interest. There was one incident where the Prophet (*s.a.w.*) appointed a man as an administrator of *zakah* collection in one province of the Muslim state. However, while performing his administrative work of *zakah* collections, the community of the region gave him their prescribed *zakah* and some additional donations for the government's public welfare funds. When he was on his way back to the capital city of the Islamic state –Medina, the man thought that since his duty was to collect only the official *zakah* for the government, the additional donations could be his own. When he arrived at Medina he sent only the collections of the official *zakah* and kept the additional donation for himself. When the Prophet (*s.a.w.*) heard this, he outrageously expressed his anger about such action and asked the man to give all the collection and put in the government's account. The Prophet termed such act as a conflict of interest between the public duties and personal interests, thus, rejected and reminded the Muslim public administrators not to do such act again in any circumstance. The Prophet (*s.a.w.)* said:

> *"...I (the Prophet) have appointed a person from among you to do some duty on my behalf for which I have been assigned by Allah. On the completion of his mission that man comes back and says: "this is yours (the public) and that has been presented to me as a gift." If he is telling the truth then why does he not stay in the house of his father or mother, until some body comes to him and presents him gifts? By Allah, if any one of you takes anything without its proper ways* (haqqiha*), he will have to face Allah on the Day of Judgement, with the burden of such things....".*[40]

Likewise, with regard to the administrative authority, the *Qur'an* commands its adherents to respect and obey (*ta'ah*) their leaders (*ulul -amr, i.e.*, those charged with authority) and follow their orders as far as they are not commanding the outlawed things.[41] Additionally, the Prophetic narrations inform us that the Prophet (*s.a.w.*) never send a delegation or never ask a group of people to accomplish certain task without appointing a leader for them. This is understood as a clear message of performing administrative matters with responsibility and authority.

Furthermore, with respect to the human resource dimension of administration, Islam believes the overall well being of employees such as paying their salary on time,[42] giving them enough workloads,[43] providing incentives according to their work and productivity,[44] and enhancing the employees' team spirit[45] and clear set of communication language, will have greater contribution to maintain effective public administration. In addition, on the personal traits of administrators, interestingly enough, when such titles *ajir*, *ulul-amr* and *ra'i* are mentioned in the *Qur'an* and *sunnah*, the same managerial ethics are applied to all; to the physician, teacher, or engineer; the baker, butcher, or carpenter; the factory or agricultural worker; the corporation or government employee; the caliph and his ministers.[46]

Such administrative and professional ethics are integrity (*amanah and ikhlas*), transparency (*bayan and adam al-ghish*), good governance (*amal salih*), accountability (*mas'uliyah*), commitment and continuation of work (*quwah* and *itqan*), professional attitude (*hafiz and alim*), team spirit or collective oriented (*shu'ra*), reasonableness or fairness (*adalah*) and to avoid of conflict of interest (*Qist and qawwama*). These administrative and professional ethics are categorically analyzed in the following sub-topics.

Tawhidic Worldview and Public Administration

What makes Islamic ethics in general and administrative ethics in particular unique is the concept of oneness of God (*tawhid),* which binds everything to Allah (*s.w.t.*), the Creator of everybody and everything. It combines into a homogeneous whole all of the different aspects of a Muslim's life, including economic, political, religious, and social life, and stresses the idea of consistency and order throughout the Islamic thought.[47] With regards to the job of public administration, the *tawhidic* worldview of Islam teaches us that "public administration" is both noble and dedication to the job. It is noble because public administration was the profession of the Prophets delightfully provided a divine leadership of public administration throughout the history of mankind. Furthermore, both the *Qur'anic* dictums and Prophetic pronouncements teach us that every human individual is individually a *khalifah* (vicegerent or trustee) on the earth. In this capacity, duties of a man are only actualized through the job of public administration. The job of planning, organizing, controlling and leading, which is normally done by the administrators or managers, is achievable through a meaningful participation in the social reality of the community. Moreover, it is dedicatory because religious and social rewards of effective public administration are everlasting. In various occasions the *Qur'an* states the necessity of obeying the Al-Mighty God (*s.w.t.*) and following the path of the Messenger (*s.a.w.*), and obeying the *ulul-amr*, i.e., those who are in charge for the public affairs or leaders. Stating the obedience of *ulul-amr* subsequent to the obedience to Allah (*s.w.t.*) and his Messenger (*s.a.w.*), show the importance that Islam invested in the job of public administration. Besides the fact that the *tawhidic* worldview balances the administrators' ultimate objectives of administration,[48] the *tawhidic* worldview motivates the just managerial behaviour:

> *"...since a Muslim administrator looks upon every thing in the world as belonging to Allah, the same lord to Whom he himself belongs, he cannot be biased in his thinking and behaviour. His vision is wider, and his sense of service is not restricted to any specific sphere or group. Any thought of racism or caste system is inconsistent with his thinking."*[49]

The belief in unity of God requires the Muslim public administrators not to discriminate among his employees, suppliers, buyers, or any other stake-holders on the basis of race, colour, sex, or religion. He or she follows the same unified code of behaviour whether he is in the mosque, earning a living or acting out other aspects of his life. Islam does not distinguish society into employer and employed, capitalists and workers, rather it declares all human are "workers"; and, as such, responsible before God, His Prophet and the society. Thus, a Muslim public administrator is not solely guided by benefits, and is not seeking to accumulate wealth at any cost.[50]

Continuation of Good Deeds (Amal salih) and Commitment (Itqan) to Work

Besides the tawhidic worldview, which balances the administrators view towards the public and the whole universe, *Qur'an* requires the Muslim public administrators to work continuously hard and be committed to the quality of their profession. Various Qur'anic verses and the Prophetic tradition state "singular: '*imal*" or "plural: '*imalu*", i.e., keep working or work continuously, individually and collectively.[51] According to *Qurlubi*, the command "'*imalu*",[52] i.e., to work continuously, generally demands every believer (including administrators and professionals) to continue their work with commitment and consciousness.[53] Hence, administrators' commitment to their work (*amal*)[54] and successful delivery of public responsibility with full trust and honesty is strongly demanded and advised.[55] Though generally continuation of work means enhancing individual's ability to govern meaningfully life and work for change, the greater part of such work lies on the shoulder of the public administrators. Moreover, while the *Qur'an* teaches that Allah (*s.w.t)* will not change a community unless they make efforts for change to the betterment of their lives, such change for betterment is not conceivable without effective public administration. Therefore, the community might be left behind in terms of economic, political and administration, if laziness and inefficiency of decision making spread in their decision making process. According to the Prophetic tradition, inefficiency or lack of public administration is tantamount to a boat full of passengers in an ocean. If the passengers of such boat are able to manage the boat and the affairs of the passengers well, they will reach to their destination safely. However, if they fail to administer it, then their live is at risk.[56] Hence, coping with the rapidly changing natural and social environments demand leaders and public administrators to be continuously vigilant and act accordingly. It has been narrated in the tradition of the prophet Muhammad (*s.a.w*) that three kinds of people shall get double rewards. One of them is the worker, who is discharging his responsibilities towards his master or head efficiently and serving God at the same time.

On the other hand, Islam views work as necessary capital for human's survival, and, therefore, continuation of *amal* is prescribed. Allah (*s.w.t.*) has commanded every human individual to work and produce; and has promised that work will indeed earn merit for the worker, materially as well as spiritually. He warned that no one will receive any more or any less than what he has worked or earned for himself. He described the true believers as those who establish faith on earth and reconstruct the world around them so as to make it a place of plenty and peace for all. The messenger of Allah said:

> *"No one eats a better-food than what he has attained through his manual work".*[57]

Answering about the question of what is the best livelihood (*rizk*) that some may have, the prophet said:

> *"That which proceeds from the work of your hand, as well as every legitimate business."*[58]

On another occasion, he indicated that whoever returns home at the end of the day exhausted from his labour, will be forgiven. Furthermore, the Prophet also said that the hand which shows the effect of hard work is worthy of being kissed. While on other occasions he said:

> *"It is better for anyone of you to carry a bundle of wood on his back, and sell it than to beg of someone whether he may give or refuse to give him".*[59]

Thus, man is required to work from cradle to grave continuously.[60] It was narrated from the Prophet (s.a.w.) saying that:

> *"If the last hour strikes and finds you holding a nursling in your hand go ahead and plant it".*

All these prophetic narrations recommend the ethics of working hard and continuation of *amal* until the last minutes of someone's life. Thus, administrators should work hard and continuously with perfection (*itqan*) and quality (*amal salih*). According to the Islamic *tawhidic* conception of life, if man's work including doctrinal statements, rites and rituals, professional and other daily activities of life, are not done with full intention and perfection, such works will not be productive. Productivity and quality is related to the perfection,[61] while sustainable social progress and durable economic prosperity are achievable through striving hard for good work.[62] The Qur'anic term *amal* is always followed with the description "*salih*, i.e., good" and is always stated as *amal salih* which means "good work". The *Qura'nic* dictums like "*wa amilu as-salihati*",[63] and "*wa amila amalan salihan*"[64] constitute the basic guidelines for professionals to strive for quality in administration and production. In one hand the Qur'an states that man's deeds are wasted except the good deeds,[65] while on the other hand man's deeds, including public administration, are counter productive except the good deeds.[66] In the *Qur'an itqan* in administration is promoted through different ways; teleologically[67] and professionally. At the teleological level the *Qur'an* reminds the Muslim to reflect the perfection of Allah's actions in the creation of the universe and the natural environment. In chapter *al-Mulk,* we are informed to reflect on the architectural design of the natural phenomena and how Allah (s.w.t.) perfected their creation. According to the *Qur'an,* it is He Who created the seven heavens one above another, no cracks or inefficiency in both the design and order of the universe, are there.[68] Hence, man should also perfect his professional duties, in order to enjoy durable and sustainable social and economic life. Professionally, the Prophet (*s.a.w*) commanded the Muslims to perform their daily works, perfectly, with quality.[69]

Integrity (Quwah) and Trustworthiness (Amanah)

Public administration without integrity (*quwah*) and reliability (*amanah*) may be described as a counterproductive. We might, in the professional sense, agree that integrity denotes the character of being steadfastly adherent to strict ethical values. Besides implying following steadfastly the professional norms, integrity in this regard also means to be conscious of the rapid environmental and social changes. Some ethicists employ integrity interchangeably with trustworthiness. However, integrity is more than trustworthiness in the sense that it is the balancing or controlling factor of trustworthiness. As strength without trust is hard to imagine, hence the person could be trustworthy but to maintain the trustworthiness he or she needs to have strength or integrity. Therefore, administrators of public and private sectors need to be and remain strong and trustworthy.[70] Hence, according to the *Qur'an* the best person to hire for public or private office (*inna khayra man ista'jarta*) is he who has integrity and trust (*al-qawi al-amin*). Good example of this is the story of the Prophet Shu'aib (*a.s*) with Prophet Moses (a.s). According to the *mufasirun*, Prophet *Shu'aib*, who was living in the remote area between Egypt and Arabian Peninsular,[71] was depending on the seasonal rains for his cattle, but, because of his age, he faced certain difficulties related to the administration of the family as well as the livestock, thus needed to hire someone for the job.[72] Such profession includes making environmental assessment of postural life and managing the seasonal changes, and their impact on the livestock. However, Prophet Shu'aib (a.s) was convinced that the candidate of such profession should possess the professional characteristics of trustworthiness and integrity.[73] Prophet Moses (*a.s*) arrived and met with Shu'aib (a.s), after quick check and evaluatior of Moses' professional behaviour, Prophet Shu'aib was convinced that Prophet Moses was fit for the job, thus, offered him the job and explained to him the terms and conditions of the job in terms of its nature and duration of the contract.[74] What is interesting in this contract is that while Moses (the employee) was required to work professionally with integrity and honesty, Prophet Shu'aib (the employer) promised that he would remain patient and tolerant. Accordingly, the *Qur'an* teaches that mutual understanding and accommodative behaviour are necessary elements of effective public administration.

Similarly, it has also been narrated that one of the Companions of the Prophet (*s.a.w*) came to the prophet and asked the Prophet to let him hold a public office; however, the Prophet rejected such application. The Prophet (*s.a.w*) immediately informed the candidate the reason of such refusal that because holding public office required integrity and strength while he (the candidate) was not strong enough.[75] On another occasion, the Prophet announced that the believer who lived and involved positively in the community in terms of administration and development was better than the person who isolated himself from the community, while the believer with strength and integrity (*al-mu'min al-Qawi*) was better than the believer who lacks such strength (*al-mu'min ad-da'if*).

Professional Attitude (makin, amin, hafiz and Alim)

Characteristics of skilful (*alim*) and professionalism (*makin*)[76] must be possessed by a public administrator. According to the *Qur'an,* the first professional attitude that public administrators should obtain, are: *makin* (strong professional), trustworthy (*amin*), *hafiz* (integrity), and *alim* (skilful or professional. In this sense, the Qur'an advises public administrators to be *makin*, i.e., mentally and professionally talented and *alim*, i.e., skilful and professional. It is the administrative character in which an administrator remains in control of managerial duties while holding the ethical and moral values. Lawyers, judges, engineers, managers and other professionals of public administration are required to acquire skills that facilitate them to deliver their public duty sufficiently. To achieve the well being of the society, public administrators should undergo an extensive period of training of both intellectual and technical aspects. Such attitude will enable the public administrator to eliminate corruption and coping with new social circumstances.

Historians of Egyptology agreed that the Egyptian dynasty of the 17th and 18th centuries,[77] B. C. E faced economic and financial crisis which threatened the life of millions of Egyptians both in urban and rural areas. The then powerful Egyptian ruler was very keen to regenerate and reenergize the administrative path of his government to cope with the difficulties ahead. He had announced that the kingdom will undergo economic recession. He laid out seven years of financial plan and some administrative methods of wealthy management. However, he was strongly convinced that such plans and methods will not be effective without proper expertise that are free of corruption, thus decided to handover the ministry of finance and other financial offices to someone who is trustworthy and free of corruption. Prophet Yusuf (*a.s*) who was aware of the case realized that he can fulfil such conditions and informed the king his candidacy for the ministry of finance (*ij'alni ala khaza'in al-Arl̀i, i.e.,* set me over the store-houses of the land or the agricultural sector), which was the main source of financial income at that time.[78] He (*a.s*) submitted his résumé to the ruler, reminding the ruler that what makes him outstanding candidate for such public duty is that, first he (*a.s*) was skilful or professional (*alim*), and second, he (*a.s*) was trustworthy (*hafiz*).[79] With such skills and traits prophet Yusuf (*a.s*) was able to successfully manage the economic recession period and led the nation back into the stable conditions of prosperity.[80]

Avoiding Conflict of Interest (qisÏ and qawama) Transparency (bayan)

Qist (faire-mindedness), *Qawama* (consistency) and *bayan* (clarity and transparence) are all related to justice and avoiding conflict of interest or nepotism when performing administrative and professional activities. According to the dictionary of "Professional Business Terms" conflict of interest is the state of disharmony between antithetical individual's interest or a clash between individual's interest and professional requirement and obligations.[81] It is the divergence between a person's private interests and his/her public obligation. It takes place when someone is in a position of professional trust, such as lawyer, medical doctor or an executive or director of a corporation, has competing professional and personal interest which risks the normal procedures of his public duty. Whatsoever form might the conflict of interest be, the *Qur'an* strongly opposes it and requires public administrators to avoid it, and be resolute and stand out firmly for justice (*qawwamina bil qist*), even if the cases which are against your interest or that of your family and relatives.[82] The combination between the terms *qist*, i.e., fair-mindedness and *qawwama*, i.e., consistently uprightness, denotes that the public administrators should not incline to injustice or any sort of conflict of interest in their administrative practices. No nepotism or any other form of administrative injustices should public administrators be involved in.

On the other hand, since public administrators have taken the professional oath to execute their professional duty fairly, they are duty bound to improve their profession, give measure and weight with (full) justice, speak justly, even if a near relative is concerned, and fulfil the covenant of Allah.[83] Public administrators are informed to remain transparent and honest in their interpretation of facts and scientific data obtained through their professional endeavours. In this sense, according to the *Qur'an,* public administrators are *umna* or trustees and should not hide anything that can jeopardize the well being of the community. The public deserves to be aware of what is happing in the decision making authorities to either correct the path of the direction of certain policies, or take action against professional misconducts.[84] This necessarily means that professionals including administrators should display integrity and remain without deception or fraud, thus neither *kitman*, i.e., hiding or concealment, nor *libs*, i.e., to mix-up and intentionally falsify with regard to the dispersal, is expect from the professionals.[85]

Team Spirit or Collective Decision (shura)

In the Islamic faith, Prophecy is understood within the concept of infallibility of the Prophets." Prophets are guided by Allah (*s.w.t*), therefore, He protected them from committing any sin in any manner.[86] And through His revelation to them, He provided ready-made answers to the most of the cases. However, one might wonder why the Prophet (*s.a.w.*) was commanded in the *Qur'an* to consult the companions in the administrative matters of the nation. Does consulting the companions-who are basically fallible human beings - mean that the revelation was not enough to guide the Prophet to make the right administrative decisions for the public? Another question is: if the infallible Prophet was required to consult the fallible companions, does this mean promoting human rationality over the revelation? According to ar-Razi and Qurtubi, the aim was neither to prefer the human intellect over the revelation nor to doubt the administrative ability of the Prophet (*s.a.w.*), but was to teach the Muslim administrators the importance of human element in the administration process, particularly, the significance of collective decisions and consultation (*shu'ra*) in the decision-making process.[87] Additionally, both Zamakhshari and Wahba az-Zuhaily state that another objective was to highlight the imperative role of human resource and team-spirit dimensions of the public administration.[88]

However, reading inductively the *Qur'anic* verses we find that the term *Shu'ra* and its derivatives are directly stated in the *Qura'an* three times only.[89] Moreover, through topical reading of the three verses we realize that the first verse is about "family issues or family level",[90] the second is about "social and cultural issues"[91] and the third is about "administration and political issues"[92] of the community. This means *Shu'ra* is not only a political term but rather cultural and administrative term. Thus, *Shu'ra* should be practiced at all levels of the community: between the administrative heads of the state, father and mother or husband and wife, child and parent, teacher and student, chief administrator and his subordinates. Furthermore, this means when the child grows up in a family where the *shu'ra* is the mechanism to solving familial issues, educates in a school or university where teachers allow students to express themselves freely in the class, and in a society that is consultatively interconnected, then the team spirit of the administrator or the head of the state is demonstrated and with the result of that healthy minds grow. Besides the fact that this shows the gradual psycho-social formation of administrative character of the administrator, it also shows the importance of manpower in crisis management and the administration of the problematic social issues. Many examples of effective public administration are there in the *Qur'an*. Of which, good example of this is the story of *Balqis* with Prophet Sulaiman (*a.s*).

Though many Muslim jurists debate about the role of gender (masculine or feminine) in public administration, specifically, whether to outlaw a woman to head a public office or not, in this story the *Qur'an* states and praises the story of the stateswoman, the queen Balqis, who had wisely administered her nation, even when her close male advisors become emotional and lost the futuristic vision of making decisions. Initially, the *Qur'an* states how consultative she was, and how she had mobilized the manpower of her administration towards making the right decision. This is when Prophet Sulaiman's bilateral contract reached the Queen's office, and she immediately, as the head of the state, called for a cabinet meeting, saying that it was: "delivered to me a letter worthy of respect", thus I seek your (ministers, chiefs and executives) advice in this matter for I have: "not decided any affair unilaterally without your presence and consultation. However, the chiefs gave mixed response to the issue and most of them preferred war and military confrontation than bilateral relations based on mutual respect.[93] Nonetheless, she was able to manage their opinion and intelligibly reminded them the grave consequences of wars and the destruction that follows invasions and conflicts. She said: "Kings, when they enter a country, they despoil it, and make the noblest of its people its meanest thus do they behave". Hence, in her opinion military confrontation was not a solution, thus, she suggested exhausting the other diplomatic ways first.[94] Perhaps there are many reasons why the *Qur'an* narrated this story, one of them could be to show the Muslim administrators the importance of consultation, regardless of gender, colour and ethnicity. Thus, sheikh al-Ghazali (d. 1997), concludes that, according to the above mentioned story, feminine and masculine had nothing to do with who is going to hold a public office. According to him, the question is who can exercise *shu'ra* and provide justice to the public.[95] Thus, the best administrators are those who are team oriented when making decisive decisions for the public.

Conclusion

According to the *Qur'an* social harmony and sustainable economic prosperity is unachievable without practicing managerial ethical values in all administrative activities of the society. Administrative activities of the heads of states, directors of companies and corporations, chancellors and vice-chancellors of educational institutions as well as the welfare organizations which are termed as *ra', ulul-amr* and *ajir* in the *Qur'an*, should be in accordance with managerial ethics. These include integrity, transparency, good governance, accountability, commitment, attitude, reasonableness, fairness and devoid of conflict of interest. In the Islamic perspective of administration, such managerial ethics of administrators and managers, address three interrelated aspects of administration. *First,* is the ethics towards work structure, *second,* is the ethics towards manpower and human resource, and *third,* is the ethics towards the personality of the administrators. Thus, the *Qur'anic* managerial ethics encompasses both *micro* and *macro* levels of administrative behaviour. In the micro level it includes perception, motivation, personality and career development are concerned, while in the *macro* level of managerial behaviour it includes crises management, human resource management and coping with new social changes and development, are encouraged.

It is clear that ethical rules, enshrined in the Qur'an and *Sunnah,* are eternal, universal and most of them are immutable. Thus, a large part of administrative and managerial ethical rules are based on divine wisdom and they instil quality administration in states and companies. This is a mark difference when we compare the Islamic administrative law with that of various civil laws governing administrators and managers.

Notes

1. The Qur'an reminds its adherents that their nationhood existence and security is in their hands or how they handle the public affairs. Additionally, committing immoral actions in the public affairs' administration will cause them to loose their social harmony and spiritual happiness on earth. The Qur'an states:

   "وَلاَ تُفْسِدُوا فِي الأَرْضِ بَعْدَ إِصْلاَحِهَا وَادْعُوهُ خَوْفًا وَطَمَعًا إِنَّ رَحْمَتَ اللهِ قَرِيبٌ مِّنَ الْمُحْسِنِينَ."

   "Do no mischief on the earth, after it hath been set in order, but call on Him with fear and longing (in your hearts): for the Mercy of Allah is (always) near to those who do good." (see: *Surah al-A'raf*, verse: 56)

2. The Qur'an advises man not to let your hands or actions contribute to your destruction; but do good and set up firmly the ethical values that are required from you. The Qur'an reads:

"وَأَنفِقُوا فِي سَبِيلِ اللهِ وَلَا تُلقُوا بِأَيْدِيكُمْ إِلَى التَّهْلُكَةِ وَأَحْسِنُوَا إِنَّ اللهَ يُحِبُّ الْمُحْسِنِينَ"

"And spend of your substance in the cause of Allah, and make not your own hands contribute to (your) destruction; but do good; for Allah loveth those who do good." (*Surah al-Baqarah*, verse: 190).

3. The Qur'an states that unethical individuals will not only destroy other people's life, but they destroy themselves too. The Qur'an states:

اسْتِكْبَارًا فِي الأَرْضِ وَمَكْرَ السَّيِّئِ وَلَا يَحِيقُ المَكْرُ السَّيِّئُ إِلاَّ بِأَهْلِهِ فَهَلْ يَنظُرُونَ إِلاَّ سُنَّتَ الأَوَّلِينَ فَلَن تَجِدَ لِسُنَّتِ اللهِ تَبْدِيلاً وَلَن تَجِدَ لِسُنَّتِ اللهِ تَحْوِيلاً.

"On account of their arrogance in the land and their plotting of Evil, but the plotting of Evil will harm in only the authors thereof. Now are they but looking for the way the ancients were dealt with? But no change wilt thou find in Allah's way (of dealing): no turning off wilt thou find in Allah's way (of dealing)." (*Surah Fatir,* verse: 43)

4. He informed them that even the agricultural and the natural environment will be more prosperous and fruitful, where Allah (*s.w.t*) will send down the rain to enhance their economic and social well beings. And he finally warned them that, failure to maintain the administrative ethics, the price will be higher, where they may no longer exist in the future; perhaps some other groups will replace them. (*Surah Hud*, verses: 51-58.)

5. He said weigh the goods for sale properly (*wala tanqusu al-mikyala*) and do not cheat the people when measuring the scale (*mizan*) in selling the goods to the customers.

6. To the extent that even their existent will depend on carrying on their good ethical codes. In case of failure to fulfil this He warned them the painful and destructive consequence of such failures. (See: *Surah* Hud, verses: 89-93).

7. See *surah ash-Shu'ara*, verses: 146-152. We read in the same connotations the story of a prophet *(pbuh)* who commanded his society to administer the marital issues with balance. (See: Surah *ash-Shu'ara*, verses, 165-173).

8. The Prophet (s.a.w) stated:

سبعة يظلهم الله في ظله يوم لا ظل إلا ظله، إمام عادل، وشاب نشأ في عبادة الله عزوجل، ورجل قلبه معلق بالمساجد، ورجلان تحابا في الله وتفرقا عليه....."

"...Seven kinds of people will be sheltered under the shade of Allah on the Day of Judgment when there will be no other shade, besides His shade. They are A just ruler or administrator; a young man who passed his youth with the worship and service of Allah (*s.w.t*), one whose heart is perpetually attached with the mosque; two such persons who love each other for the sake of Allah, they joined together for His sake and parted each other for the sake of Allah...." (reported by Bukhari and Muslim)

9. In many occasions the Prophet reminded the public official to deal with the members of the community and their job with sincerity and responsibility. Abdullah b. Amar b. As (r.a.) reported that:

   قال رسول الله صلى الله عليه وسلم، إن المقسطين عند الله على منابر من نور: الذين يعدلون في حكمهم وأهليهم وما ولوا.

   "The Prophet said: the just and fair persons (ruler and administrators) will be seated on chairs of light before Allah. Such persons are those who decide justly and deal justly in the matters relating to their families and other affairs entrusted to them." (reported by Muslim).

10. The Prophet once stated that:

    "أكمل المؤمنين إيمانا أحسنهم خلقا ، وخياركم خياركم لنسائهم"

    Abu Huraira (r.a.) narrated that the Messenger of Allah (s.a.w) had said: the most perfect man of the believers in their faith is that whose behaviour is the most excellent and the best of you are those who are the best to their wives." (reported by At-Termizi).

11. Gary Dessler, Management: principles and Practices for Tomorrow's Leaders, (New Jersey: Prentice Hall, 3rd ed. 2004), p. 255.

12. Gary Dessler, Management: principles and Practices for Tomorrow's Leaders, p. 3.

13. The adjectival expression of the term denotes: Of, concerning, or affecting the community or the people. It also means maintained for or used by the people or community, while it also indicates participated in or attended by the people or community. (See: A. S. Hornby, Oxford Advanced Learner's Dictionary of Current English, (London: Oxford University Press, 1974).

14. Public is literally expressed to denote a group of people sharing a common interest. (A. S. Hornby, Oxford advanced learner's Dictionary of current English).

15. English synonyms of administrator are; executive, director and manager.

16. The Prophet (*s.a.w*) said:

"Every-one of you is a protector and every-one of is guardian of his or her responsibility. A ruler or administrator is also *ra'i,* .i.e., accountable or steward for those who are under his or her charge, a man is a steward in respect of his family members of his house, a woman is a steward in respect of her house and children. In short every one of you is steward and is accountable for those who are placed under his care. (Reported by Bukhari and Muslim).

17. Though man is theologically known as the "*khalifah*" or vicegerent of Allah, however, politically it is applied to any one who holds administrative and religious leadership of the Muslim society.
18. In the Islamic political thought *wali, imam* and *amir* are synonymously used besides *ajir* and *ra'i*. However, the former terms usually indicate political leadership; the later two terms are inclusively employed for all public administrators and professionals.
19. *Imam* is also known to be the person who leads the prayers of the devotees in the mosque or any other place. This according to the Muslim theologians and expositors of the *Qur'an* shows how religion and administration of the state affairs are interconnected.
20. See: Ar-Razi, *at-Tafsir al-Kabir*, v. 18, pp.111-112, al-Qurtubi, *Al-Jami' li Ahkam al-Qur'an,* (Beirut: *Dar al-Kutub al-Ilmiyah,*1993), and Gary Dessler, Management: principles and Practices for Tomorrow's Leaders, pp. 255-258.
21. See the critics of these theories in: Gary Dessler, Management: principles and Practices for Tomorrow's Leaders, pp.257 onwards.
22. The principles of his theory are: division of Work, authority and responsibility, unity of command, subordination of personal interests, chain of command and centralization of decisions. (See: Gary Dessler, Management: principles and Practices for Tomorrow's Leaders, (New Jersey: Prentice Hall, 3rd ed. 2004), pp. 256-257.
23. Among basic tenets of this theory are:, a clear hierarchical system of authority, division of labour according to specialization, a complete system of rules, comprehensive outline of work performance selection and promotion on the basis of technical ability. (See: Max Weber, T*he Protestant Ethic and the Spirit of Capitalism,* Translated by Talcott Parsons, (New York: Scribner, 1976).
24. This theory made various suggestions regarding the best way of performance, selection of personals, compensation and incentives and division of labour. (See: Karen M. Hult and Charles Walcott, *Governing Public Organizations: Politics, Structures and Institutional Design,* (California: Brooks/Cole Pub. Co, 1990)).

25. *Ibid.*
26. According to trait theory, leaders of both public and private sectors, are people, who are able to express themselves fully. They also know what they want, why they want it, and how to communicate what they want to others, in order to gain their co-operation and support.
27. Contingency theory suggested that previous theories such as Max Weber's bureaucracy and Frederick Taylor's scientific management had failed because they neglected the point that management style and organizational structure were influenced by various aspects of the environment: the contingency factors. There could not be "one best way" for leadership or organization. (for more reading on this see: Lex Donaldson, The contingency theory of organizations, (California: Sage Publications, 2001), and Thomas E. Harris, Applied organizational communication: principles and pragmatics for future practice, (New Jersey: Lawrence Erlbaum Associates, 2002).
28. The behavioural theory holds that human action is guided by three kinds of considerations: first, beliefs about the likely outcomes of the behaviour and the evaluations of these outcomes. Second, beliefs about the normative expectations of others and motivation to comply with these expectations. Third, beliefs about the presence of factors that may facilitate or impede performance of the behaviour and the perceived power of these factors. (for more details see: George Wright, Behavioural decision theory : an introduction, (Penguin Books, 1984).
29. Karen M. Hult and Charles Walcott, 1990.
30. In his book Kitab al-Kharaj (book of Land Tax), he highlighted the basic framework of leadership and state policies and its political limitations.
31. In his two correlated books, *Adab al-Kabir and Adab as-Saghir, Ibn al-Muqafa* dealt with the various aspects of state, ruler's attitude, the administrator's behaviour, obligation and his bureaucratises through religious sentiment.
32. In his two theological books, *Kitab al-Irshad Ila Qawati' al-Adilah* (book of guidance to the concrete evidences), and *Tamhid al-Awail wa Talkhis ad-Dala'il* (prelude to the previous ideas and summary of the evidences), al-Juwaini dealt with leadership characteristics. With exclusive chapter of *imamah* is found in the each of these two books, where he analyzed the characteristic and traits of the sultan al-Adil in the Islamic political thought.
33. Abu al-Hassan Ali Ibn Muhamad b. Habib al-Mawardi, made a considerable contributions on the Islamic administration, tafsir, ethics and many other fields. Among many of his works are: *Al-Aĺkam al-*

Sultaniya wal Wilayah al-Diniyya, i.e., the Ordinances of Government. *Qanun al-Wasarah*, i.e., Laws regarding the Ministers, and *Kitab Nasihat al-Muluk*, i.e., The Book of Sincere Advice to Rulers.

34. See for example the works of "al-Mawardi, *Al-Ahkam aÎ-Øultania wal Wilayat al-Diniyah*,".
35. See: Syed Muhammad al-Naquib al-Attas, *Islam: the Concept of Religion and the Foundation of Ethics and Morality* (Kuala Lumpur: Dewan Bahasa dan Pustaka, 1992.)
36. See: Shaukat Ali, Administrative ethics in a Muslim state (Lahore: Publishers United, 1975).
37. See: Al-Qardhawi, Yusuf, *Dawr al-Qiyam wa al-Akhlaq Fi al-Iqtisad al-Islami*, (Cairo: Maktabat Wahbah, 1995).
38. Al-Faruqi, Isma'il Raji,, and Gamal al- Banna, *Towards Islamic Labour and Unionism*, Pub: the international Islamic Confederation of Labour, Cairo, p. 13-14.
39. See the Qur'an, (Surah al-Anbiya, verse: 7).
40. Reported by Bukhari and Muslim.
41. (4:59).
42. The Prophet (s.a.w) once said: " *'Atu al-Ajira Haqahu qabla an-Yajifa Araqahu*", i.e., give the salary of the employee his or her salary on time, even before his or her swat dries.
43. Work, in the Islamic view, is to be done according to some one's ability and capacity, where Islam teaches that every one is charged with the capacity that he or she could. Hence: "No soul shall have a burden laid on it greater than it can bear." (2:233).
44. The Prophet (*s.a.w*) said: "if a person does something good for you, reward him or her, however, if you do not have any incentives to him or her, say to him "*Jazaka Allah Khairan*", i.e., God might reward you". This includes the professionals who show commitment to their work and contributed to the process of achieving the goals of the organization, should be reworded by the administration.
45. According to the Islamic perspective of administration disunity among the colleagues damages the reputation of the organization and nullify the productivity of the team. Thus, to follow the guidelines of the authority, and to remain united will strengthen the credibility of the organization and its product. Strengthening team spirit includes coordination, cooperation and maintaining healthy relationship. The *Qur'an* reads:

"And obey Allah and His Messenger. and fall into no disputes, lest ye lose heart and your power depart; and be patient and persevering: For Allah is with those who patiently persevere." (8: 46).

46. M*as'ul* which is another term employed together with *ijir* and *ra'i*, denotes the same meaning and further indicates "responsibility", "accountability" and "transparency".
47. Maududi, Sayyid Abul A'la, *Towards Understanding Islam*, pp.74-7. See also: Rafik, p. 21.
48. According to al-Faruqi the ultimate objectives of public administration is not only the financial outcome of the organization, but to win the rewards of God. Man as vicegerent must deliver his duties with intention that he is serving under the guidelines of his or her Lord. The *tawhidic* view affects the administrator to think with equality and justice towards all subordinate and staff. *Tawhidic* administration system teaches us to treat the manpower of the organization equally, regardless of color, ethnic background or culture. (See: Al-Faruqi, Isma'il Raji, Al-Tawhid: its implications for thought and life, (Herndon: International Institute of Islamic Thought, 1982).
49. Beekun, Rafik Issa, *Islamic Business Ethics, International Institute of Islamic Thought* (Virginia, USA, 1997), p. 18.
50. Rafik, p. 22-23.
51. The *Qur'an* reads:

    "And say: "Work (righteousness and continuously): Soon will Allah observe your work, and His Messenger, and the Believers: Soon will ye be brought back to the knower of what is hidden and what is open: then will He show you the truth of all that ye did." (*Surah at-Tawbah*, verse: 105).
52. The term *'Imalu* is the plural form of the Arabic word *amal* which literally means deed, work and profession. However, in the professional usage, the term *amal*, and all of its ramifications, are equally applicable to all manifestations of "work and profession".
53. Al-Qurĭubi, Mohamad b. Ahmad, *Al-Jami' li Aĭkam al-Qur'an* (Beirut: Dar al-Kutub al-Ilmiyah,1993), 8th volume, p. 160.
54. *Qur'an* says that if the person calls for Allah and at the same time fulfils the good work; there is none nobler then him. Furthermore, Allah (*s.w.t*) promised in the *Qur'an* that if anyone among you; whether he or she engage good deeds and maintain the faith in Allah, he will enjoy good life here and hereafter. (*Surah al-Nahl,* verse: 97).

55. Furthermore, they should be conscious of their responsibilities and of their own abilities, mental resourcefulness and experience. (See: *Surah al-Qasas*, verse: 26).

56. The Prophet (*s.a.w*) said:

    "The example of a person who obeys injunction of Allah and the one who disregard these limits is like passengers on a boat who decide by drawing lots as to who should occupy the upper deck and who should go to the lower deck. Those in the lower deck had to pass through the upper deck to fetch water which caused some inconvenience to occupants of the upper deck. So they suggested to the occupants of the upper deck to allow them to bore a hole in the lower deck and draw water without causing any inconvenience to them. If the occupants of the upper deck were to leave those in the lower deck to carry out their design, they would all perish together; but if they were to stop them from carrying it out they would save themselves and all others." (Reported by Bukhari).

57. قال رسول الله صلى الله عليه وسلم: "ما أكل أحد طعاما قط خيرا من أن يأكل من عمل يده..." رواه البخاري.

58. "عمل الرجل بيده وكل بيع مبرور". رواه البخاري ومسلم.

59. "قال رسول الله صلى الله عليه وسلم: "لأن يحتطب أحدكم حزمة على ظهره، خير له من أن يسأل أحدا، فيعطيه أو يمنعه". متفق عليه.

60. This based on the *Qur'anic* teachings in which Allah says that He has created every thing on earth for your consumption and utilization, therefore, go and work seeking his *rizk* from the earth. (See: *Qur'anic* chapters: 2:29, 6…: 15)

61. If you engage with unethical practices to increase your wealth, such as not weighing or measuring enough on the scales, it will never increase or benefit, but you do every thing properly for the sake of countenance of Allah (*s.w.t*), will increase it. (30:39).

62. The *Qur'an* teaches that the deeds which involved unethical behaviour involves will not be productive, while those deeds which are carried out with morality and ethics will increase such as *sadaqah*, for He (*s.w.t)* loves not ungrateful and wicked personalities. (2: 276).

63. See: (102: 3).

64. See: (25:70).

65. The *Qur'an* reads:

    "إِنَّ الإِنسَانَ لَفِي خُسْرٍ ، إِلاَّ الَّذِينَ ءامَنُوا وَعَمِلُوا الصَّالِحَاتِ..."

    "Verily Man is in loss, except such as have faith, and do righteous deeds.." (*Surah al'Asr*, verses: 2-3)

66. The *Qur'an* reads:

    "إِلَّا مَن تَابَ وَءَامَنَ وَعَمِلَ عَمَلًا صَالِحًا..."

    "Unless he repents, believes, and works righteous deeds..." (*Surah al-Furqan,* verse: 70)

67. The *Qur'an* calls the architectural design of the natural physics as both purposive and evocative. The enduring attractive architectural design of the natural physics, the diversity of its subject matter and the expediency of its environmental climate is not without philosophy and aim according to *Qur'an*.

68. The Qur'an reads: "He Who created the seven heavens one above another: No want of proportion wilt thou see in the Creation of (Allah) Most Gracious. So turn thy vision again: seest thou any flaw? Again turn thy vision a second time: (thy) vision will come back to thee dull and discomfited, in a state worn out." (Surah at-Tabarak, verses: 3-4)

69. The Prophet (*s.a.w*) stated that:

    "Verily Allah has prescribed proficiency (*itqan*) in all things. Thus, if you kill, kill well; and if you slaughter, slaughter well. Let each one of you sharpen his blade and let him spare suffering to the animal he slaughters." (reported by Muslim).

70. Perhaps this is the reason why the *Qur'an* used the terms (*qawi and amin*) successively.

71. According to the *Qur'an,* Prophet Sha'aib was living in Madyan which is between Egypt and Arabian Peninsular.

72. The *Qur'an* mentions that while other people were successful providing water and other needs for their livestock, Prophet shu'aib, due to his age was not able to do so, and that his daughters wait until others pour the water from underground wells to their livestock. Thus Prophet Shu'aib needed to hire someone who will administer and management the family and the livestock. [See: Al-QurÏubi, *Al-Jami' li AÍkam al-Qur'an,* (Beirut: Dar *al-Kutub* al-Ilmiyah, 1993)].

73. See the *Qur'an* verses: (*Surah al-Qasas*: 22-25)

74. Prophet Shu'aib informed Moses the duration of the current contract is eight years but extendable to ten if Moses want to extend.

75. Abu Úar (r.a.) narrated that:

    "I ask the Prophet (*s.a.w*), why do you not appoint me as an administrator of some place? He (s.a.w) patted his hand on my shoulder and said: "O Aba Úar you are weak and holding of public administration is a (huge) trust." (Reported by Muslim.)

In another narration Aba Zar (*r.a.*) relates that the Prophet (*s.a.w*) replied to his request for public office the same answer and added:

" ... Do not desire authority even over two persons, nor take up the guardianship of the property of an orphan." (Reported by Muslim).

76. Professionalism is defined as the professional status, methods, character and standards. The expertness characteristic of a professional person, or skilful, by virtue of possessing special knowledge. (The English-Arabic dictionary of professional business terms, Saba and Co. (London: Middle East Economic Digest: 1987, p. 104).
77. See ar-Razi, *at-Tafsir al-Kabir*, v. 18, pp. 111-112.
78. *Surah Yusuf*, verse: 55.
79. *Surah Yusuf*, verse: 55.
80. See the *Qur'anic* verses: (*Yusuf*: verses: 53-55).
81. The English-Arabic dictionary of professional business terms, Saba and Co. (London: Middle East Economic Digest: 1987, p. 104).
82. The Qur'an reads:

    "O You Who believe stand out firmly for justice as witnesses to Allah, even as against yourselves, or your parents, or your kin..."

    See: *Surah an-Nisa*, verse: 135.
83. *Surah al-An'am*, verse: 152.
84. According to the *Qur'an* a public administrator should discharge his/her trust with deep sense of the presence of Allah (*s.w.t*). The *Qur'an* adds "*wala Taktumual shahadah*", i.e., conceal no evidence" because for whoever conceals it will inherit a durable feeling of guiltiness "*Athimun Qalbuhu*".
85. *Surah al-Baqarah*, verses: 42, and 283.
86. This is because if mistakes are contributed to the Prophets this will in turn means questioning the credibility of the Prophets and message from Allah, thus, never the Prophets are not infallible nor they are forgetful in conveying the message of Allah in all matters of life.
87. They agreed the verse to show: "*jawaz al-Ijtihat fi al-umuri wa al-Akhzi bi Al-zununi ma imkan al-wahyi*, i.e., the permissibility of using the human intellect to extract an idea or solution for the binding issues other than the *wahy*. (See: Al-Qurïibi, *Al-Jami' li Aĺkam al-Qur'an*, v.4, pp.191-194. See also: Ar-Razi, Fakhar ad-Din Mohamad b. Omer, *At-Tafsir al-Kabir* (Beirut: Dar al-Fikr, 1978), v. 3, pp. 79-80.
88. Az-Zamakhahari, Mohmud b. Omer, *al-Kashaf an Haqa'iq at-Tanzil wa uyun al-Aqawil fi wujuh at-Ta'wil* (Beirut: Dar Ihya at-Turath al-

Arabi, 1st ed. 1997), v.1, p. 459. See also: Wahbah az-Zuhaili, *at-Tafsir al-Wasit* (Beirut: Dar al-Fikr al-Mu'aÎir, 1st ed. 2001), v.1, pp. 254-255.

89. I am saying directly because, there are many other forms in which the Qur'an promoted shu'ra without mentioning the term *Shu'ra* directly. The three places in which the *Qur'an* mentioned the term *shu'ra* and its derivatives are: (2:233, 3:159 and 42: 38).

90. The issue is about managing the breast feeding which is related to both the growth of the child and health of the mother. According to the medical doctors breast feeding is good for the child in terms of biological, mental and the growth of the immune system and the parental relationship between the child and the mother becomes strong if the child is breast fed enough. Thus the *Qur'an* advices the mothers to continue breast feeding the child until two years, however, it is up to the mother and father to decide whether to complete such breast feeding duration or not, and it is up to them whether or not to seek a foster-mother for breast feeding. What is important according to the verse, is that there should be no force or dictatorship in the family. According to the *Mufassirun,* this means that familial issues are, not only breast feeding, but other issues should be settled on mutual understanding between the father and mother. (2:233).

91. In this verse the Qur'an highlights various interrelated values and principles that identify the real Islamic culture. The first principle is that Muslims always submit themselves willingly to Allah (*istijabah*), second, they establish prayers (*aqamu as-salat*), they conduct the affairs through mutual consultation (*shu'ra*) and finally, for meaningful co-existent and social welfare they pay their *zakat* or spend their wealth wisely (*wa mima razaqnahum yunfiquna.*) These four principles are among basic principles that constitute the Islamic identity, however, seemingly *shu'ra* is mentioned in the middle between *Øalat* and *Nafaqah*, and this means, that as we obey Allah (*s.w.t*), establish *salat* and pay *zakat* we should also practice *shu'ra* for sustenance. (42:38).

92. *Surah Ali Imran*, verse: 159.

93. Most of them emotionally responded and feel proud of their military might and skill of fighting. They said "We are endued with strength, and given to vehement war: but the command is with thee; so consider what thou wilt command."

94. See: *Surah an-Naml*, verses: 29-37.

95. There is one *Íadith*, narrated by Abi Bakrah, which states that any community that appoints a woman as the head of the state or public office (*wallaw amrahum ibra'ah*) will never succeed. According to

some Muslim jurist the *íadith* directly prohibits a woman to hold a public office, however, such narration is not authentic according to sheikh al-Ghazali, thus have no authority to state such issue. Al-Ghazali contends that, according to the methods of *íadĭth* authentication, *íadith* is valid if two conditions are there. First, its chain of narration should be connected to the Prophet (s.a.w) without any disconnections, second, it should not contradict with the *Qur'an*. Accordingly, sheikh al-Ghazali, Abi Bakrah's *íadith* is not valid because it directly contradicts with the story of the stateswoman in surah an-Naml. Hence, though the *Qur'an* denied the Queen's pagan faith, but praised and admired her administration and ethics. Thus, gender has a role in leadership why the *Qur'an* praised this woman's leadership, which occupies more than two pages of the *Qur'an*. For him we cannot accept the authority of such while ignoring the teachings of the *Qur'an*. The skill and qualification, not gender, are what determine who will hold the public office. (Sheikh Mohamad al-Ghazali, *as-Sunnah an-Nabawiyah Bayna Ahl al-Hadith wa Ahl al-Fiqh* (Cairo: Dar ash-Shuruq, 1989), pp. 49-51.

Index